IMPORTANT.

W9-AYF-842

HERE IS YOUR REGISTRATION CODE TO ACCESS
YOUR PREMIUM McGRAW-HILL ONLINE RESOURCES.

For key premium online resources you need THIS CODE to gain access. Once the code is entered, you will be able to use the Web resources for the length of your course.

If your course is using **WebCT** or **Blackboard**, you'll be able to use this code to access the McGraw-Hill content within your instructor's online course.

Access is provided if you have purchased a new book. If the registration code is missing from this book, the registration screen on our Website, and within your WebCT or Blackboard course, will tell you how to obtain your new code.

Registering for McGraw-Hill Online Resources

TO gain access to your McGraw-Hill web
resources simply follow the steps below:

1. USE YOUR WEB BROWSER TO GO TO: **www.mhhe.com/parkba4**
2. CLICK ON **FIRST TIME USER**.
3. ENTER THE REGISTRATION CODE* PRINTED ON THE TEAR-OFF BOOKMARK ON THE RIGHT.
4. AFTER YOU HAVE ENTERED YOUR REGISTRATION CODE, CLICK **REGISTER**.
5. FOLLOW THE INSTRUCTIONS TO SET-UP YOUR PERSONAL UserID AND PASSWORD.
6. WRITE YOUR UserID AND PASSWORD DOWN FOR FUTURE REFERENCE. KEEP IT IN A SAFE PLACE.

TO GAIN ACCESS to the McGraw-Hill content in your instructor's **WebCT** or **Blackboard** course simply log in to the course with the UserID and Password provided by your instructor. Enter the registration code exactly as it appears in the box to the right when prompted by the system. You will only need to use the code the first time you click on McGraw-Hill content.

Thank you, and welcome
to your McGraw-Hill
online Resources!

REGISTRATION CODE

JD0G-G92F-NE2K-HF22-74R0

Mc Graw Hill Higher Education

* YOUR REGISTRATION CODE CAN BE USED ONLY ONCE TO ESTABLISH ACCESS. IT IS NOT TRANSFERABLE.

0-07-296312-3 T/A PARK: BIOLOGICAL ANTHROPOLOGY, 4E

BIOLOGICAL ANTHROPOLOGY

Published by McGraw-Hill, a business unit of the McGraw-Hill Companies, Inc., 1221 Avenue of the Americas, New York, NY 10020. Copyright © 2005 by the McGraw-Hill Companies, Inc. All rights reserved. No part of this publication may be reproduced or distributed in any form or by any means, or stored in a database or retrieval system, without prior written consent of The McGraw-Hill Companies, Inc., including, but not limited to, in any network or other electronic storage or transmission, or broadcast for distance learning.

This book is printed on acid-free paper.

1 2 3 4 5 6 7 8 9 0 VNH/VNH 0 9 8 7 6 5 4

ISBN 0-07-286312-9

Editor-in-chief: *Emily Barrosse*
Publisher: *Phil Butcher*
Sponsoring editor: *Kevin Witt*
Permissions coordinator: *Marty Granahan*
Marketing manager: *Dan Loch*
Project manager: *Christina Gimlin*
Design manager: *Cassandra Chu*
Designer: *Anna George*

Art editor: *Robin Mouat*
Manager, photo research: *Brian Pecko*
Production supervisor: *Richard DeVitto*
Compositor: *The GTS Companies, Los Angeles*
Typeface: *10.5/12.5 Goudy Old Style*
Printer and binder: *Von Hoffmann Press*
Cover photo: *Conservationist with Chimpanzees.*
   © Yann Arthus-Bertrand/Corbis

Because this page cannot legibly accomodate all the copyright notices, credits are listed on page C-1 and constitute an extension of the copyright page.

Library-of-Congress Cataloging-in-Publication Data
Park, Michael Alan.
   Biological anthropology/Michael Alan Park—4th ed.
      p. cm.
   Includes bibliographical references and index.
   ISBN 0-07-286312-9 (softcover)
      1. Physical anthropology.   I. Title.

GN60.P35 2004
599.9—dc22

www.mhhe.com

BIOLOGICAL
ANTHROPOLOGY

FOURTH EDITION

MICHAEL ALAN PARK

CENTRAL CONNECTICUT STATE UNIVERSITY

Boston   Burr Ridge, IL   Dubuque, IA   Madison, WI   New York   San Francisco   St. Louis
Bangkok   Bogotá   Caracas   Kuala Lumpur   Lisbon   London   Madrid   Mexico City
Milan   Montreal   New Delhi   Santiago   Seoul   Singapore   Sydney   Taipei   Toronto

To the Instructor

Contemporary biological anthropology is a dauntingly broad field. It studies humans in the same way that zoologists study their subject species—from a perspective that includes *all* aspects of the species' biology and that emphasizes the interrelationships among those aspects. In addition to encompassing the traditional topics of the human fossil record and human biological variation, bioanthropology includes primatology, modern technologies in molecular genetics, human demography, disease and medical issues, development of the individual, life histories, and such applications as forensic anthropology. Bioanthropology also appreciates that our cultural behavior is an integral part of our behavior as a species.

No wonder, then, that I (and others I have spoken to) have had difficulty in covering the entire field in a one-semester course. We have ended up leaving out important aspects (or paying them little more than lip service), or we have sacrificed the sense of bioanthropology as an integrated whole for a rushed and encyclopedic inventory of all the field's current topics.

As modern bioanthropology increased in breadth and complexity over the past several decades, so too did the size and detail of introductory texts. Several are now more than 600 pages long. Attempts to produce shorter introductory texts have consisted of simply cutting out parts of these tomes, resulting in rather uneven, sometimes oddly organized, presentations of the field.

I wrote this text in order to present a diverse scientific field to beginning students. Here are the major assumptions that guided my writing:

- Because this is a text for introductory courses, I have tried to reduce the field to its most basic information. No part of the discipline has been left out; instead I have achieved brevity by managing the level of detail and including only the information necessary to clearly and accurately convey the basic themes, theories, methods, and facts of bioanthropology.

- The text assumes that students have limited background knowledge of the material and little understanding of what science is and how it works. The text *explains* rather than simply itemizes facts and ideas, and it does so, as much as possible, in a narrative format. A lesson from the study of folklore is that a story is far more easily understood and retained than is a list of facts.

- I want students to feel that they are reading a text written by a real person who has participated in the field. I have tried to achieve a balance between an informal style and a formal style, and I have not shied away from the occasional colloquialism or personal comment.

FEATURES

I've included a number of features that I hope will make this text a more useful learning tool for students.

- *I use the scientific method as a theme throughout the book to demonstrate the integrity and nature of bioanthropology.* I describe the scientific method and then, because this *is* anthropology, compare science with knowledge garnered from belief systems, discussing the relationship of these two spheres of inquiry within cultures. I try to show specifically how scientific reasoning has provided us with the knowledge we have about the topics in bioanthropology. For example, I present extended discussions of bipedalism and the issue of modern human origins by posing questions, suggesting answers, and then testing the logic of and evidence for those answers.

- *The text is organized to help students navigate their way through what is still a fairly hefty amount of information.* To help students feel a little less at sea in the midst of new facts and ideas, I regularly refer back to previous topics and ahead to topics that will be covered. The headings I use as signposts are as descriptive as possible (for example, "Natural Selection: The Prime Mover of Evolution").

- *Within chapters, a consistent format helps students better understand material new to them.* Each chapter starts with an **introduction,** which sets the stage and context for what's to come, followed by a series of **questions** that the chapter will answer. Because science proceeds by asking and answering questions, this format is also used within the body of the text. **Key terms** are boldfaced in the text and defined in the margins at their first appearance. Each chapter concludes with a list of key terms and a **summary** that not only recaps the important points of the chapter but also provides some new ideas and thoughts that help put the chapter into context within the whole discipline. Also concluding each chapter are **questions for further thought,** which are designed to help students explore the real-world ramifications of the chapter's topics. And a list of **suggested readings,** made up mostly of nontechnical works, tells interested students where to find more information on the material discussed.

- There is a new Appendix that focuses on population genetics (formerly part of Chapter 13) and an Exercises section that allows students to try their hand at applying the concepts of Mendelian genetics, taxonomy, skeletal identification, and population genetics.

- *Two glossaries, a reference list, and a comprehensive index make information more accessible.* A Glossary of Human and Nonhuman Primates, with pronunciations for each term, defines and describes the taxonomic groups discussed in the text. In addition to the running glossary within chapters, a comprehensive Glossary of Terms appears at the back of the book. The References section contains complete sources for the suggested readings and also lists technical works referred to within the text. The Index helps students access information quickly.

- *The text's visual appeal enhances its readability.* Detailed, colorful charts and drawings, as well as full-color photographs, underscore significant points in the text. Captions for the artwork add information rather than simply label the pictures.

NEW TO THIS EDITION

The book has been updated throughout, and the discussions of many topics have been expanded and clarified. Highlights include the following:

- The text focuses more specifically throughout on the *biocultural* nature of anthropology as a whole and bioanthropology in particular.

- Chapter 1, "Biological Anthropology," includes a revised discussion of the nature of "theory" within science.

- Chapter 2, "The Evolution of Evolution," now includes William "Strata" Smith and Thomas Malthus in its discussion of the history of evolutionary thought.

- Chapter 3, "Evolutionary Genetics," has a new section, "An Overview of the Human Genome," that summarizes the latest information about the number and nature of genes in the human genetic code. This chapter also has a new Contemporary Reflections box on genetic cloning.

- In Chapter 5, "The Origin of Species and the Shape of Evolution," the concepts of gradualism and punctuated equilibrium have been further clarified, and the issue of so-called intelligent design has been added to the discussion of scientific creationism.

- Chapter 7, "The Primates," has a clarified discussion of Linnaean versus cladistic taxonomies, along with new diagrams to better explain the implications for classification. There is also a new Contemporary Reflections box on the endangered status of the great apes.

- Chapter 9, "Studying the Human Past," clarifies some of the data concerning the genetic closeness between humans and chimpanzees.

- Chapter 10, "Evolution of the Hominids," is reorganized to better discuss the wealth of new fossil data and interpretations from early hominid evolution. Included are a new *Ardipithecus* and *Sahelanthropus tchadensis*. A new section, "Putting It All Together," has diagrams to explain some of the phylogenetic schemes proposed for this period. Finally, the section on the first members of genus *Homo* has been moved to the following chapter.

- Chapter 11, "The Evolution of Genus *Homo*," includes the new *Homo erectus* fossils from Bouri, Ethiopia; East Turkana, Kenya; and Dmanisi, Georgia; as well as the new modern human finds from Herto, Ethiopia.

- Chapter 12, "The Debate over Modern Human Origins," updates some of the genetic data brought to bear on the debate and, while keeping the point-by-point comparison of the two major models, now ends with a description of a new and viable alternative, the "Mostly-Out-of-Africa" model.

- In Chapter 13, "The Study of Living Peoples," the section on population genetics has been moved to the Appendix, and population and AIDS statistics have been updated. Data on human genetic variation has been clarified.

- Chapter 14, "Human Biological Diversity," has new discussions on the nature and meaning of human genetic variation, in light of recent research and interpretations.

- Chapter 15, "Biological Anthropology and Today's World," covers new information on the "Ice Man" and a forensic example from the 9/11 terrorist attacks.

- "Exercise 2: Taxonomy" now has accompanying photographs, and the trees in the Discussion and Answers section for that exercise have been corrected.

- The Glossary of Human and Nonhuman Primates and Glossary of Terms have been updated, and the References section (formerly the

Bibliography) has seventy-five new entries, including twenty-five from 2003 and 2004.

SUPPLEMENTARY MATERIAL

The **Instructor's Manual** includes a test bank of about 500 multiple choice and short-answer/essay questions, as well as chapter overviews, suggested activities, and lists of key terms.

A **Computerized Test Bank** is available free of charge to qualifying adopters. It is a powerful, easy-to-use test-generation system that provides all test items on computer disk for IBM-compatible or Macintosh computers. Instructors can select, add, or edit questions; randomize them; and print tests appropriate to their individual classes.

There is a Web site (www.mhhe.com/parkba4) that includes an online study guide and other interactive aids, downloadable illustrations, and a Late Breaking News feature.

Physical anthropology is eminently visual. This sample of the images available on the Online Learning Center Web site at www.mhhe.com/parkba4 show some of the thirty images available for instructor and student alike. These images can help make the course more concrete and vivid.

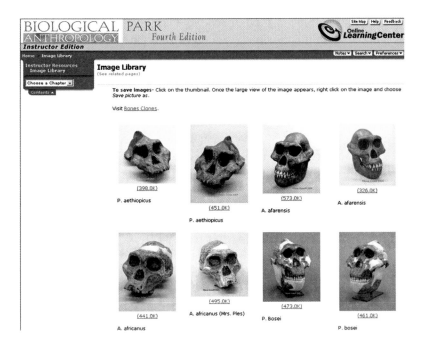

ACKNOWLEDGMENTS

Thirty-one years now since leaving Indiana University, I still feel a profound debt to my first teachers there in bioanthropology, Robert Meier, Paul Jamison, and Georg Neumann. This book, I trust, reflects some of the knowledge and inspiration I received from them.

It was Jan Beatty who first brought me to Mayfield Publishing Company (which has since joined forces with McGraw-Hill) eighteen years ago. She was the sponsoring editor of ten editions of my books. It is an understatement to say that her knowledge of all aspects of publishing, combined with her understanding of anthropology and the needs (and quirks) of us academic types has been a major influence on all my written work. Although I consider this book the result of a collaboration of many capable people over the years, it owes its heart (in every way) to Jan.

Thanks to the able staff at McGraw-Hill for once again transforming my ideas and words into an attractive and useful finished product. They are: Kevin Witt, sponsoring editor; Christina Gimlin, project manager; Cassandra Chu, designer; Robin Mouat, art editor; Brian Pecko, manager, photo research; Rich DeVitto, production supervisor; Louis Swaim, supplements producer; and Dan Loch, marketing manager.

Special thanks to copyeditor Andrea McCarrick, who has a singular knack for understanding what I'm trying to say with some of my words and turning them into actual sentences.

Since I wrote the previous edition of this book, the world of science lost one of its most articulate voices with the death of Stephen Jay Gould. If you look in the references section you will see that he has more entries than anyone else. This is with good reason. I didn't know him personally (we corresponded by letter just once) but it is no exaggeration to say that he was a primary inspiration for me to even think about trying my hand at writing about my field.

The manuscript was reviewed by the following people: Deborah E. Blom, University of Vermont; Mary Glenn, Humboldt State University; Steve Gravely, Solano Community College; Ronald Hicks, Ball State University; Joel D. Irish, University of Alaska—Fairbanks; Deborah Overdorff, University of Texas—Austin; and John F. Scarry, North Carolina State University. I thank them all for their helpful and insightful contributions. All final content, decisions, and errors are, of course, my own.

To the Reader

The broad field of biological, or physical, anthropology deals with everything from evolutionary theory to the human fossil record to the identification of human skeletal remains from crime scenes and accidents. A detailed account of this whole field would result in an unwieldy text that would be a tough assignment for a one-semester introductory course, especially if it were assigned in its entirety.

This text is intended to truly be an *introduction* to biological anthropology. It will tell you about the many different kinds of studies bioanthropologists participate in and how they conduct them; you'll also learn about the scientific theories and data they use. All the important aspects of bioanthropology are covered here but with just the essential amount of detail. An understanding of the ideas presented in this book will provide you with the basis for delving more deeply into those aspects of bioanthropology that interest you.

A major theme of this book is the scientific method. Biological anthropology is a science, so an understanding of how science works is essential. Because the field of anthropology studies the human species in its entirety, however, the text will examine science as a human endeavor, seeing where it fits in the realm of human knowledge.

HOW TO USE THIS BOOK

Each chapter starts with an **introduction** that sets the stage and context for what's to come, followed by a series of **questions** that the chapter will answer. Because science proceeds by asking and answering questions, this format is also used within the body of the text. **Key terms** are boldfaced and defined in the margins at their first appearance. Each chapter ends with a **summary** that not only recaps the important points of the chapter but also provides some new ideas and thoughts that help put what you have just learned into the context of the whole discipline of bioanthropology. There are also **questions for further thought** that will help you explore some of the real-world ramifications of the chapter's topics. A list of **suggested readings,** made up mostly of non-technical works, tells you where to find more information on topics of particular interest.

A Glossary of Human and Nonhuman Primates defines taxonomic (scientific) names for species discussed in the text—names like *Homo sapiens* and *Australopithecus afarensis*—and tells you how to pronounce them. In addition to the running glossary within chapters, a comprehensive Glossary of Terms appears at the back of the book. The Exercises will allow you try your hand at applying some of the concepts from the text. The References section contains complete citations for the suggested readings and also lists technical works referred to within the text. The Index will help you more quickly access information.

For an online study guide and a Late Breaking News feature, see our Online Learning Center: www.mhhe.com/bioanth4.

To help you visualize specific fossils, a wealth of images is available on the Online Learning Center Web site at www.mhhe.com/parkba4. The images on page ix show a sample of the web site photos. Physical anthropology is eminently visual and these images can help bring the course alive for you.

Contents

13 THE STUDY OF LIVING PEOPLES   *349*

14 HUMAN BIOLOGICAL DIVERSITY   *387*

CHAPTER

1

BIOLOGICAL
ANTHROPOLOGY

Anthropologists study
spiders, right?
—Anonymous caller

If you asked twenty people to define anthropology, you would probably get twenty different answers. Anthropology is such a broad field that many people, understandably, are not sure just what an anthropologist studies. People have brought me rocks to identify and have asked me about the accuracy of the dinosaurs in *Jurassic Park*. One man even called me for information on black widow spiders—and he was referred to me by someone within the university where I teach.

In this chapter, we will define anthropology in general and then focus on the subfield of biological anthropology (also called *bioanthropology* or *physical anthropology*). Because fieldwork—where anthropologists make their observations and collect their data—is perhaps the best-known aspect of anthropology and is the part that attracts many students to the discipline, I will begin with a brief description of two of my fieldwork experiences.

As you read, consider the following questions:

What is anthropology, and what are its subfields?

What is biological anthropology?

How does the scientific method operate?

In what way is bioanthropology a science?

What are belief systems, and what is their relationship to scientific knowledge?

IN THE FIELD: DOING BIOLOGICAL ANTHROPOLOGY

The wheat fields on either side of the long, straight road in western Saskatchewan, Canada, stretched as far as the eye could see. I found myself wishing, on that June day in 1973, that the road went on just as far. I was on my way to visit with my first real anthropological subjects, a colony of people belonging to a 475-year-old religious denomination called the Hutterian Brethren, or Hutterites.

Up to this point, I had not felt much anxiety about the visit. Accounts by other anthropologists of their contacts with Amazon jungle warriors and New Guinea headhunters made my situation seem rather safe. The Hutterites are, after all, people who share my European American cultural heritage, speak English (among other languages), and practice a form of Christianity that emphasizes pacifism and tolerance.

At this point, though, those considerations, no matter how reassuring they should have been, didn't help. Nor did the fact that I was accompanied by the wife of a local wheat farmer who was well known and liked by the people of this colony. I simply had that unnamed fear that affects nearly all anthropologists under these first-contact circumstances.

Finally, the road we traveled—which had turned from blacktop to dirt about 10 miles back—curved abruptly to the right and crested a hill. I saw below us, at the literal end of the road, a neat collection of twenty or so white buildings surrounded by acres of cultivated fields. This was the Hutterite colony, or *Bruderhof,* the "place where the brethren live" (Figure 1.1).

As we drove into the colony, not a soul was in sight. My companion explained that it was a religious holiday that required all but essential

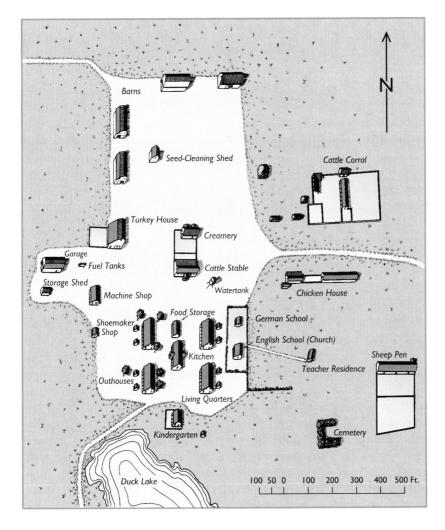

FIGURE 1.1
Diagram of typical Hutterite colony. The variety of buildings and their functions are indicative of the Hutterites' attempt to keep their colonies self-sufficient and separate from the outside world.

work to cease. Everyone was indoors observing the holiday, but the colony minister and colony boss had agreed to see me.

We entered one of the smaller buildings, which I recognized from pictures and diagrams of "typical" colonies as one of the residential buildings. The interior was darkened in keeping with the holiday. A few minutes later, having gotten my bearings, I explained the reason for my visit to two men and a woman.

The men were dressed in the Hutterite fashion—black trousers and coats and white shirts—and they wore beards, a sign of marriage. The older, gray-haired man was the colony minister. The younger man, who happened to be his son, was the colony boss. The woman, the minister's wife, also dressed in the conservative style of the Hutterites and related groups. She wore a nearly full-length sleeveless dress with a white blouse underneath. Her head was covered by a polka-dot kerchief, or *shawl*, as they call it (Figure 1.2).

My contacts, the wheat farmer and his wife, had arranged the visit and had already given the Hutterites an idea of what I wanted to do. But if the colony members didn't like me or my planned study, they could still decline to cooperate. The three listened in silence as I went through my well-rehearsed explanation. When I had finished, they asked me only a few questions. Was I from the government? (My study involved using fingerprints as hereditary traits, and they apparently associated fingerprinting with law enforcement and personal identification.) Did I know Scripture? (My equivocal answer created no problem.) What would I use this study for? Was I going to write a book? Did I know so-and-so, who had been there two years ago and done medical examinations?

I expected them to confer with one another or ask me to come back when they had decided if they would allow me to conduct the study. Instead, the minister, who was clearly in charge, simply said, "Today is a holiday for us. Can you start tomorrow?"

And so, for the next month I took part in my personal version of fieldwork—taking fingerprints, recording family relationships, observing colony life, and getting to know the Hutterites of this and one other Canadian Bruderhof (Park 1979; Figure 1.3).

What exactly had brought me 1,300 miles from my university to the northern plains, to this isolated community of people whose way of life has changed little over the past 475 years and whose lifestyle and philosophy differ so much from those of North Americans in general? Essentially, it was the same thing that takes anthropologists to such locations as the highlands of New Guinea, the caves of the Pyrenees, and the street corners of New York City: the desire to learn something about the nature of the human species.

FIGURE 1.2
Hutterite women in typical dress.

In my case, I was pursuing an interest I had developed early in graduate school—to study the processes of evolution and how they affect humans. I was curious about two of these processes: gene flow and genetic drift (see Chapter 4 for details). Both topics had been described half a century earlier, but their workings and importance, especially with regard to living human populations, were still poorly understood.

To examine the actions of these processes on human populations and to determine their roles in human evolution, I needed to find a human group with a few special characteristics. The group had to (1) be genetically isolated, (2) be fairly small as a whole but with large families, and (3) consist of individual populations that resulted from the splitting of earlier populations.

The Hutterites exhibited all these characteristics. (I'll elaborate later.) I discovered them through library research on genetically isolated

FIGURE 1.3
Author (*right*) and Hutterite informant. I already had the beard, but it was suggested that I keep it so I would look more familiar to the Hutterite children.

groups. My opportunity to study them was greatly enhanced by a stroke of luck. A fellow graduate student was the daughter of the wheat farmer and his wife who became my "public relations advisors."

Exactly twenty years after my fieldwork with the Hutterites, I found myself standing over an open grave in an old cemetery in the wooded hills of northwest Connecticut. Our team of anthropologists was hoping to find the remains of a native Hawaiian who had been buried here in 1818 and who was now, after 175 years, going home.

A few weeks earlier, Nick Bellantoni, the Connecticut state archae-ologist (and a former student of mine), had called me with a fascinating story. In 1808 a young Hawaiian named Opukahaia (pronounced *oh-poo-kah-hah-ee'-ah*) escaped the tribal warfare that had killed his family by swimming out to a Yankee whaling vessel, where he was taken on board as a cabin boy. Two years (and many adventures) later he ended up at Yale University in New Haven, Connecticut. He took the name Henry, converted to Christianity, and became a Congregational minister who helped build a missionary school in Cornwall, Connecticut. His dream

FIGURE 1.4
Headstone of Henry Opukahaia.

was to return to Hawaii and to take his new faith to the people there (see his portrait in Figure 1.6).

Sadly, Henry's dream was never realized. He died in a typhoid epidemic in 1818 at the age of 26, but his vision inspired the missionary movement that was to change the history of the Hawaiian Islands forever. His grave in Cornwall became a shrine both for the people of his adopted land and for visiting Hawaiians, who would leave offerings atop his platform-style headstone (Figure 1.4).

Nearly two centuries after his death, a living relative of Henry's had a dream that she would honor Henry's final wish to return to his native land. After almost a year of raising funds and making the necessary arrangements, her dream was to come true. And this is where anthropology comes in.

Old New England cemeteries tended to be inexact in the placement of headstones relative to the bodies buried beneath them, and the acidic New England soil is unkind to organic remains. Both logically and legally, this was a job for the state archaeologist, and Nick wanted my help in recovering and identifying whatever remains we might be lucky enough to find. He also wanted my help, it turned out, in moving several tons of stone.

Henry's tomb had been carefully and lovingly assembled by the people of Cornwall. They had placed the inscribed headstone on a pedestal

FIGURE 1.5
Nick Bellantoni excavating the grave of Henry Opuka-haia. The pattern on the floor of the excavation marks the coffin outline.

of fieldstone and mortar. We dismantled this with care, labeling each stone and diagramming its position, since it was to be rebuilt in Hawaii by a stone mason. Under the pedestal and going down about 3 feet into the ground, we uncovered three more layers of fieldstone, which acted as a foundation for the monument and protection for the coffin and the remains we hoped were still below. When all the stones had been removed and we were into a layer of sandy soil, Nick worked alone, delicately scraping away the dirt inch by inch (Figure 1.5).

Late on the second day of our excavation, the remnants of the coffin came into view. In fact, the wooden coffin itself had long since decayed. All that was left was the dark stain of its outline in the soil. We began to despair of finding much else, but an hour later Nick's trowel grazed something hard, and in a few minutes the apparent remains of Henry Opukahaia saw the light of day for the first time in 175 years.

We soon learned that the skeleton was virtually complete. But was it *Henry*? As Nick slowly freed each bone from the soil and handed it up to me (see chapter-opener photograph), we recorded it and compared it with what we knew of Henry from written descriptions and a single portrait. The skeleton was clearly that of a male and, at first glance, conformed to that of a person in his late 20s of about the right size. Henry had been described as being "a little under 6 feet," and the long bones of the arms and legs appeared to be just a bit shorter than mine, though much more robust. The skull, however, confirmed our identification. As the dirt was brushed away, the face of Henry Opukahaia emerged, the very image of his portrait. (The family has requested that, for religious reasons, photographs of Henry's remains not be published.)

We spent two more days with the bones, this time in the garage of a Hartford funeral home. We cleaned, photographed, measured, and described each bone. Finally, we placed each bone in its proper anatomical position in spaces cut into heavy foam rubber that lined the bottom of a *koa*-wood coffin, specially made and shipped from Hawaii. The following Sunday we attended a memorial service in Cornwall, and then Henry's remains began their long journey back home (Figure 1.6).

FIGURE 1.6
Reverend David Hirano, from Hawaii, speaks over the remains of Henry Opukahaia at his "homegoing" celebration in Cornwall, Connecticut. The *koa*-wood coffin, *ti* leaves, and flowered *lei* all have symbolic meaning in Hawaiian culture.

WHAT IS BIOLOGICAL ANTHROPOLOGY?

My experiences as a biological anthropologist range from examining the esoteric detail of evolutionary theory to using my knowledge of the human skeleton for a very personal endeavor. These are just two examples of the many things that biological anthropologists do.

Biological anthropology (or **bioanthropology** or **physical anthropology**) needs to be defined within the context of anthropology as a whole, and doing this is both simple and complex. **Anthropology,** in general, is defined as the study of the human species. Simply put, anthropologists study the human species as any zoologist would study an animal **species.** We look into every aspect of the biology of our subject—genetics, anatomy, physiology, behavior, environment, adaptations, and evolutionary history—stressing the interrelationships among these aspects.

This kind of approach—examining a subject by focusing on the interrelationships among its parts—is called **holistic.** The holistic approach is the hallmark of anthropology. We understand that all the facets of our species—our biology, our behavior, our past, and our present—interact to make us what we are. But we need to study some topics separately, since they can be so complex—just as you may be taking courses in history, economics, psychology, art, anatomy, and so on. What anthropologists do, though, is seek the connections among these subjects, for in real life they are not absolutely separate.

But here's where it gets complicated. The most characteristic feature of our species' behavior is **culture,** and cultural behavior is not programmed in our genes, as is, for example, much of the behavior of birds and virtually all of the behavior of ants. Human culture is learned. We have a biological potential for cultural behavior in general, but exactly *how* we behave comes to us through all our experiences. Take language, for example. All humans are born with the ability to learn a language, but it is the language spoken by our respective families and our broader cultures that determines what language we actually speak.

Moreover, cultural knowledge involves not just specific facts but also ideas, concepts, generalizations, and abstractions. For example, you were able to speak your native language fairly fluently before you were ever formally taught the particulars of its grammar. You did this by making your own generalizations from the raw data you heard and the rules they followed, that is, from the speech of others and from trying to make yourself understood. Even now when you speak, you are applying those generalizations to new situations. And each situation—every

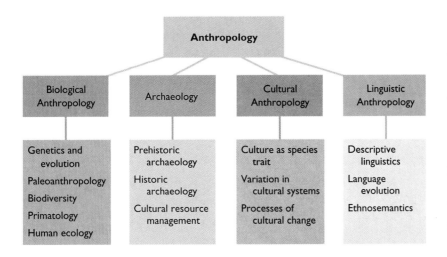

FIGURE 1.7
Major subfields of anthropology with some of their topics. The topics of each subfield may be applied to various social issues (see Chapter 15); this is collectively called *applied anthropology*.

biological anthropology: A subfield of anthropology that studies humans as a biocultural species.

bioanthropology: Another name for biological anthropology.

physical anthropology: The traditional name for biological anthropology.

anthropology: The holistic study of the human species.

species: A group of organisms that can produce fertile offspring among themselves but not with members of other groups.

holistic: Assuming an interrelationship among the parts of a subject.

culture: Ideas and behaviors that are learned and shared. Nonbiological means of adaptation.

biocultural: Focusing on the interaction of biology and culture.

cultural anthropology: A subfield of anthropology that focuses on human cultural behavior and cultural systems and the variation in cultural expression among human groups.

conversation you have, every essay you write, every book you read—is a new situation.

In addition, because culture exists in the context of human social interactions, it must be shared among members of a social group. The complexity of cultural ideas requires this sharing to involve symbols—agreed-upon representations of concepts and abstractions. Human language, of course, is symbolic, as are many visual aspects of our cultures.

In short, culture is highly variable and flexible. It differs from society to society, from environment to environment, and from one time period to another. It even differs in its details from one individual to another. We continually modify our cultural behaviors to fit the unique circumstances of our lives.

So another characteristic of the field of anthropology is its **biocultural** approach. That is, anthropology seeks to describe and explain the interactions between our nature as a biological species and the cultural behavior that is our species' most striking and important trait. We will encounter plenty of examples of these interactions as we continue.

But all these different dimensions make the study of the human species complex and challenging, and so anthropology, the discipline that takes on this challenge, is typically divided into a number of subfields (Figure 1.7). Biological anthropology looks at our species from a biological point of view. This includes all the topics covered in this book. **Cultural anthropology** is the study of culture as a characteristic of our species and of the variation in cultural expression among human groups. This includes human language, although sometimes linguistic anthropology is considered a separate subfield. **Archaeology** is the study of the human cultural past and the reconstruction of past cultural systems. It also involves the techniques used to recover, preserve, and interpret the material remains of the past. The theoretical basis for these activities is the study of the relationship of material culture with cultural systems as a whole.

Each subfield has many specialties. For biological anthropology, these specialties are best expressed in terms of the questions we seek to answer about human biology:

1. What are the biological characteristics that define the human species? How do our genes code for these characteristics? Just how much do genes contribute to our traits? How much are traits shaped by the environment? How does evolution work, and how does it apply to us? (These were the questions I was pursuing in my study of the Hutterites.)

2. What is the physical record of our evolution? This is the specialty referred to as **paleoanthropology,** the study of human fossils based on our knowledge of skeletal biology, or **osteology.**

3. What sort of biological diversity do we see in our species today? How did it evolve? What do the variable traits mean for other aspects of our lives? What do they *not* mean?

4. What can we learn about the biology of our close relatives, the non-human **primates,** and what can it tell us about ourselves? This specialty is called **primatology.**

5. What do we know about **human ecology,** the relationships between humans and their environments?

6. How can we apply all this knowledge to matters of current concern? This is often called **applied anthropology** and can refer to all the subfields. (The story of the exhumation of Henry Opukahaia is an example.)

Individual biological anthropologists undertake numerous and diverse studies. I took fingerprints of members of a centuries-old Christian group to learn something about the processes of evolution that have affected our species. Paleoanthropologist Donald Johanson was with the team that discovered and identified the famous fossil of "Lucy," a 3.2-million-year-old human ancestor. Paleontologist Elwyn Simons studies fossils of nonhuman primates that go even further back in evolutionary time—to the dawn of the apes more than 30 million years ago. Other anthropologists study living nonhuman primates. Shirley Strum, Barbara Smuts, and Linda Fedigan, for example, have all observed troops of baboons to understand what their behavior can tell us about our own.

Clyde Snow is a **forensic anthropologist.** He applies his knowledge of the human skeleton to solving crimes and identifying missing persons. He has worked to identify the remains of death squad victims in Argentina and has tried (so far without success) to locate the bones of Butch Cassidy and the Sundance Kid in Bolivia.

Melvin Konner has examined the lifestyles of contemporary **hunter-gatherers,** including their diet and exercise, to show how those lifestyles differ (mostly for the better) from those of people in industrial societies.

We'll discuss these people and their studies, and many more, as we survey the field of bioanthropology. As we do, keep in mind that what connects these varied activities is their focus on *learning about human beings as a biocultural species.*

The studies of bioanthropologists are also connected in that they are all scientific. In many cases, they may not seem to fit the common conception of science. Most anthropologists don't wear white lab coats or work with test tubes and chemicals. Many anthropologists study things that can't be directly observed in nature or re-created in the lab because they happened in the past. But bioanthropology *is* a science, just as much as chemistry, physics, and biology. We'll see how this is so, and we'll also look at some nonscientific ways in which people try to understand their world.

BIOANTHROPOLOGY AND SCIENCE

A popular image of a scientist is that of a walking encyclopedia. Science is often seen as fact-collecting. While it's fair to say that scientists know a lot of facts, so do a lot of other people. Winners on the TV quiz show *Jeopardy* are not usually professional scientists.

Facts are certainly important to science. They are the raw material of science, the data scientists use. But what scientists really do is *explain* facts, not simply collect them. **Science,** in other words, is a method of inquiry, a way of answering questions about the world. But how does science work? Is science the only valid and logical method for explaining the world around us?

The Scientific Method

The world is full of things that need explaining. We might wonder about the behavior of a bird, the origin of the stars in the night sky, the identity of a fossil skeleton, the social interaction of students in a college classroom, or the ritual warfare of a society in highland New Guinea. As people, we strive to understand such phenomena, to know why and how

archaeology: A subfield of anthropology that studies the human cultural past and the reconstruction of past cultural systems.

paleoanthropology: A specialty that studies the human fossil record.

osteology: The study of the structure, function, and evolution of the skeleton.

primates: Large-brained, mostly tree-dwelling mammals with three-dimensional color vision and grasping hands. Humans are primates.

primatology: A specialty that studies nonhuman primates.

human ecology: A specialty that studies the relationships between humans and their environments.

applied anthropology: Anthropology used to address current practical problems and concerns.

forensic anthropologist: A scientist who applies anthropology to legal matters.

hunter-gatherers: Societies that rely on naturally occurring sources of food.

science: The method of inquiry that requires the generation, testing, and acceptance or rejection of hypotheses.

FIGURE 1.8
Steps in the scientific method. Science is a cycle of asking questions, finding patterns, generating hypotheses, and testing those hypotheses. Even when a hypothesis is well supported, it still must be subjected to scientific inquiry to check its validity and explain its details. Science should always be skeptical, always open to questioning and self-examination. All science is conducted by individuals within the context of a culture and so is affected by preconceptions. It is an important part of the scientific method to be aware of these preconceptions.

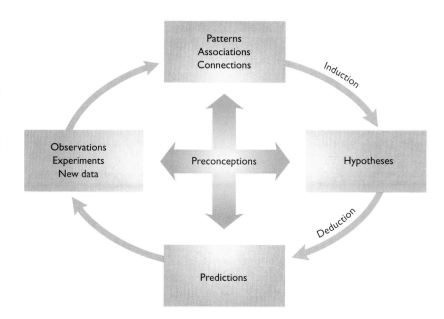

these things occur. As scientists, we must answer these questions according to a special set of rules—the **scientific method.**

The scientific method involves a cycle of steps, and in reality, one may begin anywhere on the cycle (Figure 1.8). The most basic step is asking the questions we wish to answer or describing the observations we wish to explain. We then look for patterns, connections, and associations so we can generate educated guesses as to possible explanations. These educated guesses are called **hypotheses.** In other words, we try to formulate a *general* explanatory principle that will account for the *specific* pieces of real data we have observed and want to explain. This process of reasoning is called **induction.**

Next comes the essence—indeed the defining characteristic—of science. We must attempt to either support or refute our hypothesis by testing it. Tests may take many forms, depending on what we are trying to explain, but basically we reverse the process of induction and go from the general back to the specific by making predictions: *If* our general hypothesis is correct, *then* what other specific things should we observe? This process is called **deduction.** For example, we look for:

Repetition: Does the same phenomenon occur over and over?

Universality: Does the phenomenon occur under all conditions? If we vary some aspect of the situation, will the phenomenon still occur? How might different situations change the phenomenon?

Explanations for exceptions: Can we account for cases where the phenomenon doesn't appear to occur?

New data: Does new information support or contradict our hypothesis?

If we find one piece of evidence that conclusively refutes our hypothesis, we consider it disproved. But if it passes every test we put it to, we elevate it to a *working hypothesis* and use it as a basis for further induction and testing. Notice that I didn't say we *prove* a hypothesis. Good science is skeptical, always looking for new evidence, always open to and, indeed, inviting change. The best we should honestly say about most hypotheses is that, so far, no evidence has been found that *disproves* them.

When, through this process, we have generated an integrated body of ideas forming a general concept that coordinates, explains, and interprets a wide range of factual patterns in a given area, we refer to this body of ideas as a **theory.** In science, *theory* is a positive term. The theories of gravity, relativity, and evolution are called *theories* because they are general ideas that explain a large number of phenomena and are themselves made up of interacting and well-supported hypotheses. All the facts of biology, for instance, make sense within the general theory of evolution—that all life has a common ancestry and that living forms change over time and give rise to new forms by various natural processes.

We don't stop when we have developed a theory, however. No theory is complete. The theory of gravity establishes that some force we call *gravity* exists, but we still don't understand exactly what gravity is and how it works. In other words, we still have questions to answer and observations to explain to complete the theory. Scientists are now testing hypotheses that attempt to explain the origin, nature, and operation of gravity.

Another popular conception of science is that it only studies visible, tangible, present-day things—chemicals, living organisms, planets and stars. But notice that gravity is neither visible nor tangible. We can't see gravity, but we know it exists because all our deductive predictions support its existence. We see gravity work every time we drop an object or jump up in the air and come back down to earth instead of flying off into space. We logically predict that if gravity is the property of objects with mass, the bigger the object the more its gravity. We saw this clearly when we watched the astronauts walk around on the moon; they were literally lighter (about one-sixth their earthly weight) because the moon, being smaller than the earth, has less gravity. We also see the increased effects of the gravity of very massive objects (Figure 1.9). We can even explain exceptions *within the context of our general idea.* The reason a

scientific method: The process of conducting scientific inquiry.

hypotheses: Educated guesses to explain natural phenomena.

induction: Developing a general explanation from specific observations.

deduction: Suggesting specific data that would be found if a hypothesis were true.

theory: A well-supported general idea that explains a large set of factual patterns.

FIGURE 1.9
Light bent by gravity. Einstein predicted in 1905 that a strong gravitational field could bend light. His prediction was verified in 1919, when light from stars that should have been blocked by the sun could be seen during a solar eclipse. The effect is greatly exaggerated in this drawing.

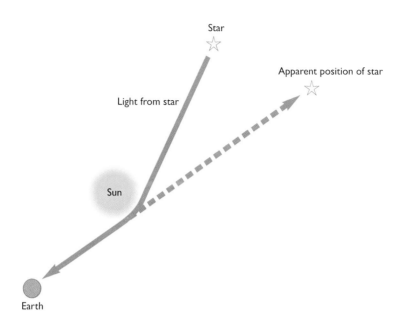

helium-filled balloon seems to violate gravity can be explained by our theory of gravity: helium is less dense than the surrounding air and so responds relatively less to the earth's gravity (that is, it is lighter). In other words, the balloon exhibits buoyancy like a boat on water.

Similarly, past events can't be seen or touched. They can't be experimented on directly or repeated exactly. The evolution of plants and animals is an example. But again, we know that evolution occurred because the idea has passed all our tests. The idea of evolution explains observations of the real world. We have observed everything we predicted we would *if* evolution occurred. (We'll look more closely at how science has generated and supported the theory of evolution in Chapter 3.)

I noted that scientists may begin their investigations at any point on the cycle diagrammed in Figure 1.8. For instance, we might have a flash of inspiration for some overarching concept that might explain many different phenomena. In other words, we might dream up a potential theory. We then, of course, would have to go through all the other steps: making observations, generating individual hypotheses, and testing those hypotheses. As an example, Albert Einstein was working on the nature of light waves when he came up with the idea of the equivalency of matter and energy, his famous formula $E = mc^2$. It was only later that this relationship was experimentally verified and all its implications and applications were understood.

Finally, what about the label "Preconceptions" in the middle of Figure 1.8? Don't scientists search for truths—truths that are objective and not influenced by preconceived notions or prejudices? Ideally, yes. But in fact, scientists are members of their societies and participants in their cultures, and science is always conducted within the context of a particular culture at a particular point in time. Thus, science—as objective as we try to make it—is always constrained by what we already know, by what we still don't know, by the technology available to us to gather and test data, by existing theories, and even by certain influential social or cultural trends.

For example, I remember back in the mid-1950s, when one of my elementary school teachers pointed out that the east coast of South America and the west coast of Africa seemed to potentially fit together like a giant jigsaw puzzle (Figure 1.10). Of course, she had said, there's no way the continents could move around, so it must just be a coincidence. In fact, she was reflecting our scientific knowledge of the time. There was plenty of geological and fossil evidence suggesting that the continents had moved around, but we knew of no way then that such movement could possibly occur. Although the idea of continental drift had been proposed in 1912, there was no mechanism to explain it. Beginning in the 1960s, however, new technologies gave us new evidence that provided such a mechanism. We now have a well-verified theory of continental drift by the process of plate tectonics.

An interesting example of an influential social trend comes from a hypothesized explanation for the famous Salem witch trials in Massachusetts in 1692, when a group of young girls accused some adults of witchcraft, with the result that twenty people were executed. The idea was that the people of Salem had consumed bread made from grains tainted with ergot, a fungus that contains alkaloids, some of which are derivatives of lysergic acid, which in turn is used in the synthesis of the hallucinogenic drug LSD. In other words, maybe the young girls who made the witchcraft accusations were experiencing substance-induced hallucinations. I need not tell you in which recent decade this idea arose. By the way, there is no evidence for this explanation. These examples show us why scientific skepticism is so important and why we should always question and re-examine even our most well-supported ideas.

So, science answers questions about our lives and about the world in which we live. For an answer to be defined as scientific, it must be testable—and must be tested. Put another way, it must be possible to find data that would *disprove* it. For an answer to be accepted, it must pass all tests and be refuted by none.

FIGURE 1.10
Topographic map of the Atlantic Ocean floor showing the correlating outlines of the edges of the Eastern and Western Hemispheres. Also shown is the Mid-Atlantic Ridge—evidence for the plate tectonics that pushed the once-connected continents apart.

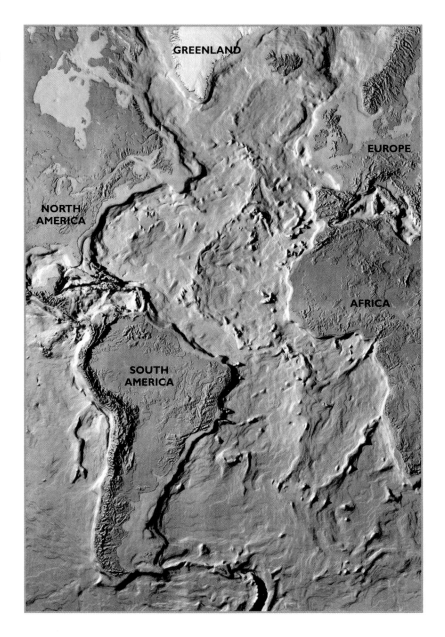

Belief Systems

Some questions about the world, even in a technologically complex society like ours, remain beyond the scope of science.

Scientific inquiry, as powerful and important as it is, doesn't answer everything. Although we have some well-established theories about how the universe evolved once it began, the ultimate origin of the universe remains, for the moment at least, outside the realm of science. For most human societies throughout most of our species' history, many questions could not be addressed scientifically.

Nor does science tell us how to behave. In our society, for example, we treat medical matters scientifically. But science does not, and cannot, inform us how best to apply medical knowledge. Who should practice medicine? How are medical practitioners trained and administered by society? How should they be compensated? What should their relationship be with their patients? Is everyone equally entitled to medical care? Society and the medical profession answer these questions through laws and regulations. For example, one version of the Hippocratic oath (there are several forms) taken by doctors says in part, "I will not permit considerations of religion, nationality, race, party politics or social standing to intervene between my duty and my patient."

Finally, there are questions that can never be answered by science—matters such as the meaning of life, the existence of a higher power, the proper social relationships among people within a society, or the purpose of one's own life.

All these sorts of questions are addressed by **belief systems**—religions, philosophies, ethics, morals, and laws. Belief systems differ from science in that they cannot be tested, cannot be disproved. Their truths are taken on faith, and that, of course, is the source of their power. They provide stable bases for our behavior, for explanations of what is beyond our science, and for the broad, existential questions of life. Belief systems change, but they only change when *we* decide to change them, either as a society or as individuals.

The existence of a supreme being is an example of a value inherent in one's belief system. Two of us with opposite views on the subject could debate the issue endlessly, but no scientific test could support or refute either view. If I were to change my mind on the matter, it would be because of a personal decision. The supreme being is not to be found in a test tube or through a telescope.

Belief systems don't apply only to these big questions. I had a friend in graduate school from a West African society that is polygynous—men may have several wives. Having more than one wife is normal in his society, whereas in mine, one wife (at least one at a time) is the norm. We discussed the pros and cons of these two systems at length one day, but we never, of course, arrived at any "answer." His belief was the norm for his society as was mine for my society. We each took it on faith that this was so.

belief systems: Ideas that are taken on faith and cannot be scientifically tested.

Contemporary Reflections

Is Evolution a Fact, a Theory, or Just a Hypothesis?

It may surprise you that the answer is "all of the above." Evolution, as a broad topic, incorporates theory, fact, *and* hypothesis. This is because the scientific method is not a nice, neat, linear series of steps from first specific observation to final all-encompassing theory. Rather, science works in a cycle (see Figure 1.8), and the inductive and deductive reasoning of science is applied constantly to the different aspects of the same general subject. Data and hypotheses are always being re-examined, and each theory itself becomes a new observation to be questioned, tested, explained, and possibly changed.

A theory is a well-supported idea that explains a set of observed phenomena. Evolution is a theory in that all our observations of life on earth—fossils, the geological formations in which they are found, and the biology of living creatures—make sense and find explanation within the concept of evolution, the idea that living things change through time and that organisms are related as in a huge branching bush, with existing species giving rise to new species.

Moreover, there is so much evidence in support of evolution that this tried-and-tested theory may reasonably be considered a fact. Of course, new data could conceivably change that, but with an idea as well supported as evolution, it is highly unlikely. A good analogy is the accepted fact that the earth revolves around the sun and not, as people thought for so long, the other way around. But how do we *know* the earth revolves around the sun? It certainly appears upon daily observation to do just the opposite. We accept the heliocentric (sun-centered) theory because there is so much data in its support. It makes so much sense and explains so many other phenomena that we consider it a fact and take it for granted, never giving it much thought on a regular basis. I would be very surprised to read in tomorrow's newspaper that some new evidence refuted the idea. Similarly, that evolution occurs and accounts for the nature of life on earth is, for all intents and purposes, a fact.

But that fact poses more questions. A big one (the one that confronted Darwin) is *how* evolution takes place. The fact of evolution now becomes a new observation that requires explanation through the generation of new hypotheses and the subsequent testing and retesting of those hypotheses. Darwin proposed a mechanism he called *natural selection* and then, over many years, examined this hypothesis against real-world data. The mechanism of natural selection is now so well supported that we call it, too, a fact.

But an overall explanation for how evolution works—a theory (or set of theories) to explain the observed fact of evolution—is far from complete. We know that mechanisms in addition to natural selection contribute to evolution. The relative importance of all these mechanisms is still being debated. The broad picture of evolution—the "shape" of the family bush of living things—is a matter of much discussion. The specific genetic processes behind all evolutionary change are really only beginning to be revealed as new technologies are letting us look at the very code of life. In other words, we are still examining hypotheses to account for *how* evolution takes place.

Evolution—like any broad scientific idea—involves a complex and interacting web of facts, hypotheses, and theories. It is the never-ending nature of scientific inquiry that can make science so frustrating, but that also makes it so exciting and so important in the modern world.

Although we often perceive science and belief systems as being eternally and inevitably at odds with one another, nothing could be further from the truth. Conflicts arise among facets of all societies. But it should be apparent that for a society to function, it needs both scientific knowledge and beliefs, because neither by itself addresses all the questions.

▽   ▽   ▽

SUMMARY

Anthropology is the holistic study of the human species from the biocultural perspective. Cultural anthropology studies human culture, cultural systems, and their variation. Our species' most characteristic feature today is our cultural behavior, which is expressed in a great variety of ways among different societies.

The majority of human cultural systems that ever existed did so in the past and so have left us only meager physical remains of their presence and nature. A second major subfield of anthropology recovers and interprets these remains; this subfield is archaeology.

Biological anthropology studies the human species the way biology studies any species, examining our biological characteristics, our evolution, our variation, our relationship with our environment, and our behavior, including our ability to have culture.

Bioanthropology, as a scientific discipline, asks questions about the human species and then attempts to answer them by proposing hypotheses and by testing those hypotheses, looking both for evidence in their support and for anything that would refute them.

Scientific knowledge is important for any society, but it must be mediated by the nonscientific values of belief systems—the untestable ideas of philosophy, law, and religion that are taken on faith. Societies need both science and belief systems, interacting in harmony, to fully function.

QUESTIONS FOR FURTHER THOUGHT

1. Anthropologists have special responsibilities when studying other human beings. What sorts of issues do you think I had to take into account when conducting my research among the Hutterites? What

issues would have been involved in the exhumation of Henry Opukahaia? Consider another culture you are familiar with, and imagine what particular issues would be involved in studying it as an anthropologist.

2. Because of anthropology's wide scope of interests and its overlap with other scholarly disciplines, anthropologists have sometimes been described as "jacks of all trades and masters of none." How would you respond to this?

3. Our impression that science and belief systems are naturally at odds with one another comes largely from cases in which the two areas are forced into conflict—when, for example, a religious belief is said to refute a scientific idea or a scientific idea is said to undermine a belief. Can you give an example of such a conflict? How would you resolve the conflict, given what you now understand about these two areas of inquiry?

KEY TERMS

biological anthropology

bioanthropology

physical anthropology

anthropology

species

holistic

culture

biocultural

cultural anthropology

archaeology

paleoanthropology

osteology

primates

primatology

human ecology

applied anthropology

forensic anthropologist

hunter-gatherers

science

scientific method

hypotheses

induction

deduction

theory

belief systems

SUGGESTED READINGS

For more personal experiences of biological anthropologists, see part 1 of my *Biological Anthropology: An Introductory Reader,* third edition. (*Complete publication details of the suggested readings appear in the "References."*)

For more information on the Hutterites, see John Hostetler's *Hutterite Society.*

For a longer discussion of the nature of science and the scientific method, see Kenneth L. Feder's *Frauds, Myths, and Mysteries: Science and Pseudoscience in Archaeology*, fourth edition. The relationship between science and belief systems is nicely covered by John Maynard Smith's article, "Science and Myth," in the November 1984 issue of *Natural History*. A more philosophical discussion can be found in *Rocks of Ages: Science and Religion in the Fullness of Life*, by Stephen Jay Gould.

The field of anthropology in general is covered in my *Introducing Anthropology: An Integrated Approach*, second edition, and in a collection of contemporary articles edited by Aaron Podolefsky and Peter Brown, *Applying Anthropology: An Introductory Reader*, fifth edition.

I've written an extended version of the story of Henry Opukahaia, "The Homegoing," which appears in *Lessons from the Past: An Introductory Reader in Archaeology*, by Kenneth L. Feder.

CHAPTER

2

THE EVOLUTION OF EVOLUTION

One touch of Darwin
makes the whole
world kin.
—George Bernard
Shaw

Evolution and its application to the human species—how we descended from nonhuman ancestors, how we have changed over time into modern *Homo sapiens*, and how we are still changing—is a central theme of bioanthropology. As noted in Chapter 1, the *fact* of evolution is well supported by scientific examination—the idea has passed every scientific test applied to it. Scientists, however, are still debating the details of evolution and refining the *theory* that explains exactly how evolution operates. It took some time, though, for the scientific method to be applied to this idea.

How did our knowledge of the history of living organisms move from the realm of belief systems to the realm of science?

How did the scientific evidence for evolution develop?

"ON THE SHOULDERS OF GIANTS": EXPLAINING THE CHANGING EARTH

The Englishman Charles Darwin (1809–1882) is usually, and correctly, associated with our understanding of biological evolution (Figure 2.1). He is also popularly given credit for the very idea of evolution and for explaining and therefore proving it. This, however, is not entirely correct. Like any great scientific accomplishment, Darwin's was based on the work of many who came before him. He stood, as Isaac Newton said of himself, "on the shoulders of giants." Darwin's genius was in being able to take massive amounts of data and assorted existing ideas and, using an imagination possessed by few humans, put them all together into a logical, cohesive theory that made sense of the world and that could be examined by the methods of science.

The idea of **evolution** is simple enough: species of living things change over time, and under the right circumstances this change can produce new species of living organisms from existing ones. This idea was not new in Darwin's time. Anaximander, a Greek philosopher and astronomer of the sixth century BC, proposed that humans had arisen from other forms of life. He incorrectly thought we arose directly from fish, but rather than explaining his idea in supernatural terms, he used reasoning to explore the question of how animals survive in their environments, a question that would form the cornerstone of Darwin's idea (Harris, 1981).

FIGURE 2.1
Portrait of Charles Darwin in 1869 by famed photographer Julia Margaret Cameron.

Many others over the next two thousand years also contemplated the origins of living things, but the modern story of evolutionary theory really began in seventeenth-century Europe, where the influence of the Bible was felt in all aspects of life, including science. Specifically, the ancient Judeo-Christian creation story—Adam and Eve, the Garden of Eden, the Flood and Noah's ark—was generally considered to be literally true. Thus, it was thought that the entire universe was created by supernatural processes over a period of six days and that, except for the matter of the great flood, the earth and its inhabitants were pretty much the same now as they were when created. One scholar, Irish archbishop James Ussher (1581–1656), even used the assumption of biblical truth, as well as certain historical records, to help him calculate the date of the Creation and thus the age of the earth. In 1650 he reckoned that the Creation began at noon on Sunday, October 23, in the year 4004 BC. The earth was thus about 6,000 years old.

The literal interpretation of the Bible, in turn, was probably influenced by two old but persuasive ideas that go back to Plato and Aristotle, Greek philosophers of the fourth and fifth centuries BC. One idea is called *essentialism*—the notion that there is an ideal, or essential, form of every natural entity and that the variations we see are largely inexact copies of the ideal. The variations among the members of some species of living organisms—for example, breeds of dogs—are just deviations from the essential form. Applied to biblical creation, essentialism promoted the idea that one ideal form of each living thing had been created and that the present-day variations—breeds of animals or races of people—are mostly departures from those ideals.

The second idea is called the *great chain of being*. It says that since there is an ideal, the various forms of things are not just a list of equals but are arranged in a ladder or chain, from least complex to most complex and from least perfect to most perfect. There are two different creation stories in Genesis, one in which humans are created last, after all the animals (Genesis 1), and one in which humans are created first (Genesis 2). Whichever order one accepts, however, there is the clear implication that humans are the most perfect form of creation. These two philosophical ideas would also have a strong influence on the later science of evolution, as we will see.

Dependence on the Bible for knowledge of the natural world was not to last. About the time Ussher was making his calculations, others were beginning to seek knowledge about the earth from the earth itself. What these "natural scientists," or "natural philosophers," saw forced them to reconsider what seemed to be the obvious lessons from the Book of Genesis.

evolution: Change through time; here, with reference to biological species.

For example, another seventeenth-century scientist, Robert Hooke (1635–1703) recognized **fossils** of plants and animals—once thought to be mere quirks of nature—as the remains of creatures that had become extinct or that still existed but in different form. Living things, in other words, had changed.

Moreover, Hooke attributed these extinctions and changes to the fact that the earth itself had been continually undergoing change since the Creation. He even proposed a naturalistic explanation for Noah's flood; it was, he said, probably caused by earthquakes. So, since the earth is in a continual state of change, so are its inhabitants, changing as their environments are altered or becoming extinct if that alteration is too great.

Evidence for this idea of a changing earth came from the examination of the layers of rock and soil below the earth's present surface. These layers are the earth's **strata** (singular, *stratum*), and their study is called **stratigraphy** (Figure 2.2). One of the earliest scientists to discuss this was a Dane, Nicholas Steno (1638–1686). He suggested that the strata represented layers of sediments deposited by water in a *sequence*, the lower layers earlier and the higher layers later. The nature of the rock and soil of each stratum, and its fossil contents, showed the natural conditions at the time the stratum was deposited: what creatures existed, whether the area was under sea or on land, and so on. It became clear that neither the earth nor its inhabitants were stable and unchanging. It was also clear that the record of past change could be read by observing the present-day world.

Steno and Hooke, however, still believed in a biblical chronology. To Steno, the water-deposited layers of the stratigraphic sequences represented two events—the original water-covered earth on which God created land and plants and animals (Genesis 1) and the waters of Noah's flood (Genesis 6–8). The geological record, however, shows a vast amount of change, and the Bible provides only 6,000 years of the earth's history. To bring about so much change in such a short time, thought Steno and Hooke, required the presence of global catastrophic events—such as earthquakes and volcanoes—associated with the Creation and the Flood. Steno and Hooke and others who subscribed to this explanation are often referred to as **catastrophists.**

One well-known proponent of catastrophism was the French naturalist Georges Cuvier (1769–1832). Cuvier thought that a "prototype" of each creature had been created and that it and its environment had been planned to fit each other. The influence of essentialism is obvious here. Cuvier believed that differences in climate could bring about alterations in these prototypes but that such changes were limited, producing minor variations in the created types. He also thought that he could reconstruct

fossils: Remains of life-forms of the past.

strata: Layers; here, the layers of rock and soil under the earth's surface.

stratigraphy: The study of the earth's strata.

catastrophists: Those who believe the history of the earth is explained by a series of global catastrophes, either natural or divine in origin.

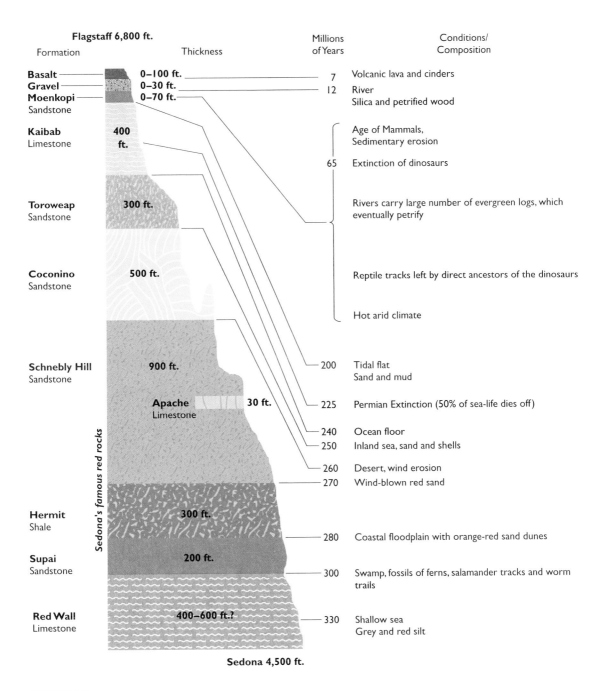

FIGURE 2.2

This geological cross section of the area around Sedona and Flagstaff, Arizona, shows the variation in composition and thickness of the strata and some of the events represented in those strata.

✳ the prototypes by using fossil remains of creatures. He compared the fragments of ancient creatures to living ones to try to picture what the whole organism looked like. In so doing, he pioneered the method known as **comparative anatomy,** still used today to infer missing parts of fossil organisms.

Cuvier also knew that life on earth had undergone major changes. He believed that the entire plan of the Creation had been changed several times by the Creator and that the changes were manifested in a series of global catastrophes that brought about the extinction of existing forms of life and prepared the way for newly created forms. Thus, as science historian John Greene put it, Cuvier "recognized change but not development" (1959:130). In other words, he accepted that the world had changed but not that it had evolved, with new forms of life being modifications of older forms. Moreover, since humans were only included in the latest Creation (although Cuvier did admit that they might have been around before), there was the implication that humans were somehow the Creator's highest, most perfect form of living thing—an idea clearly influenced by the great-chain-of-being concept.

Catastrophism enjoyed a degree of popularity because it seemed to reconcile natural evidence with a biblical time frame. But strict catastrophism did not stand up to further scientific observation and examination. The French scholar Comte Georges-Louis Leclerc de Buffon (1707–1788) concluded that although catastrophic events do occur, they are rare and so "have no place in the ordinary course of nature." Instead, the earth's history is mainly explained by "operations *uniformly* repeated, motions which succeed one another without interruption" (emphasis mine). The motions Buffon spoke of were mainly the motions of the sea—tides and currents—operating to form the earth while the earth was still completely covered by water and while the strata were still being deposited. Phenomena occurring on land, such as wind and water erosion, he thought, were not particularly important. But he did establish a new model: much of the earth's geological history could be explained by normal, everyday, uniform processes—the things taking place before our eyes. This idea is called **uniformitarianism.** For such processes to account for all the changes recorded in the earth's strata, however, the earth would have to be older than 6,000 years. Buffon was among the first to propose a longer history for the planet.

It was a Scotsman, James Hutton (1726–1797), who brought uniformitarianism onto the land. Hutton said that the history of the earth, as seen in its strata, is the result of three general processes: (1) the deposition of strata under the waters of the oceans; (2) the compacting of these strata by pressure and their uplifting above sea level by subterranean heat; and (3) the erosion of land by water, wind, and decay. Hutton saw these processes as part of a self-regulating system: Erosion produced the soil in which plants grew. Plants, in turn, fed animals and humans (for whom, he thought, all this had been created in the first place). New land was continually being formed under the sea from sediments produced by erosion, which would ultimately provide new sources of soil. And so on. Again, such a system would require far more than 6,000 years, and Hutton suggested that the earth was much older. Indeed, he thought it was virtually timeless, having "no vestige of a beginning—no prospect of an end."

The English surveyor and geologist William Smith (1769–1839) formalized the description of the evidence for change in the earth—the strata and their fossil content. Smith, whose work earned him the nickname "Strata," documented the patterns of strata and fossils across England, Wales, and Scotland and produced the first geological map of any area of the world.

Charles Lyell (1797–1875), born in Scotland the year Hutton died, is usually associated with uniformitarianism as it applies to geology. This is in part because his version of that idea was so extreme. He advocated, as had Hutton, the uniformity of processes throughout time, that is, that present-day processes are the key to explaining the past. He also believed that the rate of geological change was uniform—slow and steady through countless eons, with no need to invoke global catastrophes. He wasn't too far off.

But he also believed that the earth itself was fairly uniform through time, that the earth has been, and always will be, basically the same. Changes certainly occur, but they occur, said Lyell, just in the details, not in the overall appearance of the earth or in its life-forms. Moreover, these changes occur in great cycles. He thought, for example, that dinosaurs, though extinct at the moment, would eventually reappear.

At this point, it would be a good idea to briefly describe what modern scientific knowledge has to say about these issues. We now agree with the major parts of the uniformitarian position:

1. Processes that formed and changed the earth in the past—as seen in its stratigraphic record—are the same processes that take place in the present.

2. By studying the stratigraphic record, we can reconstruct the history of the earth (an idea that goes back to Steno).

3. For known geological processes to account for the changes recorded in the strata, an immense amount of time would have been required; we know now that the earth is about 4.5 billion years old (Figure 2.3).

comparative anatomy: Comparing the anatomical features of various species. Used to reconstruct a fossil species from fragmentary remains.

uniformitarianism: The idea that present-day geological processes can also explain the history of the earth.

FIGURE 2.3
Utah's Bryce Canyon shows the results of geological processes, especially the laying down of strata and subsequent erosion, over millions of years.

We also now understand that Lyell was far too restrictive in his idea about uniform rate. Not all processes are slow and steady. Catastrophic events may seem relatively rare to us, but they do take place and have occurred many times during the history of the earth. Even Lyell acknowledged that most are localized events, such as volcanoes and earthquakes that affect the geology and life of a particular area. However, some events are catastrophic on a global scale. At least five major catastrophes have occurred during the 3.5-billion-year history of life on earth—in one case, bringing about the extinction of over 90 percent of the earth's species. The most famous of these cataclysms (though not the biggest) occurred 65 million years ago when at least one asteroid collided with the earth and caused such radical environmental change that 75 percent of the world's marine species became extinct, along with many terrestrial species, including the dinosaurs. (See Chapter 6.) These are not the series of biblically associated catastrophes proposed by Steno, Hooke, and Cuvier; rather, these catastrophes occur irregularly and are of natural origin. They have, nonetheless, radically altered the history of the planet.

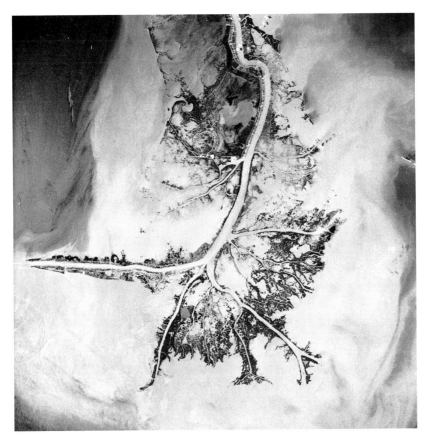

FIGURE 2.4
Aerial view of the Mississippi Delta. By estimating the amount of material deposited in the delta (the delta-shaped [Δ] deposit of sand and soil at the mouth of a river), Charles Lyell concluded (although incorrectly) that it was 100,000 years old. (For orientation, the town of Venice, Louisiana, is the light patch just above the center of the photograph.)

Today we understand that Lyell's idea about the earth changing only in its details and in great cycles is also incorrect. The earth's history is a complex chain of events leading to other events, a continual sequence of changes—major and minor—never to be repeated. The dinosaurs are extinct; they will never return.

Despite what turned out to be some incorrect notions, Lyell's influence was great. Not only did he expand on the work of Hutton and others, he also began the explicit examination of geological data, bringing it fully into the realm of natural science. For example, he attempted to estimate the age of the Mississippi Delta (Figure 2.4). Because the rate of deposition of sediments at the mouth of the river can be measured and because the size of the existing deposit in the delta can be estimated, the time required for the delta to be formed can be reckoned by assuming a uniform rate of deposition. Lyell arrived at an age of about 100,000 years (1873:44–47). (Lyell was incorrect; the delta is not that old. Deposition rates are not constant, nor were existing measurement techniques precise enough.)

Through the work of Hooke, Steno, Hutton, Smith, and Lyell—and many others—the study of the earth shifted from the supernatural to the natural. Scientists sought data about earth's history from the earth itself, not from the presuppositions of belief systems. As a result, by the early nineteenth century, our world was viewed through the interacting perspectives of constant change brought about by observable processes over vast amounts of time.

Lyell put these ideas down in a major scientific work, his three-volume *Principles of Geology,* first published between 1830 and 1833. The book was highly influential. It was enthusiastically received by supporters of the uniformitarian approach, strongly criticized by those who continued to explain earth's history as a series of global catastrophes, and pored over by those still examining the data. Among those weighing Lyell's ideas was a young British naturalist who took the first volume of Lyell's book with him as he embarked, in 1831, on a round-the-world voyage of scientific exploration. This was Charles Darwin.

"COMMON SENSE AT ITS BEST": EXPLAINING BIOLOGICAL CHANGE

The view of life on earth as static and unchanging is exemplified by the work of Carl von Linné (1707–1778), better known to us as Carolus Linnaeus, whom we will discuss in detail in Chapter 7. Linnaeus, who devised the system of scientific names we still use to classify living things, initially thought that all species of plants and animals had been divinely created in their present forms and numbers. But Linnaeus, a keen observer of nature, came to recognize (as had Hooke before him) that some sort of change had taken place—that fossils, for example, represented species that had become extinct and that new species could arise. Still, Linnaeus saw any change as divinely preordained and as taking place within the constraints and limits of the original Creation—he thought, for example, that new species arose through hybridization between originally created species. This is another example of essentialism.

Gradually, though, through the observations and interpretations of all the scientists discussed so far, it became clear that life on earth had undergone change, just as had the earth itself, and that this change required scientific explanation using a uniformitarian approach. But this idea—then referred to as the *transmutation of species*—was a more controversial matter than the idea of a changing earth. For if other forms of life had arisen and changed over eons of time by uniform natural processes, then it followed that the same should apply to humans. It was, in part, in reaction to this idea that Cuvier attempted to apply catastrophism with a divine basis to an explanation of biological change. So, even after it became obvious that life had "evolved" (as we now phrase it), just *how* this had taken place mattered a great deal.

There were many who addressed this issue from a uniformitarian position, including Charles Darwin's grandfather, Erasmus Darwin (1731–1802), but one of the most influential was the French naturalist Jean-Baptiste de Lamarck (1744–1829). Lamarck emphasized Hooke's conclusion that plants and animals are **adapted** to their environments; that is, each kind of living organism has physical traits and behaviors that allow it to survive under a given set of natural circumstances. When environments change—as the stratigraphic record shows they do—organisms must change if they are to continue to exist.

Lamarck was quite correct that organisms undergo "possibly very great" change and that this change is connected to the environment. He erred, however, in his explanation of how this change occurs and in his idea as to the overall direction of evolution. Like others, he could not bring himself to see biological change as lacking a particular direction. Rather, he saw it as **progressive,** going from imperfect to perfect by a process of increasing complexity. This is another example of the influence of the great-chain-of-being concept. It should be obvious which species Lamarck thought was the most perfect and complex. This was the appeal of the idea of progressive evolution: if life itself changed through time, at least *we* were what it was changing toward.

Moreover, Lamarck's mechanism for this progressive change was fairly foolproof. It is called the **inheritance of acquired characteristics,** an old idea that Lamarck formalized in his 1809 *Philosophie zoologique*. He wrote:

> When the *will* guides an animal to any action, the organs which have to carry out that action are *immediately stimulated* to it by the influx of *subtle fluids*. . . . Hence it follows that numerous repetitions of these organised activities strengthen, stretch, develop and *even create* the organs necessary to them. . . . Now every change that is wrought in an organ through habit of frequently using it, is subsequently *preserved by reproduction*. . . . Such a change is thus handed on to *all succeeding individuals* in the same environment, without their having to acquire it in the same way that it was actually created. (Harris 1981:116–17; emphases mine)

adaptation: The state in which an organism is adjusted to and can survive in its environment through its physical traits and behaviors. Also, the process by which an organism develops this state through natural processes.

progressive: In evolution, the now-discounted idea that all change is toward increasing complexity.

inheritance of acquired characteristics: The incorrect idea that adaptive traits acquired during an organism's lifetime can be passed on to its offspring.

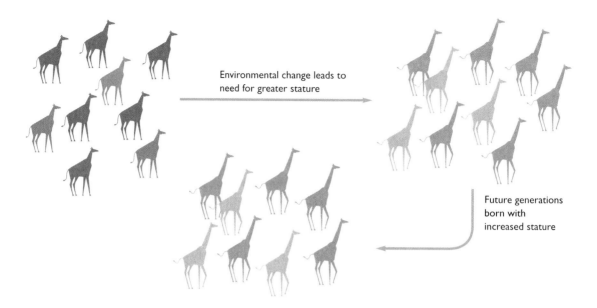

Environmental change leads to
need for greater stature

Future generations
born with
increased stature

FIGURE 2.5

Lamarck's model of inheritance of acquired characteristics applied to the evolution of long necks and tall bodies in giraffes. In the past, giraffes were short, but environmental change altered their food source, placing the foliage they ate high up in the trees. Confronted with this problem, *each giraffe* was able to stretch its neck and legs enough to reach the leaves. This greater height was automatically passed on to the giraffes' offspring, which had to make themselves even taller, and so on, giving rise to the 18-foot-tall giraffes of today.

As a famous (and probably over-used) example, Lamarck explained the long necks and legs of giraffes in the following way: In the past, giraffes were short, but some environmental change altered their food source, placing the foliage they ate high up in the trees. Confronted with this problem, each giraffe was able to stretch itself enough to reach the leaves. This greater height was automatically passed on to the giraffes' offspring, which had to make themselves even taller. And so on (Figure 2.5).

One reason that Lamarck's idea was popular was that it was one of the first detailed, lengthy, scientific treatments of evolution. Lamarck even spelled out how he used the scientific method by specifying the data that would be required to falsify his model. It was also a comfortable explanation for an uncomfortable topic. It had become clear that life was capable of change over time. At least, according to Lamarck's hypothesis, life changed in a particular (and very human-oriented) direction, and it changed by a process that was unfailing and dependent on something inherent to the organism—Lamarck called it "will." It even followed that no organisms ever become extinct. Creatures represented only by fossils were simply creatures that had undergone so much change they now looked very different.

But observation and logic produced some major objections to Lamarck's concept. For example, traits acquired during an organism's lifetime cannot be inherited by its offspring. A bodybuilder's children will not automatically be born with bulging muscles. Further, it was hard to

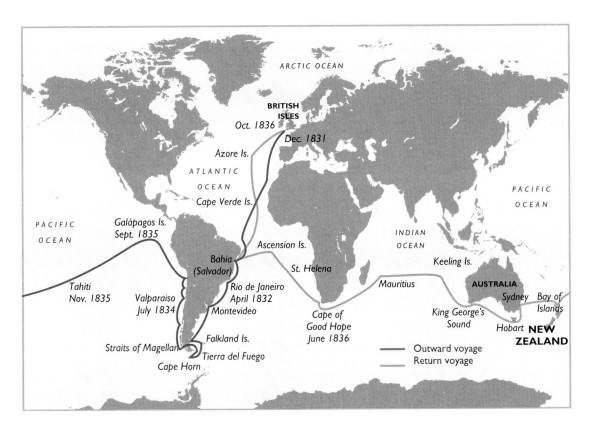

FIGURE 2.6
Route of Darwin's voyage
aboard the HMS *Beagle* from
1831 to 1836. This trip provided Darwin with observations and thoughts vital to his
formulation of the theory of
natural selection. Especially
famous and important was
his visit to the Galápagos
Islands in the eastern Pacific.

see how an organism's "will" could change its color or produce a new
organ or make a giraffe taller. And just what is the "subtle fluid" that is
supposed to bring all this about?

Thus, Charles Darwin was born (in 1809, the same year Lamarck's
book was published) into a world that accepted the *fact* of biological
change but was still in search of a *mechanism* for that change. Although
many, including Lamarck, held to a uniformitarian position, others, such
as Cuvier, still adhered to a catastrophic explanation. It was Darwin who
would provide the mechanism that has withstood over a century of
scientific examination.

The story of Darwin's life and scientific work is a fascinating one
(see, for example, Bowlby 1990). For the purpose of our story, however,
we can simply say that Darwin recognized an important fact not fully
appreciated by many of his predecessors or contemporaries. In his work
in his native England and especially on his famous voyage around the
world on the HMS *Beagle* (1831–1836; Figure 2.6), Darwin realized

the incredible degree of variation that exists within each living species (Figure 2.7). If Lamarck were correct, one would expect every member of a particular species to look pretty much the same because they all would have responded identically to the same environmental circumstances. Darwin saw this was clearly not the case. Variation always exists, no matter how well adapted a species might be. What tipped Darwin off to this fact of nature were his observations of domestic species such as pigeons, carefully bred for certain features but still showing physical variation every generation. Therefore, in each generation, breeders would have to choose for mating only those individuals possessing the features they desired, using the assumption that offspring tend to resemble parents. The goal was to eliminate undesirable traits and accumulate desirable ones.

Darwin also took a clue from the work of English economist Thomas Malthus (1766–1834). Malthus argued that in "animate nature" populations, if unchecked, increase at a more rapid rate than do resources. Thus, there is competition within any population over those resources, and this is what keeps populations in check.

Darwin reasoned that the same things happened in nature. Some of the natural variation within a species would make a difference in the success, or **fitness,** of individuals. The better-adapted individuals would tend to be more reproductively successful. Their traits would be passed on to more offspring than would those of the less well adapted. Over time, then, some traits would accumulate while others would decrease in frequency or even be eliminated. If the environment to which a species is adapted changes, it stands to reason that the fitness value of certain traits might also change, so the process described might proceed in a different adaptive direction—what was once adapted might now be neutral or perhaps even poorly adapted.

So, while Lamarck thought that variation *arose when it was needed,* Darwin understood that variation *already existed.* Because Darwin lived before the processes of genetics were understood, he did not know where this variation came from, but his observations showed it was a fact; and he realized that nature, like a plant or animal breeder, "selects" better-adapted individuals for more successful reproduction. Darwin called this process **natural selection.**

Thus, according to Darwin's model, giraffes didn't become steadily taller and taller in response to one environmental change. Rather, over many millennia, various environmental factors selected for certain expressions of many traits, resulting today in these tallest of living mammals.

fitness: The relative adaptiveness of an individual organism, measured ultimately by reproductive success.

natural selection: Evolutionary change based on the differential reproductive success of individuals within a species.

FIGURE 2.7

Variation within a population represents the raw material for natural selection. The tiger swallowtail butterflies *(upper right and bottom)* are members of the same species. The dark tiger swallowtail is a mimic of the pipe-vine butterfly *(left),* which is protected from predation by its foul taste.

Several important ideas follow from natural selection:

1. It becomes clear that evolution by natural selection has no particu-
    lar direction. Organisms do not "progress" to increasingly complex
    forms, as Lamarck thought, but evolve to simply stay adapted to their
    environments or, if possible, become readapted to changed environ-
    ments. Variation is not "willed." It results from random processes
    that we now understand from the study of genetics (see Chapter 3).

2. It is also clear that such a process, using random rather than directed
    or "willed" variation, is not foolproof. It doesn't always work. Species
    do become extinct, usually when the environment changes so exten-
    sively or rapidly that none of the existing variation within a species
    is adaptive. Extinction is, in fact, the norm. Nine-tenths of all
    species that have ever lived are now extinct.

3. It follows that *new* species can arise from this basic process. If pop-
    ulations within a species become environmentally separated, these
    populations will exist under different selective pressures—different
    traits will be differently adapted to each environment. Moreover,
    different variations will be produced in each population. Natural
    selection will have different raw materials to work with. Over time,
    then, a single species may give rise to one or more new species. This,
    in fact, was what Darwin was ultimately trying to explain, as indi-
    cated by the title of his most famous work, *On the Origin of Species by
    Means of Natural Selection*, first published in 1859. (See Chapter 5.)

Darwin's idea generated some controversy, which was perhaps why
he delayed publishing his book. We know he understood natural selection sometime in the late 1830s, yet it was not until more than twenty
years later that he made it public. Even then, he did so only because a
younger, less well-known naturalist, Alfred Russel Wallace (1823–1913),
independently came up with the same idea, and Darwin was urged by
friends to rush his conclusion into print.

The controversy centered not around the idea of uniformitarian evolution itself—which was generally well accepted by that time—but
around the fact that Darwin's idea, unlike Lamarck's, did not involve a
particular progressive direction nor the direct control or will of the
organism. Darwin also acknowledged extinction. These ideas were not
always comfortable. But to Darwin's surprise, by the time his book sold
out on its first day of publication, the scientific community and much of
the informed public were ready to accept the idea, even with its implications. Natural selection—the mechanism of evolution—was hailed as
a major scientific breakthrough and remains today a classic example of

Contemporary Reflections

Has Science Dehumanized Society?

To many, the story recounted in this chapter is one of science *versus* belief systems, specifically religious belief. A popular assessment of Darwin's contribution is that by "proving" evolution he "disproved" the Bible. As we will see in Chapter 5, there is still a substantial contingent today who feel that the very idea of evolution is antireligious.

And it's not just the science of evolution. From Mary Shelley's *Frankenstein* (published in 1818) to modern blockbuster movies such as *Jurassic Park* and *The Lost World*, science in general is seen as a potential evil, something that is far too easily abused and that, when abused, wreaks havoc on people and their societies. People often use the phrase "playing God" when referring to scientific endeavors—genetics studies in particular—that they perceive as affronts to human spirit and individuality. Science is blamed for many of today's social and environmental ills—and there *are* plenty of them—from global warming to radioactive contamination to the proliferation of weapons of mass destruction.

There are three errors in this view of science. First, although science has put forth, and scientists have embraced, ideas that resulted in human suffering, one of the hallmarks of science is its ability for self-correction. The eugenics movement, for example—which held that many human behaviors were hereditary and that therefore selective breeding could improve the species—resulted (even in the United States) in the forced sterilization of many individuals who were deemed less fit because of some characteristic that society felt undesirable (below-average intelligence, for instance, or having borne illegitimate children). This practice is abhorrent, but through scientific progress we now know much more about the nature of human heredity, and such mistakes are at least unlikely in the future.

Second, this view of science ignores the fact that *anything* may be a danger if used incorrectly or for nefarious purposes. One has but to examine world history to see that religious ideals are not always put to positive use. Indeed, many of today's bloody hostilities are the result of religious conflict—often involving religions that specifically prohibit the taking of human life.

Third, in focusing on the negative results of science, we all too easily forget about the positive results. Today's most vocal critics of science still promote their ideas on television and over the Internet; they travel in airplanes and enjoy all the medical and nutritional benefits of a modern scientific society. The astronomer Carl Sagan (1934–1996) once asked a group of people how many of them would not be alive today if it weren't for modern medical technology. Most raised their hands. (I tried this with a class of undergraduates, average age about 20, and still about half raised their hands.)

But still, didn't Darwin set the stage for this seeming conflict by disproving the Bible with his theory of evolution? Not at all. He *did* show that one literal interpretation of one part of one book of the Bible failed to account for observations of biology in the real world. In no way, however, did his idea of evolution refute a whole religious worldview, nor need it conflict with one's personal sense of the spiritual.

It is not knowledge or ideas, scientific or otherwise, that are dangerous, but how they are used. Ignorance is far more dangerous. It is ignorance that dehumanizes us.

TABLE 2.1
Important People and Ideas Associated with Evolution

	Approx. Date of Publication	Contribution
James Ussher (1581–1656)	1650	Calculation of the age of earth, using biblical data
Robert Hooke (1635–1703)	1660s–90s	Fossils as evidence of change Importance of environmental change
Nicholas Steno (1638–1686)	1669	Stratigraphy
Carolus Linnaeus (1707–1778)	1758	System of scientific names Recognition of extinction and possibility of new species
Comte Georges-Louis Leclerc de Buffon (1707–1788)	1749	Uniformitarianism Longer time frame for age of earth
James Hutton (1726–1797)	1795	Uniformitarianism Natural cycles Longer time frame for age of earth
Jean-Baptiste de Lamarck (1744–1829)	1809	Adaptation Inheritance of acquired characteristics Progressive evolution
Thomas Malthus (1766–1834)	1789	Relationship between population and resources
William Smith (1769–1839)	1815	First geological map showing strata
Georges Cuvier (1769–1832)	late 1700s, early 1800s	Ideal prototypes Climatic alterations Extinction Catastrophism
Charles Lyell (1797–1875)	1830–33	Uniformitarianism Scientific investigation
Charles Darwin (1809–1882)	1859	Natural selection Origin of species
Gregor Mendel (1822–1884)	1860s	Laws of inheritance
Alfred Russel Wallace (1823–1913)	1859	Natural selection

scientific reasoning, what Darwin's friend Thomas Henry Huxley called "common sense at its best."

At about the time Darwin was writing *Origin of Species,* a monk in what is now the Czech Republic was answering Darwin's question about the source of variation. After years of undocumented research on several species of plants and animals, Gregor Mendel (1822–1884) derived the basic laws of genetics by experimenting with pea plants in the garden of his monastery. These laws (which we'll cover in the next chapter) not only explained one source of biological variation but also showed why and how offspring tend to resemble their parents. Basic laws of genetics and biological variation are crucial to natural selection and the origin of new species.

Mendel died in relative obscurity (Darwin never learned of his work), and his writings languished in libraries until 1900, when they were rediscovered independently by three European scientists who realized that Mendel's work carried implications far beyond some interesting facts about pea plants. (This had been the reaction to Mendel's work during his life—that he had found some interesting facts about peas.) They understood that genetics filled in those pieces that Darwin acknowledged were missing from his process.

Over the past century, many scientists have added to Darwin's idea of natural selection and Mendel's work on genetics. There have been new details, changes of emphasis, and major discoveries, such as the breaking of the genetic code in the early 1950s. But all the work of the past hundred years has been built on the thoughts and discoveries of people such as Darwin and Lyell and Hooke, and many others. All the men and women whose investigations have led to our modern theory of evolution (which we will cover in the next three chapters) would freely agree that they have stood on the shoulders of these giants (Table 2.1).

▽   ▽   ▽

SUMMARY

The Judeo-Christian belief system, as set down in and interpreted from the Bible, was long seen as both a belief system and a source of literal knowledge. As scholars began looking more objectively at nature itself, however, their observations and the rational conclusions they drew from them showed clearly that knowledge of the heavens, the earth, and the earth's inhabitants required the methods of science. As the scientific method was applied to the study of the earth, scientists gradually learned to give up their presuppositions.

Charles Darwin, adhering faithfully to the spirit of scientific methodology, was able to synthesize his observations and thoughts with those of many others and to formulate a theory that made possible the work that has led to our modern knowledge of the nature and evolution of living things.

QUESTIONS FOR FURTHER THOUGHT

1. The scientific research and ideas of many early biologists and geologists were influenced by philosophical concepts. Do you think such influences ended with people like Darwin? Can you think of a modern scientific matter that may be influenced by beliefs?

2. Whereas biological evolution is not Lamarckian, the evolution of culture is. How so?

3. There are those who say that certain areas of scientific research should be avoided either because their results might be misused or because the facts generated might be unpleasant. What sorts of research do you think these people might be referring to? How would you respond to such cautions?

KEY TERMS

evolution	comparative anatomy	inheritance of acquired characteristics
fossils	uniformitarianism	
strata	adaptation	fitness
stratigraphy	progressive	natural selection
catastrophists		

SUGGESTED READINGS

The history of the study of evolution is covered in C. Leon Harris's *Evolution: Genesis and Revelations*, which contains numerous sections from original works, and in John C. Greene's *The Death of Adam*. The impact of Darwin's work on modern knowledge in general is the theme of Philip Appleman's *Darwin: A Norton Critical Edition*, second edition.

My favorite biography of Darwin, which focuses on the man as well as the scientist and nicely shows how the two aspects of his life were related, is John Bowlby's *Charles Darwin: A New Life*.

For more on the fascinating life and work of Alfred Russel Wallace, see *Bright Paradise: Victorian Scientific Travellers*, by Peter Raby, and *In Darwin's Shadow: The Life and Science of Alfred Russel Wallace*, by Michael Shermer.

William "Strata" Smith's eventful life is chronicled in Simon Winchester's *The Map That Changed the World: William Smith and the Birth of Modern Geology*.

Paleontologist and science historian Stephen Jay Gould wrote many wonderful essays about the history of evolution and other scientific topics and the personalities involved. These can be found throughout his books *Ever Since Darwin*, *The Panda's Thumb*, *Hen's Teeth and Horse's Toes*, *The Flamingo's Smile*, *Bully for Brontosaurus*, *Eight Little Piggies*, *Dinosaur in a Haystack*, *Leonardo's Mountain of Clams and the Diet of Worms*, *The Lying Stones of Marrakech*, and *I Have Landed*. These are all highly recommended.

EVOLUTIONARY GENETICS

The laws governing
inheritance are for the
most part unknown.
—Charles Darwin

wo important features of Darwin's natural selection were the seemingly contradictory facts that offspring tend to resemble their parents but that, at the same time, there is continual production of biological variation among members of a species and from generation to generation. Both facts were obvious enough to careful observers such as Darwin. But, as Darwin freely admitted, science was largely ignorant of the source of those facts, in other words, of how inheritance worked.

A popular idea of Darwin's time assumed that inheritance was a "blending"—a mixture of some material from both parents. Certainly there are sufficient examples of offspring with combinations of parental traits to make this idea seem logical. For example, new flower colors can be produced by crossbreeding other colors, much like paints are mixed to make new shades. Breeds of dogs can be crossbred to get combinations of the parents' physical and behavioral characteristics in the hybrid offspring. But offspring are often born with characteristics that resemble neither parent's or, as with one's sex, that are definitely *not* mixtures.

Observations of nonblending traits like sex may have led Gregor Mendel to begin experiments to determine just how inheritance operates. The laws he derived are still recognized today as the basis of genetics, although, of course, they have been added to greatly. The most basic and perhaps most important of Mendel's contributions was his conclusion that inheritance does not involve the blending of substances but, rather, is **particulate.** He showed that traits are passed on by individual particles according to very specific principles. Mendel called these particles "factors"; we call them **genes.** We'll now survey the aspects of modern genetics pertinent to bioanthropology by addressing the following questions:

> **What are genes, and how do they produce the traits that make a pea plant or a human being?**
>
> **What do we know about the nature of the human genome?**
>
> **What are the basic laws of inheritance?**
>
> **What processes bring about the variation we see among members of a species and between parents and offspring?**

HOW GENES WORK

We begin to see how genes work with something Mendel could not possibly have understood. Although he concluded that the particulate factors we now call genes produce the features of an organism and he provided us with the basic model for how traits are inherited, Mendel possessed neither the background knowledge nor the technology to figure out just how the genetic code operates at the chemical level.

We now understand that the genetic code is a set of instructions for the production (or synthesis) of **proteins** from **amino acids,** which we obtain from the foods we eat and which are found in the cytoplasm of the cell. Proteins are the basic building blocks of an organism's cells, shaping the cells, supporting the cells' internal structure, linking cells, and building membranes, muscles, and connective tissue. In a form called **enzymes,** proteins are responsible for the cells' chemical reactions. All organisms are composed of cells (Figure 3.1), so it can logically be said that all living things are based on proteins. Even the nonprotein substances found within a living organism—like the calcium in your bones—are regulated by proteins.

The genetic code is found in the nucleus of cells, on long strands called **chromosomes** (see Figure 3.6). A chromosome is made up of a protein core and strands of nucleic acid. It is the nucleic acid—**deoxyribonucleic acid (DNA)**—that carries the code.

DNA is like a ladder with its ends twisted in opposite directions (Figure 3.2). This shape is referred to as a *double helix.* The sides of the ladder provide structural stability. The rungs of the ladder carry the code. They are made up of pairs of bases (a family of chemicals) bonded in the middle. Each base, along with the portion of the side of the ladder to which it is connected, is called a **nucleotide.** Only four bases are involved: adenine (A), thymine (T), cytosine (C), and guanine (G), and they are only paired in A-T or T-A and C-G or G-C combinations. Thus, if we know the sequence of bases on one side of the DNA helix, we can correctly predict the sequence on the other side.

The first function of this pairing is to enable the DNA molecule to make copies of itself during cell division. During cell division the helix unwinds, and each strand, with its now unpaired bases, picks up the proper complementary bases, which are in solution in the cell. This is called **replication.** Thus, when the whole cell divides, each new *daughter cell* has a complete set of DNA base pairs (see Figure 3.2).

We refer to each consecutive sequence of three DNA bases as a **codon.** Codons are like words made up of three letters. Each word stands for a particular amino acid. A string of words—a genetic sentence—thus stands for a chain of amino acids. A chain of amino acids is a protein. Therefore, a sequence of codons codes for the linking together of amino acids to make a protein. This process is known as **protein synthesis** (Figure 3.3).

particulate: The idea that biological traits are controlled by individual factors rather than by a single all-encompassing hereditary agent.

genes: Those portions of the DNA molecule that code for a functional product, usually a protein.

proteins: Molecules that make cells and carry out cellular functions.

amino acids: The chief components of proteins.

enzymes: Proteins that control chemical processes.

chromosomes: Strands of DNA in the nucleus of a cell.

deoxyribonucleic acid (DNA): The molecule that carries the genetic code.

nucleotide: The basic building block of DNA and RNA, made up of a sugar, a phosphate, and one of four bases.

replication: The copying of the genetic code during cell division.

codon: The three-base sequence that codes for a specific amino acid. Technically, the sequence on the mRNA.

protein synthesis: The process by which the genetic code puts together proteins in the cell.

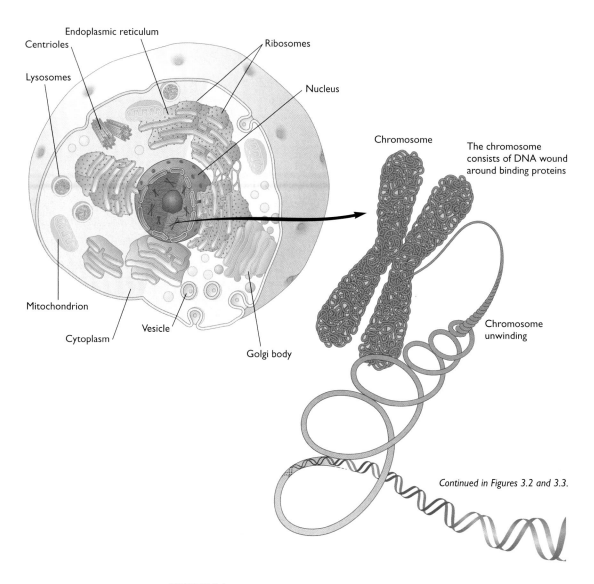

FIGURE 3.1
Typical cell and its important parts. This cell represents all types of cells, from the more complex single-celled organisms such as amoebas to the cells in the human body. The ribosomes are the sites of protein synthesis (see Figure 3.3). The mitochondria are the cells' energy factories, converting energy stored in nutrients into a form the cells can use to perform their various functions.

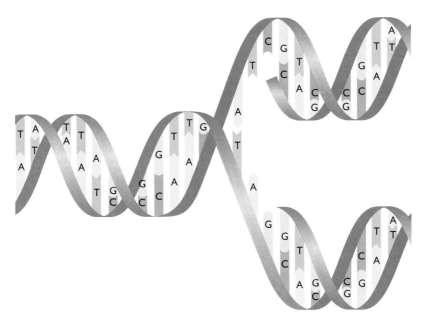

FIGURE 3.2
DNA molecule. This molecule is shown in the process of unwinding and copying itself prior to cell division (see Figure 3.7).

For our purposes here, we will define *gene* in a functional way, that is, as that portion of the DNA molecule that carries the codon sequence for a particular protein. To summarize:

FEATURE	ANALOGUE	MEANING
base (A, T, C, G)	letter	
codon	word	amino acid
gene	sentence	protein

How does protein synthesis work? As you read this description, follow along in Figure 3.3. During protein synthesis only a portion of the DNA molecule is unwound (in contrast to the complete unwinding seen in replication). **Messenger ribonucleic acid (mRNA)** is assembled against one strand of this unwound DNA. (Only one strand carries the code; the other is structural.) The mRNA **transcribes** the gene by matching complementary bases to those exposed in the coding strand of DNA, except that uracil (U) replaces thymine (T).

After mRNA has transcribed the code, it leaves the nucleus of the cell and moves to specialized structures in the cell called *ribosomes*, where the message is decoded and **translated** into an actual protein. Another type of RNA called **transfer RNA (tRNA)** reads the three-letter codes, or codons, as instructions for assembling a chain of amino acids. Each set of three exposed RNA bases codes for one amino acid. Thus, for

messenger ribonucleic acid (mRNA): The molecule that carries the genetic code out of the nucleus for translation into proteins.

transcription: The process during which messenger RNA is formed from the DNA code.

translation: The process during which the mRNA code builds a protein using amino acids supplied by tRNA.

transfer ribonucleic acid (tRNA): RNA that lines up amino acids along mRNA to make proteins.

1. Section of DNA molecule with base pairs.

2. DNA molecule temporarily separates at bases. mRNA lines up its bases (with U replacing T) with their complements on the coding side of the DNA.

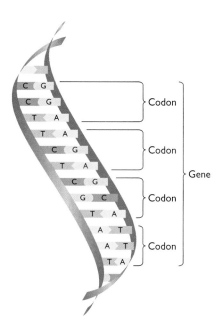

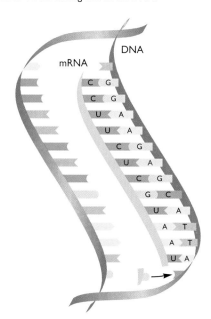

3. mRNA moves out of cell nucleus to ribosomes. As ribosomes move along mRNA, tRNA picks up amino acids and lines up along mRNA according to base complements. Each tRNA transfers its amino acid to the next active tRNA as it leaves, resulting in a chain of amino acids.

4. This chain of amino acids forms a protein.

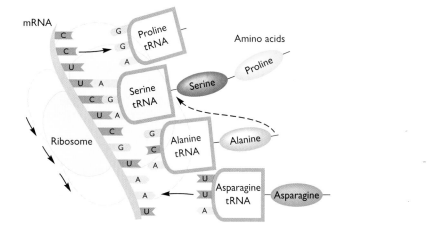

FIGURE 3.3
Protein synthesis. In reality, no protein is only four amino acids long, but the process works exactly as shown.

FIGURE 3.4
Skin color variation in humans is an example of a polygenic trait with a wide range of phenotypic expressions.

example, a sequence of 300 bases codes for a sequence of 100 amino acids. A sequence of amino acids is a protein. Although there are only about twenty or so types of amino acids, it is possible to arrange them in a nearly infinite variety of sequences and lengths. In this way, the sequence of DNA bases represents a sequence of amino acids, and it is this sequence that determines the shape and function of the protein.

It's still a long way from a protein to a trait—the observable, measurable physical or chemical characteristics of an organism. Some traits are fairly simple. Hemoglobin, the chemical on red blood cells that carries oxygen, is a protein. It is made up of two chains of 141 and 146 amino acids. In other words, it is coded for by two genes—two sentences with 141 and 146 words.

Skin color, by contrast, is not a simple trait. It involves three different pigments (including red hemoglobin) and other factors such as skin thickness. The color of a person's skin is thus a trait produced by the complex interaction of many proteins and so is coded for on many genes. Such traits are called **polygenic** (Figure 3.4). Traits coded for by a single gene are called **monogenic.** Most traits of complex organisms are polygenic.

polygenic: A trait coded for by more than one gene.

monogenic: A trait coded for by a single gene.

AN OVERVIEW OF THE HUMAN GENOME

As of spring 2003, nearly the entire human **genome** has been sequenced. What this means is that we know the sequence of the 3.1 million base pairs (the As, Ts, Gs, and Cs) of two representative humans' DNA. (There were two organizations working on the genome sequence, each primarily focusing on a different participant's DNA.) We now have a baseline from which scientists will be able to further research the genome and compare other people and populations.

There is still much to learn. We need to figure out just where in that 3.1-billion-base-pair sequence the genes are, what proteins they code for, what those proteins do, and what functions the other nongene DNA serves. In other words, we still need to discover how the DNA "builds" an organism. But in the last few years, some remarkable new information has come to light.

It turns out that most of the genome is not composed of genes. That is, most of the genome—possibly 98 percent—doesn't code for proteins. We refer to this nongene material as *noncoding* DNA. Although this DNA used to be referred to as "junk DNA," we now know that much of it is not *without* function. Some of it acts as punctuation, marking the beginnings and ends of coding sequences. Some serves to regulate gene function and activity level. Some jumps around carrying other DNA with it, allowing the genetic code to reshuffle its elements; this provides a partial explanation for why a surprisingly small number of genes (20,000 to 40,000 by current estimates) can produce such a huge variety of proteins (around 50,000) in an organism as complex as a human being. Some noncoding DNA is made up of repetitive sequences, some hundreds of thousands of base pairs long, that may do nothing. Some of our DNA may be very ancient, from a remote common ancestor, and some may have been transferred from microbes.

Moreover, we have learned that the coding sequences are not lined up neatly together but are scattered and interrupted by noncoding sequences. A single coding sequence might code for more than one protein, depending on just which part is transcribed.

And recently it was discovered that RNA is more than just the means of converting the DNA code into proteins. Some classes of RNAs have other functions, such as turning on or off some genes, blocking the action of mRNA in producing a protein (which may be important in disease research), shutting down genes and thus operating as a defense against harmful DNA or viruses, and even shaping the genome itself by keeping and discarding certain genes. Realizing that at least some of these noncoding RNAs are produced by the DNA genome has expanded the definition of a *gene*. Some genes (that is, coding DNA sequences) produce proteins as their end products, but others have noncoding RNAs as end products. By this definition, then, the estimated number of genes in the genome would increase.

Thus, the nice neat view we've had of the genetic code and how it works, even until recently, has radically changed. In the words of Lewis Carroll, the nature and operation of the human genome keeps getting "curiouser and curiouser" and will be an important area of study for years to come. (We'll return to some of this new information in Chapter 14.)

FROM GENE TO TRAIT

If Mendel possessed neither the technology nor the background knowledge to understand the structure of the genetic code and the process of protein synthesis, what then did he discover about the processes of genetics? We refer to his contribution as **Mendelian genetics.** It involves the basic laws of inheritance, which we will take up in the next section, and some general principles about the relationship between the genetic code and the traits that are the end product of that code.

Mendel conducted at least eight years of extensive breeding experiments, the most famous on pea plants. He crossed plants that exhibited different expressions of a trait and then crossed hybrids with each other and back with the original plants.

Mendel used only traits that were monogenic (Figure 3.5). He carefully picked these after considering other traits, many of which were polygenic and so were rejected because, like skin color, they did not appear in simple either/or variation. While no modern scientists would simply leave out what didn't fit their expectations, we forgive Mendel because, in fact, all *genes* work the way he thought even if some *traits* are more complex.

Mendel reached the conclusion that *each organism possesses two genes for each trait—one from each parent*. Not only does each organism possess two of each gene, but genes may come in different versions. We call these **alleles.** Although Mendel used pea plants, it might be more interesting for us to use a human example. There is a chemical called PTC (phenylthiocarbamide) that people can either taste or not. (For those who can, it has a dry, bitter flavor. If you find brussels sprouts bitter, you are tasting a thiocarbamide.) This "taster trait" is monogenic, but the gene for the trait has, as you might suspect, two alleles: *T*, which codes for the ability to taste PTC, and *t*, which codes for the inability to taste the chemical.

Because we each possess two genes for the taster trait—one from our father and one from our mother—we have one of three possible combinations. These combinations are called **genotypes.** We may have

genome: The total genetic endowment of an organism.

Mendelian genetics: The basic laws of inheritance discovered by Gregor Mendel in the nineteenth century.

alleles: Variants of a gene.

genotypes: The alleles possessed by an organism.

Seeds	Seed Interiors	Seed Coats	Ripe Pods	Unripe Pods	Flowers	Stems

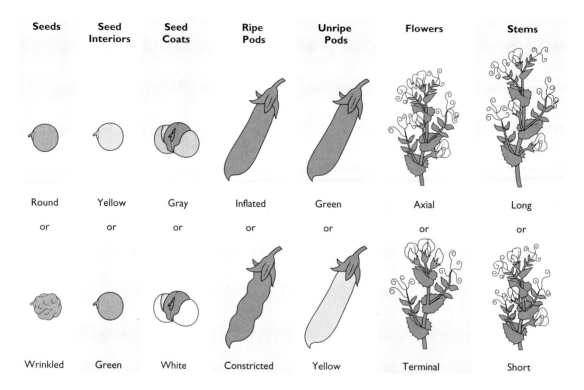

Round	Yellow	Gray	Inflated	Green	Axial	Long
or	or	or	or	or	or	or
Wrinkled	Green	White	Constricted	Yellow	Terminal	Short

FIGURE 3.5

These are the traits of the pea plant that Mendel observed in his famous experiments.

two of the same allele: *TT* or *tt*, a condition known as **homozygous** (from the Greek root *homo*, "the same"). Or we may have a pair of non-matching alleles: *Tt*, a condition known as **heterozygous** (from the Greek root *hetero*, "different").

These genotypes are responsible for producing either a taster individual or a nontaster. The observable trait—the result of the genetic code—is the **phenotype.** What phenotype does each genotype produce?

Genotype	Phenotype
TT	taster
tt	nontaster
Tt	taster

Why does the heterozygote *Tt* produce the same phenotype as the homozygote *TT*? Because, as Mendel also reasoned, some alleles are **dominant** and some are **recessive.** In this case, the allele for tasting is dominant (that's why it's written as a capital letter), and so, in the heterozygous genotype, it hides the action of the allele for nontasting. The only way a phenotype can reflect a recessive allele is if the genotype is homozygous for the recessive (*tt*).

It is very important to understand that the words *dominant* and *recessive* have no value attached to them. Dominant alleles are not necessarily better or more common. There are, for example, quite a few human genetic diseases, some lethal, caused by dominant alleles. The terms *dominant* and *recessive* simply mean that if two alleles in this relationship are in a heterozygous genotype, the action of the dominant will be expressed and the action of the recessive will be hidden.

Alleles for most traits do not, in fact, work this neatly. In most cases, heterozygous genotypes result in phenotypes that exhibit some action of both alleles. (This is, in part, what led to the mistaken concept of "blending" inheritance.) Such alleles are said to be **codominant,** and they result in a greater number of possible phenotypes. In addition, many genes have more than two possible alleles, resulting in even more potential phenotypes. (Remember, however, that each individual can only possess a *pair* of alleles.)

A single example can demonstrate both these concepts. Your blood type for the ABO system is coded for by a single gene, the *I* gene, which has three possible alleles: I^A, I^B, and I^O. So we have six possible genotypes but only four possible phenotypes. (We can designate the genotypes using only the superscript, but remember that these are alleles of a single gene, not separate genes.)

GENOTYPE	PHENOTYPE
AA ⎫ AO ⎭	type A
BB ⎫ BO ⎭	type B
AB	type AB
OO	type O

It's clear that both A and B are dominant over the recessive O. The AB genotype, however, expresses the action of both alleles. The A and B alleles are codominant. (We will discuss the ABO system in greater detail in Chapter 13.)

Most phenotypic traits are coded for by multiple genes, some of which may have more than three possible alleles. In addition, some alleles have an even more complex relationship, where the action of both is expressed in the phenotype but one more so than the other. Some of the pea plant traits that Mendel rejected were probably traits like these. He rejected them because their phenotypic expressions were too complex for him to easily see any regularities. We still have this problem today, although, of course, we don't simply ignore data we can't explain. The genetic bases for most phenotypic traits have eluded us because there are multiple genes

homozygous: Having two of the same allele in a gene pair.

heterozygous: Having two different alleles in a gene pair.

phenotype: The chemical or physical results of the genetic code.

dominant: The allele of a heterozygous pair that is expressed in the phenotype.

recessive: The allele of a pair that is only expressed if homozygous.

codominant: When both alleles of a pair are expressed in the phenotype.

involved and because the alleles of those genes are not in a simple dominant/recessive relationship to one another.

There is a further complication, and it's an important one. The path between the genetic code and the resultant phenotypic expression can be influenced by outside factors, that is, factors that are not directly part of the reading of the genetic code and the synthesis of proteins. We can call these nongenetic influences **environmental.** Certainly, some traits are unaffected by environmental influences. Your ABO blood type is a direct product of your genetic code—there's nothing that can change what those genes code for except a change in the code itself. Such a change is called a **mutation,** literally a mistake in the genetic code. (We will discuss mutations in the next chapter.)

Other traits, however, are influenced by environmental factors. Your skin color, for example, is certainly coded for in your genes (there are at least four genes involved and probably more). Your specific skin color phenotype at any point in time, however, is influenced by a number of nongenetic factors: the amount of exposure to ultraviolet radiation from the sun, your health status, even your psychological condition (blushing from embarrassment, for example). In other words, two of us might have exactly the same genes for skin color but still differ in our phenotypic expression of that trait. In fact, different parts of your own body can have different skin colors at the same time depending on environmental influences, as many of us learn every summer when we're not careful about exposure to the sun. Mendel noticed such variation even in some of the simple traits he worked with in peas, some of which may have been the result of different environmental effects on individual plants.

HOW INHERITANCE WORKS

Genes come in pairs. So do the chromosomes that carry these genes. Thus, the members of a pair of genes are found on a pair of chromosomes. Species differ in number of chromosomes. In humans, there are forty-six chromosomes, which come in twenty-three pairs (Figure 3.6). Chimpanzees have forty-eight chromosomes, wheat plants have forty-two, and dogs have seventy-eight. One species of amoeba has several hundred chromosomes.

When cells divide—as the organism grows or to replace cells that have died or been lost—each chromosome copies itself. It does this by unwinding and splitting at the bond between the bases A, T, G, and C, as in the first step of protein synthesis. Each strand now picks up nucleotides with the proper complementary bases (which are in solution within the cell) and thus replaces its other half. There are now *two* pairs

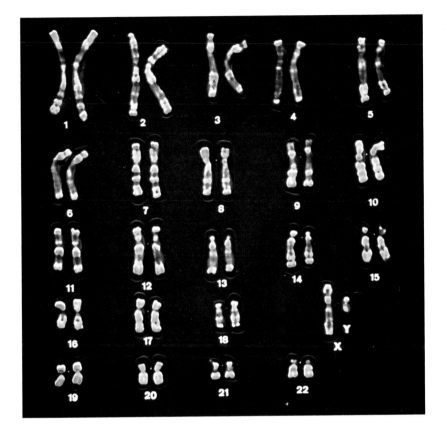

FIGURE 3.6
The twenty-three pairs of chromosomes typically found in a human being. This set of chromosomes came from a man—note the last pair has an X chromosome and a Y chromosome. A woman would have two X chromosomes.

of each chromosome. When the cell divides, each daughter cell receives a full set of chromosome pairs. This process is known as **mitosis** (Figure 3.7).

Some single-celled organisms reproduce in this fashion, but other single-celled organisms and nearly all multicellular organisms reproduce sexually, that is, by the joining of specialized cells from two parents. Such specialized sex cells are called **gametes** (sperm and egg in animals, for example). Now, if each gamete had a full set of chromosome pairs and thus a full set of gene pairs, the resultant fertilized cell, the **zygote,** and all the cells of the offspring, would have *twice* the normal number of chromosomes and *twice* the normal number of genes.

This duplication does not occur, however, because when gametes are produced, the chromosome pairs—and thus the gene pairs—separate. Mendel called this **segregation.** Each gamete, then, has only one member of each chromosome pair and so only one member of each pair of genes. The process of producing gametes is **meiosis** (see Figure 3.7). When the gamete from the male fertilizes the gamete from the female, the zygote once again has two of each chromosome and two of each gene. But because

environmental: Here, any nongenetic influence on the phenotype.

mutation: Any mistake in an organism's genetic code.

mitosis: The process of cell division that results in two exact copies of the original cell.

gametes: The cells of sexual reproduction, which contain only half the chromosomes of a normal cell.

zygote: The fertilized egg before cell division begins.

segregation: In genetics, the breaking up of allele pairs in the production of gametes.

meiosis: The process of cell division in which gametes are produced.

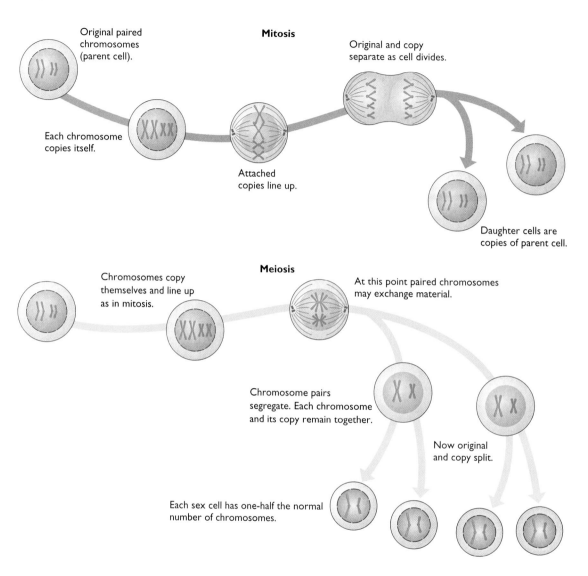

FIGURE 3.7

Simplified diagrams of mitosis and meiosis. Cell division occurs in two ways. Mitosis produces exact copies of the parent cell and is the most common form of cell division. Meiosis results in four daughter cells, each with one-half the genetic content of the parent cell. Meiosis is the process by which gametes, or sex cells (sperm and egg), are manufactured. It ensures that when fertilization occurs, the new individual has a complete set of genes, one-half from each parent.

the members of each pair come from different parents, the combination of alleles for each gene may well be different from that of either parent.

Adding to the differences between parents and offspring that result from fertilization are differences caused by two other phenomena, independent assortment and crossing over. **Independent assortment,** described by Mendel, says that as long as genes are on different chromosomes, their alleles will segregate independently during the production of gametes. For example, all the traits Mendel observed in pea plants (see Figure 3.5) are on different chromosomes and therefore assort independently. One expression of stem length is not linked to a particular expression of seed texture or to a particular expression of seed color. All combinations are possible. If, on the other hand, two genes are on the same chromosome, they are said to exhibit **linkage;** therefore, their alleles will not assort independently, and variation is reduced.

But sometimes during meiosis portions of chromosome pairs break and are "spliced" back together, but to the *other* member of the pair. This is **crossing over.** Thus, alleles are exchanged between chromosome pairs, and this adds to the possible genotypic combinations that linkage reduces. This phenomenon is called **recombination.**

Independent assortment, crossing over, and recombination, (together with mutations, the mistakes that change the code itself) account for much of the variation within a species that Darwin observed but could not explain. Recall that without the continuous generation of variation, natural selection—and therefore evolution as we know it—could not take place.

We can demonstrate Mendelian inheritance using the taster trait. Suppose we have two individuals who are both phenotypic tasters and who are both heterozygotes, that is, their genotypes are *Tt.* Because chromosomes carrying allele pairs segregate during meiosis, each person will produce some gametes that receive the dominant allele and some that receive the recessive. At fertilization, then, depending on which sperm fertilizes which egg, three possible genotypic combinations are possible in the zygote. A device called a *Punnett square,* named after an English geneticist, illustrates this (Figure 3.8).

The cells of the Punnett square represent the possible fertilizations. If a *T* sperm fertilizes a *T* egg, the zygote is homozygous dominant. If a *T* sperm fertilizes a *t* egg, the zygote is heterozygous, and so on. Notice that two individuals with exactly the same genotype and phenotype can produce offspring with all three possible genotypic combinations and even, in the case of the homozygote *tt,* a different phenotypic expression. Two tasters, in other words, can give birth to a nontaster. This variation between parents and offspring is the result of the processes of segregation and fertilization. Variation is the raw material of evolution, the topic of the next chapter.

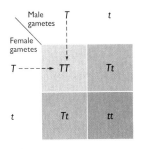

FIGURE 3.8
This Punnett square illustrates the possible genotypic combinations when two heterozygotes for the taster trait reproduce. Note that because of the hidden recessive, two tasters have a one-quarter chance of producing a nontaster offspring.

independent assortment: When genes on different chromosomes segregate to gametes independently of one another.

linkage: When genes occur on the same chromosome and are inherited together.

crossing over: When sections of chromosomes switch between chromosome pairs during meiosis.

recombination: The exchange of genetic material between pairs of chromosomes during meiosis.

Contemporary Reflections

What Is Genetic Cloning?

Since advances in genetic technology enabled the cloning of Dolly the sheep in 1997, that ability and its potential applications have been areas of both great scientific interest and heated controversy, much of the latter due to a poor general understanding of what the term *cloning* means. What immediately comes to mind are the plots from popular science fiction novels and movies. For example, in Ira Levin's *The Boys from Brazil*, a Nazi scientist produces clones of Hitler, each, of course, with Hitler's personality.

Not only is something like that impossible, but it doesn't even come close to exemplifying the scientific meaning of cloning. The term *clone* simply refers to an exact or nearly exact copy of a biological entity, whether an individual or a cell. Identical twins, by that definition, are natural clones because they began life as a single fertilized egg cell and are, essentially, genetically the same.

In terms of artificial cloning, there are two main types. And the distinction is important. Dolly and members of at least seven other species are examples of *reproductive cloning*. Here, the goal is the production of a genetic duplicate of an organism. Motivations range from increasing productivity of food animals to producing organs for transplantation to replicating pets. Not only are the functions of reproductive cloning open to ethical considerations, but at present there are severe limitations on its success, including the fact (probably mercifully) that it doesn't seem to work with primates (Simerly et al. 2003).

Specific techniques differ, but in the most widely used method, the chromosomes are removed from an unfertilized egg shortly after ovulation, when it would be ready to develop if stimulated by the sperm. The donor cell, the one to be copied, is a somatic (body) cell, often a skin cell or a mammary cell. It is fused with the egg cell with the help of electric pulses, which also mimic the stimulation of fertilization. After about four or five days in a chemical solution, if all goes well, the fused cells will have developed into an embryo of several hundred cells. At this point the embryo is transferred to the uterus of a surrogate mother of the species in question with the

> (*Following Chapter 15 is a series of exercises that should add to your understanding of some of the concepts discussed throughout the book. The first is on Mendelian genetics as covered in this section.*)

SUMMARY

This brief account of the basic facts of genetics demonstrates two important points relative to evolution:

1. It is important to understand that all phenotypic traits are, initially, the products of the genetic code. Thus, evolutionary change is at its most

hope that it will develop normally. If it does, as was the case with Dolly, the new organism will be an exact genetic copy of the individual from whom the donor cell was taken.

One misconception about this technique is that the clone will be a phenotypic duplicate of the donor. To be sure, clone and donor will be very much alike. But genes do not act alone in producing phenotypic traits, and many variables are involved in the path from single egg to multicellular organism. The more complex the trait, the more variable the potential results. So a clone of me would look like me but would not have all my personality traits. Even if we could clone humans, we would not be making exact copies.

The second type of genetic cloning is *therapeutic cloning*, in which cells and eventually tissues are grown *in vitro* (in a chemical culture) for medical purposes. No reproduction of individuals is involved. The idea is to make copies of stem cells. These are cells, like a fertilized egg and cells from early in embryonic development, that have the potential to become all the different cell types in the body. In a few days, cells begin to specialize. At this stage (which is the same stage an embryo is implanted into a surrogate in reproductive cloning), certain cells are removed from the embryo in the hope of differentiating them into specific types of tissues to replace or repair a patient's tissue damaged by certain diseases, including Parkinson's disease, muscular dystrophy, and diabetes.

An objection to stem cell cloning is that an embryo—a potential life—is intentionally created only to be destroyed when the wanted cells are removed. But a new technique can "trick" an egg cell into "thinking" it has been fertilized so that it clones itself into an embryo. Such embryos are nonviable and could not lead to a pregnancy. In addition, there are stem cells still present in adult animals, and these could potentially be cloned and artificially differentiated. Ethical objections to stem cell research seem easier to overcome than those to reproductive cloning, and the benefits to human health are of potentially inestimable value.

Both research and debate will continue on cloning, as well they should. But the former should be done with clear and beneficial goals in mind and the latter with sound, accurate knowledge of the science involved.

basic level genetic change. But the pathway from the genetic code to phenotypic traits is a complex one. A gene simply codes for the synthesis of a protein. Proteins build cells, run their chemical reactions, link them together, and help them communicate; cells make up tissues, which in turn make up the body of a living organism—humans as well as pea plants. Moreover, this complex process is affected by environmental factors, so that the genetic code is most definitely *not* solely responsible for the final form and function of a living being. As we try to explain the phenotypic changes we see in evolution, we must keep these ideas in mind, for if the genetic process itself is complex, so, then, are the processes of evolution that act to change it.

2. The very process by which organisms pass on traits from parent to offspring also accounts for the variation seen between generations

and among members of a species. If inheritance produced offspring that were exact copies of their parents, no change would ever take place and there would be no evolution—no adaptation, no change through time, and no new species. But segregation, independent assortment, crossing over, and recombination mix existing genetic combinations (sort of like shuffling a deck of cards), and mutation produces new genetic variation.

We will look more closely at sources of variation and the processes of evolution in the next chapter.

QUESTIONS FOR FURTHER THOUGHT

1. New information about the specific nature of the human genome indicates, among other things, that we are, from several perspectives, not all that different from other organisms. We have far fewer genes than would be expected given our complexity. We share a great many of those genes with other organisms, from mice to bacteria. What philosophical issues might follow from these facts? How might these facts be practically applied?

2. We've considered some of the ethical concerns regarding cloning. How do you feel about the goals of reproductive cloning? Are they all equally worthwhile? What constraints should be placed on cloning? Should *any* reproductive cloning of humans be allowed? What about stem cell research? Do the same issues apply? Should companies be allowed to "own" certain lines of stem cells that came from a human and would be used to improve the health of other humans?

KEY TERMS

particulate
genes
proteins
amino acids
enzymes
chromosomes

deoxyribonucleic acid (DNA)
nucleotide
replication
codon
protein synthesis

messenger ribonucleic acid (mRNA)
transcription
translation
transfer ribonucleic acid (tRNA)

polygenic	phenotype	zygote
monogenic	dominant	segregation
genome	recessive	meiosis
Mendelian genetics	codominant	independent assortment
alleles	environmental	linkage
genotypes	mutation	crossing over
homozygous	mitosis	recombination
heterozygous	gametes	

SUGGESTED READINGS

For additional details on the workings of genes and inheritance, try the genetics chapter of John H. Relethford's *The Human Species: An Introduction to Biological Anthropology,* fifth edition, or the genetics section of any good introductory biology text.

For a brief discussion of Mendel and an excerpt from his writing, see C. Leon Harris's *Evolution: Genesis and Revelations.*

For the original announcement of the completion of the human genome, see the "Science Times" section of the 3 February 2001 *New York Times,* the 15 February 2001 issue of *Nature,* and the 16 February 2001 issue of *Science* (in the last publication, see page 1163 for a list of Web sites on the genome project and data).

A nice history of and update on genetics can be found in a special insert in the 23 January 2003 issue of *Nature* called "The Double Helix—50 Years." It contains facsimile articles from 1953 announcing the discovery of the structure of the genetic code, as well as pieces on historical perspective, DNA in medicine and society, and current knowledge of DNA itself.

An interesting short piece on metaphorical descriptions of our current knowledge of the genome is "Evolving Genomic Metaphors: A New Look at the Language of DNA," by John C. Avise, in the 5 October 2001 *Science.* For more on the new discoveries about RNA see "Small RNAs Make Big Splash," by Jennifer Couzin, in the 20 December 2002 *Science.*

Cloning technology is summarized in "Cloning for Medicine," by Ian Wilmut (who cloned Dolly), in the December 1998 *Scientific American.*

THE PROCESSES OF EVOLUTION

I am convinced that
Natural Selection has
been the most
important, but not the
exclusive, means of
modification.
—Charles Darwin

One of the scientists who "rediscovered" Mendel's work in 1900 was the Dutch botanist Hugo de Vries (1848–1935). De Vries had been trying to explain the variations that sometimes spontaneously appear in plants (and, of course, in animals)—such as a single flower of the wrong color or one that was much smaller or larger than other members of its species. At that time breeders called these oddities "sports." De Vries called them *mutations*. When he read about Mendel's experiments, de Vries realized that these mutations resulted from sudden changes in Mendel's "factors." We now say that a mutation is any change in the genetic mechanism.

With de Vries's contribution, all the major pieces were in place to articulate a *basic theory of evolution*, often referred to as the *synthetic theory of evolution* because it synthesizes Darwin's theory with genetics. It may be stated as follows:

A particulate genetic code is initially responsible for the form and function of an organism. Mutations in the coding portion of DNA continually add genetic, and therefore phenotypic, variation to a species. Segregation, independent assortment, recombination, and crossing over shuffle existing genotypic combinations at reproduction and thus provide additional genetic and phenotypic variation. Phenotypic variation is affected by the process of natural selection, where the better-adapted individuals will be more reproductively successful and will thus disproportionately pass on their phenotypic traits to future generations. The results of natural selection are the maintenance of a species' adaptive relationship to existing environmental conditions, the potential alteration of a species' phenotypic variation under circumstances of changing environmental conditions, and, ultimately, the development of new species.

As research continued throughout the twentieth century, scientists realized that other processes also play roles in the production of the variation on which natural selection acts. Research still goes on into the relationships and relative importance of all these processes in the evolution of species.

In this chapter, we will address the following questions:

What are species?

What are the processes of evolution?

How do these processes interact to bring about evolution as we understand it today?

SPECIES: THE UNITS OF EVOLUTION

We observe evolution as the change in species over time and the development of new species. Evolution does not take place in individuals. You and I don't evolve in this sense. Evolution takes place in *populations* of organisms, and the basic population in nature is the species.

A species may be defined as *a population of organisms whose members can, under natural circumstances, freely interbreed with one another and produce fertile offspring*. Humans and chimpanzees, despite our genetic similarity, cannot (even under *unnatural* circumstances) interbreed and produce offspring because our two species have different numbers of chromosomes. We are separate species. But any two normally healthy humans of opposite sex, no matter how different they may appear phenotypically, can reproduce and generate fertile offspring. Thus, all human beings are members of a single species, *Homo sapiens*.

Horses and donkeys can mate and produce offspring, known as mules. But mules are nearly always sterile. Two mules can't reproduce and make more mules. Thus, horses and donkeys are considered separate species that are unable to combine their genetic endowments for more than one generation.

In captivity, lions and tigers have been known to produce hybrid offspring that are, in many cases, fertile. But lions and tigers don't interbreed in the wild. Although their ranges overlap (in India), the specific environmental **niche** of each animal is different, as are their behaviors, including mating behavior. Thus, lions and tigers are separate species.

Domestic dogs and wolves can and will mate and produce hybrid offspring that are fertile. To be sure, such hybridization is not common. And some breeds of dogs (thanks to human breeding efforts) are so small that they could not possibly mate with a wolf (or with some other dog breeds for that matter), nor could they carry and give birth to the fetuses from such matings. But the reality of hybridization and the genetic similarity between dogs and wolves have recently led authorities to lump the dog into the wolf species. Formerly *Canis familiaris*, your family pooch is now *Canis lupus*, technically a wolf. (Coyotes and jackals are also able to hybridize with dogs and wolves, but those two groups are still given different species names.)

It is not surprising to us that humans and chimps are separate species because, very simply, we don't *look* like the same species; although we do differ in only a small percentage of our genes. Horses and donkeys, on the other hand, do look pretty similar yet are different species. Lions and

niche: The environment of an organism and its adaptive response to that environment.

FIGURE 4.1
Wolflike and very unwolflike
dogs. The German shepherd
(*top*) closely resembles the
wolf, the ancestor of all dog
breeds. The West Highland
terrier (*bottom*) bears little
resemblance to that ancestor.
Both breeds, however, are
genetically the same as
wolves and could potentially
interbreed with them.

FIGURE 4.1
Wolflike and very unwolflike dogs. The German shepherd (*top*) closely resembles the wolf, the ancestor of all dog breeds. The West Highland terrier (*bottom*) bears little resemblance to that ancestor. Both breeds, however, are genetically the same as wolves and could potentially interbreed with them.

tigers look like different species but can still produce fertile offspring, although only under artificial conditions. And some breeds of dogs look so similar to wolves as to obviously belong to the same species, although other breeds only faintly resemble their wild ancestors (Figure 4.1).

If the species is the natural basic unit of evolution, then why is the distinction among various species sometimes so vague? Why aren't all species equally distinct—separate from one another to the same degree and for the same reasons? And why are scientists who specialize in classifying species (called **taxonomists** or **systematists**) sometimes at odds with one another over which populations belong to the same species?

The answer to all these questions is that while the origin of new species from existing species usually happens relatively quickly, it does not happen instantly. It is a *process* that takes place over time (a subject we'll examine in Chapter 5). Thus, there is usually a period when an emerging species still can interbreed with its ancestral species and is therefore difficult to define.

In addition, all species did not emerge at the same time. They appeared at different times, they evolve at different rates, and they continue to evolve. Species thus change in relation to one another as time goes on.

We established in the last chapter that although evolution results in phenotypic change, it must also involve genetic change. So, if species change over time, we need to characterize populations within a species in genetic terms in order to fully examine their evolution. We do so by using the concept of **gene frequency,** which is more accurately called **allele frequency.**

Going back to our example in Chapter 3 of the taster trait, suppose every human on earth were homozygous for the dominant (*T*) allele. The allele frequency would be $T = 1.0$ (or 100 percent). The phenotypic result of this would be that every member of the species would be a taster.

Now, suppose that a mutation occurred somewhere that changed a *T* allele to a *t* allele and that, over time, the mutated allele was passed on over many generations of offspring so that at some point 25 percent of the alleles of the taster gene were recessives (*t*). Now the allele frequencies for this gene would be .75 (75 percent) *T* and .25 (25 percent) *t*.

This change in frequency would, of course, have a phenotypic effect. Most individuals would still be tasters since *T* would still be the most frequent allele—and, as you recall, heterozygotes are phenotypically tasters. But there would be some homozygous recessives (*tt*) who would be nontasters. The species would have changed phenotypically over time as a result of a genetic change. Thus, evolution operates by *changes in allele frequency through time.* Anything that changes allele frequency is therefore a process of evolution. (See the Appendix for more on the quantification of evolutionary change.)

We will now describe those processes that produce evolutionary change within species and that, ultimately, bring about the origin of new species.

MUTATIONS: NECESSARY ERRORS

A mutation is any change in the genetic code. Some mutations involve a single incorrect base in a codon (one letter of one word). These are known as **point mutations.** Some point mutations are inconsequential, but some result in the wrong amino acid in a protein, which could have

taxonomists: Scientists who classify and name living organisms.

systematists: Another name for taxonomists.

gene frequency: The percentage of times a particular allele appears in a population.

allele frequency: Another name, and the preferred term, for gene frequency.

point mutations: Mutations of a single base of a codon.

FIGURE 4.2
This child with Down syndrome has the characteristic facial features that are some of the multiple phenotypic effects of the presence of the extra chromosome 21. This girl has just won medals in swimming at a Special Olympics event.

disastrous results for the organism. (An example is sickle cell anemia, a genetic disease, which we'll cover at the end of this chapter.)

Other mutations involve a whole chromosome or a large portion of one. These are called **chromosomal mutations.** They are almost always deleterious because many genes are involved. For example, humans who have three copies of chromosome 21, instead of the usual pair, have trisomy 21, or Down syndrome, which results in mental retardation and other phenotypic effects (Figure 4.2). This mutation most commonly takes place as a result of a failure of a pair of parental chromosomes to segregate in the production of gametes.

Mutations are random; that is, a specific mutation doesn't occur at a specific time or for a specific reason. In other words, mutations don't occur because they are needed. They occur continually, but exactly *what* mutation occurs is totally unpredictable. Some mutations are the result of environmental influences such as cosmic radiation, other forms of radioactivity, or chemical pollutants. Most, however, are simply mechanical errors that occur during the complex process of gene replication at cell division or during the even more complex process by which the genetic code is read, translated, and transcribed into proteins.

As you might imagine, then, mutations arise frequently. They are occurring in the cells of your body as you read this sentence. The mutations that occur during the reading of the code affect just the individual since they cannot be passed on. The process of aging, for example, is partly due to an accumulation of cells with mutations that make them in some way abnormal, though they are still alive and able to divide.

The only mutations that concern us in an evolutionary sense are those that occur in the gametes or in the specialized cells that produce gametes. These mutations are the ones that are passed on to future generations and thus bring about genetic change through time. Therefore, mutations change allele frequency through time by making new versions of a gene (as in the taster trait example above) or by otherwise altering the details of the genetic code. Mutation is a process of evolution.

Because mutations are mistakes—deviations from the normal genetic code—many mutations in coding regions are deleterious. They produce a phenotypic result that is abnormal and therefore, to one degree or another, maladaptive. Individuals with such traits may not be as reproductively successful as most members of their species, and so the mutant gene or genes will not be passed on as often, if at all. In other words, natural selection will select *against* those genes. But mutations may also produce alleles that are neutral, making no difference to an individual's fitness, or they may produce alleles that result in even *better-adapted* phenotypes and are thus selected *for* by being passed on more often.

Mutation, in other words, changes allele frequency and, as it does so, adds genetic variation to a species' **gene pool.** Mutations are the price living things pay for the process of evolution. Without mutation—if the first life-forms had reproduced themselves absolutely without error—nothing would have changed, and the first living things would be the *only* living things. Mutations are thus one of the basic processes of evolution. They are necessary errors.

NATURAL SELECTION: THE PRIME MOVER OF EVOLUTION

By now, you should have a pretty good idea how natural selection operates. The genetic variation produced by mutation, segregation, independent assortment, and recombination results in phenotypic variation within a species. Much of a species' phenotypic variation may make little difference to the fitness and reproductive success of individuals. We have come to see that nature is more tolerant of variation than Darwin thought. He felt that *every* variation made a difference. We now know this is not the case.

At the same time, however, some phenotypic variation *does* make a difference. How much of a difference, of course, depends on what traits are important for the adaptation of a particular species to a particular environment at a particular time. What's adaptive for one species—say, large size or a certain color—will not necessarily work for even a closely related species. As environments change, a trait that *was* adaptive for a species may no longer be adaptive, or a trait that was once neutral, or even nonadaptive, may now be adaptive.

A striking example of natural selection in changing environments comes from the pioneering work of Rosemary and Peter Grant and their colleagues (Grant and Grant 2000, 2002; Weiner 1994). These scientists have studied the famous birds of the Galápagos Islands collectively known as Darwin's finches (Figure 4.3; see also Figure 5.3). Among the important adaptive features of these birds are their beaks, which have evolved to help each species of finch exploit particular food sources. In 1977 there was a severe and nearly yearlong drought on one of the small islands that the Grants' team was using as a study area. Insects virtually disappeared, and the only plant seeds available were larger than average and had tougher than average exteriors to preserve their moisture. The finches on the island suffered a serious food shortage.

The next year, when the rains returned, the researchers found that just one finch in seven (a mere 14 percent) had made it through the drought.

chromosomal mutations: Mutations of a whole chromosome or a large portion of a chromosome.

gene pool: All the alleles in a population.

Moreover, the surviving birds of one species common to the island (the medium ground finch) were 5 to 6 percent larger than those that had perished and had beaks that were slightly (in fact, less than a millimeter) longer and deeper than the average before the drought. These are not big differences on a human scale, but the beak-size difference helped some of the finches crack open the larger, tougher seeds during the drought, enabling them to survive. As a result, many more males survived than females because they are about 5 percent larger overall than females.

Now, however, because evolution takes place across generations, it had to be seen if this change would be passed on to the offspring of the surviving finches. This was, indeed, the case. It is the female finches who select males for mating. The males that the few surviving females selected were the largest and had the deepest beaks. As a result, the finches of the next generation were both larger and had beaks that were 4 to 5 percent deeper than the average before the drought. Moreover, when conditions, and thus food sources, returned to normal for a time, the average beak size decreased over several generations toward its previous dimensions. Larger beaks were no longer a distinct advantage and so were no longer selected for. These changes showed natural selection in action. Because of the severity of the situation, it took place rapidly enough for human observers to measure and record it.

It is important to note that in this case, as in any example of natural selection, the variation that proved useful under changed circumstances was already present. It did not appear when it was needed or because it was needed. The finches that survived *already* had larger bodies and beaks; they did not develop these after the drought altered their food source. It was, in other words, already an aspect of their variation, although only a small number of finches possessed large beaks and bodies because under usual conditions they conferred no distinct advantage and may even have been disadvantageous. This is the essential difference between Lamarck's inheritance of acquired characteristics and Darwin's natural selection.

It follows from these points that natural selection is not always successful in maintaining a species' adaptation and survival in the face of environmental change. If a change is too rapid or too extensive, the natural variation within a species simply may not be enough to provide any individuals with sufficient reproductive success to keep the species going. When one or more asteroids hit the earth 65 million years ago and radically altered the earth's climate, perhaps hundreds of thousands of species—the dinosaurs and many others—were unable to adapt and thus became extinct. Natural variation within a species cannot predict what environmental change may take place in the future. Adaptation to change is a matter of luck. Indeed, for 90 percent of all species that have ever existed, luck has run out; they are extinct.

Recognition that extinction is commonplace was another reason for Charles Darwin's delay in making his idea of natural selection known to the public. Natural selection does not produce change in a particular direction, nor is it always successful in ensuring the survival of a species. Darwin thought, perhaps correctly at first, that these implications were too uncomfortable for most people to accept. By 1859, however, the Victorian world of rapid social, industrial, economic, and political transformation had come to accept change as the norm, for nature as well as for itself. Moreover, the logic of *Origin of Species* was so lucid and well presented that its conclusions were seen as obvious. Darwin's book was a best seller, and his idea was, except for a few holdouts, well accepted, at least within science.

Mutation and natural selection are the major processes of evolution. Mutation provides new genetic variation. Natural selection selects phenotypes for reproductive success based on their adaptive relationship with the environment. But because evolution is technically defined as change in allele frequency, two other processes must also be considered as processes of evolution: gene flow and genetic drift (Figure 4.4).

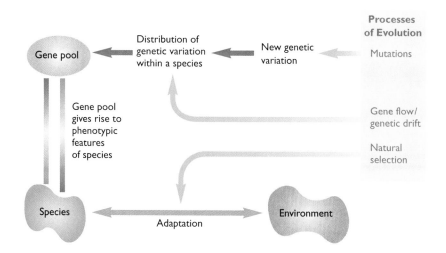

FIGURE 4.4

Processes of evolution. A species is in an adaptive relationship with its environment. This relationship is maintained by natural selection. Environments, however, are constantly changing, so the adaptive characteristics of species change through time. In addition, the gene pool of a species is always changing, altering the phenotypes on which selection acts. Processes that alter a species' gene pool are also, by definition, processes of evolution because they change allele frequency. Mutation provides new genetic variation by producing new alleles or otherwise altering the genetic code. Gene flow and genetic drift mix the genetic variation within a species, continually supplying new combinations of genetic variables.

GENE FLOW: MIXING POPULATIONS' GENES

By definition, members of a species can and do interbreed with one another. The members of a species, however, are usually unevenly distributed over that species' range. Populations within a species can be to some degree separated from other populations by environmental barriers, geographic distance, or, in the case of our species, social and cultural distinctions such as political, religious, and ethnic boundaries. Such populations are called **breeding populations.** Individuals tend to find mates within their own breeding population (Figure 4.5).

Although belonging to the same species, breeding populations may exhibit genetic differences. There are two reasons for this. First, breeding populations may exist in somewhat different environmental circumstances from each other, as illustrated in Figure 4.5. Natural selection will have been favoring different phenotypes, and thus different allele frequencies, in adaptive response to these environments.

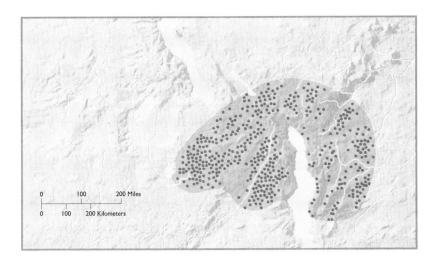

FIGURE 4.5
Breeding populations. The members of a species of lowland, nonaquatic animal (represented by the dots) are unevenly distributed within that species' range because of mountain and water boundaries. The separate population concentrations—the breeding populations—may show genetic and phenotypic differences.

Second, other genetic events (such as mutations and the evolutionary processes we're about to discuss) tend to be concentrated within breeding populations because that is where breeding is concentrated. What happens genetically in one breeding population will differ from what happens in another.

However, because breeding populations *are* still members of one species, interbreeding between them does take place as populations and individuals migrate and as neighboring populations exchange genes. This is called **gene flow.** When members of different breeding populations interbreed, new genetic combinations are produced in the offspring. In other words, genes within a species "flow" among the populations of that species, altering the allele frequencies in those populations and adding still more genetic—and thus phenotypic—variation to the species as a whole (Figure 4.6).

This process of evolution is particularly effective in a mobile species like ours, with populations that are continually moving around and mixing genes. For example, about half of Hutterite marriages (see Chapter 1) take place between colonies, the bride moving to the colony of her husband. The woman thus brings her genes into the population and contributes them to subsequent generations. In one of the colonies I visited, 70 percent of the female parents came from other colonies, and marriages involving these women produced nearly 60 percent of the children of the next generation. In the other colony, 75 percent of female parents "flowed" in, and their marriages produced 47 percent of the next generation. Changes from one generation to the next in a Hutterite colony are greatly affected by this continual mixing, or flowing, of genes among populations, and it is the same for the human species as a whole.

breeding populations:
Populations within a species that are genetically isolated to some degree from other populations.

gene flow: The exchange of genes among populations through interbreeding.

FIGURE 4.6
Simple example of gene flow. The dots represent the relative frequencies of two alleles.

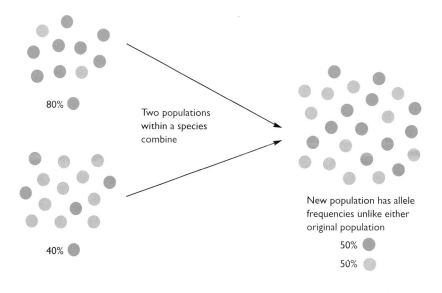

80%

Two populations within a species combine

40%

New population has allele frequencies unlike either original population

50%

50%

GENETIC DRIFT: RANDOM EVOLUTION

One form of genetic drift can be demonstrated by the following experiment: Take 100 coins and arrange them so that 50 heads and 50 tails are showing. Mix them up and without looking (that is, at random) set aside 10 coins. The 10 coins you've chosen will probably *not* be 5 heads and 5 tails, 50 percent of each as in the original group. The odds are against it (about 4:1). Your sample of 10 will probably not be representative of the whole population of coins. It will probably be a non-representative sample, and this effect is called **sampling error.**

Similarly, when a population within a species splits, each new population will exhibit a nonrepresentative sample of the genes, and therefore the phenotypes, of the original. The splitting of a population is called **fission** and is the opposite of gene flow (Figure 4.7). When one of the new populations is drawn from a small sample of the parental population, it will be strikingly different genetically (as with the coins above). This phenomenon is called the **founder effect.**

The Hutterites again provide an example. Hutterites have one of the highest recorded birth rates, an average of about 10 children per family. After such rapid population growth for about 15 or 20 years, a colony becomes so large (130 to 150 people) that social and administrative problems arise, and there is increasing duplication of labor specialists. The colony will then fission, or as they call it, "branch out." Half the colony families will stay in the original location, and half will found a new colony. As a result, the 3 original North American Hutterite colonies,

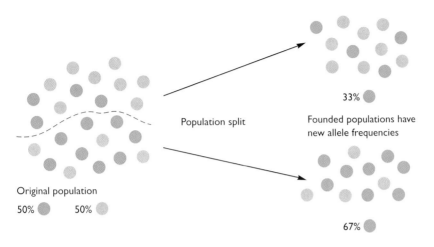

Population split

Original population

50% ● 50% ○

33% ○

Founded populations have
new allele frequencies

67% ○

FIGURE 4.7
Fission and the founder
effect. Notice that this diagram is basically the reverse
of that representing gene
flow (Figure 4.6).

founded in 1874 and 1875, have now increased to more than 380, and the original 300 Hutterite immigrants now number 35,000.

In fact, the situation is more pronounced than that. Of the 300 original North American Hutterites, only 90 contributed genes to future generations. So most of the 35,000 present-day Hutterites can trace most of their genes back to fewer than 100 ancestors. (A small number of people have joined the group from the outside over the past 120 years.) When a founder population constitutes a small percentage of an original group, it is referred to as a **bottleneck.** Other bottlenecks may take place as a result of an epidemic disease, natural disaster, or overexploitation by humans.

The founder effect can have interesting and sometimes tragic results. In a population of 333 Pennsylvania Dutch, nearly one-third (98) were found to have the gene for Tay-Sachs disease, a fatal condition that kills recessive homozygotes by their fourth year of life (see also Chapter 15). The high frequency of this lethal recessive allele can be explained by the fact that these 333 people were all descended from one couple who founded the group in the nineteenth century. One of them, no doubt, by sad circumstance, carried the gene (Diamond 1991).

Fission, the founder effect, and gene flow are particularly important in the evolution of our species. For most of human history we have been divided into many populations, defined by such things as religion, politics, and ethnicity; and, of course, we have been separated by our ability to live all over the globe in nearly all natural environments. Our populations, however, have always mixed genes, and they have often split up to found new populations. Cultural boundaries, in addition, are temporary, so the definitions of populations change. Gene flow and fission are processes caused by population movement, and our species is

sampling error: When a sample chosen for study does not accurately represent the population from which the sample was taken.

fission: Here, the splitting up of a population to form new populations.

founder effect: Genetic differences between populations produced by the fact that genetically different individuals established (founded) those populations.

bottleneck: A severe reduction in the size of a population or the founding of a new population by a small percentage of the parent population that results in only some genes surviving and characterizing the descendant population.

among the most mobile. This is the essential reason why our species cannot be divided into biologically meaningful racial groups, a topic we'll discuss in detail in Chapter 14.

Another form of genetic drift is called **gamete sampling.** Just as genes are not sampled representatively when a population fissions, they are not sampled representatively when two individuals produce offspring. An organism passes on only one of each of its pairs of genes at a time, and only chance dictates which one will be involved in the fertilization that produces a new individual.

For example, two humans who are each heterozygous for the taster trait (see Figure 3.8) will possess one of each allele of the taster gene (*Tt*). But they will not necessarily, in their reproductive lifetimes, pass on an equal number of each allele. It's a matter of chance. It's possible that they could pass on only their dominant allele or only their recessive— or both, but in a proportion other than 50:50. In other words, the very act of reproducing—with the genetic processes of segregation and fertilization—can change allele frequency from one generation to the next.

This example refers to a single set of parents, but the combined effects of this phenomenon on a whole population can bring about a great deal of change between generations. This is especially true in small populations of 100 or fewer (about the size of the average Hutterite colony). Here, the change produced by one set of parents is not likely to be balanced by change in the opposite direction produced by another set.

Allele frequencies, then, may change at random across generations, "drifting" in whatever direction chance takes them. The change may be great enough that certain alleles may be completely lost, while others may reach a frequency of 100 percent—all with no necessary relationship to natural selection based on the fitness of those alleles.

SICKLE CELL ANEMIA: EVOLUTIONARY PROCESSES IN ACTION

We can now take the ideas covered in Chapters 2 and 3 and see how they work in a real example. Sickle cell anemia is a genetic blood disorder; it is often associated with Africans and African Americans because it is found in high frequency in a band across the center of Africa. It is also found in North Africa, Southwest Asia, India, and Southeast Asia.

Sickle cell anemia is the result of a mutation affecting hemoglobin, the protein on the red blood cells that carries oxygen from the lungs to the body's tissues. Hemoglobin, as you recall, is made up of two pairs of amino acid chains, the alpha chain of 141 amino acids and the beta

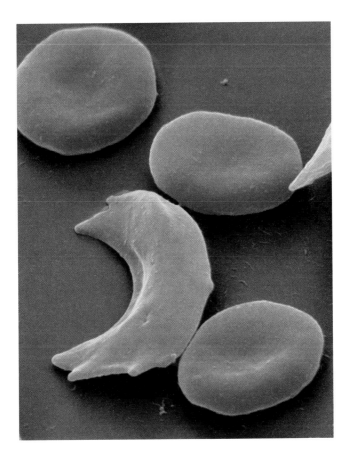

FIGURE 4.8
Normal red blood cells and one with the abnormal shape (*bottom left*) that results from the presence of hemoglobin with one incorrect amino acid. Such cells fail to transport oxygen properly to the body's tissues.

chain of 146. Mutations no doubt occur all along the codes for these proteins. But if the codon CTC for glutamic acid mutates to CAC for valine in the sixth position of the beta chain—one particular wrong word in a sentence of 287 words—an abnormal form of hemoglobin results.

When this abnormal form is present and stress, high altitude, or illness lowers an individual's oxygen supply, the red blood cells take on peculiar shapes, some resembling sickles (Figure 4.8). These misshapen cells cannot carry sufficient oxygen to nourish the body's tissues and can also block capillaries. Symptoms include fatigue, retarded physical development in children, increased susceptibility to infection, miscarriage, fever, and severe pain. Sickle cell kills about 100,000 people a year, 85 percent of whom die before their 20s. Those who live longer experience constant pain and have very low reproductive rates. In terms of evolutionary fitness—that is, reproductive success—sickle cell anemia may be considered nearly 100 percent fatal. (It should be noted that

gamete sampling: The genetic change caused when genes are passed to new generations in frequencies unlike those of the parental generation. An example of sampling error.

FIGURE 4.9
Distribution of frequencies of the sickle cell allele. Compare this with the map of endemic malaria (Figure 4.10).

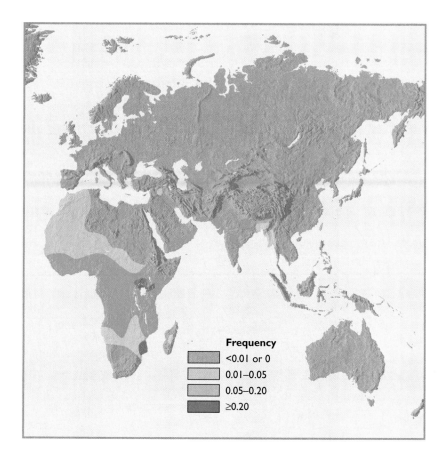

Frequency
<0.01 or 0
0.01–0.05
0.05–0.20
≥0.20

there have been recent breakthroughs in the treatment of this disease, including a means of repairing the messenger RNA so that it produces normal hemoglobin. This new technique, however, remains out of reach for most people suffering from the disease.)

The abnormal allele for sickle cell is an example of a codominant allele. An individual who is homozygous for the allele will have sickle cell anemia. A heterozygote, who inherits one sickle cell allele and one allele for normal hemoglobin, will possess only about 40 percent abnormal hemoglobin. These people are said to have the sickle cell *trait*. In extreme conditions of low oxygen, they may experience symptoms of the disease but usually not as severe as homozygotes and with a great deal of variation from person to person. The heterozygous condition is not normally fatal.

For a disease that kills its victims, usually without allowing them to pass on their genes, sickle cell is found in unexpectedly high frequencies in parts of the world (Figure 4.9), in some areas as high as 20 percent.

FIGURE 4.10
Distribution of endemic (consistently present) malaria. Compare with the map showing high frequencies of the sickle cell allele (Figure 4.9).

One would expect such an allele to be selected against and to virtually disappear.

The answer to this puzzle is a perfect example of the complexity of natural selection. Not only do heterozygotes experience less severe episodes of the disease, they also have a resistance to malaria, an often fatal infectious disease caused by a parasitic single-celled organism and transmitted by mosquitoes. Malaria, though now treatable, still infects over 400 million and kills 1 million to 3 million people a year, mostly African children younger than 5. Red blood cells with abnormal hemoglobin (recall that heterozygotes have about 40 percent of this) take on abnormal shapes when infected by the malaria parasite and die, thus failing to transport the parasite through the body. Sickle cell is thus found in highest frequencies where malaria is found in highest frequencies (Figure 4.10).

In no environment is there any advantage to being homozygous for sickle cell. In most environments, being heterozygous also confers a

~~~~~~

Contemporary Reflections

Are Humans Still Evolving?

As asked by most people, the question has two meanings. Perhaps the most common refers to the direction of future human evolution; in other words, how will we look in so many millions of years? As our minds do more and more of our work—and our bodies do less and less—will we eventually be great big heads atop short, spindly bodies? (This is the image we are often given of aliens from more advanced civilizations. Think of *Close Encounters of the Third Kind*, *E.T.*, or *The X-Files*.)

The answer to this first meaning of the question is, obviously, who knows? Evolution is so complex, so dependent on multiple, interacting series of events, that there is really no way of predicting the evolutionary future of any species, especially ours, with its ability to control its behavior, the environment, and, indeed, its genes through culture. If we could take a time machine back to the Cambrian period 543 million years ago and look at its animal life (see Figure 6.5), made up mostly of primitive arthropods (ancestors of modern insects, spiders, and crustaceans), who would predict that a rare little wormy creature only about 2 inches long, called *Pikaia*, would be the earliest-known representative of the chordates, the important group of organisms now represented by fish, amphibians, reptiles, birds, and mammals (Gore 1993; Gould 1989)?

A second, more sophisticated meaning of the question concerns whether we humans have stopped our evolution by so controlling our environment that natural selection is no longer in operation, that genetic variation is no longer an important factor in reproductive success. There are two parts to the answer. First, as we discussed, there are processes other than natural selection that bring about genetic change from generation to generation in a species. Our control over our environment certainly won't halt the processes of mutation, gene flow, and genetic drift. Indeed, one might argue that we have increased mutation rates through some of our environmental

~~~~~~

disadvantage. But in malarial areas, heterozygotes do have an advantage. They are resistant to malaria, and they exhibit a variable and nonfatal form of the anemia. If heterozygotes are the healthiest in such environments and thus are relatively more successful at passing on their genes, then more sickle cell alleles will be inherited than would be expected if sickle cell had no benefit in any environment. Whenever two heterozygotes mate, they stand a one-quarter chance of producing an individual with normal hemoglobin, a one-quarter chance of producing an offspring who will die from sickle cell, and a one-half chance of producing an offspring who will die neither from sickle cell nor from malaria but who will possess one sickle cell allele that can be passed on (Figure 4.11). This shows dramatically how adaptive fitness is related to specific environmental conditions. Even a lethal allele may be adaptive under certain circumstances.

The connection between sickle cell and African Americans is an example of the founder effect. African Americans can trace at least some manipulations and that our increasing mobility makes gene flow ever more powerful. So, by its genetic definition, evolution will always be taking place in our species.

But have we buffered ourselves against natural selection? For some genetically based characteristics, yes, we have. Remember that fitness is measured against a particular environment. If, through culture, we change the environment, we then change the adaptive fitness of certain phenotypes and thus of the genes that code for them. If I had lived in, say, *Homo erectus* times (1.8 million to 100,000 years ago), I'd no doubt be dead by now. If my infected appendix hadn't killed me (which it would have), my nearsightedness would have prevented me from being a very effective hunter or gatherer. Our present environment, however, has available all sorts of techniques and devices to improve one's eyesight. I wear glasses and see my optometrist once a year, so my poor vision (which, for the sake of the example, we'll say has a genetic basis) does not put me at any survival or reproductive disadvantage. You can probably think of dozens of other examples.

We have not, however, completely eliminated all relevant genetic variation. There are plenty of genes for diseases that place severe, or absolute, limits on a person's ability to reproduce and thus pass on those genes. Tay-Sachs disease, for example, is lethal well before reproductive age. Sickle cell anemia lowers reproductive rates in the few individuals who live long enough to reproduce.

And let's end on a hypothetical note (keeping in mind my precaution about predicting future evolution). There could well be some genetic variables that will make some difference in reproductive success in the near future. Suppose there is genetically based variation in humans' abilities to withstand less-than-optimal air quality or severely crowded living conditions or high levels of noise pollution. As these conditions worsen, it is certainly conceivable that genes for such tolerances will become more frequent as their possessors become less reproductively affected by the modern environment.

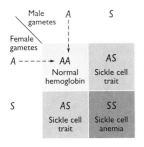

FIGURE 4.11

Punnett square for sickle cell anemia showing the potential offspring of two heterozygotes. Because heterozygotes have an adaptive advantage in malarial areas but stand a one-quarter chance of producing an offspring with sickle cell anemia, the allele for sickle cell is maintained and passed on in such populations and the disease exhibits high frequencies.

of their ancestry back to the populations from West Africa that provided much of the slave trade to North America. The African American population was thus, in part, founded by individuals from an area where sickle cell already existed in high frequencies.

But sickle cell is less frequent among African Americans than it is among certain populations of Africans. Moreover, sickle cell is not limited to persons of African descent in this country. One only has to have the alleles to have the disease. Persons of largely European American background can also have sickle cell. Both these facts can be explained partly as a result of gene flow. There has been a good deal of genetic mixing between European Americans and African Americans over the past several hundred years. The addition of European genes would have lessened the frequency of the sickle cell allele in African Americans because Europe is largely free of the disease. The presence of the disease among a small number of persons of largely European descent might be the result of their having an ancestor of African descent who carried the allele. Of course, the mutation that produces the sickle cell allele can occur in people of any geographic or ethnic background, European Americans included.

Moreover, because malaria is less common in the United States and Canada than in central Africa (although it was a problem in the southern United States until about twenty years ago), there has been less of an adaptive advantage in possessing the sickle cell trait. Natural selection has thus been producing lower frequencies of the sickle cell allele, even in persons whose ancestors are from one of the areas of highest frequency.

Finally, while we're on the subject, there is evidence (Livingstone 1958; Pennisi 2001; Relethford 2003b) that the frequency of malaria increased when people began farming in Africa several thousand years ago. Clearing and planting the land provides the sunlight and the pools of stagnant water that are ideal breeding grounds for the mosquitoes that carry the malaria parasite. An increase in malaria would result in an increased selection for the sickle cell allele, which, in heterozygotes, confers an immunity to the infectious disease.

Thus, the full story of this lethal disease shows the interaction of the forces of evolution and involves not only the genetics behind the cause of the disease but also a single-celled parasite, an insect, and human demographic and cultural practices. The story of sickle cell is a perfect example of the holistic perspective of anthropology.

▽　　　▽　　　▽

SUMMARY

A basic theory of evolution involves the production of new genetic variation by mutation and the continual mixing of that variation at reproduction. Gene flow and the forms of genetic drift (fission, the founder effect that results from fission, and gamete sampling) act to randomly change allele frequencies within populations of a species. The resulting phenotypic variation becomes the raw material for natural selection that selects individuals for reproductive success, thus accumulating adaptive traits across generations and decreasing the frequency of poorly adapted traits.

The basic unit of evolution is the species, an interbreeding population that is reproductively isolated from other populations. Because the evolution of new species is a process that occurs over time and at differing rates, species are not always equally distinct from one another and can often be difficult to define. Species are characterized genetically by allele frequency, the percentage of times each possible allele of a gene occurs. Evolution is thus technically defined as a change in allele frequency over time.

The processes of evolution, based on this definition, are:

1. *Mutation*—mistakes in the genetic mechanism that add new variation to a species' gene pool.

2. *Natural selection*—the differential reproduction of individuals based on the relative adaptive value of their traits.

3. *Gene flow*—the mixing of genes as populations within a species move about and interbreed.

4. *Genetic drift*—the splitting of populations to found new populations with new sets of allele frequencies (fission and the founder effect) and the nonrepresentative sampling of genes as each new generation is produced (gamete sampling).

Sickle cell anemia is not only an example of the processes of evolution at work but also an example of anthropology's holistic approach—the search for connections among the various aspects of its subject.

QUESTIONS FOR FURTHER THOUGHT

1. Domestic dogs are now classified in the same species as wolves, but we humans have been able to produce through selective breeding hundreds of different dog breeds, each with its own phenotype and behavioral attributes—many decidedly unwolflike. Given what you know about the processes of evolution, how do you think we've accomplished this?

2. Severe bottlenecks can pose a serious problem for a species. We are seeing this now among such species as cheetahs and elephant seals.

What do you think the problem is with a severe bottleneck, in some cases even after the species regains a fairly large population? Why is it actually threatening some species with extinction?

3. If I were an African American planning on having children, I might want to be screened to see if I were heterozygous for sickle cell. (I could be without ever having exhibited noticeable symptoms.) But since I am a European American, there is virtually no need for me to do so. Some people object to such reasoning, saying that it is potentially racist because it makes an assumption about one's health based on one's race. What do you think? Do you know of any other diseases that are statistically linked to certain populations?

KEY TERMS

niche

taxonomists

systematists

gene frequency

allele frequency

point mutations

chromosomal
    mutations

gene pool

breeding populations

gene flow

sampling error

fission

founder effect

bottleneck

gamete sampling

SUGGESTED READINGS

An extended discussion of genetics and evolutionary processes within the context of anthropology can be found in John H. Relethford's text, *The Human Species: An Introduction to Biological Anthropology*, fifth edition. It includes a chapter on sickle cell and many additional examples of evolution in action within human populations.

A highly technical but very readable text on all aspects of evolution is *Evolution*, second edition, by Mark Ridley. The nature of species and the evolutionary processes that affect them are nicely covered in Edward O. Wilson's *The Diversity of Life*, a book about the importance of maintaining the biological diversity of the planet.

The reseach on Darwin's finches and the people who conducted it are the subjects of Jonathan Weiner's Pulitzer Prize–winning *The Beak of the Finch: A Story of Evolution in Our Time*. For an update, see Peter and Rosemary Grant's article "Non-Random Fitness Variation in Two Populations of Darwin's Finches," in the 22 January 2000 issue of the *Proceedings of the Royal Society of London: Biological Sciences* and their "Unpredictable Evolution in a 30-Year Study of Darwin's Finches" in the 26 April 2002 issue of *Science*.

For a discussion of the definition and origin of species, which also relates to the next chapter, see Stephen Jay Gould's article, "What Is a Species?" in the December 1992 issue of *Discover*.

THE ORIGIN OF SPECIES AND THE SHAPE OF EVOLUTION

Endless forms most beautiful and most wonderful have been, and are being evolved.
—Charles Darwin

The examples of evolution in action that we discussed in the previous chapter—the finches responding to climatic changes on the Galápagos and populations of our own species interacting with malaria—focused on changes within single species. Darwin's book, however, was called *Origin of Species.* What Darwin was ultimately trying to explain was how new species arise, the "mystery of mysteries" as he called it in his introduction.

We will address the following questions in this chapter:

How do existing species give rise to new species?

How do the processes of evolution contribute to the origin of new species?

How do species diversify?

What does the "family tree" of species look like?

Are there any challenges to the idea of evolution? Are they valid?

NEW SPECIES

Species are, by definition, reproductively isolated from other species. Members of two species cannot mate and produce fertile offspring. Members of the same species can. What prevents interbreeding between species?

Any difference that prevents the production of fertile hybrid offspring between two populations under natural conditions is called a **reproductive isolating mechanism.** These isolating mechanisms fall into several general categories (based on Dobzhansky 1970):

1. *Ecological.* Members of the populations are adapted to different environmental niches. Even though their ranges may overlap, their specific environments don't—as is the case with lions and tigers in India. Ecological isolation probably explains the origin of the **hominids,** the group to which our species belongs (see Chapter 10).

2. *Seasonal.* Mating within each population or the flowering of plants of two related species takes place at different times of the year.

3. *Sexual.* Behaviors that attract one sex to the other (called *courtship behaviors*) are different in the two populations.

4. *Mechanical.* The organs of reproduction (genitalia or flower parts) are incompatible.

5. *Different pollinators*. In flowering plants, different species, even if closely related, attract different insects, birds, or bats to facilitate pollination.

6. *Gamete isolation*. The cells of reproduction may be incompatible or may not be able to survive within the body of a member of the other species, thus preventing fertilization even if mating takes place.

7. *Hybrid inviability*. Fertilization may occur, but the hybrid zygotes do not survive.

8. *Hybrid sterility*. Hybrids survive but do not produce functional gametes. Mules are normally an example, although in some cases they are fertile.

The origin of new species, then, is the evolution of *any* of these differences between populations that prevent the production of fertile offspring. As biologist Edward O. Wilson puts it, "In order to spring forth as a species, a group of breeding individuals need only acquire *one* difference in *one* trait in their biology. . . . When that happens, a new species is born" (1992, 68; emphases mine).

How do such differences arise? It is important to understand that reproductive isolating mechanisms do not evolve *in order* to produce a new species. It is an accident when the differences in traits are isolating mechanisms. The differences themselves evolve through the processes of mutation, gene flow, genetic drift, and natural selection acting differently on different populations.

To take the simplest model, a species inhabits a wide geographic range, and populations at opposite ends of the range exhibit slightly different adaptive responses to particular environmental circumstances (Figure 5.1). Now, some environmental change—say, a river changing its course, the destruction of some important resource, or the advance of a glacier—splits the species, geographically isolating one population from another. Over time, each population will continue to adapt to its environment but without being able to exchange genes with the other population. In other words, there will be no gene flow. Each population will accumulate different genetic and phenotypic traits. Quite possibly one or more of these traits will, by chance, be a reproductive isolating mechanism. If at some later point the geographic barrier were removed and the two populations *could* mix, they would not be able to interbreed. They would be separate species, and we would say that **speciation** had occurred.

Even if there are no distinct geographic barriers separating portions of a species, speciation can still take place. For example, in Nicaraguan lakes there are two closely related species of cichlid fishes that are

reproductive isolating mechanism: Any difference that prevents the production of fertile offspring between members of two populations.

hominids: Modern human beings and our ancestors, generally defined as the primates who habitually walk erect.

speciation: The evolution of new species.

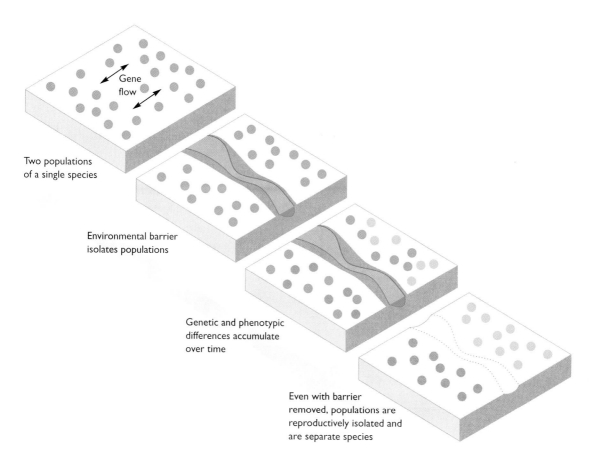

Gene flow

Two populations
of a single species

Environmental barrier
isolates populations

Genetic and phenotypic
differences accumulate
over time

Even with barrier
removed, populations are
reproductively isolated and
are separate species

FIGURE 5.1

Simple example of speciation
through environmental
isolation.

distinguished by color (Figure 5.2). Since cichlids mate according to color, these two groups don't hybridize. They apparently evolved from an original species when a new color arose through mutation, and because of the importance of color in mate choice, those with the new color were reproductively isolated (Kirkpatrick 2000).

In another striking example, a recent study (Johnson et al. 1996) has indicated that the basin of Lake Victoria in East Africa was completely dry only 12,000 to 14,000 years ago (ya*). And yet there are 300 distinct but closely related species of cichlid fishes in the lake, species found *nowhere else*. Clearly all these species have arisen fairly recently from, according to DNA studies, a single ancestral species. Apparently,

*By convention, I will use the following abbreviations throughout the remainder of the book: *ya* for "years ago," *mya* for "million years ago," and *bya* for "billion years ago."

FIGURE 5.2
Two cichlids of different species, one from Central America and one from South America, illustrating the sometimes slight differences in color that the cichlids themselves respond to in mate selection.

cichlids are poor swimmers that prefer certain habitats and don't move around much. They may also have a tendency not to select mates outside their local group. So small populations could quickly become isolated, and this could account for what seems to be the world's fastest speciation rate in a vertebrate (Yoon 1996a).

Ocassionally speciation may be accelerated when a breeding group within a species shares a mutation with extensive phenotypic effects. Such mutations are called **macromutations.** Most macromutations are, as you would expect, deleterious. But by chance, some macromutations might be neutral or even beneficial. In such a case, they would be retained by natural selection, and they might serve to very rapidly make a small population within a species adaptively isolated from the rest of the species. Speciation is given a "head start" by the macromutation, especially if it involves a gene that influences the development of an individual during its life. A mutation of one of these genes could have important consquences for the structure and function of the adult organism.

macromutations: Mutations with extensive and important phenotypic results.

The processes of evolution that bring about genetic and phenotypic variation are constantly in action (see Figure 4.4). So are the processes that alter environmental circumstances. It stands to reason, then, that the conditions that produce new species are ever-present and that speciation must be a very common occurrence indeed.

▸ ADAPTIVE RADIATION: THE EVOLUTION OF LIFE'S DIVERSITY

No one is sure how many species of living things inhabit the earth, and we have no idea how many have *ever* lived on this planet. There are about 1.5 million *named* species living today; the total is certainly many times that number, possibly 100 million.

Even in modern times, new species are still being discovered. In 1997, for example, a new species of marmoset (a type of monkey) was discovered in Brazil—the seventh new monkey species found in that country in a decade. New species of small mammals, mostly rodents and bats, are described at an average rate of sixteen per year. In 2002 a whole new order of insects was discovered. (Orders are groups of many related species. See Table 7.1.) New species of bacteria are being found by the thousands, including some recently discovered bacteria living in small spaces within rocks nearly 2 miles below the surface of the earth and at temperatures of more than 235°F.

Indeed, some microbes (single-celled organisms) that live at extreme conditions in superheated water near volcanic vents on the ocean floor, for example, or in water so salty it would kill most creatures, have been shown to be far more common than previously thought. Genetic tests of these and other microbes have shown them to belong to a whole new branch of life and have indicated that microbes compose the bulk of the world's *biomass*—a measure of the weight of organic matter (Gould 1996a). The actual number of species in the world must be, as one scientist put it, "staggering."

Despite the great array of living creatures, however, there is a high degree of similarity among them all. All living things, for example, use the same genetic code; they are built from the proteins that are the products of that code, using the same basic twenty amino acids. We assume, then, that life on earth had a single origin. This being the case, all those millions upon millions of species have descended from a common ancestor and have come about by the process of speciation.

For a potential new species to persevere, it must survive the adaptive trials of natural selection. Put another way, it must have a place to go, an environment to which its traits are adapted, an *ecological opportunity*. When such opportunities are extensive, speciation may take place numerous times, and a group of related species may spread into a number of niches. This spread of related species is called **adaptive radiation.** Evolution has been a story of the adaptive radiation of species into different environments and the subsequent actions of the processes of evolution on those species.

Ecological opportunities come about and can foster adaptive radiation under these three general circumstances:

1. When an environment supports no similar and therefore competing species

2. When extensive extinction empties a set of environments of competing species

3. When the new group of related species are adaptively **generalized** (as opposed to **specialized**) and are able to disperse successfully into different niches and displace species already there

An example of the first circumstance is the famous case of Darwin's finches (introduced in Chapter 4), a group of thirteen related species that inhabit the Galápagos, the volcanic archipelago of some nineteen islands in the Pacific about 600 miles west of Ecuador (Figure 5.3). This was one of Darwin's stops on his voyage around the world. There is a fourteenth related species that lives on Cocos Island, north of the Galápagos.

From a small group of original migrants of an ancestral species, blown out to the islands from the mainland of Central or South America no more than 3 mya, these birds have radiated into niches that were pretty much unoccupied by other birds. Today there are species of ground-dwelling finches that feed on seeds of different sizes and have bills shaped accordingly. There are several species that feed on cactus and several that live in trees and eat insects. Their beaks, too, as noted in Chapter 4, are adapted for the specific foods they eat. One species is a tool-user, holding a cactus spine or twig in its bill and using it to probe for insects in tree trunks. The ground finches on two of the smaller islands peck the skin of larger birds and drink the surfacing blood. Not surprisingly, they are referred to as "vampire finches."

Moreover, there is new evidence that beak form influences the songs of the various finch species, which could also affect species distinction (Podos 2001).

adaptive radiation: The evolution and spreading out of related species into new niches.

generalized: Here, species that are adapted to a wide range of environmental niches.

specialized: Here, species that are adapted to a narrow range of environmental niches.

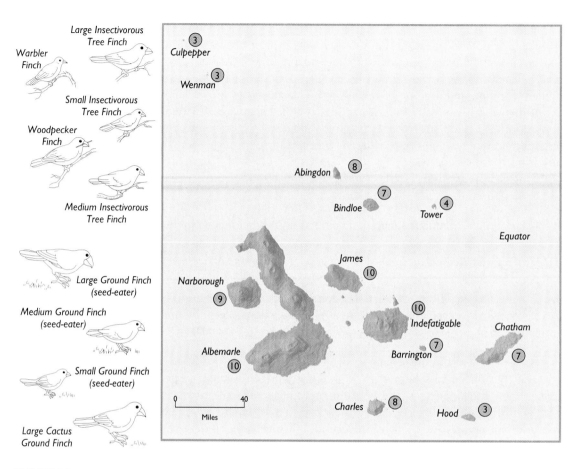

FIGURE 5.3

The various species of Darwin's finches evolved when small groups from an original species underwent adaptation to the varying environmental conditions found throughout the Galápagos Islands. The numbers on the map represent the number of finch species found on each major island. The bird drawings illustrate some of the variations observed among the species of Darwin's finches.

In fact, birds in general are an example of adaptive radiation into empty niches. Birds first evolved some 150 mya from a group of dinosaurs (Figure 5.4). There was little competition for species possessing the new attributes of feathers and, for some, flight. This evolutionary novelty radiated into a wide variety of niches, resulting currently in about 9,000 species of birds of incredible diversity. All are variations on the same basic theme.

Mammals are an example of a group of species that were able to take advantage of the niches vacated by a major extinction—the one that killed off all the dinosaurs and many other species 65 mya. Mammals were among the survivors. At the time they were mostly small **nocturnal** shrewlike or rodentlike creatures, but they now had a world of niches open to them that were free of many previous competitors. The mammals radiated rapidly, and by about 40 mya most major types of mammals we

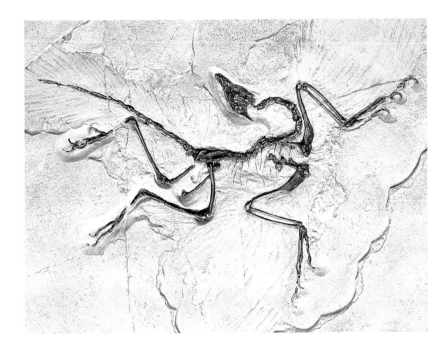

FIGURE 5.4

Fossil remains of *Archaeopteryx* ("ancient bird"), about 150 million years old, in appearance a small bipedal dinosaur with feathers. The feathers, modifications of dinosaurian scales, are an example of an alteration in a species' genetic makeup that eventually gave rise to a whole new group of organisms.

know today had evolved. (The ancestors of all modern birds, too, survived this extinction.)

We can look to our own group of mammals, the primates, for examples of species that were able to radiate because they were generalized and could fairly easily disperse into diverse niches. When monkeys first evolved, about 40 mya, they proved more generalized than their **prosimian** ancestors, the so-called primitive primates. The monkeys were larger-brained, **diurnal,** and well adapted to an active **arboreal** life, eating a mixed diet of leaves, fruits, and insects. As the monkeys underwent speciation and radiated into new niches, they displaced the prosimians. In the New World (Central, South, and North America), there are only monkeys, which inhabit Central and South America (prosimians apparently became extinct in North America). In the Old World (Europe, Africa, and Asia), prosimians were pushed into marginal areas. A few species live on the mainland of Africa and the mainland of Southeast Asia, but most inhabit isolated islands of Southeast Asia and the island of Madagascar, which separated from mainland Africa prior to the monkeys' evolution (see Chapter 10 for more detail).

On a smaller scale, we will see this pattern repeated when we look more closely at our own evolution. At least once during the evolution of our group of primates, a new and more generalized species of hominid

nocturnal: Active at night.

prosimian: A primate with primitive features, most closely resembling the ancient primates.

diurnal: Active during the day.

arboreal: Adapted to life in the trees.

spread geographically and ecologically, displacing an existing hominid species (see Chapters 10, 11, and 12).

THE SHAPE OF THE FAMILY TREE

What is the pattern of speciation, and what, as a result, is the shape of the evolutionary family tree of species?

Charles Darwin felt that natural selection was directly responsible for speciation and that it was a process of almost unlimited power. He said that natural selection brought about "the accumulation of innumerable slight variations, each good for the individual possessor." He added:

> What limit can be put to this power, acting during long ages and rigidly scrutinizing the whole constitution, structure, and habits of each creature,—favoring the good and rejecting the bad? I can see no limit to this power, in slowly and beautifully adapting each form to the most complex relations of life. (1898:267)

In other words, Darwin saw natural selection as "fine-tuning" each species to its environment, constantly favoring or rejecting any difference among individuals, no matter how "slight." This constant selection eventually changes one species so much that it may be considered a new species. In addition, such constant selection, Darwin said, will also produce variation among populations within a species in response to slight differences in their environments. He referred to these populations as "varieties." Eventually, selection brings about such marked distinctions in varieties that two or more new species branch from the old one. These species, said Darwin, "are only well-marked varieties, of which the characters have become in a high degree permanent" (1898:285).

According to this model, referred to as **Darwinian gradualism,** the family tree of species has relatively few gracefully diverging branches (Figure 5.5). These represent the slow but steady pace at which individual species change through time and at which populations within species slowly become distinct from one another under the "scrutiny" of natural selection. The tree of evolution represents, in Darwin's words, "an interminable number of intermediate forms . . . linking together all the species . . . by [fine] gradations" (1898:271–72). In modern terms, we would say that most of the evolutionary change we see, in a broad geological time frame, is the result of **microevolution,** a "continuous transformation of a unitary population through time" (Gould 2002:775).

Here, however, Darwin's model has been challenged. For one thing, the fossil record has failed to show intermediate forms with fine gradations

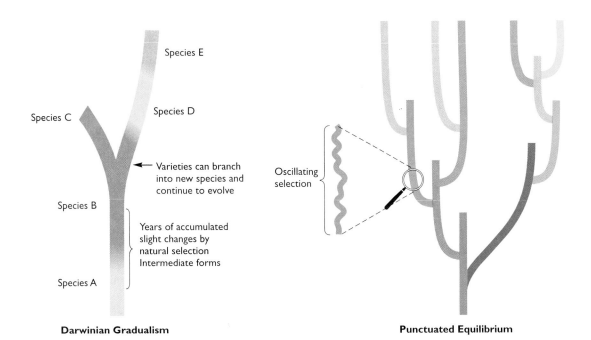

Darwinian Gradualism

Species E

Species C

Species D

← Varieties can branch into new species and continue to evolve

Species B

Years of accumulated slight changes by natural selection Intermediate forms

Species A

Oscillating selection

Punctuated Equilibrium

FIGURE 5.5

Models of evolution through geological time. According to Darwinian gradualism, the evolution of species through time is a slow, steady process. By contrast, according to the punctuated equilibrium model, major evolutionary change is the result of speciation, the branching of new species from existing ones. Individual species change relatively little through time, although natural selection still acts constantly to maintain a species' adaptation to its environment.

Darwinian gradualism: The view, held by Darwin, that evolution is slow and steady with cumulative change.

microevolution: Evolutionary change within a single species through time.

for all evolutionary lines. Instead, fossil species often tend to remain relatively stable for long periods of time, and changes—new species—show up rather suddenly.

The origin of our own group, the hominids, did not occur slowly and steadily, gradually producing a humanlike form from an apelike one. The first fully accepted hominid fossils, from over 4 mya, are, to exaggerate only slightly, apes that stood upright (see Chapter 10). The change was not gradual but was focused on bipedalism and was quick enough so that few other evolutionary changes had time to occur. (It is important to remember that "quick" in evolutionary perspective is, of course, a relative term and may mean *tens* of thousands of years or more.)

Another problem with Darwin's model is more theoretical. If, as according to Darwin, each "slight variation" that natural selection favors is "good for the individual possessor," then we have to assume an adaptive benefit for *each small step* in the development of some trait. But could one-tenth of a wing, or one-hundredth of an eye—like a millimeter in those finches' beaks—*always* convey to its possessor a reproductive advantage over the members of its species that lack this trait?

Finally, there is the problem of determining at which point in the microevolution of one species enough change has occurred to warrant calling it a new species. In fact, if species are defined as natural populations capable of interbreeding, then there is *no point* in a species' evolution when—barring one of those rare macromutations—a member of one generation could not interbreed with a member of the previous generation. As Stephen Jay Gould put it (2002b:775), "A true continuum cannot be unambiguously divided into segments with discrete names."

It would seem, then, that evolutionary change over great spans of time is not the result of gradual change *within* species (individual species changing so much they become new species) but, rather, the result of new species *branching from* existing species, the process of **macroevolution.** Indeed, natural selection is not the creative "scrutinizing" force that Darwin envisioned but a more conservative force, eliminating what doesn't work adaptively and allowing to reproduce what does. Change *within* a species is limited.

This does not mean that natural selection has *no* effect on a species over time. Traits that are important may change back and forth as environmental conditions change. Recall the changes in beak size among the Darwin's finches that the Grants and their team studied. The data indicate that a slight difference in beak size among members of one species—as little as a millimeter or two—can be of adaptive importance during sudden, prolonged, or radical environmental changes such as droughts. In fact, small differences made the difference between life and death, and so, after such an environmental episode, the average beak size of an affected finch species could be significantly altered. When conditions—and thus food sources—returned to normal, the average beak size returned to its previous measurement. The average expression of important traits of a species, then, may change back and forth as environmental conditions change. This is called **oscillating selection.** But it is adaptive variation around a norm, rather than continual change in a particular direction—a sort of nondirectional fine-tuning.

So, the role of natural selection is basically to maintain the adaptation of a species to its environment. Natural selection is not the author of evolution so much as the editor. Thus, species normally change little over the course of their tenure on earth, and new species seem to arise fairly quickly as a result of the isolation of populations within species through geographic or ecological separation, mutation, or a combination of both. Natural selection, of course, *then* plays an important role in screening the isolated population in terms of adaptive fitness.

We may describe this model of evolution as follows: The adaptive equilibrium of species with their environments is punctuated (interrupted) by the evolution of a new species from a population of the parent species. The parent species, in the meantime, may remain unchanged, at least for a time. This model is called **punctuated equilibrium** and is represented not by a tree with gracefully diverging branches but by a bush with many twigs (see Figure 5.5). These twigs are evolution's experiments, potential new species. Many twigs are short, since the species they represent became extinct over a short time. Some are longer, however, and give rise to yet more new species.

So, the evolution of life on earth cannot be depicted as a ladder or a chain representing the steady march of progress toward complexity, as Lamarck and other early scientists believed. Nor is it a gracefully branching tree, as Darwin pictured it. Instead, it is, in the words of Stephen Jay Gould (1994b:91), a "luxuriant bush," more complex than we will probably ever know—a "blooming and buzzing confusion" (1985:355).

EVOLUTION QUESTIONED: THE PSEUDOSCIENCE OF "SCIENTIFIC CREATIONISM"

All the information about the theory of evolution presented in Chapters 3 and 4 has been developed and tested, using the methods and principles of science, over the past several hundred years by many people and from many different perspectives. Evolution is so well supported we consider the basic idea to be a fact, and it is the central concept of all biology, although we continue to apply the scientific method to our investigation of specific details. Our ideas about the generation of genetic variability, adaptation by natural selection, and the origin of species from existing species—all come together to explain everything we observe and understand about the living world.

We benefit from this knowledge every day of our lives. We eat foods from species of plants and animals bred according to the principles of genetics and selection. We know the causes of many of the illnesses that beset us because we understand the genetic operations of our cells, and we have insight into how some organisms (such as viruses and bacteria) are adapted to other organisms (like us), and vice versa. Many of the antibiotics and other medicines that help us treat those illnesses work only because of the interrelatedness of all life. And this interrelatedness has also allowed us to manipulate the genes of other organisms, including bacteria, to "trick" them into producing, say, human insulin for the treatment of diabetes. This same technique is used in producing human growth hormone and interferon, a chemical found in our body's immune system. Moreover, recent advances in decoding the genome (see Chapter 3) have shown remarkable genetic similarities among even distantly

macroevolution: The branching of new species from existing species.

oscillating selection: Adaptive variation around a norm, rather than in one direction, in response to environmental variation in a species' habitat.

punctuated equilibrium: The view that species tend to remain stable and that evolutionary changes occur fairly suddenly through the evolution of new species branching from existing ones.

related species. The basic genetic code for the development of eyes, for example, is pretty much the same from humans to fruit flies. Genes that control cell division in baker's yeast (a single-celled fungus) are matched by abnormal genes in human cancer cells.

So it is truly astounding that some people, even today, question the fact that evolution actually occurred, and many of these people base their questioning on religious belief. Why is this a problem? Think back to our discussion of science from Chapter 1. Science and belief systems are both important for the operation of any society, and, ideally, they operate in harmony with one another. They are still, however, distinct realms of knowledge, distinguished by the *testability* of science and the *faith* of belief.

But what about ideas that have characteristics of both? Suppose someone holds a scientific idea (an idea that is testable) but treats it as a belief by taking it on faith and by not testing it or recognizing the results of tests that have been applied to it, even if those tests refute it. Here's an example: there are people who believe that the lines on the palms of your hands and on your fingers hold information about your personal character and even, perhaps, about your future. This belief is called palmistry, and its precepts are quite scientifically testable. In fact, I examined them scientifically (Park 1982–83) and they failed. But will palmists all over the country close up shop because some anthropologist says their ideas are false? Hardly. Palmists take their ideas on faith. In other words, they treat a scientifically testable idea like a belief system. Thus, palmistry is a **pseudoscience,** or "false science."

Although pseudoscientific ideas such as palmistry, astrology, and the power of crystals may be harmless enough, other examples have implications that may not be so benign. Some pseudoscientific ideas find support within established belief systems. There are—believe it or not—still people who think the earth is flat and who refuse to acknowledge the masses of scientific evidence to the contrary (Schadewald 1981–82). This belief stems in large part from the literal interpretations of several biblical passages, for example, Matthew 4:8: "Again, the devil taketh him [Jesus] up into an exceeding high mountain, and sheweth him all the kingdoms of the world. . . ." How, the flat-earthers ask, could Jesus have seen all the kingdoms of the earth unless the earth were flat?

Although most people recognize the allegorical sense of this and similar passages in both testaments of the Bible, there is a danger that some might find the issue terribly confusing. On the one hand, scientific evidence—not to mention photographs taken from space—tells us unequivocally that the earth is a sphere. On the other hand, an interpretation of the chronicles of two major religions seems to say the earth

pseudoscience: Scientifically testable ideas that are taken on faith, even if tested and shown to be false.

scientific creationism: The belief in a literal biblical interpretation regarding the creation of the universe, with the connected belief that this view is supported by scientific evidence.

FIGURE 5.6
Strata of the Grand Canyon in Arizona. Scientific creationists contend that these strata and all the fossils they contain are the results of the biblical flood. Scientific data show that the canyon's strata represent geological and biological events that took place over nearly 2 billion years. (See also Figure 2.2.)

is flat. Must one choose between science and religion? There are those who think so, and in the process, both science and belief suffer.

The idea of a flat earth is utterly ridiculous, but there is another pseudoscience, relevant to our topic here, that is far more complex and difficult to evaluate. It's called **scientific creationism.** It proposes that the entire universe, including the earth and all its inhabitants, were created spontaneously by untestable supernatural forces around 10,000 ya. Except for minor changes within "kinds" of plants and animals (breeds of dogs, for example, or regional varieties of a wild species), no changes in living organisms have occurred. Certainly no *new* species have arisen. But, we might ask, what about the layers of rock and soil and the fossils they contain? According to supporters of scientific creationism, those resulted from "a primeval watery cataclysm" (Morris 1974:22), a great flood in other words (Figure 5.6).

Sound familiar? It should. This argument derives directly from one literal interpretation of the first eight chapters of the Book of Genesis, and it is clearly in direct opposition to all the data and ideas accumulated and tested by science. More than 200 years of scientific inquiry tell

Contemporary Reflections

Can We See Evolution in Action?

When we look around us, it seems as if the world is a fairly stable place, biologically speaking anyway. Certainly we hear of species becoming extinct at a rapid rate (see the "Contemporary Reflections" box in Chapter 6), but otherwise we don't see much change. There doesn't seem to be any evolution still going on. But there is, of course.

The problem is one of scale. We tend to see the world from our perspective—as large mammals with large brains that afford us a great deal of control over our environments. We have an amazing ability to live in and withstand a wide variety of environmental conditions and extremes. But most creatures are a lot smaller than we are, and most are far more at the mercy of their environments.

And we rarely see things from the point of view of our genes. By definition, evolution is phenotypic change across generations, involving at the most basic level genetic change. Much genetic change is brought about by the processes of mutation, gene flow, and genetic drift (fission, the founder effect, and gamete sampling). These processes are *always* taking place. Indeed, given the mobility of our species and our proclivity for exchanging genes, gene flow and the forms of genetic drift might be seen as particularly powerful processes of evolution for us. The human species is evolving all the time, by these processes alone.

What about natural selection? As noted in the "Contemporary Reflections" box in Chapter 4, natural selection is certainly still taking place in our species, although, again because of scale— especially our long life span—we might not always perceive it. But look to some other species.

us that the universe, including the earth and its inhabitants, arose through knowable, natural processes. The universe is at least 12 billion years old, the earth 4.5 billion years old, and life on earth nearly 4 billion years old. Living organisms do change through time, and species give rise to new species. The geological and fossil records are the records of these billions of years of change. We've been covering the evidence, data, and arguments for evolution in these last few chapters.

Scientific creationism is thus a pseudoscience—a testable set of ideas that even in the face of contrary evidence is accepted on faith. But scientific creationism goes further. Its proponents claim its ideas are, indeed, supported by scientific evidence that also refutes the accepted theory of evolution. That the creation model coincides with one interpretation of Genesis merely shows, they say, the scientific accuracy of the Bible. Because advocates of scientific creationism claim both models are scientific, they feel both should be taught in science classes as viable alternative explanations for the origin and diversity of life.

The argument is persuasive, especially in a society like ours, concerned with religious freedom and with our American sense of fair play

In the woods in back of my house there are numerous small stands of young pine trees. Where the trees are very young, a foot tall or less, they can grow in quite dense concentrations. I counted six small trees growing in a 1-square-foot area of forest floor. A square foot, however, is hardly enough space for six full-grown pines. There will be fewer plants there next year, fewer still the next year, and fewer the next. Many years from now, with luck, there will be one adult tree in that space. Only one will have the characteristics that will allow it to outcompete the others—greater height to catch more sun, greater ability to withstand insects, cold, and drought—whatever makes pine trees successful. Only one will be left to reproduce and pass on those traits that made it successful. Natural selection right in my backyard. Evolution in action.

But evolution in its broadest sense involves the origin of new species. Can we see this? Think about how new species evolve, but *don't* think on our human scale. There must be new species of small organisms evolving all the time. Speciation in microbes must be very common indeed. And even with larger organisms, whose generation times are longer, we can see distinct evidence of evolution. Although we recognize and name thirteen species of Darwin's finches on the Galápagos, the Grants and their team noted that some of those species can interbreed when altered environmental circumstances cause their niches to overlap. In other words, they are still in the process of becoming completely separate species. With several species of Darwin's finches, we have caught speciation in the act. And recall the cichlid fishes mentioned earlier in the chapter, whose multiple species must have arisen from a single ancestor over a relatively brief period of time. Evolution—even the origin of new species—is happening all around us. We just have to look carefully enough.

and equal time. *But equal time is for equivalent things.* There is not a single shred of scientific evidence in support of the creation model.

To teach scientific creationism alongside evolution would be to violate the religious freedoms of those who do not subscribe to a strict creationist interpretation. It would also badly confuse those trying to learn how science really operates and what conclusions about our world science has arrived at. The distinction between science and belief would be blurred, interfering with the harmonious and important relationship between the two.

Recently, a new twist on this problem has surfaced with a new degree of complexity and, thus, a potential for unquestioned acceptance. It is generally referred to as **intelligent design.** It comes in several forms, but one will capture the idea. This version of intelligent design says that the basic chemistry of life—the cell, with its DNA, RNA, resultant proteins, and myriad reactions—is far too complex to have evolved naturally and so *must* have been designed by some intelligent entity. The more involved arguments use statistics to convey the great odds against putting together just the right combination of molecules that we now know are needed for

intelligent design: The idea that an intelligent designer played a role in some aspect of the evolution of life on earth, usually the origin of life itself.

life. Intimidated by such large numbers, many people accept the proposed improbability, if not impossiblity, of life evolving by natural processes.

There are two problems with this idea. First, the initial improbability of something happening doesn't *preclude* its happening. What was the probability at my birth that I would eventually become a biological anthropologist teaching at this university and, at this moment, writing a textbook? The answer is: infinitesimally small! And yet it happened, through all the contingent facts of my personal history—all the little things, many of them conscious decisions but many random, unpredictable, and accidental, which led to other things, and so on.

Similarly, for the evolution of life, a billion years or so passed from the formation of the earth to the first evidence of life (think of how long a billion years is). There are so many molecules, so many combinations of molecules to make compounds, so many individual chances for things to come together in different variations that we couldn't begin to even estimate the number. Among the things that did occur was the chemical combination, under just the right circumstances, that set in motion the chain of events that led to what we now call *life*. In other words, an intelligent designer is *not necessary*.

The second problem is that an intelligent designer is not a scientific (that is, testable) idea. The proposal of an intelligent designer based on supposed rational, scientific evidence (biochemistry and statistics) is just a thinly disguised version of scientific creationism. It ignores the majority of empirical evidence and substitutes an idea that cannot be tested, that *must* be taken on faith. It then becomes, by the definition I use here, a pseudoscience. There may well *be* some designer behind the universe we see, but a belief in such a designer is not a *substitute* for a scientific explanation of that universe.

The quality of our lives now and in the future depends on the continued progress of our testable scientific knowledge, mediated by the values of our belief systems. We need to understand what these two areas of knowledge are and how they interact, and we must promote free access to and sharing of all knowledge.

▽   ▽   ▽

SUMMARY

The evolution of new species is an obvious result of the interacting processes of genetic variation, natural selection, and environmental change. New species arise when a population within an existing species becomes isolated. Isolation is often geographic but may also be ecological, adaptive, or the result of a macromutation. In isolation, this new population experiences the processes of genetic variation and phenotypic adaptation separate from the parent species. Among the differentiating traits that result, some may act as reproductive isolating mechanisms, meaning that even if the populations once again have the opportunity to interbreed, they will probably not be able to do so. They will have become separate species.

The process of speciation, occurring countless times over the billions of years of life's history, has produced the incredible array of life-forms we know today and see in the fossil record. The species we know about only hint at the variety that actually exists and has existed in the past. When species have the opportunity, they are able to adaptively radiate into new niches, and the increased diversity of life-forms is the result. It must be remembered, however, that all these forms are variations on the single theme of life that originated on this planet. All life, through speciation and adaptive radiation, is descended from a single origin.

We can depict evolution as a luxuriant bush, dense with innumerable twigs, each representing a new species. We use the bush as a metaphor for evolution for two reasons. First, we realize that the conditions for speciation are continuous, so that speciation has probably taken place more often than we can imagine. Second, we understand that Darwin's model of the origin of species, driven by the steady, gradual "fine-tuning" of natural selection, is not accurate. Natural selection is a conservative force, acting largely to maintain a species' adaptation. What produces new species is geographic or genetic isolation, and these processes act relatively quickly. In other words, evolutionary change on a geological time frame is the result of macroevolution, not microevolution.

The evidence for evolution is overwhelming. We are still examining the specific details of evolutionary theory, but the idea of evolution and our knowledge of the essential processes involved are hypotheses that have passed numerous scientific tests and failed none. Evolution itself is a *theory* in the scientific sense of the word. The evidence for evolution is as strong as, say, the evidence for the theory that the earth revolves around the sun. Nonetheless, some people, for reasons that have nothing to do with science, claim that evolution did not occur. These claims have been examined scientifically, and they have been shown to be scientifically invalid. Their proponents, however, continue to insist on their accuracy. These claims are thus pseudoscience, and they confuse the important relationship between science and belief systems; for in fact, there is no necessary conflict between the two.

QUESTIONS FOR FURTHER THOUGHT

1. Does the conflict between scientific creationism and mainstream evolutionary science mean that we must choose between science and religion? Are the two realms of knowledge, with regard to this subject, incompatible?

2. Consider the processes of evolution and speciation. Can you think of any examples of these processes in action today? How are human influences on the world part of these processes? Or are they? Do these processes still affect our species? If so, how?

3. The result of adaptive radiation is biodiversity. Human actions are threatening the rich biodiversity of the planet. Is there a real problem with this, beyond the loss of some interesting or attractive species? How might diversity in and of itself be vital to the health of the planet?

KEY TERMS

reproductive isolating mechanism
hominids
speciation
macromutations
adaptive radiation
generalized

specialized
nocturnal
prosimian
diurnal
arboreal
Darwinian gradualism
microevolution

macroevolution
oscillating selection
punctuated equilibrium
pseudoscience
scientific creationism
intelligent design

SUGGESTED READINGS

You should certainly have a look at the book that began our modern understanding of evolution, Darwin's *Origin of Species*. The last chapter, "Recapitulation and Conclusion," nicely summarizes his arguments and provides a good idea of his style.

A wonderful book on evolutionary processes, the origin of new species, and the variety of living things is Edward O. Wilson's *The Diversity of Life*.

For more on Darwin's finches, see Jonathan Weiner's *The Beak of the Finch*.

One of the originators of the model of punctuated equilibrium is biologist Stephen Jay Gould, and many of his articles concern that model. Try "The Episodic Nature of Evolutionary Change" and "Return of the Hopeful Monster," both in *The Panda's Thumb*. Gould has also addressed the shape of the evolutionary bush. See his informative books *Wonderful Life* and *Full House* and his article in the October 1994 *Scientific American*, "The Evolution of Life on the Earth." And for what many consider the "last word" on evolutionary theory in general, look at Gould's *magnum opus*, his 1433-page *The Structure of Evolutionary Theory*, with special attention to Chapter 9 on punctuated equilibrium.

For an idea of the arguments of the scientific creationists, try *Evolution: The Fossils Say No!* by Duane T. Gish. For a refutation of scientific creationism, go once again to Stephen Jay Gould and a series of articles on the subject in *Hen's Teeth and Horse's Toes*. A good example of the intelligent design argument is *Darwin's Black Box*, by biochemist Michael J. Behe. For a discussion, see the January–April 2002 issue of *Reports of the National Center for Science Education*.

The National Center for Science Education, Inc. (NCSE) works to support the teaching of evolution and to increase public understanding of evolution and science. They publish "Reports of the NCSE," which contain interesting and useful articles on all aspects of this topic. Their Web site is www.natcenscied.org.

The relationship between science and philosophical ideas, brought out so powerfully by the issue of scientific creationism, is addressed in Kenneth Miller's *Finding Darwin's God* and in Stephen Jay Gould's *Rocks of Ages;* for a very broad discussion, see *Consilience,* by Edward O. Wilson.

Data continue to come in about the cichlids of Lake Victoria. Among other things, it appears that some of the named cichlid species are not entirely reproductively isolated; that is, they are still in the process of real speciation. However, because of the increasingly murky waters of the lake, many cichlids can't discern color differences and are mating with members of other populations. This is gradually increasing gene flow and thus decreasing the variability of these fishes. See Erica Goldman's piece in the 31 January 2003 *Science*, "Puzzling Over the Origin of Species in the Depths of the Oldest Lakes."

A BRIEF EVOLUTIONARY TIMETABLE

And there is no new
thing under the sun.
—Ecclesiastes 1:9

Anthropology focuses on one group of organisms, the hominids, and deals mostly with a single species of hominid, *Homo sapiens*. Hominids have been around for 5 or 6 million years. Depending on one's interpretation (see Chapter 12), our species has inhabited the earth for 2 million years at most. Although this seems like a long time, it is really just the last tick of the earth's evolutionary clock, four-hundredths of 1 percent (0.04 percent) of the history of our planet, and one-hundredth of 1 percent (0.01 percent) of the estimated history of the universe. If the history of the universe were reduced to a single year, our species would not show up until after 11:30 p.m. on December 31.

So, although we focus on *us*, we need to appreciate the fact that all the processes of evolution apply to all forms of life on earth and that the idea of evolution—change through time—applies to the whole history of the universe.

Before we focus on ourselves, our close relatives, and our immediate ancestors, we need to put human evolution in context, to see it as part of a long and ongoing series of changes that began maybe 15 bya.

Following are two questions we will consider in this chapter:

What is the history of the universe, the earth, and life on earth?

What processes and events have affected the overall history of the earth and life on earth?

FROM THE BEGINNING: A QUICK HISTORY

The origin of the universe is shrouded in mystery. We don't, in all honesty, really know exactly how old it is, although 15 billion years is an average of recent estimates. We do know, however, that the universe is expanding in all directions. All the galaxies in the universe (an estimated 50 billion) are constantly traveling farther away from each other. A logical conclusion from this fact is that the universe began at a single location, and evidence indicates that it started as an incredibly tiny, dense, and hot speck (the proper term is a *singularity*) composed of pure energy that would one day become all the energy and space and matter—including us—of the universe we know.

At the beginning of time—we'll use 15 bya—this speck began to expand, an event commonly called the Big Bang, although it wasn't really an explosion. It was more like a balloon being rapidly inflated—a balloon that contained both energy and space. It is hypothesized that this inflation was caused by the accumulation of a material that produced

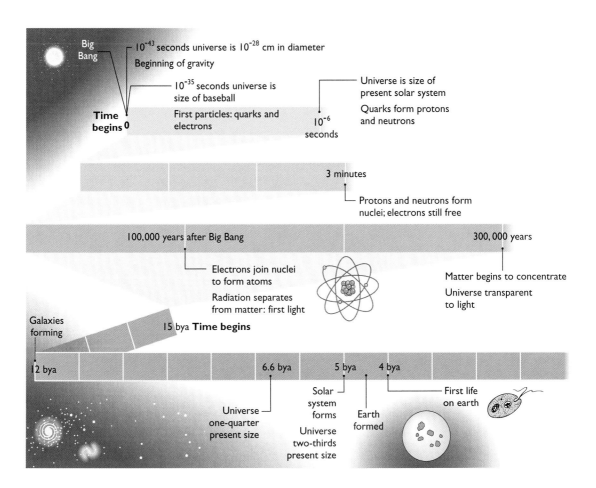

FIGURE 6.1

History of the universe, from the Big Bang to the origin of life on earth. The scale of the timeline changes because some events are condensed into incredibly small periods and others are stretched over unimaginable spans.

a repulsive force—the opposite of gravity's attracting force. The details of the Big Bang are still a matter of intense debate and are among the most complex issues in science. For our purposes here, suffice it to say that as the newborn universe expanded, it cooled, and matter quickly condensed from energy (Figure 6.1). Within 3 minutes after the beginning, protons and neutrons had formed and had joined to make atomic nuclei, but it took another 100,000 years for electrons to join the nuclei to form atoms. At about the same time, radiation separated from matter and there was light, but for the next 200,000 years the universe was still too dense for that light to travel through it.

By 12 bya, galaxies had begun to form as gravity pulled matter together into huge clusters. These were made up of stars that were mainly hydrogen, the simplest element. As a result of the nuclear reactions in these stars, heavier, more complex elements formed. When these early

FIGURE 6.2

Stromatolites in Australia, (*top*), are formed when mats of blue-green algae (single-celled organisms) are covered with sand, silt, and mud, which the algae cement down and then grow over. Fossil stromatolites (*bottom*), and thus the organisms that made them, have been dated to 3.5 bya.

stars died in tremendous supernova explosions, their elements were scattered into space, some eventually contributing to the formation of new galaxies with all their stars and, in several known cases, planets. (Planets have been discovered orbiting other stars in our galaxy.)

About 5 bya, when the universe was two-thirds its present size, our solar system formed around a medium-sized star in the Milky Way galaxy. Earth, the third of nine existing planets orbiting that star, came into being 500 million years later. Amazingly, in less than a billion years—maybe 3.6 bya—life on earth was established. We know this indirectly from fossils found in Greenland, southern Africa, and Australia (Figure 6.2). In Australia there are also actual fossils, preserved in stone, of single-celled organisms from at least 2.8 bya, many of which were probably already capable of **photosynthesis.**

Just how life came about on the earth is also a matter of debate. For over forty years, scientists have been able to produce carbon-rich **organic** compounds from **inorganic** compounds with a fairly simple laboratory procedure, showing that the process could have occurred quite easily. In fact, they have been able to produce amino acids, which, as you recall, are the building blocks of proteins. But as you also recall, proteins cannot be built without a nucleic acid code. Evidence now suggests that RNA formed very early in earth's history. RNA was able to replicate itself and act as a code for the synthesis of proteins. Later, DNA took over this role (Orgel 1994). It is still, of course, a long way from amino acids and RNA to a living organism, and the details of this path remain unclear.

Whatever happened, it happened fast (about 700 million years from the formation of the earth to life *is* fast, in the geological time scale), but once established, life at first evolved slowly. The world's first identifiable organisms were simple single cells like bacteria (Figure 6.3). It wasn't until about 2 bya that complex single-celled organisms containing nuclei and organelles evolved (see Figure 3.1). Multicellular organisms first appeared about 1.7 bya. The earliest evidence for simple life on land—bacteria—dates to 1.2 bya.

All these early single-celled organisms reproduced **asexually** by splitting and making copies of themselves. Evolutionary change relied entirely on mutations. Then about 1 bya, some organisms began to reproduce **sexually.** Sexual reproduction may have begun as a mechanism of genetic exchange to replace defective genes. Soon, however, it proved to be an accelerator of evolution. Now, in addition to mutation, fertilization also provided genetic and phenotypic variation, and evolutionary change quickly gained speed. Figure 6.4 summarizes what is known about the timing of important events in the evolution of life on earth.

About 543 mya, in the Cambrian period, complex multicellular organisms burst on the scene. Some even possessed hard parts like shells. So

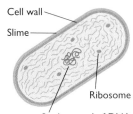

Cell wall
Slime
Ribosome
Single strand of DNA
(not in a nucleus)

FIGURE 6.3
This typical bacterium represents some of the earliest forms of life on earth and what are still—in terms of time and numbers—the dominant forms of life today.

photosynthesis: The process by which plants manufacture their own nutrients from carbon dioxide and water, using chlorophyll as a catalyst and sunlight as an energy source.

organic: Molecules that are part of living organisms. They are based on the chemistry of carbon and contain mostly hydrogen, oxygen, carbon, and nitrogen. Even carbon-based molecules that are not found in living things are sometimes referred to as organic.

inorganic: A molecule not containing carbon.

asexually: Reproducing without sex, by fissioning or budding.

sexually: Reproducing by combining genetic material from two individuals.

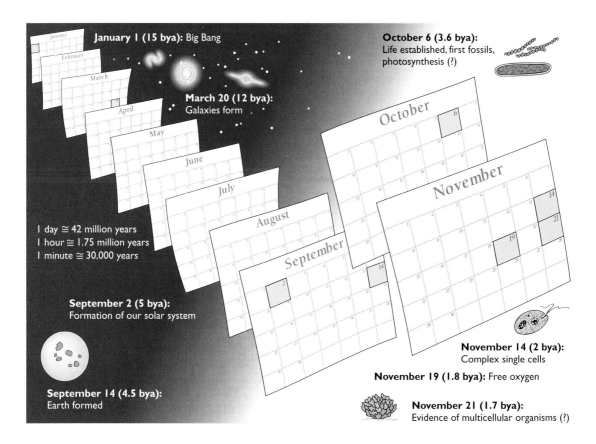

January 1 (15 bya): Big Bang

March 20 (12 bya): Galaxies form

1 day ≅ 42 million years
1 hour ≅ 1.75 million years
1 minute ≅ 30,000 years

September 2 (5 bya): Formation of our solar system

September 14 (4.5 bya): Earth formed

October 6 (3.6 bya): Life established, first fossils, photosynthesis (?)

November 14 (2 bya): Complex single cells

November 19 (1.8 bya): Free oxygen

November 21 (1.7 bya): Evidence of multicellular organisms (?)

FIGURE 6.4

Astronomer Carl Sagan likened the history of the universe to a single calendar year in his 1975 Pulitzer Prize–winning book *The Dragons of Eden*. This calendar has been recalculated to show the currently accepted dates for important events.

(Adapted from Sagan, 1977)

vertebrates: Organisms with backbones and internal skeletons.

apparently sudden and rapid was this event that it is referred to as the Cambrian Explosion. In a mere 5 million years, all major body plans of multicellular animals had evolved, including ancestors of the **vertebrates,** animals with backbones (Figure 6.5). So far, there are no agreed-upon explanations for this "explosion," but it is clearly a major event in the history of life, and it set the themes for the subsequent evolution of animals.

By 470 mya, plants and fungi had colonized the land. Fish had evolved, and land animals appeared by 425 mya. Insects appeared about 400 mya; by 350 mya, some of them had evolved wings. Reptiles showed up around 350 mya as well, and the reptilian form that is thought to have given rise to the mammals was found at about 256 mya. Dinosaurs began evolving around 235 mya, with true mammals appearing about 220 mya. Sometime around 150 mya, feathers evolved by a group of dinosaurs signaled the beginning of the evolution of birds (see Figure 5.4). Flowering plants appeared only a little more than 100 mya, and the primates, the group to which humans belong, showed up about 55 mya, perhaps earlier.

December

1

2

3

4

5

6

7

8 Sexual reproduction (1 bya)

9

10

11

12

13

14

15 Land fungi and plants (700 mya)

16

17 First soft-bodied animals (590 mya)

18 Cambrian explosion (543 mya) First vertebrates (530 mya)

19 First land plants (470 mya)

20

21 Fish, complex land plants, and land animals (425 mya)

22 Insects (400 mya)

23 Winged insects, reptiles (350 mya)

24

25 Mammal-like reptiles (256 mya)

26 Dinosaurs (235 mya) True mammals (220 mya)

27

28 Birds (150 mya)

29 Flowering plants (100 mya)

30 K/T extinction (65 mya) First definite primates (55 mya)?

31

1:00 a.m. (40 mya): First monkeys

11:00 a.m. (23 mya): First apes

9:00 p.m. (5–6 mya): First hominids

10:30 p.m. (2.5 mya): First stone tools

11:22 p.m. (0.5 mya): First use of fire

11:59 p.m. (30,000 ya): Cave paintings

11:59:35 p.m. (12,000 ya): Farming

11:59:55 p.m. (2,000 ya): Common Era begins

11:59:59 p.m. (500 ya): Renaissance

FIGURE 6.5
Cambrian fauna consisted mostly of arthropods, ancestors of modern-day insects, spiders, and crustaceans. The large creature in the center grew to 3 feet long. The flowerlike animals on the right are unclassified.

plate tectonics: The movement of the plates of the earth's crust, caused by their interaction with the molten rock of the earth's interior. The cause of continental drift.

Pangea: The supercontinent that included parts of all present-day landmasses.

DRIFTING CONTINENTS AND MASS EXTINCTIONS: THE PACE OF CHANGE

During all this time, life was not the only thing evolving on earth. The earth itself was also evolving as the continents changed shape and position, a phenomenon known as *continental drift*, which operates through the process of **plate tectonics.** The outer layer of rock on the earth, the *crust*, is in a constant state of change. It is broken into some sixteen *plates* of various sizes that fit together like a huge spherical jigsaw puzzle. The motion of the molten rock, *magma*, below the crust causes the plates to change shape and location. In some areas, magma seeps up between the plates and solidifies, pushing the plates apart. Something has to give, and at other boundaries called *subduction zones*, one plate is pushed under another and plunges deep within the earth, where it melts and adds to the magma. Clearly, then, the continents—those parts of the plates that protrude above sea level—have shifted over time and will continue to do so (Figure 6.6). It should also be noted that plate tectonics accounts for important geological phenomena. Where the plates meet and move

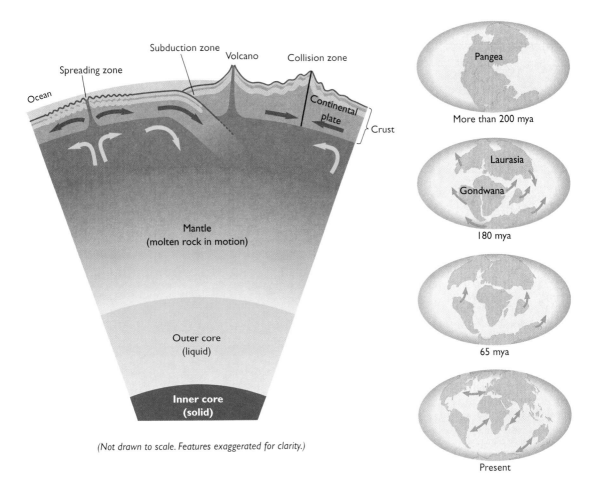

(Not drawn to scale. Features exaggerated for clarity.)

FIGURE 6.6
This cross section of the earth shows the process of plate tectonics and the resultant drift of the continents over the past 200 million years. Continental drift, of course, occurred prior to 200 mya and will continue into the future.

against one another, tremendous forces are produced that result in earthquakes and volcanoes and cause mountains to grow.

By the time the dinosaurs and early mammals had appeared, all the continents had drifted together to form a huge supercontinent we call **Pangea,** literally "all lands." This is why, for example, we find fossils of the same type of dinosaur in what are now such widely separated places as China, North America, and Antarctica. Around 200 mya, Pangea began to break up, and the resulting landmasses—the ancestors of our present-day continents—drifted over the globe, producing a diversity of environments and geographic boundaries that has profoundly affected the nature of life on earth as we know it today.

From all we've discussed so far, it would seem that the evolution of the earth and of life—influenced by continental drift and the

FIGURE 6.7

This painting, by Rudolph Zallinger, reflects some now outdated ideas about the appearance and behavior of the dinosaurs. It does show, however, some of the variety of these creatures as they existed over 170 million years of time (from left to right in the mural). The dinosaurs once dominated the earth's environments.

environmental changes it brings about—has been a steady process. And basically it has been—relative to the immense amount of time involved. But the fossil record shows that at least five times in the planet's history some change has taken place that was so rapid and extensive that it radically altered the course of biological evolution by causing a mass extinction.

For example, about the time the continents were drifting together to form the supercontinent of Pangea—at the end of the Permian period (250 mya)—over 95 percent of all species of marine and terrestrial organisms suddenly became extinct. Some changes occurred to which none of the variants within all those species were adapted. The cause for this greatest of all mass extinctions is unknown, but a new hypothesis suggests it was the result of massive volcanic eruptions, possibly initiated by a meteor impact in what is now Siberia, that altered the planet's climate. At any rate, such a catastrophe certainly had a major effect on the future course of life's evolution.

Another mass extinction directly affected the evolution of our small section of the evolutionary bush. About 65 mya, the dinosaurs were a dominant form of land animals. There were large reptiles in the seas and close relatives of the dinosaurs in the air (Figure 6.7). Mammals were also around and had been for nearly as long as the dinosaurs. In terms of ecological niches, however, mammals didn't have many places to go because other niches were already occupied.

Then one day—literally—an asteroid, thought to measure 6 miles across, crashed through the earth's atmosphere and into the crust where the north coast of the Mexican Yucatán is now. The impact made a crater 200 miles in diameter. The asteroid may have broken apart on

impact with the atmosphere, and pieces may have hit in other locations as well, or there may have been several asteroids.

This collision created a blast like that of a nuclear explosion. Thousands of cubic miles of vaporized rock, water vapor, and small particles and dust were shot into the atmosphere and carried around the world. Heat from the impact caused massive forest fires that created smoke and ash. One hypothesis suggests that the impact produced shock waves that bounced inside the earth and were focused on the opposite side of the planet, causing large-scale volcanic activity that put even more smoke and ash into the air. It has recently been noted that the Yucatán is rich in sulfur, suggesting that the impact might have produced sulfuric acid in the atmosphere, causing acid rain. All this matter created a blanket that blocked sunlight, cooling the earth and preventing green plants from carrying out photosynthesis.

These extensive environmental changes proved disastrous (a word that means, appropriately, "bad star"). Dinosaurs became extinct, along with every other species of land animal weighing more than about 55 pounds, many plants, and much of the ocean's plankton, the small organisms that provide a great deal of the world's oxygen and that act as an important source of food at the base of the food chain. This event is the famous *Cretaceous/Tertiary (K/T) extinction* (Cretaceous is abbreviated *K* to distinguish it from the earlier Carboniferous).

But many of the mammals survived. Perhaps, by a stroke of luck, they already were adapted to withstand adverse, changing conditions. Now, with the dinosaurs suddenly gone, a whole world of new niches was open to them and to many other creatures that had made it through the catastrophe. This group included some of the birds, thought by many to be the dinosaurs' only living direct descendants (Figure 6.8).

Contemporary Reflections

Are Mass Extinctions a Thing of the Past?

Extinction is part of evolution. For one reason or another, species become extinct all the time. An estimated 90 percent of all species that have ever existed are now extinct.

But the idea of some intense event that can bring about the extinction of up to 95 percent of the earth's living forms over a short period of time seems inconceivable to us. And yet, at least five such events have occurred over the 3.8-billion-year history of life on this planet. The best known of these wiped out the dinosaurs—a long-lived and very successful group of species— 65 mya. Surely, we think, these events were part of the earth's "formative" years and could not happen again. Sadly, this view is incorrect—for two reasons.

First, we know that the mass extinction that included the dinosaurs was initiated by the impact of at least one huge asteroid, and impacts are associated with some of the other mass extinctions as well. Although such impacts were more common in the past, asteroids, comets, and fragments of them are far from used up. Lots of them still orbit through our solar system. Go outside on any clear night, look up long enough, and you're bound to see one of the smaller ones burn up as it hits the earth's atmosphere. These are so-called shooting stars. Bigger ones, parts of which survive the atmosphere, hit the earth regularly (although most are neither seen nor found).

And on occasion we encounter very large ones. A few years ago an asteroid large enough to do serious damage missed the earth by a mere 250,000 miles—the distance between the earth and the moon, a near miss on the cosmic scale. It was not seen until it had already passed us!

In 1908 a large portion of an asteroid or a fragment of a comet nucleus exploded 6 miles up in the atmosphere over Siberia. The shock waves were heard 600 miles away and flattened trees

FIGURE 6.8

The wild turkey shows a striking similarity to bipedal dinosaurs, further evidence of the evolutionary relationship between dinosaurs and birds.

over 770 square miles. It's altogether possible, then, that our planet will be hit by another large object from space in the future, and if it's big enough, devastating consequences will follow, including the extinction of many species.

But there is a second reason why mass extinctions are not things of the past—a reason even more disturbing since (unlike the situation with asteroids) we *could* do something about it. There is, in fact, a sixth mass extinction in earth's history, and it is happening right now.

Starting about 10,000 ya, species began becoming extinct at a rate faster than usual. At present, species are disappearing at a rate at least as fast as, and probably faster than, during any of the previous five mass extinctions (Eldredge 1991, 1995; Leakey and Lewin 1995). Estimates vary, but the earth may be losing species at a rate of 27,000 a year—that's 3 every hour. Now, one might argue that given what we know of earth's history, extinctions—even mass ones—are "natural." Well, they have been; but this one is different. Unlike the other extinctions, where the conditions causing the problem eventually went away, this situation is unlikely to get better because, as biologist Niles Eldredge says, "the irritant . . . remains on the scene" (1995:128). That "irritant," of course, is us.

Since we figured out how to control natural food sources through farming and animal husbandry some 12,000 ya, our species' population has grown at an ever-increasing rate. Our need for resources, energy, and space has grown along with our numbers. We have pushed other species into marginal areas, destroyed their habitats and resources, and hunted or otherwise exploited them to extinction. We are well into the process of changing the very climate of the earth as our emissions into the atmosphere are causing the world's climate to warm.

Although we may or may not experience the catastrophic death and destruction of an asteroid impact, we are—*right now*—in the midst of what may be the biggest and fastest of all mass extinctions. Decidedly *not* a thing of the past.

So rapid was the mammals' adaptive radiation that within about 20 million years, all the major types of mammals we know today had appeared—everything from bats to whales to a group of tree-dwelling creatures possessed of acute eyesight, dexterous hands, and large, inquisitive brains. These were the primates, and it is this group that we shall focus on in the next chapters.

▽   ▽   ▽

SUMMARY

This narrative of the history of the universe has been necessarily brief, but it does point out three themes that are important to remember as we continue.

First, it could be said—by virtue of human numbers (over 6 billion) and our impact on the planet—that we are the dominant species on the earth today. But our evolutionary history makes up a small fraction of the whole history of the universe and even of the earth. We are the new kids on the evolutionary block, and we have not as yet even proved ourselves successful by the criterion of longevity. Cockroaches have been around hundreds of times longer than we have; bacteria have been around since the beginning of the fossil record. By these standards, our species is in its infancy.

Second, as the Bible says, "there is no new thing under the sun." Indeed, although we often speak of the "origin of the earth" or the "origin of life," the only *real* origin is that of the universe itself. All the events subsequent to that have been *rearrangements* of what already existed: matter condensing from energy as it cools; large atomic particles forming from smaller ones; stars coming together from cosmic dust; heavy elements being created from lighter ones in the nuclear furnaces of those stars; the elements of inorganic molecules being rearranged to form the molecules of life; and the shuffling of the genetic code, producing the extraordinary multitude of living things that have inhabited this planet.

Third, and perhaps most humbling, the specific history of the universe, including the earth and its life, could have happened in countless other ways. Each event in our story is contingent on preceding events. Even our evolution is dependent on the specific sequence of events that came before it. If those events had been different, *we* might be different— or we might not be here at all. Imagine if that asteroid had *not* hit the earth 65 mya. In other words, the evolution of humans—or anything else for that matter—was not inevitable. We're lucky we're here.

QUESTIONS FOR FURTHER THOUGHT

1. Consider a question from Chapter 5 from a more specific perspective: We humans may be bringing about the extinction of a large number of other species, but for some of them, what real difference does it make? We hear about such endangered species as the snail darter (a small North American fish), the spotted owl, and the Texas blind salamander. Would it really matter, beyond an ethical or an aesthetic consideration, if any of these became extinct?

2. The astronomer Carl Sagan once referred to human beings as "star stuff." He meant it literally. How so? What does this say about the nature of evolution, both on a biological and a cosmic level?

KEY TERMS

photosynthesis	asexually	plate tectonics
organic	sexually	Pangea
inorganic	vertebrates	

SUGGESTED READINGS

For an update on cosmology—the history of the universe—see the February 2000 issue of *Natural History*, especially "Genesis: The Sequel," by Alan Guth. For a good discussion of the science behind our understanding of the history of the universe, I recommend *Coming of Age in the Milky Way*, by Timothy Ferris.

The evolution of life is covered in the lavishly illustrated *The Book of Life*, edited by Stephen Jay Gould. For a good narrative approach, see *Life*, by Richard Fortey, and for a more technical but still readable work, see *History of Life*, second edition, by Richard Cowen. *National Geographic* has a series of articles called "The Rise of Life on Earth" in the March 1998, April 1998, May 1999, February 2000, and September 2000 issues.

The Cambrian Explosion is the subject of an article by R. Gore in the October 1993 *National Geographic*, "The Cambrian Period: Explosion of Life." It is also the focus of Stephen Jay Gould's *Wonderful Life* and Simon Conway Morris's *The Crucible of Creation*. These two well-respected authorities disagree on the meaning of the Cambrian fossils and the nature of evolution as a series of contingent events. For a summary of their debate, see "Showdown on the Burgess Shale," by Conway Morris and Gould, in the December 1998/January 1999 *Natural History*.

For a good discussion of the origin of feathers, see "Which Came First, the Feather or the Bird?" by Richard O. Prum and Alan H. Brush in the March 2003 *Scientific American*.

The subject of mass extinctions is discussed in Edward O. Wilson's *Diversity of Life* and in an article in the June 1998 *National Geographic*, "The March Toward Extinction," by R. Gore.

The link between extraterrestrial collisions and mass extinctions is explored in "Repeated Blows," by Luann Becker, in the March 2002 *Scientific American*.

To see animations of continental drift, go to www.scotese.com/pangeanim.htm. A good site on the geology of North America is tapestry.usgs.gov/Default.html. It's called "A Tapestry of Time and Terrain" and features a section called "Rocks of Ages" that discusses the different geological divisions of earth history.

CHAPTER

7

THE PRIMATES

> I confess freely to you, I
> could never look long
> upon a monkey,
> without very mortifying
> reflections.
> —William Congreve
> (1695)

he proper study of mankind is man," said the poet Alexander Pope. The last few chapters should have convinced you that even biological anthropologists, who by definition focus on the study of mankind (or, more properly, humankind), cannot limit their interests to just our own species. The processes that have produced modern *Homo sapiens* are the processes that have produced every single species that has ever inhabited this planet. Additionally, all those species are part of an integrated whole, composed of all environments and all living things in complex interaction with one another across geographical space and through evolutionary time.

Moreover, were we to limit our study just to our species, or even to the hominids in general, we would lose a great deal of perspective. We need to compare ourselves with other forms of life to see in what ways we are similar and in what ways we differ. This comparison is made all the more important because we *are* the species we are studying, and so it can be difficult to be objective about ourselves. Thus, primatology is an important part of anthropology.

In this chapter we will address several important questions:

What is our place in nature; that is, where do we fit—from a scientifically objective point of view—in the world of living things?

What are the characteristics of the primates—the group of animals of which we are a part?

In what ways are humans like the other primates? In what ways are we unique?

NAMING THE ANIMALS

We have already discussed the concept of the species, the natural unit of classification. Each organism belongs to a *specific species* (the words come from the same root), a group of potentially interbreeding individuals that are reproductively isolated from other groups.

The most cursory examination, however, shows clearly that there are larger units of classification of living things. Some species are more similar to one another than they are to other species. The book of Genesis, for example, does not name each species that God created, but it lists general categories: "the fish of the sea," "the fowl of the air," "every herb of the field," "every beast of the earth."

TABLE 7.1
Linnaean Taxonomy of Five Familiar Species

	Human	Chimpanzee	Bonobo	Gorilla	Orangutan
Kingdom	Animalia	Animalia	Animalia	Animalia	Animalia
Phylum	Chordata	Chordata	Chordata	Chordata	Chordata
Class	Mammalia	Mammalia	Mammalia	Mammalia	Mammalia
Order	Primates	Primates	Primates	Primates	Primates
Family	Hominidae	Pongidae	Pongidae	Pongidae	Pongidae
Genus	Homo	Pan	Pan	Gorilla	Pongo
Species	sapiens	troglodytes	paniscus	gorilla	pygmaeus

Linnaean Taxonomy

The idea that species shared similarities so struck Swedish botanist Carolus Linnaeus (introduced in Chapter 2) that he devised a taxonomic system to name and thus categorize all living creatures. A **taxonomy** is a classification based on similarities and differences. I have, for example, accumulated thousands of notes, articles, and other important individual pieces of paper in my years as a bioanthropologist. If I simply stored all these together randomly, I'd never find anything when I needed to refer to it. Instead, I file my papers according to general categories and subcategories nested within them. For instance, I have a file cabinet marked "Biological Anthropology." One of its drawers is marked "Evolution," and within that drawer is a file folder marked "Taxonomy," where I keep notes and copies of articles on Linnaeus and the related matters I'm now writing about.

Similarly, Linnaeus (who used Latin names and even latinized his original name, Carl von Linné) devised a system, published in final form in 1758, that used four nested categories—*class, order, genus,* and *species.* Other scientists soon added *kingdom, phylum,* and *family,* giving us the seven Linnaean categories recognized by modern taxonomy (which uses additional categories when needed). Modern taxonomy recognizes seven basic categories but uses additional categories when needed. Table 7.1 shows a traditional Linnaean taxonomy for five familiar species. We'll detail the taxonomy of our species to show what Linnaeus's system accomplishes.

It should be noted that a species is never referred to by just the species name, listed in the bottom row of the table. The species name is usually

taxonomy: A classification based on similarities and differences.

TABLE 7.2
A Linnaean Taxonomy of Humans (with defining criteria)

Kingdom	Animalia
	Ingestion
	Movement
	Sense organs
Phylum	**Chordata**
	Notochord
Class	**Mammalia**
	Hair
	Warm-
	blooded
	Live birth
	Mammary
	glands
	Active and
	intelligent
Order	**Primates**
	Arboreal
	Developed
	vision
	Grasping
	hands
	Large brains
Family	**Hominidae**
	Habitual
	bipeds
Genus	**Homo**
	Toolmaking
	Omnivore
Species	**sapiens**
	Brain size
	1,000–
	2,000 ml*

Note: This definition is a matter of controversy and will be taken up in Chapters 11 and 12.

descriptive, and so there may be many species that share the same name. Many African animals have the species name *africanus*, for example. The chimpanzee shares its species name, *troglodytes*, with the winter wren, a small North American bird (the name conveying the erroneous assumption that these species are cave dwellers). It takes *both* the genus and species names to denote a particular species. We are, for instance, *Homo sapiens*.

Humans are members of the kingdom Animalia (Table 7.2). We share this grouping with the other four species in Table 7.1 by virtue of the fact that we all ingest our food, have sense organs and nervous systems, and are capable of intentional movement. We are not members of any of the other three kingdoms of eukaryotes (organisms whose cells have nuclei): complex single-celled organisms (amoebas and the like), fungi (mushrooms, mildews, molds), and plants (roses, ferns, broccoli, pine trees). There are, in addition, two main groups of prokaryotes, single-celled organisms that lack nuclei: bacteria and archaea. These are the microbes, referred to in Chapter 5, that make up the bulk of the earth's biomass.

Within kingdom Animalia are about thirty *phyla* (singular, *phylum*), groups such as sponges, jellyfish, starfish, three types of worms, mollusks, arthropods (insects, spiders, crustaceans), and chordates. We are members of phylum Chordata because we have a bony spine, the evolutionary descendant of a **notochord,** a long cartilaginous rod running down the back to support the body and protect the spinal chord, the extension of the central nervous system (Figure 7.1). Chordates with a bony spine are grouped into a subphylum, Vertebrata. All five species in Table 7.1 are chordates and, more specifically, vertebrates.

There are seven classes within the vertebrates: the jawless fishes (an ancient group represented by only a few existing species), cartilaginous fishes (sharks and rays), bony fishes (guppies, tunas, and so on), amphibians (frogs and salamanders), reptiles (snakes, lizards, and alligators), birds, and mammals. All our sample species are members of class Mammalia because they maintain a constant body temperature (commonly called *warm-blooded*), have hair, give birth to live young, nourish the young with milk from mammary glands, and have relatively large, complex brains.

We need to stop here for an important point. You may have noticed that some of the traits listed for mammals are also possessed by other classes. Birds, for example, are also warm-blooded; so, according to many, were some of the dinosaurs, and so are a number of other creatures, including great white sharks. Some sharks, some bony fishes (such as guppies), and some snakes give birth to live young. By the same token, you might know two mammals that do not possess all the mammalian traits. The spiny anteater (or echidna) and the duckbill platypus, both from Australia, lay eggs. Obviously, though, birds, dinosaurs, and great white

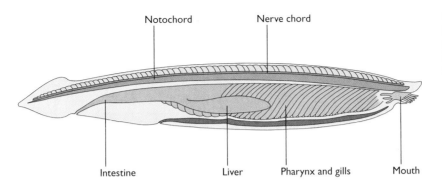

sharks are *not* mammals, while the spiny anteater and platypus *are*. What's the resolution to this seeming contradiction?

The answer is that inclusion into a taxonomic category is more than simply a matter of possessing a list of traits. The traits of an organism make possible that organism's *adaptation,* and it is adaptation, measured by reproductive success, that is the criterion of natural selection. Thus, taxonomic categories become statements about adaptation, as well as biological relationships, with each taxonomic level becoming more specifically focused. Mammals, whether they lay eggs or not, are animals that are adapted through active lifestyles and a reliance on learned behavior facilitated by a set of shared traits. Mammalian young, therefore, require a great deal of direct care and nurturing. Mammals also require a constant body temperature to sustain their level of activity, and they require hair (or in the case of whales, a thick layer of fat) to maintain that temperature. That's not a very concise definition of a mammal, but the real world doesn't always make things easy for those of us who try to describe it.

Within class Mammalia are about nineteen existing orders—nineteen rather specific adaptive strategies and resulting sets of characteristics. There are, for example, the flying bats; the fully aquatic whales and dolphins; the partially aquatic seals, sea lions, and walruses; two orders of hoofed plant eaters (the difference being a skeletal feature of the feet); the rabbits and hares; the rodents; the meat eaters; the insect eaters; the pouched marsupials (kangaroos and opposums); and a group of large-brained tree-dwellers with three-dimensional vision and dexterous hands. These last mammals are the members of order Primates.

All the species in Table 7.1 are primates, but they differ at the level of family. Humans traditionally have been classified in family Hominidae, while the other four are members of family Pongidae, the great apes. Within the pongids we recognize three *genera* (singular, *genus*). The only Asian species, the organgutan is placed in genus *Pongo*. The African

notochord: The evolutionary precursor of the vertebral column.

FIGURE 7.2

Evolutionary tree based on phenetic analysis. We infer the evolutionary relationships from the taxonomic classifications.

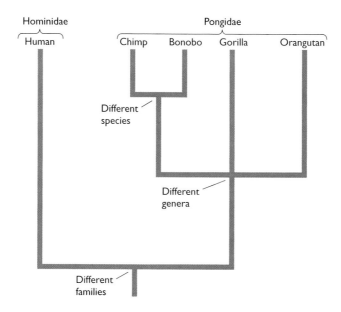

gorilla, although similar to the other African apes, is different enough to be placed in a separate genus, *Gorilla*. The chimp and bonobo are recognized as two species within the same genus, *Pan*. A Linnaean taxonomy thus indicates the relative relationships among named organisms.

Linnaeus's goal was to describe the system that, as he believed, God had in mind when he created all the earth's living things. Linnaeus was a creationist, as were just about all scientists of his time. But as you can probably see, to modern scientists his taxonomy indicates not only present-day similarities and differences but evolutionary relationships as well. For example, the reason the chimp is more similar to the bonobo than to a human is that the chimp and bonobo diverged from each other more recently than they did from humans. The chimp and bonobo are thought to have had a common ancestor from which they split less than 1 mya. Humans and the chimp/bonobo line branched about 5 mya. Humans and chimps have had a longer time to evolve in different ways than have the bonobo and chimp, which is why they are more different and why they are placed in different taxonomic families.

So, a Linnaean taxonomy, or **phenetic taxonomy** (one based on existing phenotypic features and adaptations), can be translated into an evolutionary tree, showing the relative order of branching of the classified species and other **taxa** (categories; singular, *taxon*). Figure 7.2 shows an evolutionary tree derived from the classification of the five species in Table 7.1.

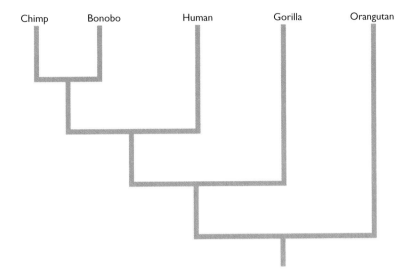

Cladistics

The tree in Figure 7.2 demonstrates the basis of a current debate within taxonomy. The tree was *inferred* from phenetic categories—physical comparisons of living species. Many such evolutionary trees prove quite accurate with regard to relative branching times and, thus, the overall pattern of branching. But as we learn more about the fossil ancestors of living species and as we improve our techniques of genetic comparison, we also learn more about the details of the evolutionary relationships among those species—particularly about the exact times and patterns of their evolutionary divergences.

Current knowledge from the fossil record and from genetic comparisons indicates that the organgutan line diverged earliest, the gorilla line next, and the human and chimp/bonobo lines most recently. In other words, the tree inferred from the phenetic taxonomy (see Figure 7.2) is inaccurate. The actual evolutionary tree should look like Figure 7.3. Thus, there is a contradiction between the traditional taxonomic names and categories for these species and their evolutionary relationships.

Cladistics (from *clade,* meaning "branch") works the opposite way from phenetics by starting with the evolutionary tree and placing organisms in taxonomic categories based on their order of branching, regardless of how their present-day appearances and adaptations might assort them into groups.

Branching order is determined in two ways. First, we use **shared derived characteristics.** If two groups share phenotypic features not

phenetic taxonomy: A classification system based on existing phenotypic features and adaptations.

taxa: Categories within a taxonomic classification.

cladistics: A classification system based on order of evolutionary branching rather than on present similarities and differences.

shared derived characteristics: Phenotypic features shared by two or more taxonomic groups that are derived from a common ancestor and that are not found in other groups.

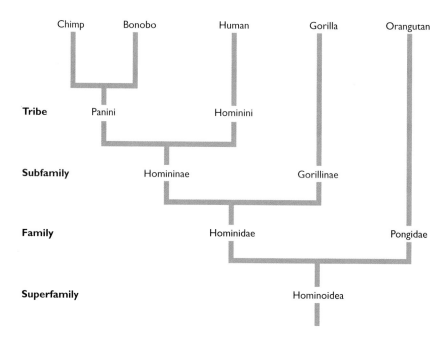

found in other groups and if it can be supported that those features were derived from a common ancestor, the groups must be lumped into the same category at whatever taxonomic level is appropriate. For example, we could justify lumping birds with dinosaurs in the same taxon and placing reptiles in a different taxon because birds and dinosaurs share a feature of the pelvis not found in any other group, including reptiles. Second, branching order is determined by genetic comparison, now done at the level of the base sequence of the genetic code itself. (See Chapter 3 and the genetics section of Chapter 9 for more detail.)

What are the implications for the primates? Under a phenetic scheme (see Figure 7.2), there is a family division between hominids and pongids—in other words, between humans and apes. This is intuitively obvious since the four ape species resemble one another in some basic phenotypic features and adaptations more than they do us humans.

But in cladistics (Figure 7.4), there is no such thing as an "ape." There is no clade that *includes* the four great apes and *excludes* humans. Cladists have proposed a number of different taxonomies to reflect this. In one taxonomy, family Pongidae includes only the orangutan, and humans and the African apes are lumped into family Hominidae. Subfamily and tribe categories are then added to make further distinctions.

Is a phenetic or a cladistic system better? Phenetics captures obvious phenotypic and adaptive relationships but may fail to accurately reflect actual patterns of branching. Cladistics is evolutionarily accurate but requires redefinition of taxonomic categories that make sense in terms of obvious adaptive focuses. For instance, if we accept the preceding cladistic taxonomy, *hominid* is no longer restricted to "the **bipedal** primate" but now includes the **quadrupedal** chimps, bonobos, and gorillas. Its definition then becomes much more complex.

The debate continues, with no consensus in sight. My own preference is to classifty taxa by branching order (that is, cladistically) and then, although it can get wordy, describe the phenotypic and adaptive differences that may have arisen within a taxon and figure out why they arose. Having said that, however, we will stick with the traditional phenetic classification for the primates in this text. My focus is to show how primate species, especially the so-called higher primates, look and behave and how those looks and behaviors have evolved. It is simpler to start with phenetic categories because they are based on looks and adaptive behaviors and *then* see how categories change under cladistic analysis. We will discuss some examples as we continue. (See Exercise 2 for some practice in constructing phenetic and cladistic evolutionary trees.)

Now, let's focus on the adaptive strategy and the phenotypic traits that characterize the members of order Primates.

WHAT IS A PRIMATE?

There are about 200 living species of primates. We're not sure how many have existed during the order's evolutionary history of more than 55 million years. Primates range from the very small, such as the mouse lemur of Madagascar, which weighs less than 3 ounces, to the gigantic— *Gigantopithecus*, an extinct ape from China, Vietnam, and India that may have stood 12 feet tall and weighed over half a ton (Figure 7.5). Some primates inhabit small, very specific environmental ranges and spend their lives slowly moving through the trees, eating fruits, leaves, or insects; one species of primate lives in nearly every environment and produces its own food.

Its wide variety makes the primate order a bit difficult to define in a simple sentence. The primates are best defined by looking at the characteristics they have in common and in seeing how these traits facilitate the primate adaptive strategy. We'll look at the primate traits by using the following categories: (1) the senses, (2) movement, (3) reproduction, (4) intelligence, and (5) behavior patterns.

bipedal: Walking on two legs.

quadrupedal: Walking on all four limbs.

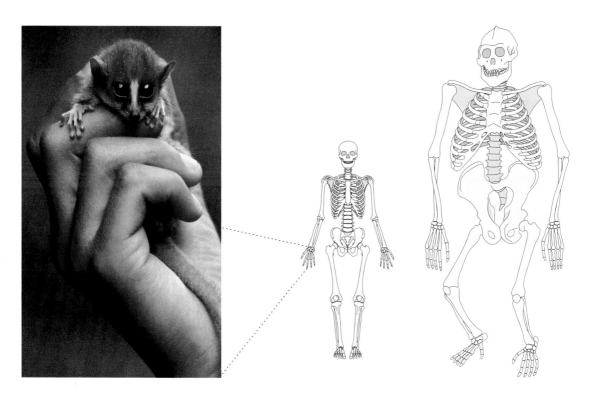

FIGURE 7.5

Here we compare a mouse lemur, the smallest living primate, with a human and with *Gigantopithecus,* now extinct, the largest primate ever (see Chapter 10).

The Senses

Bats and dolphins live in worlds of sound. Dogs live in a world of smells. The primates live in a visual world. Vision is the primates' predominant sense.

Most primates see in color, and all primates see in three dimensions. They have true depth perception (technically called **stereoscopic vision**), which is possible because the eyes face forward and see the same scene from slightly different angles (Figure 7.6). The nerves and muscles of most primate eyes are enclosed within a protective bony socket. Look at your surroundings. What you are able to see is what the majority of primates could see if they were in your place.

Other primate senses are not as acute as in many mammals. Primates lack the auditory (hearing) and olfactory (smell) sensitivity of such familiar animals as dogs, cats, and cattle. Furthermore, and obviously related to the less acute sense of smell, primates tend to lack a snout and so have a relatively flat face. There is, as you might expect for a group of 200 species, some variation among primates. Many members of one group of primates (the prosimians, which we'll discuss in the next section) are

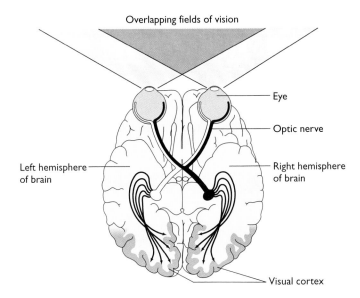

Overlapping fields of vision

Eye

Optic nerve

Left hemisphere of brain

Right hemisphere of brain

Visual cortex

FIGURE 7.6
Stereoscopic vision. The fields of vision overlap, and the optic nerve from each eye travels to both hemispheres of the brain. The result is true depth perception.

nocturnal and lack color vision, but they have better senses of smell and hearing than do monkeys, apes, and humans.

Movement

Like most mammals, primates are, with one exception, quadrupedal. Although many primates can stand or even walk on two legs for short periods, humans are the only habitually bipedal primates. Unlike most mammals, primates have extremely flexible limbs, and their hands (and in many cases their feet) have the ability to grasp objects. That is, they are **prehensile** (Figure 7.7). Primates use this trait for several forms of locomotion. Some primates, called *vertical clingers and leapers*, jump from branch to branch or trunk to trunk using the grasping ability of all four limbs (see Figure 7.14). The apes are suspensory climbers with the ability to hang and climb by the arms (see Figure 7.18). An extreme form of this mode of movement is **brachiation,** swinging arm-over-arm through the trees. When on the ground, most primates use all fours. Asia's orangutans walk on their fists. The African apes have a unique quadrupedalism, supporting themselves on the knuckles of their hands instead of the palms. Primate species may use one or more of these locomotor methods, depending on their anatomy and the situation.

In addition, most primates are able to touch their thumbs to the tips of the other fingers on the same hand, allowing them to pick up and

stereoscopic vision: Three-dimensional vision; depth perception.

prehensile: Having the ability to grasp.

brachiation: Locomotion by swinging arm-over-arm.

FIGURE 7.7
An orangutan holding its trainer's hand demonstrates the prehensile grip shared by nonhuman and human primates.

manipulate small objects. This capacity is called **opposability.** Finally, most primates have nails rather than claws on the tips of the fingers and toes. These provide support for the sensitive tactile sense receptors of the fingers. In short, primates have manual dexterity. Some have a great degree of dexterity in the feet as well (see Figure 7.14).

Reproduction

Most primate species give birth to one offspring at a time. Several primates, such as some of the marmosets from South America and some of the lemurs from Madagascar, normally produce twins or triplets. As is typical of mammals, primate parents take an active role in the protection, nurturing, and socialization of their young. Mostly because of their large, complex brains and because of the importance of learning, young primates are dependent on adults and take a long time to mature. How long, of course, varies according to the size of the primate species. The primates, relative to size, have the longest period of **postnatal dependency** of any mammal.

Intelligence

Intelligence can be defined as the relative ability of an organism's brain to acquire, store, retrieve, and process information. These abilities are related to brain size and brain complexity. A bigger brain has more room

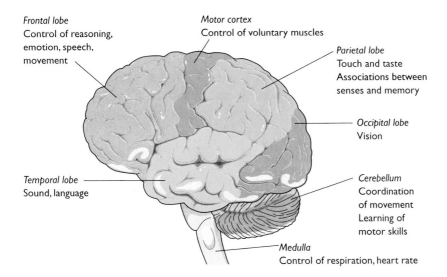

Frontal lobe
Control of reasoning, emotion, speech, movement

Motor cortex
Control of voluntary muscles

Parietal lobe
Touch and taste
Associations between senses and memory

Occipital lobe
Vision

Temporal lobe
Sound, language

Cerebellum
Coordination of movement
Learning of motor skills

Medulla
Control of respiration, heart rate

FIGURE 7.8
The human brain with major parts and their functions. The lobes and the motor cortex are all part of the neocortex.

for all the complex nerve connections that make it work, just as a very sophisticated computer must necessarily be larger than a simple one. (Brain size variation *within* a species is another matter; in humans, for example, no substantiated correlation has been shown between brain size, within the normal range, and any reasonable measure of intelligence.) But brain size must also be looked at in a relative way: How big is the brain compared to the body it runs? A sperm whale, with its 20-pound brain, has a brain ten times the size of the average human's. A sperm whale's body, however, is over *five hundred* times the size of ours. We have bigger brains than whales have *relative to* the size of our bodies; we run less body with more brain, which is true of the primates in general. Of all land mammals, the primates have the largest relative brain sizes. The human brain, however, is three times the size one would expect for a primate of our body weight (Passingham 1982:78).

In addition, the primate brain is complex, especially in the neocortex, that part of the brain where memory, abstract thought, problem solving, and attentiveness take place (Figure 7.8). In short, the primates are smart.

Behavior Patterns

Primates are social animals. Most primate species live in groups. Many other animals do too, but even those few primate species—such as orangutans—that usually remain solitary still interact with other members of their species in far more complex ways than, say, antelopes interact within a herd, or even wolves within a pack. The difference is

oppasability: The ability to touch the thumb to the tips of the other fingers on the same hand.

postnatal dependency: The period after birth during which offspring require the care of adults to survive.

intelligence: The relative ability of the brain to acquire, store, retrieve, and process information.

FIGURE 7.9

We see here some colorful primate faces, including that of one primate that purposely enhances the color. Colorful faces are evidence of the importance of individual recognition within primate societies. Shown here (*clockwise from upper left*) are a Chinese white-handed gibbon, mandrill, human, and bald uakari.

FIGURE 7.10
Male baboon protecting
mother and young. The fe-
male holding her baby at left
was being threatened by the
boisterous play of a group of
adolescent males, out of the
picture to the right. The adult
male in the center stepped in
and barked at the group,
which quickly took its play
elsewhere. (These baboons
are part of a captive troop.)

that primates recognize individuals, and the individual primate holds a particular status relative to others in its group and to the group as a whole. A primate group is made up of the collective relationships among all its individual members. We will see these relationships in action when we examine primate behavior more closely in Chapter 8.

As physical evidence of the importance of these relationships, it may be noted that primates are among the most colorful of mammals, and most of the color patterns of many primates, especially monkeys, are displayed on their faces (Figure 7.9). The attention of one primate to another is drawn to the face, to the primate's identity as an individual.

In some primates—baboons and chimpanzees, for example—each individual may have rather specific status within the group. Some have more social power and influence than others. They are said to be dominant, and the structure of the relative power and influence of a group's individuals is called a **dominance hierarchy.** In addition, most primate species recognize a special status for females with infants, and these mother-child units are well protected by other members of the group, even those that are not directly related to them (Figure 7.10). Among

dominance hierarchy: Individual differences among
group members in terms of
power, influence, and access
to resources and mating.

FIGURE 7.11
Primate communication and grooming. (*Top*) A chimp exhibits a *pant-hoot*, a call used when a food source is found, when two groups join together, or to communicate over distances. (*Bottom*) Grooming serves not only to rid these Francois's langurs (monkeys from Southeast Asia) of parasites and dirt but also to maintain group unity and harmony.

chimpanzees and baboons we even see lasting relationships that can only be described as friendships.

Primate social groups are maintained through communication. Primates have large repertoires of vocalizations, facial expressions, and body gestures. Touch is also an important form of communication among primates and often takes the form of **grooming,** an activity that serves not only the practical purpose of removing dirt and parasites but also as a source of reassurance to maintain group harmony and unity (Figure 7.11).

How, then, may we characterize the primate adaptive strategy? It is important to acknowledge the environment that the primates are adapted *to.* The basic primate environment is arboreal. To be sure, several species—gorillas, for instance—spend more time on the ground than in the branches, and we humans are thoroughly terrestrial. But the majority of primates spend most of their time in the trees, and the primate traits in the preceding discussion all evolved in response to an arboreal environment. Even the partially and completely terrestrial primates possess features that are variations on the arboreal adaptive theme. So, we can define primates in the following way:

> The primates are mammals adapted to an arboreal environment through well-developed vision, manual dexterity, and large, complex brains; their adaptation relies on learned behavior, which is aided by the birth of few offspring at a time and the direct and extensive care of those offspring during a long period of dependency while they are socialized into groups based on differential relationships among individuals.

Such a complex group of organisms requires a lengthy description.

A SURVEY OF THE LIVING PRIMATES

Figure 7.12 is a simplified phenetic taxonomy of the approximately 200 species of living primates. For the sake of space, some categories are indicated only by the number of groups within them; for instance, there are six families of prosimians. One of the first things you should notice is that there are new categories here as compared with those shown in Table 7.1. *Suborder, infraorder,* and *superfamily* have been added between the traditional Linnaean categories of *order* and *family.* A cladistic taxonomy may add more. Sometimes a taxon of organisms has many species adapted to a wide variety of geographic locations and environmental niches; consequently, additional taxonomic categories need to be added to accurately capture what seem to be natural divisions. (A complete

grooming: Here, cleaning the fur of another animal, which promotes social cohesion.

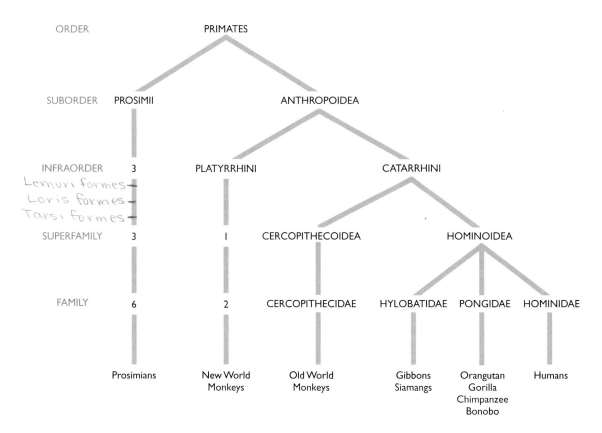

FIGURE 7.12
Primate taxonomy using traditional phenetic categories. Some categories are indicated by the number of living primate groups within them rather than the specific group names.

taxonomy of insects, for example, a class with over 750,000 *known* species, is, as you can well imagine, incredibly complex.)

Prosimians

The order Primates is traditionally divided into two major suborders, Prosimii and Anthropoidea. Prosimians ("pre-apes") represent the most primitive primates, that is, those that most closely resemble the earliest primates. At first widespread, prosimians were pushed into marginal areas as newer, more adaptively flexible primates evolved. Some modern prosimians live on the mainlands of Africa, India, and Southeast Asia and on the isolated islands of Southeast Asia, but the majority inhabit the island of Madagascar (Figure 7.13).

The 40 or so living species of prosimians exhibit a number of differences from the general primate pattern. About half of the prosimian

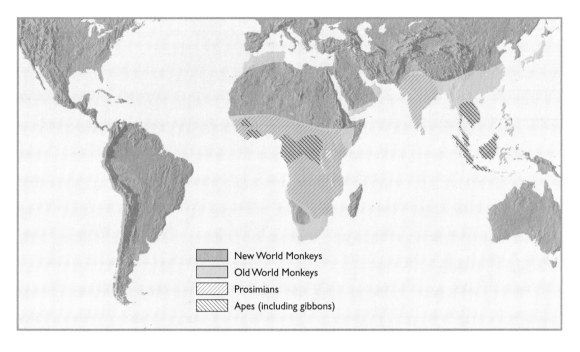

New World Monkeys
Old World Monkeys
Prosimians
Apes (including gibbons)

FIGURE 7.13
Distribution of living nonhuman primates.

species are nocturnal and so lack color vision. They have large eyes that can gather more light, as well as better than average senses of smell and hearing (Figure 7.14). To aid their olfactory sense, they have a protruding snout with a large smell receptor area (the mucous membranes within the nose) and a moist, naked outer nose (like that of a dog or cat) to help pick up the molecules that make up olfactory signals. Prosimians do have the stereoscopic vision characteristic of primates because they need to judge distances in bushes and trees, and their three-dimensional vision helps them catch insects, a favorite food of many prosimian species.

Prosimians have prehensile hands and feet, but the opposability of their thumbs is limited. Many can only touch the thumb with the other four digits together; their digits don't move independently. Some prosimians have claws instead of the typical primate nails on a couple of fingers or toes. These are known as *grooming claws* and are used both for that purpose and to help acquire food.

A few species of lemurs from Madagascar give birth to twins or even triplets on a regular basis. Transporting the infants through the trees, however, is no problem because an adult male or an older sibling often helps the mother carry and care for her infants. At other times, the infants are kept in a nest.

FIGURE 7.14

Two prosimians. The slender loris of India and Sri Lanka (*left*) has the large eyes and moist, naked nose characteristic of this suborder. Note also the prehensile hands and feet and the grooming claw on one toe of the foot at the top of the picture (*see arrow*). The crowned lemur of Madagascar (*right*) displays a posture that is typical of the locomotor pattern called *vertical clinging and leaping*. All the Madagascar primates are endangered.

A particularly interesting primate is the tarsier of Southeast Asia (Figure 7.15). Weighing just 4 or 5 ounces, this little insect eater has powerful hind limbs for jumping, enlarged fingertips and toetips for added friction, and the ability to turn its head 180 degrees in either direction, like an owl. Its name comes from its elongated ankle (or *tarsal*) bones, which make its legs look like they bend too many times.

The tarsier is another example of the debate within primate taxonomy. Because of its flat face, upright posture when clinging to trunks and branches, lack of the moist, naked nose of other prosimians, and some recent genetic comparisons, some authorities suggest placing the tarsier in the second primate suborder, Anthropoidea. Cladists go further. Focusing on the fact that all prosimians have the moist nose but that no anthropoids do, they suggest dividing order Primates into suborders based on that trait. The former prosimians would thus be in suborder Strepsirhini ("nose with curved nostrils"), and the anthropoids would

FIGURE 7.15
Philippine tarsier. Note the huge eyes (each eyeball is as big as the entire brain) for nocturnal vision, the enlarged finger- and toetips, and the powerfully built legs.

become suborder Haplorhini ("simple nose"). The latter group would include the tarsier because of its nose, color vision, and other traits.

Anthropoids

The anthropoid ("humanlike") primates include monkeys, apes, and humans. Suborder Anthropoidea is further divided into two infraorders, Platyrrhini and Catarrhini. This division is based on a geographic separation of early primates into a Western Hemisphere (or New World) group and an Eastern Hemisphere (or Old World) group. All the New World platyrrhine primates are monkeys. The Old World catarrhine primates comprise monkeys, apes, and humans. Despite the fact that humans now inhabit the entire globe, we first evolved in the Old World, in Africa.

Several features distinguish New World from Old World primates. The most obvious is the nose. *Platyrrhine* means "broad-nosed," and the noses of the Central and South American monkeys have widely spaced nostrils separated by a broad septum (Figure 7.16). By comparison, *catarrhine* is translated "hook-nosed." The typical Old World nose has closely spaced nostrils that face downward. Just look in the mirror.

FIGURE 7.16
Northern woolly spider monkey, a platyrrhine primate from Brazil. Note the prehensile tail with the bare strip of skin on the inner surface to enhance its grasping ability. Note also the typical platyrrhine nose (see also Figure 7.9 *bottom left*).

New World and Old World anthropoids also have different dental formulas, that is, the number of each type of tooth in each quadrant of the mouth. Old World anthropoids have two incisors, one canine, two premolars (bicuspids), and three molars. This is written as $\frac{2.1.2.3}{2.1.2.3} \times 2 = 32$. Some New World anthropoids have four extra premolars: $\frac{2.1.3.3}{2.1.3.3} \times 2 = 36$. Other New World anthropoids have four fewer molars: $\frac{2.1.3.2}{2.1.3.2} \times 2 = 32$.

Moreover, because New World monkeys are almost entirely arboreal, they have evolved long limbs, and some have clawlike nails. Several species also have evolved prehensile tails and thus effectively have five grasping limbs. No Old World monkey evolved this adaptation. Finally, two groups of platyrrhines, the marmosets and tamarins, normally give birth to twins.

The Old World primates are divided into two superfamilies. The monkeys of Europe (now limited to Gibraltar), Africa, and Asia make

FIGURE 7.17
Rhesus monkey, a catarrhine primate from Asia. Note the more closely spaced nostrils as compared to the platyrrhine (New World) monkey in Figure 7.16. (See also Figure 7.9, *top left and right and bottom right,* and Figure 7.11, *bottom.*) The rhesus has been important in medical and behavioral experimentation. The Rh blood factor was named after it.

up superfamily Cercopithecoidea. Apes and humans are in superfamily Hominoidea, which is further divided into three families.

There are about 75 species of cercopithecoids (Figure 7.17). They have the nasal shape and tooth number of all Old World primates, and most have tails. Males tend to be larger than females, a trait not common in New World species. Also unlike the platyrrhines, the Old World monkeys have fully opposable thumbs. The monkeys of the Eastern Hemisphere seem more adaptively flexible than those of the New World. At home in the trees, many cercopithecoids are equally comfortable on the ground. They live everywhere from the deserts of Africa and the Middle East to the mountains of northern Japan.

Superfamily Hominoidea contains the larger, tailless primates. The hominoids—the apes and humans—are generally larger than the monkeys and have larger brains, both relatively and absolutely. Their brains also have larger neocortexes, meaning that the hominoids are more intelligent, as we have defined that term. Finally, a series of traits make the hominoids good suspensory climbers and hangers; they are adapted to an arboreal environment through the ability to climb and hang from branches with their arms. The traits behind this ability are a flexible shoulder joint, a more posterior shoulder blade than in monkeys, and a stronger collarbone (clavicle) for added support. Although modern humans do not display the ability to climb or hang using the arms as

FIGURE 7.18
White-handed gibbon from Southeast Asia. Note the long, hooklike fingers and the grasping feet.

often or as well as the apes, we still possess it, as demonstrated by gymnasts on the high bar or rings.

Family Hylobatidae includes the gibbons and siamangs of Southeast Asia and Malaysia. Sometimes referred to as *lesser apes*, they are noted for their brachiating mode of locomotion (Figure 7.18). They also have an unusual social organization for primates. Male and female hylobatids form a monogamous pair, though not neccessarily a permanent one.

There are four species within traditional family Pongidae, known collectively as the *great apes:* the orangutan of Southeast Asia and the gorilla, chimpanzee, and bonobo of Africa (Figure 7.19).

FIGURE 7.19
The great apes. Shown here (*clockwise from top left*) are the orangutan of Southeast Asia and the gorilla, bonobo, and chimpanzee of Africa.

FIGURE 7.20

Chimps using tools they have made to extract termites from their mound.

The pongids are large (a male gorilla in the wild may weigh 450 pounds), with heavy, powerful jaws used for eating a wide range of fruits, nuts, and vegetables. Chimps and bonobos also eat meat on occasion. The apes are quadrupeds, although chimps, gorillas, and especially bonobos are fairly good at upright walking for short distances. Orangutans are solitary, but the other apes live in social groups marked by some degree of dominance but otherwise with fairly loose organization and changeable group membership.

The apes have relatively large brains; a large chimp may have a brain half the size of the smallest modern human brain. Apes are intelligent. They have, for example, an intimate knowledge of a large number of food sources, many of which ripen seasonally or grow in limited areas.

Some chimpanzees can make simple tools, the best known of which is their termite "fishing stick," a modified twig or blade of grass they insert into a hole in a termite mound and wiggle around to stimulate an attack by the insects. The termites cling to the "invader," and the chimps draw out a tasty meal (Figure 7.20). Other chimps have been seen using rocks to break open hard-shelled nuts. Chimps are also known to cooperatively hunt small animals, including other primates, and meat is the one food source that chimps will share with one another (see Chapter 8).

Finally, apes have a large repertoire of calls, facial expressions, and body gestures with which they communicate information, mostly about emotional states. Although this form of communication is nothing like human language, some individuals from all the great ape species have been taught to use nonvocal versions of human languages, most notably American Sign Language (Ameslan), developed for the hearing impaired. It is said by some researchers that with this skill they can communicate at the level of a 4- or 5-year-old human.

The third traditional hominoid family is Hominidae, the hominids. This includes all living and extinct species of habitually bipedal primates. We need, of course, to detail the traits of this group.

THE HUMAN PRIMATE

Each of the 200 living primate species has its own unique expression of the primate adaptive strategy. Humans are no exception. Let's describe ourselves by using the same categories with which we characterized primates in general.

The Senses

Our senses are essentially the same as those of the anthropoid monkeys and the apes. There may be some minor differences, but basically all these species hear, smell, and, especially, see the same world.

Movement

Bipedalism is the characteristic that in broad evolutionary perspective defines the hominids. We are the only primate that is habitually bipedal, and we have been for over 4 million years. (Our big brains came along much later.) The bones and muscles of our back, pelvis, legs, and feet are all structured to balance us and hold us upright. Because our legs are the limbs of locomotion, they are longer and more muscular than our arms—just the opposite of the arms and legs of the apes. Completely freed from locomotor functions, our hands have become organs of manipulation. We

Contemporary Reflections

What Is the Status of Our Closest Relatives?

In a nutshell, the answer is, not good. The International Union for Conservation of Nature and Natural Resources (www.redlist.org) recognizes 182 species of primates. Of these, 19 are listed as "critically endangered," 46 as "endangered," 53 as "vulnerable," and 43 as "near threatened." The rest are of "least concern" or "data deficient" (which is not necessarily a good sign).

And it's getting progressively worse, especially in Africa and especially among the great apes. An estimated 80 percent of the world's gorillas and most chimpanzees live in the West African countries of Gabon and the Republic of Congo. In Gabon, the populations of those species have decreased by more than half over the last twenty years. Two-thirds of the gorillas in a sanctuary in Congo have died in the last year alone. At its present rate of decline, the bonobo will be extinct in the wild in a decade. In the mountains east of those countries, the population of the rare mountain gorilla (made famous by the book and film *Gorillas in the Mist*) is thought to be down to fewer than 650 individuals.

What is causing this disastrous decline? Worldwide we humans threaten the primates, as well as other endangered species, through our overpopulation, depletion of resources, warfare, habitat destruction, pollution, hunting, and other direct exploitation of innumerable species, both plant and animal. In the case of the African apes, the effects of hunting have been recently exacerbated by the "bushmeat" trade, targeting any number of large native animals, including chimpanzees, bonobos, and gorillas. The encroachment of logging and mining into these animals' habitats (particularly in Congo, which is rich in coltan, an ore used in the production of cell phones and laptops) has brought an influx of workers, who subsist on the meat of whatever animals are available to hunt, whether endangered or not. Elsewhere, local peoples in need of food in their poverty-stricken countries are also turning to hunting. And most egregiously, and the main motivation for hunting, there is a lucrative commercial market for bushmeat in African cities and towns as well as abroad. Some believe that hunting caused the

have the most precise opposability of any of the primates and the relatively longest and strongest primate thumb.

Reproduction

Like most primates, we usually have one offspring at a time. Although we are not the largest living primate (the gorilla is), we have the longest period of postnatal dependency, and we take the longest time to mature. Chimps, for example, reach sexual maturity at about 9 years and physical maturity at about 12. For humans, the averages are 13 and 21. In addition, we are born more helpless than other primates.

first recorded primate extinction—of the wonderfully named Miss Waldron's red colobus, an African monkey.

Related to the bushmeat trade is a threat that is also a serious problem for humans—the virus that causes Ebola, the hemorrhagic fever whose origin is still unknown (Walsh et al. 2003; and see Chapter 13). Ebola decimated the gorillas at the sanctuary in Congo and is now spreading toward a national park that has one of the largest, densest ape populations in the world. Outbreaks of the disease in apes coincide with outbreaks in human populations, so it is likely that humans are contracting Ebola from apes, largely as a result of hunting and eating them. It's unclear whether the apes are transmitting the disease to one another or are, because there are more and more humans in the forests, being forced into closer contact with the source of the virus (hypothesized to be bats, mice, or birds). But we do know that outbreaks have occurred among apes in regions remote from human habitation as well.

The debate now centers on what action to take. Walsh and his colleagues (2003) recommend that the apes' status be changed from "endangered" to "critically endangered." They also suggest that only a "massive investment" in law enforcement to prevent hunting will stem the bushmeat trade. As for Ebola, some have suggested transporting apes to a safe area or otherwise dividing infected groups from noninfected groups. If, however, the apes are continually contracting the disease from its still-unknown source, these measures won't do much. There is an experimental vaccine that works on monkeys, but it still requires testing, and administering it to wild animals would be a difficult task.

The prospects, in other words, don't look good—either for the apes of West Africa or, in the long run, for the world's other primates and all the other endangered species of life. The situation can seem hopeless, but various organizations are working tirelessly to prevent the local zoo from ultimately being the *only* place to see the apes and other species. For more information on the crisis, what is being done, and how we can help, see www.primate.wisc.edu/pin; go to the conservation page by clicking on "PIN Index" and then "Conservation." Also see www.unep.org/grasp for information on the United Nations Great Apes Survival Project. To paraphrase Gandhi, whatever we do might be insignificant, but it is very important that we do it.

Our sexual behavior, too, is different. Most other primates, like most mammals, engage in sexual activity, for the most part, only when it can lead to reproduction. Thus, mating tends to occur when a female has ovulated, that is, when an egg has matured and is ready to be fertilized. She undergoes hormonal changes that make her sexually receptive and lead her to solicit male attention by giving off sexually stimulating signals. During this time, the female is said to be in **estrus** (popularly, "in heat"). In many mammals, the estrus signals are in the form of olfactory stimuli; in some primates, they are also visual (Figure 7.21).

Humans, of course, have lost the signals of estrus, a condition best referred to as *nondetectable ovulation* (A. Fuentes, personal communication).

estrus: In nonhuman primates, the period of female fertility or the signals indicating this condition.

FIGURE 7.21
Baboon in estrus. The skin around this female's genital area is swollen, a clear visual sign that she is fertile and sexually receptive. In baboons and other primates, this area may also be brightly colored.

Human males don't automatically know when a human female is fertile. This may seem a rather inefficient way to perpetuate the species, but as we are all aware, humans have replaced unconscious, innate sexual signals with sexual consciousness. Sexuality has become part of our conscious thought, tied up with all the other reactions and attitudes and emotions we have toward other members of our species and toward ourselves. You might say we are potentially continually in estrus. Although humans exhibit the most extreme form of this reproductive behavior, we will see it foreshadowed, in the next chapter, in some of our close relatives.

Intelligence

We are clearly the most intelligent primate, as we have defined that term. We can store, retrieve, and process more information in more complex ways than all the other primates. Our cultural behaviors—our languages, societies, belief systems, norms of behavior, and scientific knowledge—all attest to these abilities. Our intellect is made possible by our large, complex brains, especially our neocortex, the outer layer where abstract thought takes place.

Behavior Patterns

Like most Old World primates, humans live in societies that are based on the collective conscious responses of a group of individuals. The difference is that our groups are structured and maintained by cultural values—ideas, rules, and behavioral norms that we have created and shared through complex **symbolic** communication systems.

SUMMARY

The study of the nonhuman primates has been a traditional aspect of biological anthropology. Humans *are* primates, after all, and the characteristics of our relatively new species have evolved out of the basic primate traits and the adaptive strategy that they facilitate. We can only fully comprehend ourselves as a biological species by understanding where we fit into the natural world.

Taxonomy provides us with a way of naming and categorizing species so as to indicate their biological relationships. It also gives us an idea as to the evolutionary relationships among species. At present, there are two major schools of thought about taxonomy. One (phenetic) names and classifies according to comparisons of phenotypic features and adaptive behaviors. The other (cladistics) uses the actual evolutionary pattern of branching.

The primates are one of nineteen orders of mammals. They may be characterized as being adapted to arboreal environments through manual dexterity, visual acuity, and intelligence. There are about 200 living species of primates, each a unique manifestation of the general primate theme. The human primate's major uniqueness is its form of locomotion; we are the only primate that is habitually bipedal, a trait that evolved more than 4 mya. Since then, our other distinguishing feature has evolved—our big brain, capable of such complex functions that we can create our own adaptive behaviors, expressed as our various cultural systems. It is to the possible precursors of our behaviors that we will turn next.

QUESTIONS FOR FURTHER THOUGHT

1. Birds evolved from a group of small bipedal dinosaurs. Cladistic analysis justifies lumping birds and dinosaurs into the same taxon. Some have taken this to mean that the caged parakeet in your living room

symbolic: Here, a communication system that uses arbitrary but agreed-upon sounds and signs for meaning.

is a dinosaur. What do you think of this? Is your dog, then, really a wolf? Are humans apes? How far can we take cladistic taxonomies in our popular nomenclature? Is there some inherent contradiction in cladistic taxonomies, or can you see a resolution?

2. The primates come in a wide variety of shapes and sizes and live in a broad range of environments. It's tempting to attribute this adaptive success to the primates' big brains. But it's more complex than that. Thinking about the processes of evolution, speciation, and adaptive radiation, how would you account for the seeming success of the primate order?

3. Given the problems that now beset the human species on the African continent—AIDS and other diseases, poverty, civil unrest, and warfare—how can we justify expressing so much concern for the plight of the nonhuman primates, much less expending money and time on their behalf? Are these separate concerns that should be considered in order of priority? Or are they actually inextricably linked?

KEY TERMS

taxonomy	bipedal	postnatal dependency
notochord	quadrupedal	intelligence
phenetic taxonomy	stereoscopic vision	dominance hierarchy
taxa	prehensile	grooming
cladistics	brachiation	estrus
shared derived characteristics	opposability	symbolic

SUGGESTED READINGS

For information on the three major groups of living things, focusing on the bacteria that live under extreme conditions, see "Extremophiles," by Michael Madigan and Barry Marrs in the April 1997 *Scientific American*.

Noel Rowe's *The Pictorial Guide to the Living Primates* is a beautifully illustrated, up-to-date, and informative reference to all living primate species. For a look at the endangered lemurs of Madagascar, see the article in the August 1988 *National Geographic* by primatologist Alison

Jolly, "Madagascar's Lemurs: On the Edge of Survival." The National Geographic Society has also produced a beautifully illustrated book on the great apes; *The Great Apes: Between Two Worlds*, by Michael Nichols, Jane Goodall, George Schaller, and Mary Smith, not only discusses the four species of apes but also talks about the scientific studies conducted on them in the wild, as well as the dangers they now face from their close relative.

More on the linguistic abilities of the apes can be found in "Chimpanzee Sign Language Research," by Roger and Debbi Fouts, in *The Nonhuman Primates*, edited by Phyllis Dolhinow and Agustín Fuentes. A more detailed treatment is Roger Fout's *Next of Kin*.

A comprehensive and readable book comparing humans with other primates is Richard Passingham's *The Human Primate*. For an interesting though somewhat speculative discussion of the evolution of the human brain, try Carl Sagan's Pulitzer Prize–winning *The Dragons of Eden*.

For more on cladistics, see "Evolution by Walking," by Stephen Jay Gould, in the March 1995 *Natural History*, and "Why Cladistics?" by Eugene Gaffney, Lowell Dingus, and Miranda Smith, in the June 1995 issue of the same magazine.

For conservation information, try the Web sites listed in this chapter's "Contemporary Reflections" box, as well as www.tsidy.com/lemurs and www.duke.edu/web/primate.

I'll recommend some more books on the behavior of humans and our fellow primates in the next chapter.

CHAPTER

8

PRIMATE BEHAVIOR AND HUMAN EVOLUTION

Often I have gazed
into a chimpanzee's
eyes and wondered
what was going on
behind them.
—Jane Goodall (1990)

Just as we look to the anatomy of our close relatives to get some idea about the basic set of phenotypic traits from which we evolved, we may also look at the behavior of the other primates to gain some insight into why we behave the way we do. Because we share common ancestors, some of our behavior patterns—just like some of our physical features—may be variations on the same evolutionary theme.

In this chapter we will look at several nonhuman primates, particularly the several species collectively called baboons (genus *Papio*) and the two species of genus *Pan*, the common chimpanzee and the bonobo. The reasons for choosing these primates will be explained as well.

We will address the following questions:

How do we organize a study of something as complex as behavior?

What are some of the scientific cautions that must be exercised in doing so?

What are some of the relevant behaviors of our close relatives?

What do they tell us about the evolution of behavior in the hominids?

STUDYING BEHAVIOR

Studying nonhuman primate behavior to shed light on human behavior is based on the same premise as studying the physical traits of nonhuman primates and comparing them with our own: we share a common heritage with the other primates and so have inherited our shared features from the same source, a common ancestor. It is not a coincidence, for example, that all the primates have prehensile hands. Our common prehensile ability is a *shared derived characteristic* (see Chapter 7), coming from the same ancient ancestor and, in this case, serving the same basic function. Thus, we gain some perspective on our prehensile hands by fully examining the prehensile appendages of species with whom we share an ancestor from whom we all derived the trait.

But with traits like behaviors—which are polygenic, highly environmentally influenced, and phenotypically complex and variable—it is more difficult to decide which similarities *are* shared derived characteristics. So we need to expand our discussion and note that shared derived characteristics are also known as **homologies.**

Homologous traits need not serve the same function. Your arms and the wings of a bat, though they are used for different things, are homologies. The traits are similar by virtue of having evolved from the same source, an early mammal.

(a)

(b)

(c)

FIGURE 8.1
Homology and analogy. The arm of a human (*a*) and the wing of a bat (*b*) are homologous—they have different functions but share the same evolutionary source. The wing of a bat (*b*) and the wing of an insect (*c*) are analogous—they share a function but are evolutionarily different.

The wings of a bat and the wings of an insect, however, though they share a similar function, have evolved independently and are not at all similar in structure. These functionally similar but evolutionarily unrelated traits are known as **analogies.** We can certainly learn something about the physics of flight by comparing bats and insect wings, but there is a limited amount of information we can get about the wings of bats by studying the wings of insects because they evolved quite separately from one another (Figure 8.1).

homologies: Traits shared by two or more species through inheritance from a common ancestor. Such traits need not serve the same function.

analogies: Traits shared by two or more species that are similar in function but unrelated evolutionarily.

Just as organisms pass on anatomical and physiological features in their genes, they also pass on behavioral characteristics. In some groups—ants, for example—whole behavioral repertoires are passed on. Ants rely completely on built-in instinct; they don't really think or, in fact, have much of anything to think *with*. So, even though ants live in highly complex societies and act in elaborate ways, all their behaviors are coded in their genes, to be triggered by outside stimuli but with little or no flexibility or variation in their response.

Other organisms with larger and more complex brains can vary their behavior as needed to cope with specific situations. Their behavior is flexible. They have behavioral *potentials* or *themes* carried in their genetic codes, and they respond to their environments by building on these potentials—taking in information from the outside, remembering it, retrieving stored information, and utilizing it in appropriate circumstances. In other words, they *think*.

The nature of the inborn behavioral potentials in complex organisms is still a matter of debate, especially when humans are the topic. Some have argued that we are born as "blank slates" or, in a more modern image, as computers with internal hardware but nothing programmed. The extreme opposite view says that our brains come equipped with specific behaviors that are only modified to a small degree by our individual experiences—like a computer with many application programs already in the system.

The reality is no doubt somewhere in the middle. Certainly we come into this world with some basic behavioral responses built in. Facial expressions like smiling, nursing behavior among infants, the bond between a mother and her offspring, the drives to walk upright and learn language—these are all recognized as universal in our species and as preprogrammed in our biology. But just as certainly, we are not programmed for *particular* ways of expressing these and other behaviors. Language ability, for example, may be instinctive, but the specific language you speak is learned within a specific cultural and individual context.

There is a scientific study that looks for evolutionary explanations for behaviors, especially social behaviors. It is called **sociobiology, evolutionary psychology,** or **behavioral ecology,** and two of its ideas are particularly relevant here. The first, **inclusive fitness,** refers to the fact that your close relatives share many of your genes. As a result, the adaptive fitness of your genes is not just a matter of your own adaptive success (the usual definition of fitness); it also entails the adaptive success of your relatives. Thus, any behavior that has evolved through time that causes you to aid your close relations also serves to help your genes get passed on.

A good example is the case of **altruistic** behavior. If, for instance, I perform some action that saves my sister's life but costs me mine in the process, *I* might not pass on any more genes, but I have helped increase the possibility that *some of my genes* will get passed on, because my sister and I share, on average, 50 percent of our genetic endowment.

Of course, humans have moral reasons for altruistic actions, but altruistic behaviors are seen in many other species where there could be no cultural motivation. It may not seem logical that a behavior that might endanger the individual could have evolved by natural selection. But if we look at the genes rather than just the "packages" they come in, we can see how this could be the case. The altruistic behavior was selected for because it helped a group of individuals possessing genes for that behavior to be reproductively successful, even if a few individuals were sacrificed in the process.

The second idea from sociobiology relevant to our discussion concerns **reproductive strategies.** Put simply, individuals have evolved behaviors that maximize their reproductive success. Male and female mammals, however, differ in their contributions to reproduction, so their evolved behaviors may differ as well. Females, of course, carry, nurture, and raise offspring—largely by themselves in most mammalian species, including most primates. Males, on the other hand, contribute sperm. Thus, behaviors have evolved that help females raise healthy offspring and that allow males to try to impregnate as many females as possible.

For the primates, these reproductive strategies are especially important because of our order's emphasis on complex social interactions and social bonds, which in turn facilitate the primates' emphasis on relatively slow development and the focus on learned behavior as an adaptive mechanism. Because most primates give birth to a single offspring at a time, reproductive success in producing and caring for that offspring is vital, and so selection for the most adaptive traits, and the relative reproductive roles of males and females, is crucial.

If it is the case that at least behavioral themes can be inherited, then we can shed light on our behaviors by looking into those of other creatures. In doing so, however, we need to take into account the concepts of homology and analogy. In comparing the behaviors of humans and chimpanzees or bonobos, it is highly likely that a behavior is shared because it is the *same* behavior, derived by all three species from our common ancestor of 5 or 6 mya. Understanding the nature and function of that behavior in chimpanzees or bonobos is likely to provide insight into the behavior in humans because the behavior in question is homologous.

sociobiology: The scientific study that examines evolutionary explanations for social behaviors within species.

evolutionary psychology: Another name for sociobiology.

behavioral ecology: Another name for sociobiology.

inclusive fitness: The idea that fitness is measured by the success of one's genes, whether possessed by the individual or by that individual's relatives.

altruistic: Benefiting others without regard for one's own needs or safety.

reproductive strategies: Behaviors that evolve to maximize an individual's reproductive success.

By contrast, a specific behavior similar in humans and baboons is less likely to be homologous. Our two species have evolved independently for over 20 million years, so there is a greater chance that the behaviors evolved separately, under separate environmental circumstances and perhaps for different adaptive reasons. Still, the behavior may be a variation on some *general behavioral pattern* common to the primates and inherited from an early common ancestor.

The chance of two similar behaviors being analogous increases as we compare species that are less and less closely related. Some investigators have compared the behavior of humans with that of social carnivores such as lions, wolves, and African wild dogs. There are strikingly "human" behaviors in these species: All three hunt cooperatively. Lions from the same pride will eat from the same carcass, and mothers, of course, will bring food—sometimes still alive—back to their young. Wolves and wild dogs have complex social relationships, they use vocal and gestural signs to maintain these relationships, and both actively feed their young. Wolves, especially, are territorial. These collections of similarities, however, are probably not derived from a common ancestor but have, at most, evolved quite independently from some general mammalian traits of social interaction, care of young, and relatively large, complex brains that allow for flexibility of behavior. What we do learn from the behavior of such species is that one possible route to adaptive success for mammals is through complex social behavior and that this behavior is common in species that eat meat, especially meat from large animals. But it is only one route; other carnivores—the fox and leopard, for example—are solitary hunters. And lions, although they hunt cooperatively, do not share food in the sense that one actively gives a portion of a kill to another.

Comparing analogous behaviors, then, can be informative and can point out possible clusters of adaptive traits. But analogies must be used with the understanding that the more evolutionarily distant the species, the less useful the comparison. Ants live in highly complex societies, which investigators often describe in human terms (*slave, caste, queen, nurse, soldier*), but studying the social behavior of ants probably tells us nothing directly about our own societies.

We can now look at the behavior of some other species that have, to varying degrees, been used as models for the origin and evolution of our own behavior. For years, nearly all our information about the behavior of other species came from studies conducted in the artificial environments of zoos and laboratories. Only when the science of **ethology**—studying creatures in the wild, under natural conditions—became popular and possible could we see how they were *really* adapted. And

ⁿ some of the truly remarkable adapta-
ⁿossess.

BABOONS

There are five distinguishable types of baboon that live in the African woodland, desert, and **savanna,** all grouped within genus *Papio.* (Some authorities consider them to be subspecies of a single species because where their ranges overlap, they can and do interbreed and produce fertile offspring. Other taxonomists think that the physical and behavioral differences are sufficient to warrant giving them five different species names.) Although not as closely related to humans as are the apes, these primates have long been of interest to anthropologists because of their complex social organization and their savanna habitat—an important habitat for our early hominid ancestors (Figure 8.2).

Baboon groups range in size from 20 to 200 individuals. One of the most striking aspects of baboon behavior is the aggressive competition for dominance among males, who may be nearly twice the size of females and who are endowed with huge, sharp canine teeth (Figure 8.3). The male who is the largest, strongest, most aggressive, smartest (whatever traits are important to baboons) becomes, for a time, the dominant animal, a position recognized and acknowledged by the whole group. The dominant male is the group's leader and decision maker. He has first rights to food and often to females. He may produce the most offspring, perpetuating those traits that allowed him to achieve dominance. It is also the role of the dominant male and his immediate subordinates to protect the more vulnerable members of the group—the females and infants—from danger (see Figure 7.10).

Males are also, in general, dominant over females. In the hamadryas baboon of Ethiopia, males gather a group of females with whom they have exclusive mating rights. Such a group is referred to as a *harem*, and the proximity of and sexual access to the females in a harem is maintained by male aggression and violence. Many harem females show the scars of such treatment.

Observations of these behaviors led early investigators to depict baboon social organization as almost militaristic—centered around and totally dominated by a hierarchically arranged group of males and maintained through violent (though not always bloody) confrontations. Indeed, baboon groups have traditionally been called *troops*. These investigators considered the bearing and raising of offspring to be the female's

ethology: The study of the natural behavior of animals under natural conditions.

savanna: The open grasslands of the tropics.

FIGURE 8.2

Baboons on the African savanna. Our early ancestors might have witnessed scenes like this.

role; her individual identity was defined by that role, and her position in baboon society was subordinate to that of all males and specifically determined by the position of the male with whom she mated.

More recent studies have shown, however, that baboon societies are far more complex and variable (Fedigan and Fedigan 1988; Smuts 1985, 1995; Strum 1987). While male baboons do vie for dominance, achieve differential social power and influence, and protect the group from other baboons and from predators—and while hamadryas males do maintain harems through violent coercion—a formal, permanent, tightly structured dominance hierarchy among males does not seem to be at the center of social organization in all cases. Among other types of baboons—for example, the olive baboons of equatorial Africa—social structure is based on "a network of social alliances" (Fedigan and Fedigan 1988:14), including friendships between females and between females and males.

orangutan. Subsequent studies as well have contributed to our understanding of these primates. Each study is interesting in its own right and tells us something of the variations possible on the basic primate pattern of social organization.

The orangutan (*Pongo pygmaeus*) is an Asian ape and is separated from us by 12 million years or more. The gorilla (*Gorilla gorilla*) is nearly as close to us genetically as the chimp; while it exhibits many of the same basic social behaviors as the chimpanzee, it is a rather specialized ape. Unlike the chimpanzee, it spends much of its time on the ground, and its almost exclusively vegetarian diet consists largely of ground plants. This species is not known to make or use tools. (Orangutans, however, have recently been observed using simple tools.) The species most relevant to our present subject are the chimpanzee and bonobo.

Much of what we know of the ethology of the chimp (*Pan troglodytes*) comes from the forty years of research at Gombe Stream National Park in Tanzania led by Jane Goodall (1971, 1986, 1990). Goodall's studies have shown that in addition to physical and physiological traits, we share with chimps a number of behavioral characteristics. These center on aspects of social interaction and are thus instructive for understanding our own behavior.

The bond between mother and infant is strong in chimps, as it is in most mammals. These apes, though, have large, complex brains, and infants have a lot to learn about their world before they can become functioning adults. Thus, the mother-infant bond is particularly long-lived and important, and the nature of that interaction can have a lasting effect on the rest of a chimp's life. Poor treatment by its mother, for example, often makes a chimp a poor mother herself when she bears young. Chimps have been seen to help their mothers with younger siblings, and siblings often remain close into adulthood. Chimps, in other words, *raise* their young, and the family bonds that result may last a lifetime.

The chimps in a group are arranged in a dominance hierarchy. Males are generally dominant over females, but among females a loose hierarchy also exists. Males compete with one another in an attempt to achieve the highest position possible. The rewards are access to feeding places and to females, the latter being another example of male reproductive strategy. Social position, though attained in males through violent-looking but seldom injurious actions (Figure 8.4), is maintained via a series of expressions, gestures, and vocalizations. One of the most important interactions is grooming (see Figure 7.11), which maintains social cohesion and on occasion is a sign of dominance when a subordinate male grooms his superior. Other expressions of social interaction

FIGURE 8.4
A male chimpanzee showing a "full open grin." This expression is a sign of excitement, often used by a high-ranking chimp when in close contact with a subordinate. Compare this with the expression of the baboon in Figure 8.3.

include kissing, hugging, bowing, extending the hand, making sexual gestures, grinning, and vocalizing certain ways—and we can freely use these terms because the meanings of these actions in chimp society seem to be just what they are in human societies.

A chimp society, however, is in no way some sort of dictatorship. Instead, it is marked by cooperation and mutual concern, which is seen mostly within the family unit of mother and offspring (because chimps are sexually promiscuous—a female may mate with a dozen males during estrus—the biological father is unknown). Throughout their lives, members of this family unit will protect and care for each other, especially during illness and injury. Males have even been known to help brothers in their competition for dominance.

Care also extends outside the family unit. Offspring are important to the group as a whole, and adults will come to the aid or protection of a youngster threatened with some harm, possibly risking their own welfare, even if the youngster is not necessarily theirs. Goodall once observed an adolescent male adopt an unrelated youngster who had been orphaned (1990:202). This protectiveness may be another example of inclusive fitness, where genes contributing to a behavior have been selected for because they confer adaptive fitness to individuals, both to the protectors and the protected, who may share genes.

Group membership is somewhat fluid. Chimps, for various reasons, will leave a group, and outsiders will occasionally enter it. Despite this fluidity, there is a sense of group identity and territory. Small bands of males will sometimes patrol the boundaries of their group's range, and when they encounter members of other groups, they react to them as outsiders. This is another case of males performing a behavior that serves to protect their reproductive investment.

With chimps, however, we may reasonably wonder about more conscious motivation for some of these behaviors. In one chilling series of events, for example, males from Goodall's main study group attacked and killed a female and all the males of a group that had broken away to establish their own territory. Goodall thinks the motivation may have been to reclaim the area. Although other examples of similar behavior have been reported, there is still debate over whether it is typical of the species. It has been suggested (Power 1991, for example) that because the researchers at Gombe interfered with the chimps' normal activities by providing food, they may have influenced the apes' behavior, including this event. Others (Sussman 1997) question how convincing the evidence is for similar occurrences.

Among the chimpanzee's wide range of food sources is meat. Chimps from some groups, including those studied by Goodall and associates at Gombe, are hunters (Stanford 1995, 1999). Males, and occasionally females, will hunt and kill small pigs, antelopes, and monkeys, including young baboons (Figure 8.5). The Gombe chimps, sometimes hunting in cooperative groups, kill over 100 red colobus monkeys a year, nearly a fifth of the members of that species within the chimps' range. Meat is the one food that chimps will share, and male chimps are more likely to share with friends than with rivals—they will even withhold meat from rivals. There is evidence, too, that a male will hunt in order to get meat to give as an offering to a female in estrus.

FIGURE 8.5

A chimp in Tanzania eats the carcass of a baboon he has recently hunted and killed. He may share some of his prize with close friends in his group.

Much of our information about this species comes from Goodall's research, but work on other chimp groups amply bears out her general observations and conclusions and lends support to the idea that chimp behavior is flexible, adaptable, and the result of intelligence and reasoning. It is thus variable from group to group. For example, a chimp group in the forests on the west coast of Africa uses hammerstones to crack open nuts, something the Gombe chimps don't do, though the Gombe chimps are famous for their termite sticks (see Chapter 7). The West African chimps, in fact, use stone tools so regularly that they have left "archaeological sites" of the activity, made up of unintentionally broken stones and nutshells (Mercader et al. 2002). These chimps also have different hunting techniques, relying more on cooperation between hunting males than do the Gombe chimps (Boesch and Boesch-Achermann 1991).

W. C. Mc Grew (1998) has suggested that this and other observations are evidence of cultural differences. And a recent synthesis of data from seven well-established chimpanzee field sites across Africa, comprising an accumulated 151 years of observation, has shown variation in thirty-nine different behavior patterns, not including those for which there are obvious ecological explanations (such as not nesting on the ground where leopards and lions are common). These patterns include tool use, grooming, and courtship behavior, and the nature of the variation points to the chimps' ability to invent new behaviors and pass them on socially—in which case the behaviors might be thought of as "customs" (Whiten et al. 1999; Whiten and Boesch 2001). Recently, similar data for orangutans has been described, although on a less complex level than that of the chimpanzees (van Schaik et al. 2003.)

BONOBOS

Even more intriguing information has come to light about the third species of African ape, the bonobo (*Pan paniscus*; de Waal 1995; Ingmanson and Kano 1993; Kano 1990; White 1996). The bonobo lives in the lowland forests of the Democratic Republic of the Congo and has been estimated by genetic studies (see Chapter 9) to have been separate from the chimp for 930,000 years.

Bonobos are sometimes referred to as *pygmy chimpanzees*. But bonobos are not pygmies at all; they are as large as chimps, though more slender, with smaller heads and shoulders. They walk upright more often than chimps (Figure 8.6). Like chimps, bonobos do some hunting (though rarely) but show no evidence of cooperative hunting; further, females are sometimes the hunters of small game (flying squirrels or a tiny antelope; Ingmanson and Ihobe 1992). Also like chimps, bonobos use tools, but never to acquire food. Rather, the bonobos use leaves as rain hats and drag branches to serve the social purposes of initiating and indicating the direction of group movement (Ingmanson 1996).

Bonobos are more peaceful and gregarious than chimps. There is a dominance hierarchy among males, but unlike the case with chimpanzees, the hierarchy is easily established with brief aggressive chases. Female hierarchies appear to be based on seniority. Also unlike chimps, female bonobos may dominate males (de Waal and Lanting 1997).

Bonobos more readily share food with one another, and the food shared is not limited to luxury items such as meat (Figure 8.7). They have never been observed killing another of their kind, and their sexual behaviors play important roles in group cohesion. In contrast, sexual

FIGURE 8.6
Bonobo standing bipedally. This bonobo is collecting and carrying stalks of sugar cane in his hands, now freed from locomotor activities.

FIGURE 8.7
Bonobo society is character-ized by peaceful relationships, with sexual activity and—as seen here on the left—food sharing as mechanisms to maintain harmony, ease ten-sions, reassure other mem-bers, and show reconciliation.

coercion, as seen in the hamadryas baboons, has been observed among the chimps of Gombe.

Bonobos, especially when feeding, constantly posture toward one another, rubbing rumps or "presenting" themselves as if initiating sexual activity. When sex does follow, it is usually face-to-face, a behavior uncommon in other primates except humans. Sexual activity is not lim-ited to opposite-sex partners. Females commonly rub genitalia with other females, and males will mount each other.

Contemporary Reflections

Are Some Human Behaviors Genetic?

Since Darwin's time, people have speculated about the possible biological bases of some human behaviors. Over the past thirty years especially, a huge number of books have suggested biological bases for human aggression, social practices such as marriage patterns, altruistic acts, morality, territoriality, and many more. The more extreme versions of such ideas claim that we have a genetic program for such behaviors and that these programs evolved in the past and are maintained today because they confer a reproductive advantage on those who express them. In other words, they have been, and many continue to be, naturally selected for. According to opponents of this idea, a logical—and dangerous—implication of this claim is that variation in the specific expression of a behavior might reflect genetic variation among populations of our species.

Addressing this issue is complicated (and there are just as many books that take some opposing viewpoint), but there are a few guiding concepts we may use to think about it. We must remember that genes are instructions for making proteins. It's a long way from the gene to the phenotypic trait, and the more complex the phenotypic trait, the longer the path and the more genes involved. Behaviors are *very* complex phenotypes. In short, just as there is no single "stature gene" that determines my height, there is no "aggression gene," or "marriage gene," or "altruism gene." Even in creatures with less-complex nervous systems—ants, for example—whose behaviors *must* be biologically programmed, those behaviors are still complex responses of the whole organism to a whole host of environmental stimuli. There must be very many genes involved.

A behavior's biological program, then, is just a program for a potential or a general theme. Its expression requires some environmental stimulus (that is, something outside the genes themselves) and will vary as the exact nature of the stimulus varies. A biological basis for a human

Moreover, the signs of fertility, the estrus signals, seem nearly always present in bonobo females. In both chimps and bonobos, the fertile and therefore sexual period is marked by a swelling and coloration of the skin of the genital area, which stimulates sexual interest in males. In chimps, the swelling occurs only when the female has ovulated and is fertile. In bonobos, however, there is some swelling almost all the time, and they seem almost constantly sexually receptive. Sexual activity in this species has become separate from purely reproductive activity and is responded to on a conscious level. The motivation for sex may be as much psychological and social as it is reproductive.

The function of this friendly posturing and sexual receptiveness seems to be the same as that of grooming and as that of some expressions and behavior can only be for the most general potential. Our cultural environment, which pervades every aspect of our individual and social lives, is immensely complex, and so the expressions of a behavioral potential must be varied indeed. Thus, the variation in a human behavior from society to society (or even from individual to individual) is largely a result of different cultural environments—different systems of belief and knowledge that mark the variety of humans' ways of life.

Language is a perfect—and fairly uncontroversial—example. All normal humans come equipped with the ability to take in raw data—the speech of the people around them and the responses to their attempts to communicate—and turn them into a working knowledge of their native language. Think about it: You spoke your native language fluently before you ever were formally taught all the grammatical rules in school. And you did it by yourself, using some built-in "software" in your nervous system into which data were fed by your senses. The ability to learn language is biological and thus, at its base, genetic. The genetic basis for this ability was selected for during our evolution (see Chapter 11). Linguistic ability conferred a reproductive advantage on our ancestors.

However, *what* language you speak, how well you speak it, what words you know, what accent you have—these particulars are cultural. They vary from society to society and even within societies—not because of genetic differences among populations but because of variation in the cultural contexts of which they are a part.

Similarly, the social system, with its sexual consciousness, that we see in bonobos may represent a common behavioral theme that we humans have translated into various sets of learned cultural norms such as sexual ethics and marriage patterns. Nature has given us behavioral potentials, ultimately coded in our genes, that we inherited from our evolutionary ancestors and that evolved over the course of our species' history. Culture has given rise to our specific expressions of those behaviors. In this way, yes, some of our behaviors may be said to have a genetic basis—but only in this limited way.

gestures among chimps: to prevent violence, to ease tension, (especially while feeding), to serve as a greeting, to signal reconciliation, or to reassure another group member. Sex or some form of sexual activity, between opposite- or same-sex partners, has even been seen to precede food sharing.

While on the subject of bonobos, we should mention Kanzi, a male bonobo at the Language Research Center at Georgia State University (Savage-Rumbaugh and Lewin 1994). Kanzi is one of the most successful apes at communicating through a language with the characteristics of human communication. He uses symbols on a computer keyboard; he can even recognize and, using his computer, respond to a large number of spoken English words. In addition to his linguistic skills, he has been taught to make and use simple stone tools. Although not resembling even the earliest known hominid stone tools (see Chapter 10), Kanzi's tools are, nonetheless, true artifacts and so may show us what the *very* earliest stone tools of our lineage might have looked like. Neither of these behaviors—using a humanlike language or stone tool*making*—is seen among wild bonobos, but they do give us an idea as to the cognitive potentials of these apes.

Now, if all the behaviors of the chimp and bonobo sound more than vaguely human, the reason may be simple. We share certain general behavioral patterns because we inherited them from a common ancestor. To be sure, our evolutionary line and that of the chimps and bonobos have been going their separate ways for 5 or 6 million years, and even shared features have had the chance to become modified by all the processes of evolution—to be changed, eliminated, enhanced, and differently adapted to our species' different niches. Chimps and bonobos are not "living fossils" stuck in some 5-million-year-old rut while our ancestors continued to evolve. But because our common ancestor is relatively recent and there is striking similarity between the bodies and behaviors of apes and humans, we can argue that our shared behavioral themes are homologous.

This does *not* mean that humans have specific genes for friendship, food sharing, territoriality, or continual sexuality. These are complex behaviors, and humans and apes are complex species. It does, however, hint that, as with the chimps and bonobos, the focus of the human adaptation—what adapted our earliest hominid ancestors and what has been the adaptive theme of our line—is social interaction based on individual recognition, a strong bond centered around family relationships (generally mothers and their offspring), long-term friendships, sexual consciousness, mutual care within the group, and recognition of and defense of the group. It seems reasonable to assume that our hominid ancestors behaved in similar ways. As Jane Goodall says,

> The concept of early humans poking for insects with twigs and wiping themselves with leaves seems entirely sensible. The thought of those ancestors greeting and reassuring one another with kisses or embraces, cooperating in protecting their territory or in hunting, and sharing food with each other, is appealing. The idea of close affectionate ties within the Stone Age family, of brothers helping one another, of teenage sons hastening to the protection of their old mothers, and of teenage daughters minding the babies, for me brings the fossilized relics of their physical selves dramatically to life. (1990:207)

▽   ▽   ▽

SUMMARY

As we noted in the last chapter, one way to guide us as we look at our own species is to understand the context from which our species evolved. This approach works for behavior as well as for physical adaptations. The importance of a well-defined social organization is seen among one savanna primate, the baboon, and is a good hint that an analogous behavior was a key to the survival of early savanna hominids.

More useful to understanding our own behavior is to examine the behavior of close evolutionary relatives, especially the chimpanzee and bonobo. Chimp and bonobo behaviors differ in specifics from ours and have been evolving separately from ours for 5 or 6 million years. All three species have adapted to different niches. The basic patterns for the behavior of all three species, however, are homologous. They are the same because we inherited them from a common ancestor. It is highly likely, then, that our remote hominid ancestors also manifested these patterns in some way.

Such studies indicate to us that the early hominids of Africa may very well have been highly social creatures and that their social organization was built around differing interpersonal relationships, a family unit, conscious sexuality, recognition of group membership and territory, and mutual care at both the individual and the group level.

QUESTIONS FOR FURTHER THOUGHT

1. Consider the debate over the biological basis of human behaviors. Much of the debate in both the scientific and popular presses has focused on such things as human aggression, intelligence, and sexual orientation. What are the ramifications of the extreme points of view ("blank slate" versus "preprogrammed behaviors") of these topics? How might each be seen in terms of an intermediate model, as described in the chapter?

2. In fields as diverse as particle physics and cultural anthropology, it has been noted that the very act of scientific observation affects that which is being observed. Certainly this would also be the case for the ethological observation of nonhuman primates. What are the scientific as well as the ethical implications of this idea? Are some of our scientific ideas potentially inaccurate? Has studying other primates in the wild been in any way detrimental to them? benefical to them?

KEY TERMS

homologies

analogies

sociobiology

evolutionary
   psychology

behavioral ecology

inclusive fitness

altruistic

reproductive strategies

ethology

savanna

SUGGESTED READINGS

Descriptions of baboon behavior can be found in Shirley Strum's *Almost Human* and in Barbara Smuts's *Sex and Friendship in Baboons*. Jane Goodall describes her work with the chimps and her experiences studying them in *Through a Window: My Thirty Years with the Chimpanzees of Gombe*.

A good review of the biological basis of human behavior is in *The Biological Basis of Human Behavior: A Critical Review*, second edition, edited by Robert W. Sussman.

For more technical information on primate behavior, see *The Evolution of Primate Behavior*, by Alison Jolly; *Patterns of Primate Behavior*, by Claud A. Bramblett; and *The Nonhuman Primates*, by Phyllis Dolhinow and Agustín Fuentes.

Dian Fossey recounts her study of gorillas in *Gorillas in the Mist*; her own story, in turn, including her murder, is told by Farley Mowat in *Woman in the Mists* and in the 1988 movie *Gorillas in the Mist*. Biruté Galdikas tells about orangutans in *Reflections of Eden: My Years with the Orangutans of Borneo*.

Chimpanzee hunting behavior and the possible influence of meat eating on human evolution are the topic of Craig B. Stanford's *The Hunting Apes: Meat Eating and the Origins of Human Behavior*. His position—that the quest for meat was what helped select for our big brains and gave rise to many human social behaviors—is controversial. For a critique, see the review of Stanford's book "A Theory That's Hard to Digest," by Christophe Boesch in the 17 June 1999 issue of *Nature*.

For information on the cultural customs of chimpanzees, see "The Cultures of Chimpanzees," by Andrew Whiten and Christophe Boesch, in the January 2001 issue of *Scientific American*.

Bonobos are described in Frans de Waal's *Bonobo: The Forgotten Ape*, which has outstanding photographs by Frans Lanting. For more on the amazing Kanzi and other bonobos, see *Kanzi: The Ape at the Brink of the Human Mind*, by Sue Savage-Rumbaugh and Roger Lewin, and *Apes, Language, and the Human Mind*, by Savage-Rumbaugh et al.

Some interesting Web sites devoted to primate behavior are www.discoverchimpanzees.org and chimp.st-and.ac.uk/cultures3/index.html.

STUDYING THE HUMAN PAST

The present contains
nothing more than the
past, and what is found
in the effect was
already in the cause.
—Henri Bergson

he study of the human past—our evolutionary history—is a central part of biological anthropology. To understand the human species today, we need to know where, when, how, and from what we evolved. But the past *is* the past. We can't see past events as they were happening. We can't make them happen again. All we have are the present-day results of series of past events, like the living species of primates we discussed in Chapters 7 and 8. In some cases we have the physical remains of the past, such as the fossils of extinct species, but these have themselves undergone change since they were part of a living creature.

The present, however, can be a powerful tool. Recall from Chapter 2 how Hooke and Steno used fossils and stratigraphy to plot the events of the past and how Hutton and Lyell used the idea of uniformitarianism by observing present-day processes to understand how past events took place.

In this chapter we will address the methods used by bioanthropologists to answer these questions about our past:

What are the features of the primate skeleton, and how can knowledge of them help us identify fossil remains?

How do we locate, recover, and date fossil remains?

How are fossils formed, and what affects the condition of the fossils we find?

What can we learn about our past from new technologies in the study of genetics?

BONES: THE PRIMATE SKELETON

Most of the physical remains we find of the evolutionary past are in the form of preserved bone. Only in rare cases are we lucky enough to discover soft tissue remains of an ancient organism (see Chapter 15). Therefore, knowledge of the skeletal structure, or **osteology,** is vital. The first thing we need to do, of course, is determine what species the skeletal remains are from. The human skeleton is a variation on the basic mammalian skeletal theme and, more specifically, on the primate skeletal theme. Figure 9.1 compares the skeletons of a modern human, a gorilla, and a domestic cat.

When we look at a skeleton, it's easy to imagine the bones as something separate from the muscles, nerves, blood vessels, and other soft tissues of the body. But, in fact, they all develop together and are adapted to function together. For example, the skull serves to protect the brain;

osteology: The study of the skeleton.

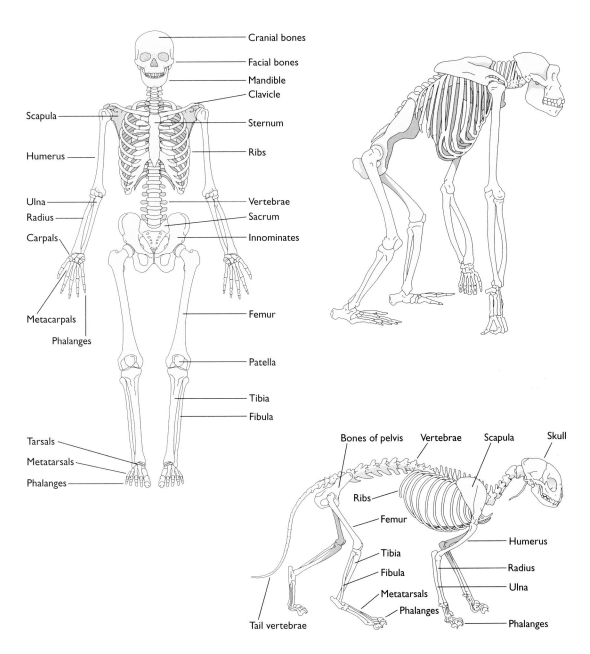

FIGURE 9.1
Skeletons of a modern human, a gorilla, and a domestic cat. (As a learning exercise, label the
gorilla skeleton yourself.)

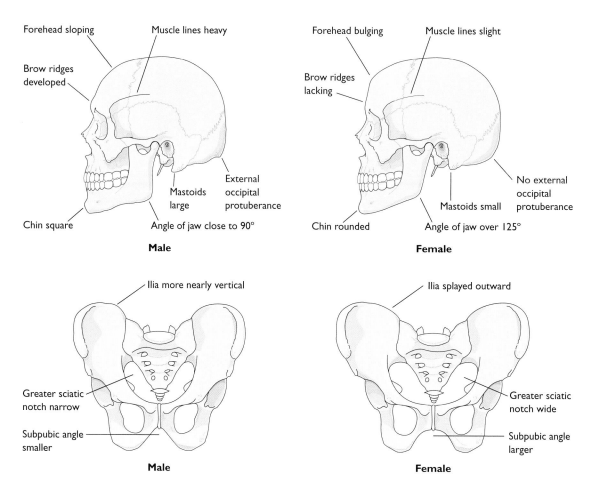

Forehead sloping   Muscle lines heavy

Brow ridges developed

Chin square   Mastoids large   External occipital protuberance   Angle of jaw close to 90°

Male

Forehead bulging   Muscle lines slight

Brow ridges lacking

Chin rounded   Mastoids small   No external occipital protuberance   Angle of jaw over 125°

Female

Ilia more nearly vertical

Greater sciatic notch narrow

Subpubic angle smaller

Male

Ilia splayed outward

Greater sciatic notch wide

Subpubic angle larger

Female

FIGURE 9.2

Major sex differences in the human skull and pelvis.

therefore, a skull fossil is a good indicator of the size and shape of the brain it once protected. Muscles are attached to bones, and so the location, size, and shape of the point where the muscle once attached to a bone will provide some indication of the size and shape of the muscle, even though the muscle itself may have decayed long ago. We can tell a lot about a creature from the bones it leaves behind.

One of the more obvious and important things we can tell about a human skeleton is its sex. Humans belong to a species that exhibits **sexual dimorphism,** notable physical differences between the sexes that are not related to reproductive traits. In general, human males tend to be larger and more heavily muscled than females, a fact that also applies to the apes and to extinct hominid species. The skull and, for obvious reasons, the pelvis are the best features for identifying the sex of a skeleton (Figure 9.2).

Age at death may also be determined from skeletal remains. The body, including the bones, goes through many physical changes as it develops, matures, and ages, and many of these changes occur at a fairly predictable rate. By determining on a skeleton which changes have already taken place and which have yet to take place, we may approximate the age at which the individual died (Figure 9.3).

The skeleton acts as a framework for the body, and thus the size and shape of the bones can reveal something of the appearance of the entire living person. We know, for example, from the sheer size and ruggedness of their bones, that a group of humans from ice-age Europe (the Neandertals, whom we will discuss in Chapter 11) were big, brawny, and extremely strong. Several investigators have attempted to reconstruct the faces of our ancestors from the shapes of skulls and facial bones. Using their knowledge of human anatomy, they artistically add missing bones, eyes, fatty tissue, cartilage, muscle, and skin to casts of ancient skulls, "fleshing out" our picture of early humans (Figure 9.4; see also Figure 15.2). This technique is also used in law enforcement to try to identify skeletal remains. We will discuss the application of human osteology to legal matters in Chapter 15.

The skeleton can also tell us something about the behavior of the deceased organism. We have mentioned the importance of bipedal locomotion as the first hominid trait to evolve. We know it was first because the nature of the bones of the pelvis and femur, along with the position of the skull atop the spine, suggests posture and movement. Thus, our analysis of the bones of our most ancient ancestors provides clues as to how they walked (Figure 9.5; see also Chapter 10 for the evolution of this behavior).

Moreover, we can discern information about a deceased organism's diet from dental and skeletal remains. Look at the dentition of a **carnivore** in your dog or cat, and compare it to the teeth of an **omnivore** in your own mouth. The teeth of the dog or cat, although they show some differentiation, are all pointed and sharp, adapted for grasping, piercing, cutting, and crushing meat. Our teeth are adapted for a greater variety of operations and, thus, a greater variety of food types. In addition, certain wear patterns on the teeth, when examined microscopically, can reveal whether the organism's diet consisted of soft foods like fruits, or more abrasive, gritty foods like grains and roots (see Figure 10.22). We can even examine the chemical content of ancient bones for the proportion of strontium, calcium, carbon isotopes, and other elements to determine whether plants or meat made up the bulk of the diet of certain populations.

Finally, we may acquire information about the health status of our ancestors, a field known as **paleopathology.** Many diseases leave

sexual dimorphism: Physical differences between the sexes of a species not related to reproductive features.

carnivore: An organism adapted to a diet of mostly meat.

omnivore: An organism with a mixed diet of animal and vegetable foods.

paleopathology: The study of disease and nutritional deficiency in prehistoric populations, usually through the examination of skeletal material.

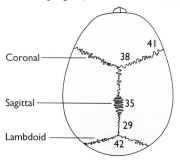

Average ages for cranial suture closure (years)

Coronal
41
38
Sagittal
35
29
Lambdoid
42

Cranial Suture Closure. The bones of the cranial vault are separate at birth and gradually fuse during a person's lifetime. The numbers indicate the average age (in years) of complete closure at different points along the lines of attachment, the sutures. There are other dates as well, on locations not shown in this view. Because of the great degree of individual variation, this is not a particularly reliable technique, but it is still used.

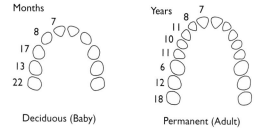

Eruption dates of deciduous and permanent teeth

Months
7
8
17
13
22

Years
7
8
11
10
11
6
12
18

Deciduous (Baby)

Permanent (Adult)

Dental Eruption. Humans have two sets of teeth: deciduous, or "baby" teeth, and permanent, or adult teeth. Each tooth erupts through the gum line at a certain average age. We determine age by seeing which tooth was the last to erupt and which unerupted tooth would have erupted next. We recognize this method in our use of the term "six year molar" for the first adult tooth to erupt. The degree of development of each tooth below the gum line (seen in broken bone or in X-rays) can also be used.

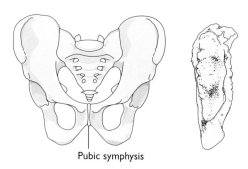

Pubic symphysis

Ages of epiphyseal union (years)

Elbow	14
Hand and foot	15
Ankle	16
Thigh (top)	17
Knee	18
Wrist	19
Shoulder	20
Hip	21
Clavicle	28

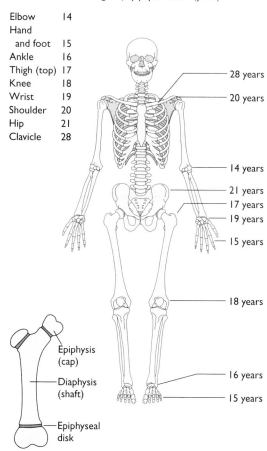

28 years
20 years
14 years
21 years
17 years
19 years
15 years
18 years
16 years
15 years

Epiphysis (cap)

Diaphysis (shaft)

Epiphyseal disk

Epiphyseal Union. The bones of the arms, legs, hands, feet, and other body parts grow in sections: a shaft, or diaphysis, and caps, or epiphyses. When growth is complete, the cartilaginous disks between caps and shaft turn to bone and a single bone results. Ages for epiphyseal union are uniform enough to provide a reliable aging method. The ages shown indicate that all the sites at any one location fuse at about the same time. For example, at the elbow, the far (distal) end of the humerus and the near (proximal) ends of the radius and ulna all fuse at approximately 14 years.

Pubic Symphysis. The inner surface of the bones where the pelvis meets in front is called the pubic symphysis. Between the ages of 18 and 50+, the appearance of this surface undergoes characteristic changes. By assessing the phase to which a specimen belongs, we can approximate the age of a specimen at death. The symphyseal face shown is a Phase VIII, giving an age of 40 to 44 years. (Redrawn from Todd 1920.)

FIGURE 9.3
Major techniques used to determine the age of hominid bones.

FIGURE 9.4
Using a cast of a fossil skull, an anthropologist adds modeling clay to flesh out the face of an ancient human ancestor.

characteristic marks on the skeleton. These include such important disorders as arthritis, tumors and other cancers, tuberculosis, leprosy, anemias, syphilis, osteoporosis, and various infections. Injuries, too, leave their marks, as do other cultural behaviors, including scalping and **trephination,** a surgical procedure that involves cutting a hole in the skull, practiced even in prehistoric times (Figure 9.6).

trephination: Cutting a hole in the skull, presumably to treat some illness.

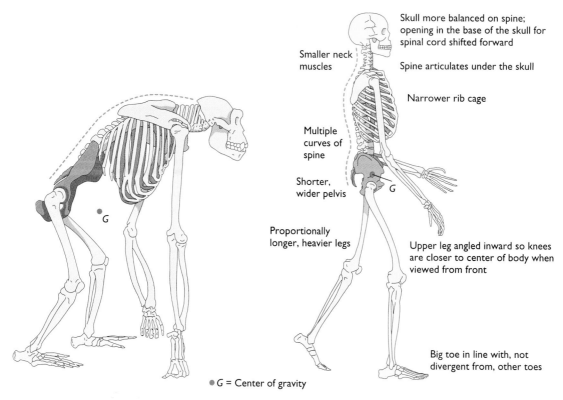

Skull more balanced on spine;
opening in the base of the skull for
spinal cord shifted forward

Spine articulates under the skull

Narrower rib cage

Smaller neck
muscles

Multiple
curves of
spine

Shorter,
wider pelvis

G

Proportionally
longer, heavier legs

Upper leg angled inward so knees
are closer to center of body when
viewed from front

Big toe in line with, not
divergent from, other toes

G

● G = Center of gravity

FIGURE 9.5
Note the anatomical changes
and, thus, the physical evidence associated with bipedalism in the human primate.
Compare human features with
corresponding ones in the gorilla. *G* represents the center
of gravity when standing
bipedally. The ape expends
much more energy to keep
from falling forward.

(Modified from John Napier, *The
Antiquity of Human Walking*, ©1967
Scientific American. Drawing by
Enid Kotschnigo)

(For some practice on analyzing skeletal remains, go to the "Exercises" section toward the back of the book.)

OLD BONES: LOCATING, RECOVERING, AND DATING FOSSILS

Most creatures that have ever lived, including humans, have left no
remains. Fossilization (which we'll discuss in the next section) is a rare
occurrence. A fossil, therefore, is really a priceless treasure, and finding
one is an uncommon event—even in those **sites** that because of their
geological history and nature yield many remains. Olduvai Gorge in
Tanzania (Figure 9.7) has provided us with some of the most important
hominid fossils, yet Louis and Mary Leakey lived and worked there for
more than twenty years before finding one. How, then, do we even
decide where to begin looking?

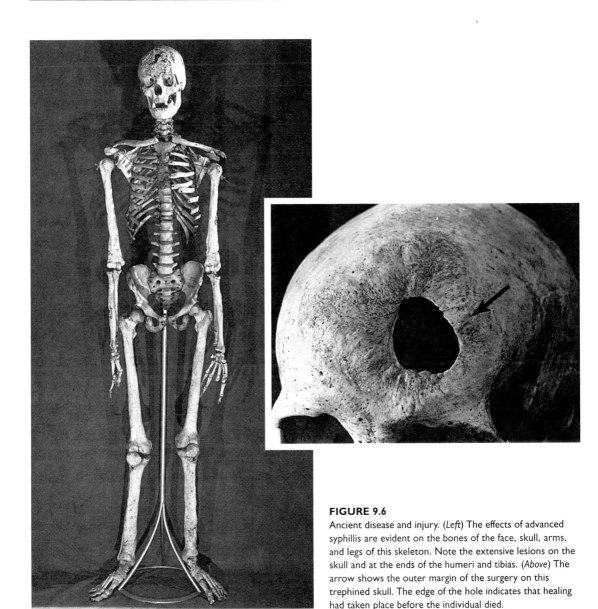

FIGURE 9.6
Ancient disease and injury. (*Left*) The effects of advanced syphillis are evident on the bones of the face, skull, arms, and legs of this skeleton. Note the extensive lesions on the skull and at the ends of the humeri and tibias. (*Above*) The arrow shows the outer margin of the surgery on this trephined skull. The edge of the hole indicates that healing had taken place before the individual died.

A lot, of course, depends on just *what* we're looking for. If it's dinosaurs we're interested in, we look in rock strata that date from the time of the dinosaurs. For hominid fossils, we need strata that were deposited in the past 5 or 6 million years.

It helps, too, if those strata are exposed by geological processes. Layers that are far under the surface might contain important fossils, but

sites: Locations that contain fossil and archaeological evidence of human presence.

FIGURE 9.7

Olduvai Gorge, Tanzania. This location is one of the world's most productive sites for paleoanthropologists. The strata represent more than 2 million years of evolution.

from a purely practical standpoint, it would be difficult, time-consuming, and expensive to dig them up. A place like Olduvai Gorge is ideal. There, an ancient river cut a canyon 300 feet into the earth, exposing layers of soil and rock that go back about 2 million years. At Omo, in Ethiopia, another important early hominid site, the strata have been tilted by geological forces, so that layers from 1 to 4 mya are all on the surface. Walking back and forth at such sites as these is like walking through time. In addition, in such places natural water and wind erosion help expose new soil and whatever fossils it may contain.

Of course, just because a location *looks* like it might easily yield fossils doesn't mean that the conditions there were always conducive to

FIGURE 9.8
Paleoanthropologist Bill Kimbel of the Institute of Human Origins uses dental tools, a small drill, and a binocular microscope to chip stone from bone on nearly sixty fragments of a fossil hominid from Ethiopia. The results of his efforts are shown in Figure 10.14.

fossilization. Paleoanthropologists might inquire as to whether fossils of *any* sort have been found in a potential area of investigation in strata from the time period they are interested in. Both Olduvai and Omo already had reputations as rich fossil areas before the search for hominid fossils began there.

Recovering fossils once they are located can be a tricky business. Fossils are old and often very fragile. Many old bones are **petrified**— turned to stone—and so can be hard to distinguish from the stone in which they were found (Figure 9.8). Raymond Dart, the discoverer of

petrified: Turned to stone.

one of the most famous hominid fossils (both of whom we shall meet in the next chapter), took seventy-three days to separate the delicate fossil from the limestone in which it was encased (see Figure 10.7). The excavation tools of the paleoanthropologist, then, are not so much the backhoe or even the shovel but rather the mason's trowel, the dentist's pick, and the artist's brush.

A fossil sitting on a shelf in a lab or on display in a museum may be beautiful, intriguing, and provocative, but it is scientifically useless unless we know precisely where it was found, its **provenience.** To keep track of the proveniences of fossils, recovery is carried out with the utmost care directed at detailed and accurate record keeping. After all, a site is destroyed in the process of removing fossils, and we must have records of the relative locations of all the important items contained in that site.

Many early hominid fossils are simply found on the surface of the ground, exposed by wind and water erosion. Many, however, are dug out of the ground or are found associated with particular strata.

The depth at which a fossil is found in the natural strata of the soil or rock is, of course, an indication of its relative age. This is the principle of **superposition**—the deeper a layer is the older it is. It is an important dating method and an example of a **relative dating technique;** that is, it indicates the age of one fossil in comparison with that of another (Figure 9.9). In the absence of any natural stratigraphy, the excavator of fossils must establish one. For example, the investigator may dig down by regular increments, perhaps only centimeters at a time, recording the precise depth of any item of interest.

Fossils can also be dated relative to their stratigraphic correlation with other fossils of known age. This is the principle of **biostratigraphy.** This dating method has been used in some of the early hominid sites in South Africa. Many of these sites are located in limestone caves, which are difficult to date by the techniques discussed in the following paragraphs. But when nonhominid fossils of known age are found in association with hominid fossils, we may infer the age of the hominids.

Similarly, the horizontal location of each fossil is important. Often a paleoanthropologist—like the archaeologist looking for human cultural remains—uses a grid system. A site is divided into squares, or grids, and each grid is excavated separately (Figure 9.10). The precise location of a fossil, relative to that of others at the same level, is recorded through photographs and maps.

Besides relative dating methods, there are also **absolute dating techniques** (also called **chronometric techniques**). These tell us the actual age of a fossil. Among the best known are **radiometric** techniques, such

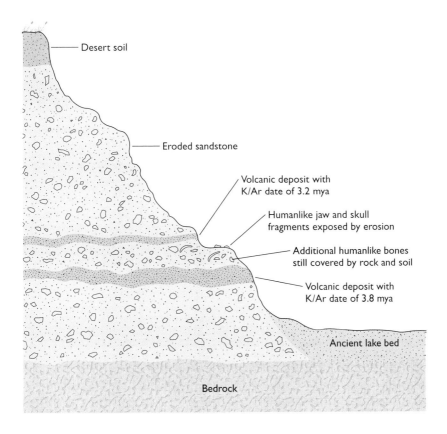

- Desert soil
- Eroded sandstone
- Volcanic deposit with K/Ar date of 3.2 mya
- Humanlike jaw and skull fragments exposed by erosion
- Additional humanlike bones still covered by rock and soil
- Volcanic deposit with K/Ar date of 3.8 mya
- Ancient lake bed
- Bedrock

FIGURE 9.9
Hypothetical stratigraphic sequence. The humanlike remains are between two layers of volcanic rock that can be dated using the K/Ar (potassium/argon) method. The remains must be younger than the volcanic deposit below and older than the one above.

provenience: Here, the precise location where a fossil or artifact was found.

superposition: The principle of stratigraphy that, barring disturbances, more recent layers are superimposed over older ones.

relative dating technique: A dating method that indicates the age of one item in comparison to another.

biostratigraphy: The study of fossils in their stratigraphic context. Used as a relative dating technique.

absolute dating techniques: Dating methods that give specific ages, years, or ranges of years for objects or sites.

chronometric techniques: Another name for absolute dating techniques.

radiometric: Referring to the decay rate of a radioactive substance.

radiocarbon dating: A radiometric dating technique using the decay rate of a radioactive form of carbon found in organic remains.

half-life: The time needed for one-half of a given amount of a radioactive substance to decay.

as **radiocarbon dating,** which can be used to date fossils back to about 40,000 ya and so is relevant to the later period of human evolution. It works as follows: Carbon, in the form of carbon dioxide, is found in all living things, which continuously exchange it with the environment through respiration and metabolism. Most carbon is ^{12}C, indicating that there are twelve particles in the nucleus (six protons and six neutrons). Some carbon, however, is called *carbon 14,* or ^{14}C, because it has two extra neutrons. It is formed when swiftly moving neutrons hit nitrogen atoms in the atmosphere. We know the proportion of each form (*isotope*) of carbon in a living organism. Once an organism dies, however, it no longer takes in new carbon, and so its ^{14}C—an unstable, or radioactive, isotope—begins to decay back into nitrogen, and it does this at a constant rate called a **half-life.** The half-life of ^{14}C is 5,730 years. In that time, one-half of the ^{14}C will have decayed. In another 5,730 years, half of the remaining half will decay, leaving a quarter of the original. And so on.

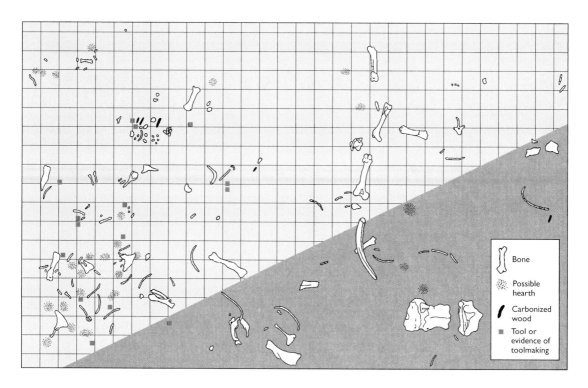

FIGURE 9.10

Grid system diagram from an excavation in Ambrona, Spain, dated at around 350,000 ya (see Chapter 11). The grid helps record the precise location of each bone and artifact. Notice how much less information is conveyed by the solid part of the drawing, which does not show the grid.

Legend:

- Bone
- Possible hearth
- Carbonized wood
- Tool or evidence of toolmaking

Now, if we find some organic remains—bone, for example, or even burnt wood from a campfire—we can test it to see how much ^{14}C is left compared to how much the organism contained when alive. We know how much ^{14}C a living organism should contain, and we test the amount left as we would test any radioactive substance, with a device that measures the amount of radiation emitted. Suppose that our specimen has one-quarter of the living amount. That means that two half-lives have passed, or $5,730 \times 2$, or 11,460 years.

In fossils older than about 40,000 years, there is not enough ^{14}C left to accurately measure. So how do we date the really old fossils, like those of the early hominids? We could use another important method called **potassium/argon,** or **K/Ar, dating.** Radioactive potassium (^{40}K), found in volcanic rock, decays into stable argon gas over time; its half-life is 1.31 billion years. Organic matter contains ^{40}K as well but loses the argon gas that it decays into. Volcanic rocks, formed during eruptions, have a crystalline structure that traps the argon. Using the same reasoning as for radiocarbon dating, we test volcanic rock for the amount of argon, work backward, and date the eruption. Then, organic remains may be dated relatively: Any fossils found in a layer of volcanic rock are as old as that rock. Fossils found just above are younger; those found just below are older (see again Figure 9.9). Recently, a technique called **argon/argon dating,** which uses the decay of radioactive ^{40}Ar into argon gas (^{39}Ar), has proved more accurate in dating volcanic rock. With the use of lasers, it can be performed on a sample as small as a single crystal.

Two other techniques have recently become more widely used and have provided new dates for some fossil sites (see Chapters 11 and 12). One is called **electron spin resonance (ESR) dating.** Natural radioactivity can excite electrons in crystalline material to higher energy levels, where they are "trapped." The number of trapped electrons in such material is related to the nature of the material, the amount of natural background radiation, and, most important, the amount of time since the material formed. By measuring the number of trapped electrons, we can calculate the age of materials such as tooth enamel, mollusk shells, cave deposits, corals, and volcanic rock. This technique has been particularly useful for sites too old (more than 50,000 years) to be dated with radiocarbon. It does not, however, work well on bone.

Luminescence dating, like ESR dating, measures electrons that have been trapped at higher energy levels by background radiation. The more energy trapped, the older the material. Here, the trapped energy is released in the lab using heat (a process called *thermoluminescence,* or *TL*) or light (*optically stimulated luminescence,* or *OSL*) and is seen in the form of a light glow (*luminescence*). It is useful to about 800,000 ya. This technique has been used to date mostly artifacts, including fired clay, pottery, bricks, and burnt rock, such as would be found lining a hearth. This technique has also been applied to soil sediments, but there is still some debate over the accuracy of this application.

Other dating techniques also exist. These are listed in Table 9.1, along with the preceding methods. Several techniques date volcanic rock; others can be used directly on organic remains. In many cases, more than one of these methods may be applied, and when they agree, we have a well-established date for a geological stratum or a fossil. Most of the dates presented in the following chapters are reasonably well confirmed through the use of one or more of these techniques.

HOW FOSSILS GET TO BE FOSSILS

As mentioned earlier, most animals and plants that have inhabited the earth have left no fossil remains. There may be whole taxonomic groups unknown to us because we've found no clues to their existence. Why is this so?

potassium/argon (K/Ar) dating: A radiometric dating technique using the rate at which radioactive potassium, found in volcanic rock, decays into stable argon gas.

argon/argon dating: A radiometric dating technique that uses the decay of radioactive argon into stable argon gas. Can be used to date smaller samples and volcanic rock with greater accuracy than K/Ar dating.

electron spin resonance (ESR) dating: An absolute dating technique that measures the number of electrons excited to higher energy levels by natural radiation and trapped at those levels. Can be used to date tooth enamel, shells, corals, mineral cave deposits, and volcanic rock, but does not work well on bone.

luminescence dating: An absolute dating technique that measures trapped electrons by releasing their energy in the form of light. Can be used to date fired clay, pottery, brick, and burnt stones. It may have some application in soil dating.

TABLE 9.1
Absolute Dating Techniques

Dating Method	Age Range	Material Dated	Basis
Accelerator mass spectrometry	70,000–100s BP*	Organic remains	Counts actual number of ^{14}C atoms
Amino (aspartic) acid racemization	1,000,000–2,000 BP	Bone	Measures shift in polarity of amino acids
Electron spin resonance	10 million–100s BP	Teeth, cave deposits	Measures electrons produced by natural radiation that become trapped in crystalline materials at a regular rate
Fission track dating	1,000,000–100,000 BP	Volcanic rock	Measures radioactive decay that leaves microscopic damage "tracks" in rock at a regular rate
Obsidian hydration	800,000 BP–present	Obsidian (volcanic glass)	Measures regular buildup of a "hydration layer," caused by the chemical reaction of obsidian to water over time
Paleomagnetism	2,000 BP–present	Material with magnetic minerals	Determines movement of earth's magnetic pole against known dates of its position
Potassium/argon and argon/argon	billions–100,000 BP	Volcanic rock	Measures decay of radioactive potassium (or argon isotope) to stable argon gas
Radiocarbon	40,000–100s BP	Organic remains	Measures decay of radioactive carbon isotope to stable nitrogen
Luminescence	To 800,000 BP	Fired clay, pottery, bricks, burned rock	Measures amount of energy captured in material from the decay of radioactive elements in surrounding soil; amount of energy captured is proportional to age
Uranium series	350,000–1,000 BP	Calcium carbonate	Measures decay of radioactive uranium to a series of other elements

*BP = "before present."

The conditions under which an organism, or some of its parts, can be preserved are quite specific. In New England, where I live, the soil is very acidic, due largely to the annual fall of leaves and pine needles. Organic remains tend to disappear very quickly. This is why we were surprised to find the intact skeleton of Henry Opukahaia (see Chapter 1). His bones were preserved because he was buried on a hill in sandy soil,

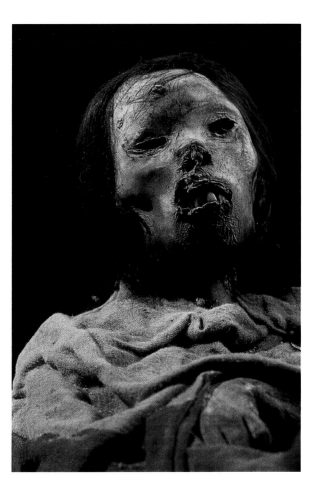

FIGURE 9.11
The Inca "Ice Maiden" is one of several naturally preserved mummies of sacrificial victims found in the Andes.

so water, with all its related chemical and biological decaying activity, could not accumulate around him; additionally, the cemetery was probably regularly cleared of leaves.

Organic remains tend to be preserved under several conditions. In cases of extreme dryness, even soft tissues—usually eaten by everything from bacteria to insects to scavengers—may mummify. Natural mummies resulted from normal burials in the desert sands of ancient Egypt, even before the Egyptians began artificial mummification. In 1995, near the summit of the 20,760-foot volcano Nevando Ampato in Peru, the naturally mummified remains of a young Inca girl were found (Figure 9.11). Sacrificed to the gods of the mountains some 500 ya, her body was preserved by the cold and dry conditions of the high altitude (Reinhard 1996). More recently, at another and even higher site in the Andes, the bodies of three more children were discovered (Reinhard 1999). (See Chapter 15 for another famous example—the "Ice Man" from the Alps.)

Lack of oxygen also contributes to preservation. Such conditions are found in the thick sediment at the bottom of some lakes and ponds. With no oxygen, there is little bacterial action, and organic remains decay very slowly. Many important fossils have been found in places that were once lake bottoms.

Of course, the longer ago an organism lived, the less likely we are to find remains, simply because there is more chance that they will have been crushed, dissolved, eaten, washed away, and so on. But in some cases, minerals may crystallize out of water around the bones or shells of a creature. In rare cases, crystals may form around slowly decaying soft tissue and fill in the spaces left by the decay of organic matter. In all these cases, the fossils become petrified. They literally turn to stone and so become harder, more resistant to processes of decay, and no longer edible—although, naturally, some anatomical detail is lost. The dinosaur fossils with which we are so familiar, as well as the remains of the earliest hominids, are all stone. Luckily for us, the creatures that left these remains perished in just the right situations. Most creatures, however, aren't so considerate.

A fossil reveals more than just the type of organism it once belonged to. A fossil also contains clues as to how the animal died and what happened to it after its death. The study of these factors is called **taphonomy** (from the Greek word *taphos*, "dead"), and it has been important in our understanding of our own evolution.

For example, some early hominid bones have been found in limestone caves in South Africa along with the bones of other mammals. These finds led investigators to believe that our early ancestors inhabited those caves and were hunters who brought their kills back home. More recent taphonomic analysis, however, reveals that the hominids were the hunted, not the hunters. The bones were the leftovers of leopard kills. Here's how scientists believe it happened: Leopards often drag their prey up into a tree, where no other predator or scavenger can get at it. Although much of South Africa is dry, trees are able to grow around the mouths of limestone caves, which hold moisture. As leopard kills hanging in the trees fell apart—after being eaten over several days or decaying over time—the bones fell into the caves. Those bones were of antelopes, baboons, and other animals leopards eat. Apparently, our ancestors were on the menu as well (Figure 9.12). One early hominid skull shows twin puncture wounds that appear to have been the cause of death. The lower canine teeth of a leopard fit exactly into these punctures, providing evidence for the preceding analysis. Although taphonomy is the study of the dead, it has told us important things about how our distant ancestors *lived*. We will describe

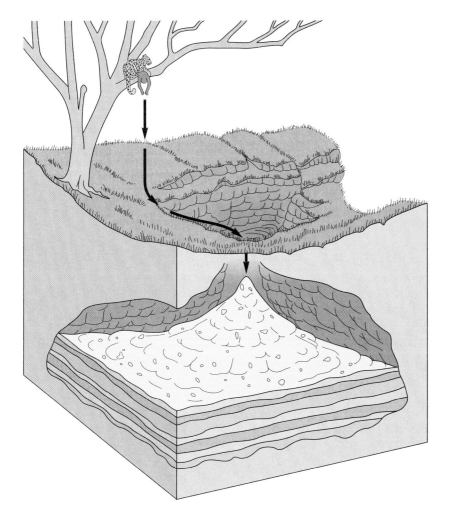

FIGURE 9.12
This artist's reconstruction shows a leopard with the remains of an early hominid in a tree above the entrance to a cave. This scenario probably accounts for the accumulation of bones, including bones of our ancestors, in South African caves.

another important conclusion from taphonomy in the next chapter, when we see how microscopic scratches on bones and teeth reveal something about the diet of the early hominids.

GENES: NEW WINDOWS TO THE PAST

Just as we can reconstruct evolutionary relationships by comparing the anatomical traits of living creatures, we may do the same by making comparisons at the genetic level. In some ways, genetic comparisons are more

taphonomy: The study of how organisms become part of the paleontological record.

accurate. Phenotypic traits are normally controlled by a complex inter-action of multiple genes, evolutionary processes, and environmental factors. As a result, a trait may look the same in two species, but the expressions of that trait in each species may be based on very different genetics, developmental processes, and environmental interactions. The two traits may also have different adaptive functions.

On the other hand, two species may *look* very different, but their differences may be the result of extensive phenotypic effects of a very small number of genes, and the species may actually be quite closely related. Humans and chimps are an example.

Comparing genetic differences among individuals, species, and higher taxa (genera, families, and so on) reveals actual biological rela-tionships, no matter what the species look like or how seemingly simi-lar or different some of their traits are. In the 1960s, Vincent Sarich and the late Allan Wilson of the University of California at Berkeley pio-neered research that used genetic comparisons to determine evolution-ary relationships. Because the technology for comparing actual genes was still unknown when they carried out their work, they compared the chemistry of blood proteins. These are large proteins, easily obtained and easy to work with and, most important, the direct products of the genetic code. This research provided some startling conclusions.

It had been assumed at the time that humans and our closest rela-tives, the great apes, were separated by 12 to 15 million years of evolu-tion. This estimate was based on the degree of phenotypic difference between us and them and on some 12-million-year-old fossils that *appeared* to show the beginnings of hominid traits. Wilson and Sarich's research showed that the blood proteins of humans and chimps are almost identical. In other words, our genes, at least for those traits, are almost the same. Comparing this difference with that between species whose evolutionary divergence time was known, Wilson and Sarich calculated that our two species had branched a mere 5 mya. These 12-million-year-old fossils, they concluded, were not hominids, no mat-ter what they appeared to be. They were right, as we will see in Chap-ter 10. Other methods for making comparisons closer to the genetic level verified this hypothesis (Figure 9.13).

Today's technology (see Chapter 3) allows us to look at and com-pare the most basic genetic components—the sequence of base pairs that make up the codons, which in turn make up the genes. This same technology has also made great strides in solving criminal and missing persons cases. For example, blood samples from crime scenes can be genetically compared with samples from suspects, virtually ensuring accu-rate identifications. DNA sequencing also helps in locating genes involved in various diseases. And, relative to our topic here, we can now

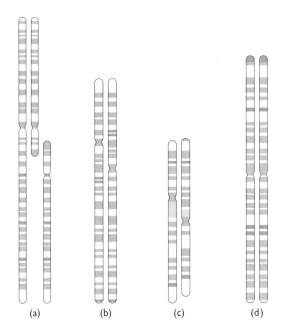

FIGURE 9.13

Comparison of human and chimpanzee chromosomes. Human chromosomes appear on the left in each pair and chimpanzee chromosomes on the right. The similarities in banding pattern (seen after applying a chemical stain) are clear. In pair (*a*) the pattern of human chromosome 2 is similar to that of two chimp chromosomes. In pair (*d*) the patterns are virtually identical. Banding patterns are the results of different concentrations of the four bases that make up the genetic code. Light bands are rich in noncoding sequences with mostly Cs (cytosine) and Gs (guanine; see Chapter 3). These tend to be associated with areas of high gene concentration. This is one piece of evidence for the genetic similarity between our two species.

more precisely compare the genetic makeup of primate species, establishing just how genetically similar or different they are, and, using the logic described above, estimate how long ago their evolutionary lines deverged. Scientists have even attempted to reconstruct the ancestral genome of all living primates (O'Brien and Stanyon 1999).

A focus of recent studies, of course, is on the genetic comparison of humans with our closest relatives, the chimpanzees and bonobos. A well-known and well-accepted quantitative expression of this comparison says that humans and these apes are 98 percent genetically identical. While this does capture the relative degree of our evolutionary closeness—which is no surprise anyway—it doesn't really tell us much (Marks 2002). For one thing, since there are only four bases in the genetic code, any two long sequences of DNA from any two species are likely to be at least 25 percent identical. Second, different sections of DNA evolve at different rates, so some portions of our two species' DNA might be

Contemporary Reflections

Who Owns Old Bones?

In 1990 the nearly complete skeleton of a *Tyrannosaurus rex*, nicknamed "Sue," was found in South Dakota and soon became the center of a controversy over ownership. After some complex legal haggling, the owner of the land on which the bones were found was granted permission to sell them. The skeleton went up for public auction in October 1997 and was purchased (with corporate help) by the Field Museum of Natural History in Chicago—for $8.36 million! It will now be available for research and is currently on public display. In this case, everybody won, but scientists worry that this could set a precedent that would remove important evidence of the past from free scientific inquiry.

The issue of ownership and availability to science becomes even more complex when the remains of the past are human. In these cases, ownership may be a matter not only of landholding but also of direct biological or cultural descent. The extreme cases are easy enough to sort out. I don't think anyone would object to the excavation and study of early African hominids, even though they are the ancestors of us all. They are simply too far removed in time, and their potential scientific value is too great. On the other hand, I would object if some anthropologist wanted to dig up my grandparents, examine their bones, and put them in a museum case—and the law would clearly be on my side. Not all situations, however, are as clear-cut.

For years, otherwise well-meaning scientists have enjoyed the freedom to recover, study, and store the skeletal remains of the remote and not-so-remote ancestors of living peoples. In North America, thousands of Native American skeletons have been recovered—many of which were exhumed from the graves into which they had been placed by members of their societies. Although these remains have provided much information about the original inhabitants of this continent, Native American groups have voiced objections, for obvious reasons. In 1990 the Native American Graves Protection and Repatriation Act (NAGPRA) was passed. It says that lineal descendants have a right to the remains of their ancestors housed in institutions or discovered on federal or tribal territory. This legislation has led to the removal of large collections of human remains and

completely identical while others would be very different. And finally, while some base sequences of human and chimp and bonobo DNA may be absolutely identical, they may show up in different numbers. For example, the base sequence of the genes for the Rh blood groups is the same in humans and chimps, but humans have two such genes while chimps have three (Marks 2002:27). There's more going on than a simple numerical statement indicates.

Far more interesting and useful questions ask just *which* genes differ between humans and chimps, *how* those genes differ, and *what* those genes do. Recent research proposes some interesting possibilities. A chemical, for example, that all mammals, including the apes, posses on associated artifacts from museums and labs and has made new excavations of Native American remains difficult, if not impossible. Indeed, before "naturally shed" remains were excluded from NAGPRA regulations, two local tribes demanded the return of some 10,000-year-old human hair found at a site in Montana, hair that could provide information on the DNA of early Americans (see Feder 1997 and references therein for a more complete discussion of this and related issues). A well-known example involves the skeletal remains discovered in 1996 in Washington State and commonly known as "Kennewick Man." A coalition of Native American tribes from the area laid claim to the 9,000-year-old bones under the terms of NAGPRA. Despite scientific testimony to the contrary, Secretary of the Interior Bruce Babbitt declared in September 2000 that the remains were culturally affiliated with the coalition and that the bones should be turned over to them. A suit by a group of scientists to gain access to the remains for study was reinstated. On February 4, 2004, a court of appeals ruled that the bones could be studied.

Is there a compromise between honoring the cultural laws and heritage of peoples and providing science with important data—data that may even shed light on the history of the people in question? Each case, in the end, must be examined and judged on its own merits. Much evidence of early America is in the form of abandoned and naturally covered-over objects and bones, not intentional burials. Many of these remains cannot be reasonably affiliated with any specific living group and, thus, should be freely open to legitimate scientific investigation. Alternatively, scientists should not go into clearly identified burial areas armed with shovels and trowels. As is most often the case, where ancient bones are uncovered by natural processes or accident (say, during a construction project), the group with which those bones are affiliated might allow scientific information to be gathered before the bones are reburied. This is the situation with the well-known African Burial Ground in New York City. A model example for me is the case of Henry Opukahaia (see Chapter 1), where the family kindly allowed us to fully examine Henry's bones before preparing and returning them for burial.

Whatever the individual cases, however, there is one overriding consideration that should guide our actions—no matter how old or from what species, bones were once integral parts of living, breathing, feeling beings. Even when we can use them as scientific specimens, they deserve respectful treatment.

the surface of all body cells is lacking in humans. This is the result of some differences in a 92-base pair section of a single gene (Gibbons 1998b; Muchmore et al. 1998; Normile 2001). One function of this chemical is cellular communication during brain development and function, so a possible result of the genetic difference could be an influence on the timing and extent of brain growth. This has obvious implications for human evolution.

Another specific difference is in some genes for enzymes called proteases, which are important to the immune system (Check 2004). This could explain why chimps are less severely affected by some diseases such as AIDS and Alzheimer's.

And most recently a difference between nonhuman primates and humans has been located on a gene for a protein important in the building of some jaw muscles. Because of a mutation, the human version of the gene is inactivated and this results in reduced muscle fibers and even a reduced size of some jaw muscles (Stedman et al. 2004). Moreover, the origin of this mutation has been placed at about 2.4 million years ago, a date, as we shall see, that is about the time of the first fossils identified as belonging to our genus, *Homo*.

In addition to these specific differences, it has also been established that five chromosomes in our two species show significant differences in the arrangement of the same genes. Some sequences, for example, have been flipped (or inverted) in one species as compared to the other. These changes could lead to different roles for those genes. Identifying their functions is a current goal, as is the establishment of a nonhuman primate genome project to provide a complete sequence of the genomes of our closest relatives (Gibbons 1998b).

In the next three chapters we will outline the story of hominid evolution. All the above scientific techniques have been applied to studying this story and have allowed us to achieve what knowledge we have of our evolutionary history. As we will see, these new technologies have also been applied to the relationships between modern humans and various groups of our ancestors (Chapter 12) and to comparisons among modern human populations (Chapter 14).

▽   ▽   ▽

SUMMARY

Often when we read a brief article in the popular press about a new fossil find, we get the impression that the scientists conducted some sort of magic to arrive at their stated conclusions. In the 3 October 1994 issue of *Time*, for example, we read that a small fossil tooth and a few other fragmentary bones from Ethiopia had been discovered, heralding "a new chapter in the history of human evolution" (Lemonick 1994). On the basis of these bones, a new species of hominid was established. According to the scientists' description, the individual was probably bipedal, stood about 4 feet tall, was "ravaged by carnivores," and lived 4.4 mya in the forests. That's pretty specific information from a handful of bones turned to stone.

You should now understand that arriving at such conclusions is not magic at all. Although data like these bones are from a creature millions of years old, we may still use scientific methodology to interpret them. We know what modern mammalian skeletons look like and what previous fossil finds look like, so we can compare our new fossils with older ones in order to give them at least a provisional taxonomic assignment. As the fossils were being recovered in Ethiopia, scientists recorded exhaustive data about their provenience, allowing us to generate hypotheses about their environment and, using technologies from physics, when they lived. We understand how fossils are formed and what their specific condition can tell us about how the organism died and became part of the fossil record. We know, for example, what bones that have been "ravaged by carnivores" look like.

Finally, combining the preceding techniques with new methods from genetics, we have been able to piece together a tentative family tree of the hominids and related primates. When a new set of fossils is found, we have a context for comparison and a taxonomic system that can supply it with a name. We will meet this 4.4-million-year-old fossil species and many others in the next chapter, as we see exactly how these fact-finding techniques are applied.

QUESTIONS FOR FURTHER THOUGHT

1. Recently the Parliament of Iceland gave a private company the right to create and maintain a database on the health records, genealogies, and DNA profiles of nearly all living and many decreased Icelanders. The intent is to better understand links between diseases and genes. But there are privacy issues and concerns that the company may sell its information to pharmaceutical and insurance companies. What issues must be taken into account so that we might benefit from such a study while still respecting the rights of individuals?

2. Read the latest information about Kennewick Man on the Web sites listed in this chapter's "Suggested Readings." What do you think about the motives of the scientists who want to use the remains for study as opposed to those of the Native Americans who want to rebury the bones with no further study? Is a compromise possible? How should we approach remains that have definite cultural affiliations but that might hold important scientific information? How far back into history must we go to find human or archaeological remains that preclude such controversy?

KEY TERMS

osteology

sexual dimorphism

carnivore

omnivore

paleopathology

trephination

sites

petrified

provenience

superposition

relative dating
    technique

biostratigraphy

absolute dating
    techniques

chronometric
    techniques

radiometric

radiocarbon dating

half-life

potassium/argon
    (K/Ar) dating

argon/argon dating

electron spin
    resonance (ESR)
    dating

luminescence dating

taphonomy

SUGGESTED READINGS

A detailed and beautifully photographed book on the human skeleton, with life-sized pictures, is *Human Osteology,* second edition, by Tim White and Pieter Folkens. Analysis of the human skeleton in anthropological context is also covered nicely in *Human Osteology: A Laboratory and Field Manual of the Human Skeleton,* by William Bass; in *Skeleton Keys,* by Jeffrey H. Schwartz; and, for comparative osteology among the primates, in *An Introduction to Human Evolutionary Anatomy,* by Leslie Aiello and Christopher Dean.

Techniques of excavation, interpretation, and dating are covered in more detail in Ken Feder and Michael Park's *Human Antiquity,* fourth edition, and in even more detail in Robert Sharer and Wendy Ashmore's *Archaeology: Discovering Our Past* and Brian Fagan's *In the Beginning.*

Taphonomy is covered by Pat Shipman in *Life History of a Fossil: An Introduction to Taphonomy and Paleoecology* and by Lewis Binford in *Bones: Ancient Men and Modern Myths.*

For information on the new techniques and discoveries regarding human genetics, see *Genome: The Autobiography of a Species in 23 Chapters,* by Matt Ridley.

More on the Ice Maiden and other mummies uncovered in the Andes can be found in three articles by Johan Reinhard in the June 1996, January 1997, and November 1999 issues of *National Geographic.*

The African Burial Ground is the topic of "Archaeology as Community Service: The African Burial Ground Project in New York City," by Warren Perry and Michael Blakey, in Kenneth Feder's *Lessons from the Past*. For the latest on Kennewick Man, see the following Web sites: www.cr.nps.gov/aad/kennewick and www.kennewick-man.com.

The Iceland genetics study is covered in "Decoding Iceland," by Micheal Specter, in the 18 January 1999 *New Yorker*.

A thought-provoking book on the genetic similarities between humans and chimps, as well as other major issues in biological anthropology (including Kennewick Man), is Jonathan Marks's *What It Means to Be 98% Chimpanzee: Apes, People, and Their Genes*.

EVOLUTION OF THE HOMINIDS

There are no final
words. Human origins
will always be
enigmatic.
—Donald Johanson

P hysicists observe and measure the universe as we see it today in an attempt to understand its origin and evolution. Their methods of observation and measurement are highly technical and are considered essentially accurate. Therefore, we know the distances to the stars, the speed with which those stars are moving away from us, and even their chemical makeup.

When these individual pieces of data are put together, however, the story is often confusing and puzzling. For example, some estimates of the age of the universe seem to indicate that the universe is *younger* than some of the stars it contains. This obviously can't be. Either some of the observational or measurement techniques were wrong, or they were less accurate than we thought, or perhaps different groups of scientists have interpreted the data differently, or—just maybe—the universe is more complicated than we imagined.

Similarly, paleoanthropologists observe present-day species and the fossilized remnants of other species to try to reconstruct the biological past. The study of human evolution is also a complicated venture. We have many thousands of individual pieces of data, each observed, measured, dated, and analyzed according to the very latest technologies. But when we try to put them all together, we come up with inconsistencies, contradictions, and often several equally plausible interpretations. This chapter and the two that follow will give you the most current ideas about our evolution, including all the missing pieces and alternative interpretations—at least the ones based on scientific inquiry. We will address the following questions:

What is the evolutionary history of the primates?

When and under what circumstances did the hominids evolve, and why was bipedalism so important?

What is the fossil record of the early hominids?

THE ORIGIN AND EVOLUTION OF THE PRIMATES

We have a large number of fossil specimens of primates, but the fossil record is still spotty. Our identifications of most of the extinct primate species are based on fragmentary remains, mostly pieces of jaws or sometimes just teeth. Although a particular extinct species may be represented by many specimens, fossils of its contemporaries are often lacking, giving us little basis for comparison. There are large gaps in the primate fossil record. Some periods are represented by many fossils, but they all come from one or two sites. Still, we can put together a general, if tentative, picture of the course of primate evolution (Figure 10.1).

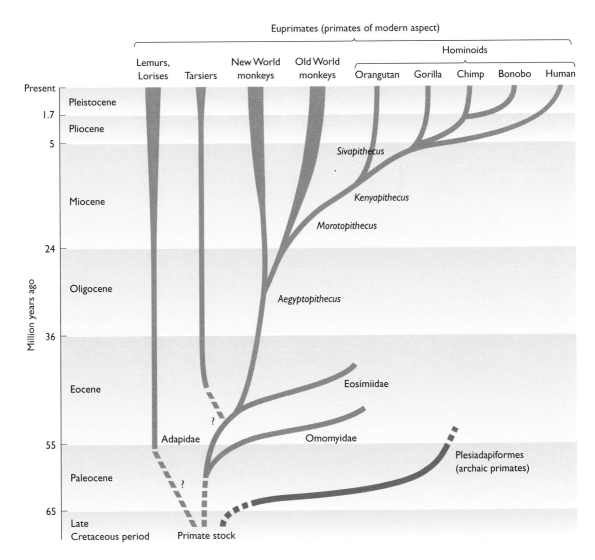

FIGURE 10.1
Simplified evolutionary tree for the primates, with major geological epochs and dates. Question marks and dashed lines indicate insufficient data to establish evolutionary relationships. This tree represents one of several possible interpretations.

We have few fossils that tell us about the earliest stages of primate evolution. Some genetic and statistical comparisons point to the origin of the primates as far back as 80 to 90 mya, well into the time of the dinosaurs (Gibbons 1998a; Tavaré et al. 2002). In terms of hard evidence, there are a few primatelike teeth from Montana dated at 65 mya and some bones from Wyoming dated at 60 mya that have primate features related to climbing behavior. Remember that at the time, North America and Eurasia were still very close together and possibly still connected in some locations (see Figure 6.6), so the primates probably

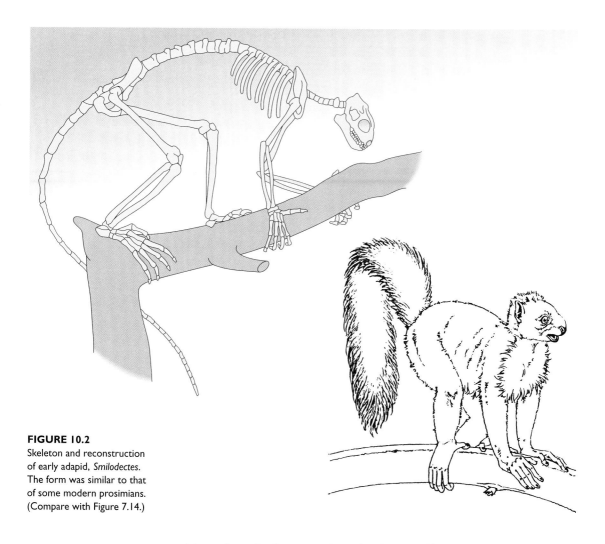

FIGURE 10.2
Skeleton and reconstruction of early adapid, *Smilodectes*. The form was similar to that of some modern prosimians. (Compare with Figure 7.14.)

originated on the large northern landmass called Laurasia, not on what is now North America.

Undisputed primates appear about 55 mya. The traits that we associate in modern primates with an arboreal environment (see Chapter 7) may not have first evolved specifically to facilitate that adaptation. After all, other mammals that do not possess these traits are also arboreal. Anthropologist Matt Cartmill (1992) suggests that prehensile extremities and stereoscopic vision may have evolved to aid leaping as a means of locomotion in the forest canopy or the shrub-layer undergrowth and to promote fruit eating and "visually directed predation" on insects. Modern mouse lemurs, lorises, and tarsiers, for example, all track insects by sight and seize them by hand. As the primates evolved, these basic traits proved a useful adaptive theme

FIGURE 10.18
The cranium of *Sahelan-thropus tchadensis.*

several teeth and dated from 7 to 6 mya (Figure 10.18; Brunet et al. 2002). It has been placed in a new genus and species, *Sahelanthropus tchadensis* (after the Sahel region of Africa that borders the southern Sahara) and is known popularly as "Toumaï" ("hope of life" in the local Goran language). This form is described as having a "mosaic" of features. It is very apelike in its brain size (estimated at 320 to 380 ml), widely spaced eye orbits, and other details of its morphology, but according to its discoverers it has a number of striking features characteristic of later hominids. These include small canines of a hominid size, shape, and wear pattern; a face with reduced prognathism; and a continuous brow ridge. The forward position of the foramen magnum, while not enough evidence to reliably infer habitual bipedalism, still makes such an inference "not . . . unreasonable" (Brunet et al. 2002:150). The primary investigators thus claim that this form represents "the oldest and most primitive known member of the hominid clade, close to the divergence of hominids and chimpanzees" (151).

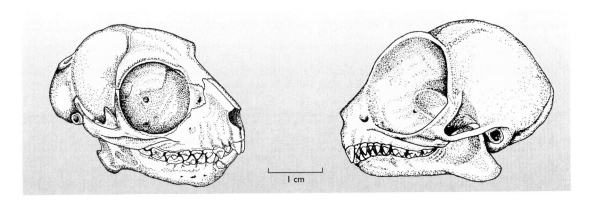

1 cm

FIGURE 10.3
Fossil omomyid, *Necrolemur* (*left*), compared with modern tarsier. (See also Figure 7.15).

for life in the trees. Some new fossil finds from Wyoming (Bloch and Boyer 2002; Sargis 2002)—representing several families of Plesiadapiformes, an extinct branch of archaic primates (as opposed to the euprimates, or primates of modern aspect)—clearly show features related to grasping, indicating that that adaptation evolved early in primate evolution.

The early primates come in two groups, both found in North America, Europe, Asia, and Africa. One group, the Adapidae, are lemurlike and so are thought to be ancestral to modern lemurs and lorises (Figure 10.2). The other group, the Omomyidae, are tarsierlike; they may date back as far as 60 mya and may be ancestral to both tarsiers and anthropoids (Figure 10.3). A recently discovered group, the Eosimiidae from Asia, may represent the more direct ancestors of monkeys, apes, and hominids (Gebo et al. 2000; Jaeger et al. 1999; Kay et al. 1997). Important evolutionary shifts that marked the origin of the anthropoids included changes to (1) a diurnal lifestyle from a nocturnal one, (2) less leaping and more climbing through the trees with all fours, and (3) a more herbivorous diet with less emphasis on insects.

By the time the omomyids were moving into Asia, the Eastern and Western Hemispheres were completely separate. We know that all modern New World primates are monkeys, but there are very few monkey fossils from the New World, mostly because the jungle environment leads to quick and complete scavenging or decay of dead animals. Thus, we don't know for sure how the evolution of the primates proceeded in the Western Hemisphere. There are two views on the subject. The first is that the early New World prosimians moved into Central and South America when those areas joined together with North America and that the prosimians subsequently evolved into modern platyrrhines, the New World monkeys.

The second view is that early monkeys from the Old World "rafted" over to the Americas, literally floating on logs and branches, or "island hopped" over a chain of volcanic islands when the two hemispheres were

FIGURE 10.4
Skull of *Aegyptopithecus* from
the Fayum in Egypt. This fossil is considered an early
monkeylike form that may
be ancestral to later Old
World anthropoids.

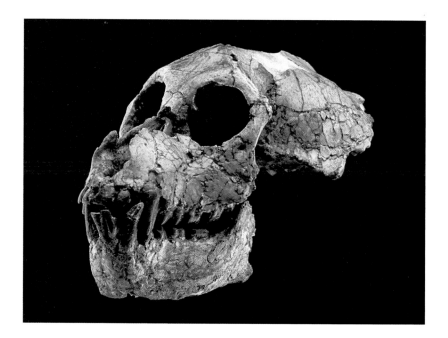

closer together. These early monkeys replaced any prosimians that still
inhabited the New World, and they eventually evolved into the modern
New World monkey species. Although there are some distinct differences
(see Chapter 7), the basic similarity between the Old World and New
World monkeys argues for a single origin and thus for the second scenario.
In addition, although most of the fossils from the New World are incomplete and therefore hard to evaluate, a recent find of a 25- to 27-million-
year-old monkey from Bolivia (Takai et al. 2000), whose teeth are very
similar to an older fossil form from Egypt, suggests that the New World monkeys originated and diversified first in Africa. That this scenario is plausible
was shown by a recent report (Yoon 1998) of fifteen iguanas (large lizards)
floating on a huge raft of trees 200 miles from their native Caribbean island
of Guadeloupe to the island of Anguilla, where they had not previously
been found. They are established and reproducing in their new habitat.

We are most interested in primate evolution in the Old World.
Much of the history of the Old World anthropoids comes from a single
site, the depression formed by an ancient lake in the desert southwest of
Cairo, Egypt, called the Fayum. Paleontologist Elwyn Simons began
extensive investigations there in the early 1960s that continue today
(Simons and Rasmussen 1994). From this valuable site come a number
of monkeylike forms dated from 40 to 25 mya. The most important, perhaps, is *Aegyptopithecus*, from about 34 mya (Figure 10.4). This 10-pound

primate shows anthropoid traits, as well as several features of the teeth, braincase, and skull that resemble later hominoids (apes and hominids). It may be ancestral, then, to all the modern Old World anthropoids.

As the early anthropoids expanded, they outcompeted the prosimians and pushed these more primitive primates into marginal areas. Most prosimians now live—as endangered species—on the island of Madagascar, which they probably reached by rafting, possibly aided by a land bridge. No other primates invaded Madagascar until humans got there.

Apes appear in the fossil record about 23 mya. We refer to these earliest apes as *dental apes* because it is their teeth, rather than their overall anatomy, that resemble those of modern apes. Especially important is a feature of the molar teeth found only in hominoids and no other primates. It is called the *Y-5 cusp pattern* (Figure 10.5).

Between 23 and 5 mya, there were an estimated thirty or more different types of apes—larger-bodied, tailless, larger-brained primates. Only one lineage, however, gave rise to the modern apes and hominids. Evidence is scanty, but new fossil finds point to two African forms as candidates for the earliest hominoid. *Kenyapithecus*, from around 14 mya, had some modern ape features of the jaw, face, and teeth. More recent finds, placed by some into a new genus, *Equatorius* (S. Ward et al. 1999), indicate similarities in the arm and ankle bones that are related to the modern chimpanzee's abilities to hang in trees and to rotate the foot, which also permits walking flat-footed on the ground and grasping (McCrossin 1997).

A more ancient and more arboreal form, *Morotopithecus* from Uganda, dated at 20 mya, also shows similarities. It had a mobile shoulder joint that would have aided in hanging from trees by the arms, as chimps and orangutans do, and vertebrae that suggest a short, stiff spine, a feature of modern apes that allows them occasional upright posture (Gebo et al. 1997).

Starting about 12 mya, we find fossils of more ground-dwelling, open-country apes, whose larger back teeth with thicker enamel point to a more mixed vegetable diet that included harder foods such as nuts. Fossils of these apes have been found in Africa, India, Pakistan, China, Turkey, Hungary, and Greece. First evidence consisted of teeth and partial jaws, and an early interpretation claimed they possessed hominid traits (see Chapter 9). We know now they are too old to be hominids, and as more complete fossils have been recovered, it has become clear they are indeed apes. One group from India and Pakistan, *Sivapithecus*, shares features with the modern orangutan and so is most likely an ancestor of that species (Figure 10.6), although a new find from Thailand, *Khoratpithecus*, has been proposed as a better candidate (Chaimanee et al. 2004.) A new form from Turkey, *Ankarapithecus*, dated at 9.8 mya, also shows similarities to this group.

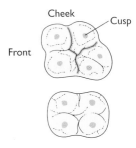

FIGURE 10.5

The Y-5 cusp pattern is found only in hominoids, and the four-cusp pattern is found in *all* anthropoids. The chewing surface is shown here. Look in the mirror, and you will probably see a Y-5 tooth, but note that not all hominid molars show this feature.

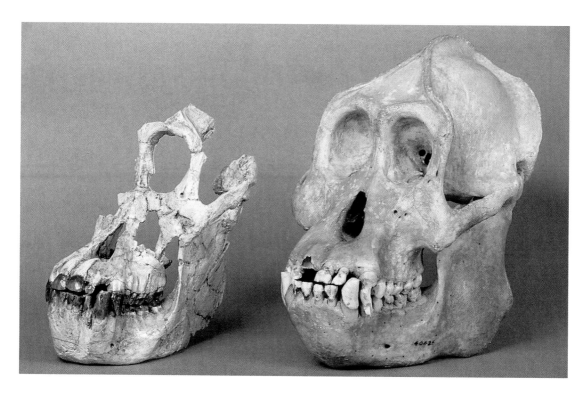

FIGURE 10.6
Skull of *Sivapithecus* (left) compared to that of a modern orangutan. They are essentially identical.

Another form, however, *Ouranopithecus*, so far only found in Greece and dated at 10 to 9 mya, shares some features with hominids. Although clearly an ape, about the size of a female gorilla, it is thought by some to be a good candidate for a member of the ape line that eventually led to the hominids (Begun 2003; De Bonis and Koufos 1994).

We can't leave this discussion without noting perhaps the most famous and the biggest sivapithecid—indeed, the biggest primate ever. This giant ape, whose fossils have been found in China, northern India, and Vietnam is called, appropriately, *Gigantopithecus* (see Figure 7.5). So far, only jaws and teeth have been found, but estimates from these indicate this primate may have been 10 to 12 feet tall when standing upright and may have weighed from 700 to 1,200 pounds. Evidence from the teeth indicate that it was, like the gorilla, a vegetarian and linked to the sivapithecid group. *Gigantopithecus* lived from about 7 mya to perhaps as recently as 300,000 ya, recently enough to have possibly encountered modern humans. (One can't help but wonder if these creatures, or at least their bones, may have given rise to legends of the famous "abominable snowman," or yeti, from the Himalayas. In any case, there is absolutely no indication that this primate still exists.)

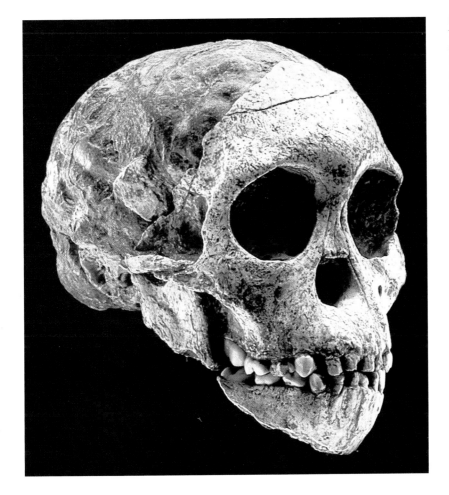

FIGURE 10.7
The "Taung Baby," the first specimen of *Australopithecus*. Note the naturally formed cast of the brain toward the back of the skull. (See also Figure 11.17.)

Current evidence indicates that apes evolved in Africa and Europe about 20 mya and diverged subsequently into a number of evolutionary lines all over the Old World. Gradually these lines decreased, leaving relatively few forms to evolve into the modern hominoids. One line that we are fairly sure of is that from *Sivapithecus* to modern orangutans. Some African form or an African population of that form gave rise to the line leading to modern African apes and hominids.

THE EARLY HOMINIDS: BIPEDAL PRIMATES

The first evidence from the dawn of hominid evolution came in 1925. South African anatomist Raymond Dart was given a fossil found in a limestone quarry at a site called Taung (Figure 10.7). It took Dart seventy-three

FIGURE 10.8
Comparison of the placement of the foramen magnum and orientation of the spinal column relative to the skull in a nonprimate quadruped and three primates. The wolf, with equally long fore and hind limbs, has a foramen magnum toward the back of the skull with an almost horizontal orientation of the spine. The chimp, still a quadruped but with longer arms than legs, has a more forward placement with the spine extending at an angle. In the bipedal hominids we see a trend toward a more forward placement and a vertical orientation of the spine.

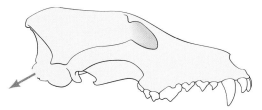

Wolf

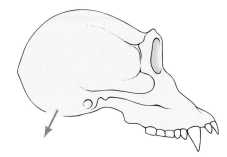

Chimpanzee

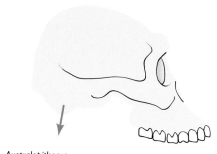

Australopithecus

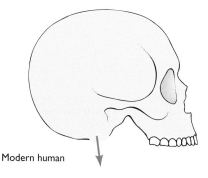

Modern human

days to separate the fossil from the limestone around it. When freed, it revealed the face, braincase, and brain cast of a young primate, apelike but for two important differences. First, the canine teeth—which are long and large in apes, with gaps to accommodate them when the jaws are shut—were no bigger than those of a human child. Second was the position of the **foramen magnum.** This is the hole in the base of the skull through which the spinal cord extends from the brain and around the outside of which the top vertebra articulates. In the Taung specimen, this hole was well underneath the skull rather than toward the back, as in apes, indicating an upright, bipedal posture rather than a quadrupedal one (Figure 10.8). Dart hypothesized that the "Taung Baby," as it came to be known, was an intermediate between apes and hominids. Nevertheless, he named it *Australopithecus africanus*, the "southern ape of Africa"; because of its many apelike traits, he wasn't ready to formally classify it in the human family.

Further finds in Africa substantiated Dart's assessment of the anatomy of his fossil and his opinion that it represented a new type of primate. Those finds also made it clear that *Australopithecus*, rather than being an intermediary, was in fact a hominid, a bipedal primate. (The rules of scientific nomenclature, or taxonomic names, however, require that first-used names stick even if they later prove to be descriptively inaccurate. Thus, these hominids are still named "southern apes.")

The story that the early hominid fossils tell is by no means clear or agreed upon by everyone. But we can begin with some reasonably well-established fossil forms and dates, which will provide a basic understanding of this period of human evolution. With these as a basis, in the following section we can examine some of the newer and more controversial fossils and consider some of the ways to put all these data together.

First, a general orientation. All the fossils discussed here belong to family Hominidae. Within that family anthropologists now generally acknowledge four defined genera: *Ardipithecus, Australopithecus, Paranthropus,* and *Homo.* Only the last genus still exists; the other three are extinct. These groups may be distinguished by the following definitions, on which I'll elaborate:

Family Hominidae: the bipedal primates (by the traditional definition we'll use here)

Genus *Ardipithecus:* the most apelike hominids

Genus *Australopithecus:* small-brained, gracile (slender) hominids with a mixed vegetable/fruit diet

Genus *Paranthropus:* small-brained, robust hominids with a grassland vegetable diet

Genus *Homo:* large-brained, omnivorous hominids

foramen magnum: The hole in the base of the skull through which the spinal cord emerges and around the outside of which the top vertebra articulates.

TABLE 10.1
Summary of Well-Established Early Fossil Hominid Species

	Ard. ramidus*	A. anamensis	A. afarensis	A. africanus	P. robustus	P. boisei
Dates	4.4 mya	4.2–3.8 mya	3.9–3 mya	3–2.3 mya	2.2–1.5 mya (?)	2.2–1 mya
Sites	Middle Awash/ Aramis	Lake Turkana	Hadar Omo Laetoli Maka Lake Turkana	Taung Sterkfontein Makapansgat Lake Turkana (?) Omo (?)	Kromdraai Swartkrans Drimolen	Olduvai Lake Turkana Omo
Cranial capacity (in ml)	(no data)	(no data)	380–500 mean = 440	370–515 mean = 440	520 (based on one specimen)	500–530 mean = 515
Estimated size (average, in lb)	(no data)	114	110	100	105	101
Skull	Canines human-shaped but large Small molars as in apes Foramen magnum forward (?)	Canines large, but hominidlike canine roots More apelike chin than A. afarensis Tooth rows parallel as in apes	Very prog-nathous Receding chin Large teeth Pointed canine with gap Shape of tooth row between ape and human Hint of sagittal crest	Less prog-nathous than A. afarensis Jaw more rounded Large back teeth Canines smaller than P. robus-tus, larger than A. afarensis No sagittal crest	Heavy jaws Small canines and front teeth Large back teeth Definite sagittal crest	Very large jaws Very large back teeth Large sagittal crest
Postcranial skeleton	(no published data)	Bipedal knee and ankle joints Fibula inter-mediate between ape and hominid	Long arms Short thumb Curved fingers and toes Bipedal	Similar to A. afarensis but possibly with longer arms and shorter legs	Hands and feet more like modern humans Retention of long arms	Similar to P. robustus

*There is another, older proposed species of *Ardipithecus*, which we will discuss in the next section under new, more controversial forms.

Table 10.1 summarizes information on the well-established species of these genera, and Figure 10.9 shows the important fossil sites discussed in this chapter.

It should be noted that authorities are about evenly divided on the issue of whether *Paranthropus* is a separate genus or is part of *Australo-*

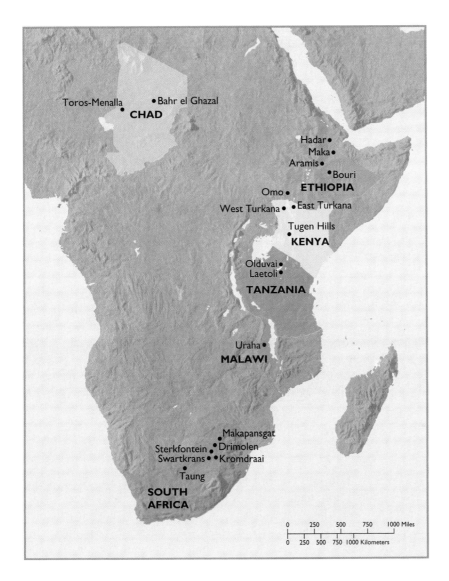

FIGURE 10.9
Map of major early fossil hominid sites.

pithecus. I will use the first option here, in part because I think the evidence warrants it but mostly because using a different name makes understanding the evolutionary trends of this complex period a little easier.

The earliest-known hominid fossils were first discovered in Ethiopia in 1992 and 1993. The finds consisted of seventeen fossil fragments, including some arm bones, two skull bases, a child's mandible, and some teeth (Figure 10.10). These fossils were different enough from any found

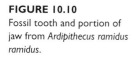

FIGURE 10.10

Fossil tooth and portion of jaw from *Ardipithecus ramidus ramidus*.

previously to warrant creating a fourth hominid genus, *Ardipithecus ramidus* (the genus name means "ground ape" and the species name means "root" in the Afar language; a second species has been added because some new finds—which we will discuss in the next section). The fossils are dated at 4.4 mya. These are the fossils mentioned in the summary in Chapter 9 that had been "ravaged by carnivores."

In 1994 more fossil bones were recovered in Ethiopia, close to the first site. These consisted of ninety fragments representing about 45 percent of a skeleton, including the telltale pelvis, leg, ankle, and foot. These new finds, however, still await published analysis.

Ardipithecus ramidus is considered a hominid because the foramen magnum is more forward than in apes and because of some detailed features of the elbow joint and the teeth. At the same time, it is "the most apelike hominid ancestor known" (White et al. 1994). Among other things, the canine teeth are larger, compared to the other teeth,

FIGURE 10.11

Mandible (*left*) and maxilla of *Australopithecus anamensis*. The chinless jaw is apelike, but the vertical root of the canine is clearly a hominid trait (the canine roots of apes are angled).

than in later hominids. It seems, then, that *Ard. ramidus* existed very close to the time when the hominids and the apes split and so may be, as the name implies, the "root" hominid species. These fossils, however, remain somewhat enigmatic for the moment. Although the evidence from the foramen magnum indicates that this species was bipedal, conclusive evidence from the legs, pelvis, and feet must wait until the newest finds can be fully examined and the results published.

In August 1995 another hominid species was announced (Leakey and Lewin 1995; C. Ward et al. 1999). Called *Australopithecus anamensis*, it consists, so far, of twenty-one specimens from the Lake Turkana region of Kenya (*anam* means "lake"), including jaws, teeth, a skull fragment, a tibia, and a humerus (Figure 10.11). The specimens are dated at 4.2 to 3.8 mya. Although they exhibit apelike features such as large canine teeth and parallel tooth rows (Figure 10.12), the root of the canine is vertical as in later hominids rather than angled as in apes, and the tooth enamel is thicker than in apes or in *Ardipithecus ramidus* and more like that in later hominids. Most notably, the leg bones are clearly those of a biped. There appears to be some consensus that *A. anamensis* may represent the ancestor of all later hominids, with *Ard. ramidus* representing a side branch of the hominid family.

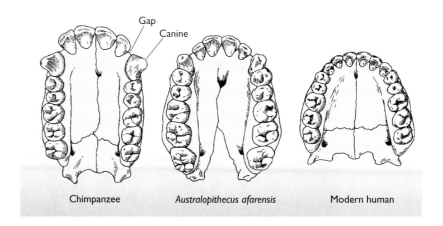

FIGURE 10.12
Comparison of upper jaws and tooth rows of chimpanzee, *Australopithecus afarensis,* and modern human. Note the parallel postcanine teeth in the chimp, the slightly divergent tooth row in the early hominid, and the divergent row in the modern human. Note also the large canines and the large gap (*diastema*) in the chimp, the lack of these in the modern human, and the intermediate state in the early hominid. *Australopithecus anamensis* has slightly larger canines than the later *A. afarensis* and tooth rows more like the ape (see Figure 10.11).

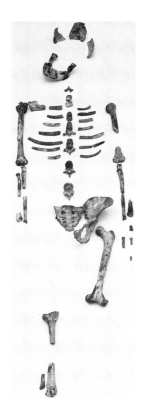

FIGURE 10.13
Skeleton of "Lucy," the first specimen of *A. afarensis.*

The next species is also well established, and its nature is generally agreed upon. The species is *Australopithecus afarensis,* and its first and most famous specimen is the 3.2-million-year-old skeleton, also from Ethiopia, known as "Lucy" (Figure 10.13), found in 1974 by Donald Johanson and his team. Lucy is remarkable because, as old as she is, nearly 40 percent of her skeleton was preserved, and all parts of her body were well represented except the cranium, the remains of which are fragmentary. We know—based on the kind of osteological analysis described in Chapter 9—that she was a female and that she stood about 3 feet 8 inches and weighed about 65 pounds. Although there is some disagreement about details, there is no doubt that Lucy and her kind were bipeds.

Other fragmentary specimens, including a portion of a skull dated at 3.9 mya, were unearthed in Ethiopia and Tanzania and assigned to this species. Based on this evidence, a reconstruction of the head of *A. afarensis* was attempted, but a single complete fossil skull was not found until 1992. In February of that year, Donald Johanson and his team discovered 200 skull fragments, again in Ethiopia. Once reconstructed, the skull closely resembled the previously discovered fragments, except that it was

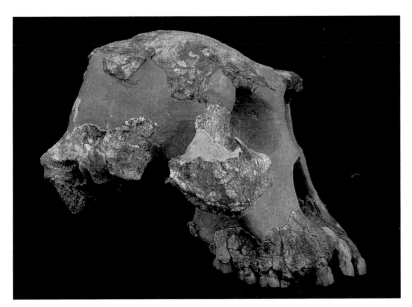

FIGURE 10.14
Side view of cranium of *Australopithecus afarensis*. Spaces between missing bones have been filled in using information from other specimens and knowledge of related species.

large and rugged, probably the skull of a male. It was dated at about 3 mya (Figure 10.14).

The evidence so far—over 300 specimens—indicates that there was a well-established hominid species, *A. afarensis*, that lived from 3.9 to 3 mya. The variation in size of the specimens fits the pattern of sexual dimorphism of apes and other early hominids. We are probably looking at the remains of both males (for example, the skull found in 1992) and females (for example, Lucy) of one species.

However, in 1995 a French team found the remains of a partial hominid jaw in Chad, in north-central Africa, dated at 3.5 to 3 mya. The team announced that this find represents a second species of hominid living during that time (Simons 1996). The species has been named *Australopithecus bahrelghazalia* (after an Arabic name for a nearby riverbed), and it suggests that early hominids were more widely spread on the continent than previously thought. Full acceptance of this classification and the implications of the fossil await further study.

What did Lucy and her kin look like? They might be described as "bipedal apes." Their average brain size was about 440 ml (a can of soda holds 355 ml), close to the average for chimpanzees and with the same maximum size of about 500 ml. *A. afarensis* had the **prognathism** (projection of the lower face and jaws), the pointy canine teeth, and the gaps

prognathism: The jutting forward of the lower face and jaw area.

FIGURE 10.15
Skull of a male gorilla. Compare the sagittal crest with those in Figures 10.23, 10.24, and 10.25.

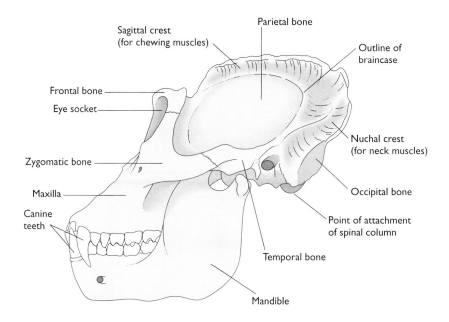

Sagittal crest (for chewing muscles)

Parietal bone

Outline of braincase

Frontal bone

Eye socket

Nuchal crest (for neck muscles)

Zygomatic bone

Occipital bone

Maxilla

Point of attachment of spinal column

Canine teeth

Temporal bone

Mandible

in the tooth rows characteristic of apes, though the canine teeth and gaps were not as pronounced as in apes. There was a hint of a **sagittal crest,** a ridge of bone along the top of the skull for the attachment of major chewing muscles. Gorillas have pronounced crests (Figure 10.15). In modern humans, these muscles are attached on the side of the head. (Put your hand on your head, about 2 inches above one ear, and then clench and unclench your teeth. You'll feel the muscle called the *temporalis.*)

At first there was some disagreement as to just how bipedal *A. afarensis* was, especially considering the apelike nature of much of the rest of its anatomy. (Disagreements continue; see Stern 2000 for a summary.) All the interpretations, after all, were based on fossilized bones; no one, obviously, had ever actually seen one walk. But in 1976 Mary Leakey recovered the next best thing at a site in Tanzania called Laetoli—a set of footprints made in a fresh layer of volcanic ash that quickly hardened and preserved for us a striking picture of an event that took place 3.7 mya. Two hominids, one large, one small, had walked side-by-side through the ash shortly after an eruption. The hominids' footprints show an anatomy and stride no different from ours today (Figure 10.16).

Thus, fossils assigned to the various species of genus *Australopithecus* are generally agreed to represent an important early stage in the establishment of the hominid family, with *Ardipithecus ramidus* being a

sagittal crest: A ridge of bone, running from front to back along the top of the skull, for the attachment of chewing muscles.

FIGURE 10.16
The larger photograph shows the Laetoli footprints from Tanzania. The inset shows a reconstruction from the American Museum of Natural History in New York City of male and female *A. afarensis*, who are thought to have made these footprints.

reasonable representative for an even earlier, more apelike stage. For many years this was all the concrete evidence we had to study our beginnings. But in the last few years mostly older fossils have been discovered, and while they will eventually shed light on hominid origins, at the moment the waters are even muddier.

SEARCHING FOR THE FIRST HOMINIDS

There are four new fossil forms that have been described and named recently. Some authorities think that each form represents an important step in the evolution of the hominids in general or of genus *Homo* in particular. As always, of course, there are disagreements and controversy.

In March 2001 Meave Leakey, daughter of Louis and Mary Leakey, announced a new hominid genus (Leakey et al. 2001). It is based on a fairly complete, although distorted cranium and a mandible, found in 1998 and 1999 in Kenya and reliably dated at 3.5 mya (Figure 10.17). The fossils show a combination of features unlike that of any other forms. The brain size, some dental features, and details of the nasal region are like those of genus *Australopithecus*. But its face appears flat, it has a tall, vertically oriented cheek area, and shows no depression behind the brow ridges. In these ways, it bears a resemblance to a later hominid form from East Africa (see Figure 11.4). This set of traits in a fossil contemporaneous with *A. afarensis* led its discoverers to give it not only a new species name but a new genus name as well—*Kenyanthropus platyops* ("flat-faced hominid from Kenya"). Some authorities have suggested that this new form may be a better common ancestor for *Homo* than any species of *Australopithecus*. More evidence, however, is needed to even establish that these fossils do represent a whole new taxon; more examples with the same set of features will have to be found (White 2003).

In March 2004 a new subspecies of *Ardipithecus* was announced (Haile-Selassie et al. 2004), *Ardipithecus kadabba* (*kadabba* means "base family ancestor" in the Afar language). Found in the same Ethiopian location as *Ard. ramidus*, these fossils are older, 5.8 to 5.2 mya, and comprise a mandible, teeth, partial clavicle, hand bones, and, most important, a toe bone. The latter is said to show an angle at the joint that indicates a "toe-off" stride, as in modern human walking—in other words, evidence of habitual bipedalism at an early date. The interpretation, of course, is not without controversy; some authorities even claim these fossils represent chimpanzee ancestors (see discussion by Gee 2001; the fossils were found earlier and originally assigned to a subspecies of *Ard. ramidus*).

FIGURE 10.17
Three-quarter view of skull
of *Kenyanthropus platyops*.

In October 2000 an even older possible hominid ancestor was proposed by French paleoanthropologists (Balter 2001a), based on thirteen fossil fragments from the Tugen Hills in northwestern Kenya. The dating of these fossils—femurs, teeth, portions of a mandible—is agreed upon; they are about 5.6 to 6.2 million years old. Their identity, however, is a matter of debate. The discoverers claim the fossils represent the real ancestor of modern humans and that the other early hominids, the species of *Australopithecus*, are side branches. *Ardipithecus kadabba,* they say, is a chimp ancestor. They base their claim on their assessment that this hominid—placed by them into a new genus and species, *Orrorin tugenensis* (*orrorin* means "original man" in the local dialect)—was bipedal and exhibited expressions of certain traits that were more modern than those of other early hominids. Features of the head of the femur and grooves for muscle and ligament attachments are said to point to bipedalism. If true, that would place the origin of bipedalism nearly 2 million years earlier than the earliest existing bipedal fossil forms. Other authorities disagree with this analysis, and some question whether this form even *is* a hominid (Haile-Selassie 2001).

The most recent candidate for "first hominid" is a find from the Toros-Menalla site in northern Chad consisting of a cranium, jaw fragment, and

This view, of course, has its detractors. One group (Wolpoff et al. 2002) claims that the supposed hominid features of *Sahelanthropus* have other explanations and, in fact, that this form was not bipedal and, indeed, "was an ape" (582). (See Brunet 2002 for a counterargument.)

Clearly, however—no matter what these fossils turn out to be—bipedalism was the first hominid trait to evolve. Those changes in posture and locomotion are essentially the only changes we see in the early hominids for a few million years, indicating that the original branching that led to the hominids occurred relatively quickly. If the branching had been a slow process, it would have involved a collection of traits in concert with bipedalism. Instead, bipedalism was strongly and quickly selected for, and all the other traits that came to be characteristic of our family of primates came later. Bipedalism is thus the first adaptation that began our family of primates.

BIPEDALISM

The Benefits of Bipedalism

What's the benefit of standing upright, an adaptation that involved major realignments of much of the body of a quadrupedal animal? Under what circumstances was it selected for in the earliest members of our lineage?

Not many creatures use this form of locomotion. Kangaroos do and birds do—and many dinosaurs did—but they also use their tails for balance and support and walk with the knees bent and the trunk sloping forward. Birds' feet are essentially prehensile; they can even sleep perched on a branch. Human bipedalism, although it obviously works quite well, involves a large number of individual physical features and evolutionary changes (see Figure 9.5) and remarkable acts of coordination. When we stand and walk, with our trunk erect and knees straight, we have to balance our bodies vertically on two relatively small points of contact with the ground. We can't run particularly fast, and we aren't very stable on rough or slippery surfaces.

What makes this adaptive change even more puzzling is some recent strong evidence suggesting that rather than evolving from completely arboreal ancestors who came directly "out of the trees," we evolved from apes with a specialized terrestrial adaptation. This adaptation, called **knuckle walking** (exhibited by modern apes), is a form of locomotion that involves placing the backs of the middle joints of the fingers on the

knuckle walking: Walking on the backs of the knuckles of the hand, typical of the African apes.

ground (see the gorilla in Figure 9.5). This adaptation allows the individual to hold a small object in its prehensile hand and walk at the same time. The wrist joints (specifically the distal portion, or hand end, of the radius) of the earliest established hominids, *Australopithecus anamensis* and *A. afarensis*, share a trait with chimps and gorillas that helps keep the arm rigid while walking in this fashion (Begun 2000; Collard and Aiello 2000; Richmond and Strait 2000). It seems reasonable, then, that the common ancestor of the African apes and hominids also had this feature. So if our common ancestor *already* had a specialized adaptation to walking on the ground (on all fours), why did our lineage evolve an even more specialized and complex one (bipedalism)?

Compare the map of early hominid sites (see Figure 10.9) with the map of Africa's climatic and vegetation zones (Figure 10.19). Note that the sites are located in savannas or tropical deciduous forests (open grasslands or woodlands more open than the rain forest and with trees that undergo seasonal cycles of growth). Where these zones meet, there is a mix of forest and open areas, as one zone grades into another.

Open areas, particularly the savannas, present a very different set of problems to a primate than do dense forests. Primates are basically vegetarian. Although there are plenty of plants on the savannas, there are not as many that can be utilized by the digestive systems of most primates. Most primates cannot digest cellulose as can the *ungulates* (grazing animals such as the African antelopes). Edible plants or plants with edible parts—at least for a hominoid primate—are not as concentrated on the open plains or even open forests. As a result, primates living in such areas have to travel over a wider area to find food. These areas are more affected by seasonal change than are the rain forests, and so there may be greater variation between the wet and dry seasons. This, too, creates the need for more traveling in search of food. Finally, there is more danger involved in acquiring these widely dispersed foods. Lions, leopards, cheetahs, wild dogs, hyenas, and other predators of the plains and open forests are more than happy to make a meal out of a small primate, as we saw in Chapter 9.

There are, of course, sources of meat, both in the forests and especially on the open savannas with their great herds of herbivores. Chimpanzees are known to hunt, kill, and eat small mammals such as monkeys. They are even known to scavenge kills that leopards have left hanging in trees—although rarely (Byrne and Byrne 1988; Cavallo 1990). While our earliest ancestors may have hunted small animals, it is unlikely they preyed on big game or even animals as large as those hunted by chimps. They were not as mobile in the trees as the chimps

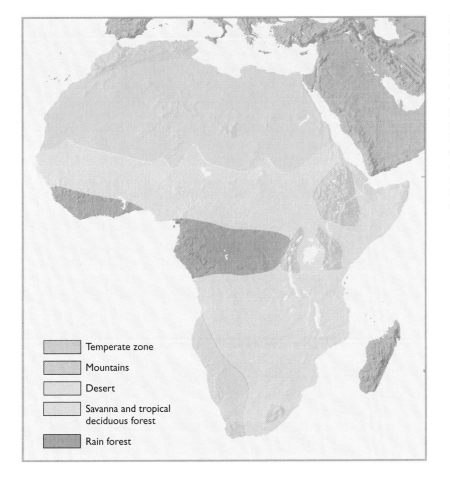

FIGURE 10.19
General climatic and vegetation zones of Africa today. Except for the large deserts in the north and south, the zones are much the same as when our evolutionary story began some 5 mya, although specific local conditions may have differed. Moreover, where zones meet, the conditions grade into one another, producing an area of mixed vegetation and other conditions.

Temperate zone

Mountains

Desert

Savanna and tropical deciduous forest

Rain forest

(having legs adapted to bipedalism), and they lacked the powerful musculature and large interlocking canine teeth of the apes (see Figures 8.4 and 10.15). And, so far at least, there is no physical evidence of big-game hunting on the plains. There is, however, evidence that they scavenged kills, which we will cover in the next chapter. Still, although scavenging provided access to meat, it was dangerous. The carcasses had to be taken away and kept away from other predators or scavenged after the predators had finished.

So, we may ask not only how bipedalism could be a benefit for terrestrial walking, but we can structure our inquiry more precisely by asking how it would be adaptive in such a mix of environments.

Explaining the Emergence of Bipedalism

Six different models have been proposed to account for the evolution of bipedalism under the environmental conditions just described.

1. *Carrying model.* Bipedalism could have allowed our early ancestors to search for and collect food in greater safety and with greater efficiency. Freeing the arms and hands from a role in locomotion would have meant that our ancestors could transport food from open areas to safer locations, such as a grove of trees or perhaps the foot of a steep hill. This would have been especially important if the food were part of an animal carcass, since other meat eaters would also have found it attractive. Moreover, bipedalism would have allowed mothers to carry children in their arms while walking in search of food. Perhaps our ancestors carried sticks and rocks to throw at predators and scavengers to scare them away from a kill. (Chimps will occasionally hurl rocks and sticks, though not particularly accurately.) Under experimental conditions (Videan and McGrew 2000), it has been shown that having something to carry is a major stimulus for bipedal locomotion in chimpanzees and bonobos (see Figure 8.6). However, Jablonski and Chaplin (2000a) claim that if bipedal carrying of anything other than small, light objects had been a major selective focus, there would have been other changes as well, such as an enlargement of the lower (lumbar) vertebrae, as seen in modern humans. But this feature had not evolved early on in our evolution, not even in the earliest members of genus *Homo* (about 2.4 mya).

2. *Vigilance model.* It has been proposed that bipedalism, by elevating the head, helped our ancestors locate potential sources of food and danger. Observe, for example, how squirrels sit upright to better look around. Videan and McGrew's (2000) experiment, just noted, showed this to be an important factor in the use of bipedalism, at least in their controlled studies among captive apes. In fact, it was the most frequent context of upright posture. It should be noted here, however, that this model only addresses upright posture, not necessarily upright locomotion.

3. *Heat dissipation model.* According to another view, the vertical orientation of bipedalism helps cool the body by presenting a smaller target to the intense equatorial rays of the sun and by placing more of the body above the ground to catch any cooling air currents. The savanna can be hot, and the heat built up by hours of walking in search of food needs to be dissipated. (This factor may also explain the adaptive significance of the relatively hairless bodies of modern

hominids. Having no hair allows sweat to evaporate more quickly and cool the body more efficiently.) This model, of course, would not apply to the forests, where primates would be sheltered by the shade of trees.

4. *Energy efficiency model.* Data indicate that although bipedalism is an energy-inefficient way of running compared to quadrupedalism, it is *more* efficient for walking. For example, a 154-pound man uses 140 more joules of energy per meter walking than standing still and 260 more joules running than standing still. A 154-pound quadrupedal mammal uses 200 more joules of energy per meter both walking and running (Alexander 1995). Long periods of steady bipedal walking in search of food, then, would seem to require less energy. Remember, however, that the first hominids may not have walked bipedally quite like later members of our family, and they may not have been any more efficient at walking upright than are chimpanzees. Moreover, it is not certain that what makes our walking more efficient is simply our upright stance. Body mass and other anatomical features may be related as well. So, as Steudel (1996) maintains, efficiency may not have been the initial key factor in selection for bipedal locomotion. It may be that bipedalism had, at first, other advantages and that once it was established, further anatomical changes made it more energy efficient.

5. *Foraging/bipedal harvesting model.* This idea refers to the benefits of standing upright to reach sources of food on bushes and trees, particularly those difficult or impossible to climb. The introduction of raised feeding structures in Videan and McGrew's experiment stimulated bipedal posture in chimps.

6. *Display model.* Jablonski and Chaplin (2000a) propose that the important factor of bipedalism was an upright display posture like that seen in chimps during dominance confrontations and, to a lesser extent, in male bonobos (who sometimes also stand erect, in both senses, as a sexual display). Among these primates, an upright display posture conveys meaning because it makes the individual seem larger; it is also directly related to mating success. Although chimps and bonobos devote relatively little time to this behavior, its adaptive and evolutionary impact among our ancestors, the authors suggest, could still have been great. In their experiment, Videan and McGrew (2000) noted that the introduction of display objects (things the animals could wave around or make noise with) increased rates of bipedalism among chimps, though not among bonobos.

Each of these models has logic and evidence in its support, and each could be argued against as being an important adaptive focus. It seems reasonable, at the moment, to provisionally suppose that *all* these factors, acting together, could have played an adaptive role in the emergence of the hominid lineage and its characteristic mode of locomotion. But do these models—other than the display model—explain why bipedalism would have made some individuals, and eventually some groups, more reproductively successful? Remember that reproductive success is the measure of natural selection. Simple survival and longevity are only part of it.

Once again, we may get a clue from our close relatives, the chimps and bonobos, the former an open-forest species and the latter an inhabitant of dense forests. Although chimps normally have no need to share resources, they do share meat from a hunt, possibly because it is—in some chimp way—considered a luxury item. Bonobos, on the other hand, share even foods that are plentiful. This serves to avoid conflict and to establish and maintain peaceful coexistence within the group. Food sharing is, in a sense, a symbol of group peace and unity. In times of need, of course, food sharing might have practical consequences. Moreover, as you recall from Chapter 8, the bonobos use sex—in various combinations and with a variety of techniques—to strengthen and maintain group unity and to defuse tension. Sex for them is separate from purely reproductive activity. It has social and psychological meaning as well.

Perhaps, then, our earliest ancestors survived by the enhancement of adaptations that promoted peaceful cooperation and group unity, including the sharing of resources. The acquisition of these resources was made easier, safer, and more energy efficient by the ability to walk habitually upright.

Such a set of adaptations would certainly have been one way of aiding survival on the floor of open forests and out on the savannas. But remember that our earliest ancestors also exhibited traits associated with an arboreal adaptation: relatively long arms; heavy shoulder girdles, arm bones, and arm muscles; and curved finger and toe bones. Perhaps in the earliest stages of our lineage our ancestors were adapted to both a tree-climbing *and* a terrestrial, open-area way of life. And environmental data bear this out.

Reassessment of the specific local environments of some important early hominid sites has shown them to be more forested than previously thought (see Shreeve 1996 for a summary and C. Ward et al. 1999 for recent descriptions). *Ardipithecus ramidus* lived in a high-altitude dense woodland and *Ard. kadabba* in a wet, wooded environment. *Orrorin* lived in a wooded habitat. *Sahelanthropus* inhabited a "swampy, vegetated" area near some open grasslands and gallery forest (Vignaud et al. 2002:155). The Lake Turkana site where *Australopithecus anamensis* was found may have been an arid area, but the lake itself was surrounded by forest, and there were woodlands associated with rivers. Lucy, the first specimen of A. *afarensis*, probably lived in a mixed forest and bushland area, and Laetoli was open grassland with scattered trees and forests nearby. A. *bahrelghazalia* from Chad is thought to have inhabited forests with grassy patches. There is, in fact, evidence that East Africa at the time was a "heterogeneous mosaic" of environments, from forests to open plains (Kingston et al. 1994:958). The same appears to be true of southern Africa, home to other early hominids to be discussed in the next section.

Indeed, Richard Potts (1996, 1998) gives evidence that the past 6 million years marks a period of increasing environmental fluctuations that produced great oscillations in moisture and vegetation in Africa. Our early ancestors, he says, encountered a variety of environments and underwent selection for the ability to live in both densely wooded and open habitats. Potts calls this "variability selection"—adaptations that result in "flexible, novel responses to surroundings and diversity" that can "buffer" a species against "episodic change" in its environment (1998:86). The retention of arboreal features accompanied by the enhancement of bipedal locomotion would seem to be a perfect example of this sort of adaptation, along with, perhaps, other changes that enhanced social cooperation and resource sharing.

Finally, the isolation of our ancestors from the ancestors of the modern African apes may have been reinforced by a geological change—the formation of the Great Rift Valley in East Africa starting about 8 mya (Figure 10.20). Tectonic movements caused some land to sink, forming the valley, with mountains on its western rim. This in turned caused a localized climatic change: the area west of the valley remained moist and heavily forested, and that east of the valley turned drier to become savanna and more open forest. Today, chimpanzees are found only in the valley or to the west. Early hominid fossils, with the exception of the Chad find, have been found only in the valley or to the east.

The details about the early evolution of our hominid family and its characteristic traits are still being debated. Clearly, however, the hominid line had emerged by perhaps 6 to 5 mya in a mixed and fluctuating woodland and savanna environment. Clearly, too, the trait that distinguishes the hominids from the other primates is bipedalism, although it first evolved in organisms that retained arboreal features as well—an adaptation to a variable and changing environment. Accompanying upright locomotion was, perhaps, an emphasis on group unity and survival facilitated by food sharing and perhaps by sexual activity separated from purely reproductive functions and linked to emotional, social, and personal relationships.

Whatever happened, it was successful. At least one hominid species was well ensconced in East Africa by 3 mya. From there our family began to branch out.

FIGURE 10.20

Portion of the Great Rift Valley in southern Kenya. The Great Rift Valley, formed some 8 mya, stretches 3,500 miles from Mozambique to the Red Sea and is over 2,000 feet deep in some places. Many lakes, such as the Little Magadi, shown in the photograph, lie in the valley.

THE HOMINIDS EVOLVE

More Australopithecines

The basic set of early hominid features represented by Lucy and her kin continued for another three-quarters of a million years. Although little changed from *Australopithecus afarensis*, the fossils representing the next period are still called by their original name, A. *africanus* (Dart's "southern ape of Africa"). The remains of this species have been found mostly

FIGURE 10.21
Skull of *Australopithecus
africanus* (female?) from
Sterkfontein, South Africa.
Note the general similarity
to *A. afarensis* (Fig 10.14).

in South Africa, but there are some fossils from Kenya and Ethiopia as well. They have the same body size and shape and the same brain size as *A. afarensis*. There are a few differences, however (Figure 10.21). Their faces are a bit less prognathous, and they lack a sagittal crest. Their canine teeth are smaller, there are no gaps in the tooth row, and the tooth row is more rounded, as in a human rather than an ape (see Figure 10.12).

The relative size and shape of the teeth of both *A. afarensis* and *A. africanus*, on the whole larger than those of modern humans, indicate a mostly mixed vegetable diet of fruits and leaves. This is confirmed by analysis of microscopic scratches and wear patterns on the teeth (Figure 10.22). There is no direct evidence of meat eating, but a recent study (Sponheimer and Lee-Thorp 1999) of a carbon isotope (^{13}C) in the tooth enamel of a sample of *A. africanus* indicated that members of this species ate either tropical grasses or the flesh of animals that ate tropical grasses or both. (Grasses have more ^{13}C in their tissues than do other types of plants.) Because the dentition examined by these researchers lacked the tooth wear patterns indicative of grass eating, the carbon may have come from grass-eating animals. While these grass-eating animals

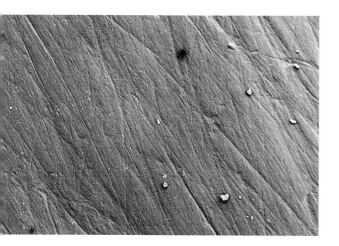 

FIGURE 10.22

Scanning electron microscope pictures of teeth surfaces of early hominids. The enamel of the teeth of *Australopithecus africanus* (*left*) is polished and scratched, while that of *Paranthropus* (*right*) is pitted and very rough. This is evidence of the hard, tough, gritty foods eaten by the latter.

may have been plant-eating insects, there is the possibility that the australopithecines either hunted small animals or scavenged the carcasses of larger ones. There is also evidence that early hominids dug up rootstocks (tubers, rhizomes, and bulbs), although prior to the use of fire for cooking, this would have required some other means of deactivating toxins found in some of these food sources, such as crushing, soaking, or drying (Ragir 2000). It is noteworthy in this regard that some early bone tools from South Africa, formerly interpreted as showing signs of tuber digging, are now seen as having wear patterns associated with opening termite mounds (Holden 2001b).

The essential similarity of A. *afarensis* and A. *africanus* suggests a plausible, and simple, interpretation: that A. *africanus* is a continuation of A. *afarensis*, more widely distributed in southern and possibly eastern Africa and showing some evolutionary changes. It should be noted that this interpretation is not agreed upon by all investigators and remains hypothetical. Moreover, this simple linear relationship is confounded by the suggestion of some older dates, of 4 mya, for the South African site of Sterkfontein (Patridge et al. 2003). So if A. *africanus* and A. *afarensis* are contemporaries, their relationship is more complex; perhaps they are either members of the same species, or of different species living at the same time.

Some recent evidence lends support to the meat-eating interpretation and to the definition of another new hominid species. The site of Bouri in Ethiopia, dated at 2.5 mya, has revealed (in separate locations) hominid cranial and postcranial bones, as well as the bones of antelopes, horses, and other animals that exhibit cut marks made by stone tools (Asfaw et al. 1999; Culotta 1999b; de Heinzelin et al. 1999). The cranial bones indicate a brain size of 450 ml, and the prognathous jaw is similar to that of *A. afarensis*. Several features of the teeth resemble those of early *Homo*, but the molars are unusually large, even larger than those of the southern African robust hominids called *Paranthropus* (to be discussed next). This set of traits led investigators to designate these bones as a new species, *Australopithecus garhi* (*garhi* means "surprise" in a local language). The postcranial remains from Bouri, not clearly from the same species as the cranial specimens, show the relative lengths of the upper arm and upper leg to be humanlike, while the lower arm remains long, as in apes. This may indicate that in the evolution of human limb proportions, the leg elongated first and the arm shortened later. Finally, the stone-tool cut marks on the animal bones show that whatever hominid (not necessarily *A. garhi*) made them was butchering animals for meat and smashing bones to get at the fat-rich marrow.

The evolutionary relationship of *A. garhi* to other hominids is still a matter of debate. Its discoverers (Asfaw et al. 1999) feel it is descended from *A. afarensis* and is a direct ancestor of *Homo*. Others disagree (Strait and Grine 1999; and see Culotta 1999a). Clearly, more evidence is needed to interpret these specimens more precisely, but they do show the extent of the variation among hominids during this period.

Still More Hominids

Between 3 and 2 mya, two new types of hominids appear in the fossil record, two new genera by the approach used here: *Paranthropus* and our genus *Homo*. One type retains the chimpanzee-sized brains and small bodies of *Australopithecus* but has evolved a notable robusticity in the areas of the skull involved with chewing. This is genus *Paranthropus*. As noted before, some authorities place these fossils in genus *Australopithecus*, but I will use *Paranthropus* both for clarity and because I lean toward that interpretation of current evidence (McCollum 1999).

The fossils representing the beginning of this genus are a single skull from Lake Turkana, Kenya—dubbed the "Black Skull" because of its dark color resulting from minerals in the ground (Figure 10.23)—and some fragmentary fossils from Ethiopia. These fossils are grouped into a separate species, *Paranthropus aethiopicus*, and are dated at between 2.8 and 2.2 mya.

The Black Skull is striking for several reasons. First, at only 410 ml, it has the smallest adult brain ever found in any well-established

hominid. Also, it has the largest sagittal crest of any hominid, the most prognathous face, and an extremely large area in the back of the mouth for the molar teeth. Although no teeth were found, its molars appear to have been four or five times the size of a modern human's.

The Black Skull represents the beginning of a second major type of hominid, sometimes referred to as "robust" hominids. Although they were pretty much the same as *Australopithecus* in brain and body size, the members of genus *Paranthropus* were considerably more robust in all those features involved with chewing. The sagittal crest; broad, dished-out face; large cheekbones; huge mandible; and back teeth that are much larger relative to the front teeth—all point to a diet of large amounts of vegetable matter with an emphasis on hard, tough, gritty items such as

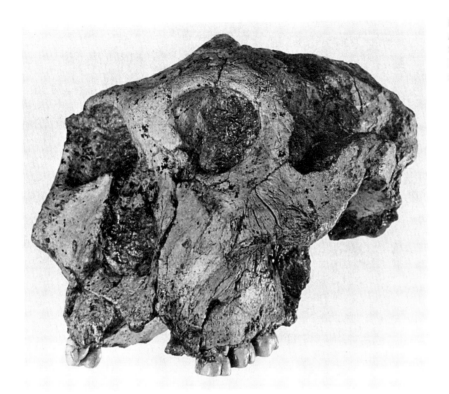

FIGURE 10.24
Paranthropus robustus from Swartkrans, South Africa. Note the remnant of a sagittal crest.

seeds, nuts, hard fruits, and tubers. This is confirmed by microscopic wear pattern analysis (see Figure 10.22).

A little over 2 mya, two more types of robust hominids appear. One species, *Paranthropus robustus*, was found in South Africa and dates between 2.2 and 1.5 mya or even later (Figure 10.24). It retains the body size of *Australopithecus*, but there is a slight increase in average brain capacity to about 520 ml. The jaws are heavy, the back teeth are large, and there is a sagittal crest—all indications of a mixed, tough vegetable diet. The crania, though, are obviously not as robust as in *P. aethiopicus*.

The second robust species continues the extreme ruggedness of *P. aethiopicus*, though it is not quite as pronounced. Found in Tanzania, Kenya, and Ethiopia and existing from 2.2 to 1 mya, *Paranthropus boisei* shows features that, along with those of *P. aethiopicus*, are sometimes referred to as "hyperrobust" (Figure 10.25). The specimen that defined the species is the famous "Zinjanthropus," found by Mary and Louis

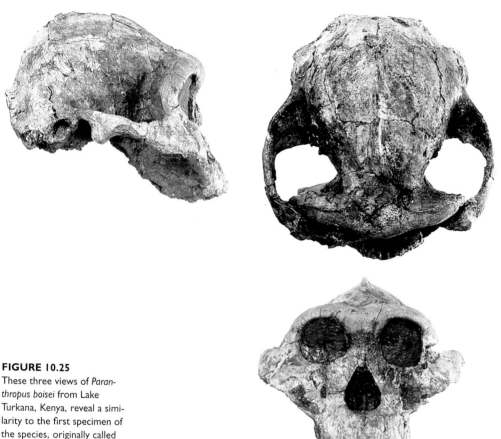

FIGURE 10.25
These three views of *Paranthropus boisei* from Lake Turkana, Kenya, reveal a similarity to the first specimen of the species, originally called "Zinjanthropus."

Leakey in 1959. Dubbed "Nutcracker Man," this specimen has extremely large jaws and back teeth and a large sagittal crest. Otherwise *P. boisei* has the body and brain size of the South African robust hominids.

A recent *P. boisei* fossil from Ethiopia (Suwa et al. 1997) consists of the first cranium of this species with an associated mandible. The largest-known skull of the species, it comes from a new site that extends the species' known range in Africa and is clearly associated with a dry grassland environment. It also shows some physical differences from existing *boisei* fossils that indicate a considerable range of phenotypic variation within the species.

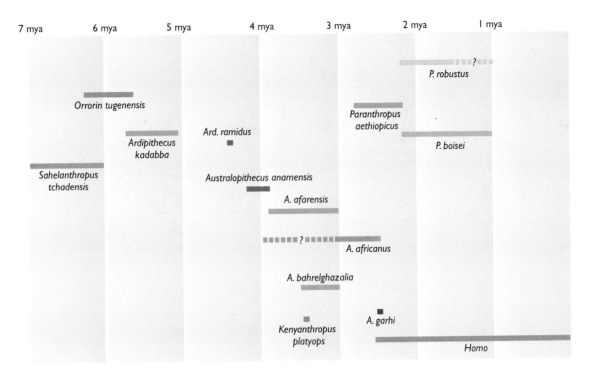

FIGURE 10.26
The fossils discussed in this chapter with their currently accepted time ranges. The dotted lines indicate possible extensions of those ranges.

The second new hominid genus that appeared about 2.5 mya is the one to which modern humans belong, *Homo*. We will discuss the early species of our genus in the next chapter. For now, however, we need to discuss the overall shape of the early hominid family tree.

Putting It All Together

Figure 10.26 shows the dates of all the established and proposed early hominid fossils discussed in this chapter (with *Homo* added for perspective and a preview of what's to come). A number of different specific models have been proposed for connecting all these fossils into an evolutionary tree. Most authorities generally agree that the hominids from about 4 mya on can be grouped into two natural categories, the gracile and the robust (here, *Australopithecus* and *Paranthropus*, although some lump them all into the first genus). I've grouped them in the timeline to reflect this. There is also general agreement that it was some member of the gracile hominids that gave rise to *Homo*. A simple tree, then, would look like this:

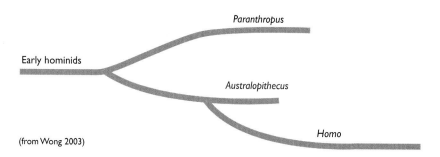

Paranthropus

Early hominids

Australopithecus

Homo

(from Wong 2003)

There is a difference of opinion as to *which* australopithecine is the direct ancestor of *Homo*, and authorities have different favorite candidates. Some have suggested that our direct ancestor was not an australopithecine at all but *Kenyanthropus platyops*, although more specimens are required to verify the validity of this taxon and its traits.

There is even more debate over the newest fossil finds: *Ardipithecus kadabba*, *Orrorin tugenensis*, and *Sahelanthropus tchadensis*. With relatively scanty evidence so far, and with different body parts represented by the existing fossils, comparison and analysis are necessarily very tentative. At one extreme (see Wong 2003) is the idea that those three are lineal descendants, all on the line to *Homo*:

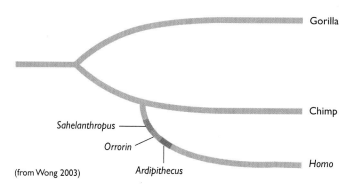

Gorilla

Chimp

Sahelanthropus

Orrorin

Ardipithecus

Homo

(from Wong 2003)

The opposite extreme has the three representing ancestors of three different genera:

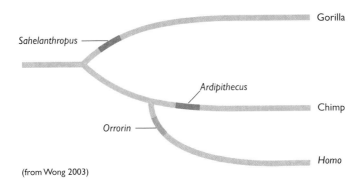

(from Wong 2003)

What *is* clear, however, is that with these three fossils (if further evidence shows they represent valid groups and are not anomalous individuals), we are close to the common ancestor of the chimps and us. Perhaps, as Bernard Wood has suggested (2002:134), none of these is *the* earliest hominid, that these fossils are "the tip of an iceberg of taxonomic diversity" during early hominid evolution and that there were many different combinations of traits in "an adaptive radiation of fossil ape-like creatures that included the common ancestor of humans and chimpanzees." Time and more fossils will presumably clarify the whole story.

We may address some other general questions about this period. What might have caused the branching that founded the new genera of *Paranthropus* and *Homo*? What caused the extinction, around the same time, of genus *Australopithecus*? Finally, what might have caused the extinction of the *Paranthropus* species about 1 mya?

We can't answer these questions with certainty, but recall Richard Potts's evidence for a sharp increase in environmental variability in Africa starting about 6 mya and continuing—and further increasing—through time (1996, 1998). There is also evidence for a major and abrupt change about 2.8 mya—an intensification of cycles that produced a shift toward grasslands. (Kerr 2001). Increased environmental variability resulting in a series of newly emerging, complex, and diverse habitats may have initially promoted different adaptations among hominid populations, as seen in the branching that gave rise to the robust hominids and to *Homo*. But if the degree of the fluctuations continued to increase,

Contemporary Reflections

Where Is the "Missing Link"?

A headline in the 19 December 1912 issue of the *New York Times* proclaimed, "Paleolithic Skull Is a Missing Link." The skull referred to was the now-infamous "Piltdown Man," discovered in England, named *Eoanthropus* (the "dawn man")—and forty years later shown to be a fraud (see Feder 2001 for details). At the time, however, it was touted as the "missing link" because it possessed traits that were a perfect mix between those of human and ape. Its cranium was the shape and size of a modern human's, and its mandible was decidedly apelike. (In fact, the cranium *was* of a modern human and the jaw *was* of a modern orangutan—modified by the still-unidentified perpetrator to appear ancient.)

For much of the history of evolutionary thought, evolution was conceived of as a ladder or a chain, progressing from primitive to modern, with living forms representing points on that chain. Even when it was generally acknowledged that humans had descended from apes, this evolution was thought of as unilinear—a single line of progress from ape to man. Thus, as we go back into the fossil record, we should eventually find something that is intermediate—half ape and half human. Since modern apes were thought of as the remnants of primitive forms that had never evolved further, the missing link (notice the chain metaphor) was conceived of as a mix of the traits of *modern* humans and *modern* apes. In our hubris, we were sure it was our big brains that separated us from the apes and that had evolved first, so the combination fabricated to concoct the Piltdown skull fit the bill perfectly. It had that big-brain hallmark of humanity, perched on top of an otherwise apelike jaw.

Indeed, even when evolution was recognized as being a branching tree rather than a ladder or chain, the idea of fossil forms that were intermediates between modern species still held. Famed anatomist Sir Arthur Keith wrote that "to unravel man's pedigree, we have to thread our way, not along the links of a chain, but through the meshes of a complicated network" (1927:8). Then, on the next page, he accepted the Piltdown find as authentic.

We recognize today that living species are not leftover primitive links on an evolutionary chain but are, themselves, the products of evolution. A missing link in the traditional sense—between modern humans and modern apes—simply does not exist. What *does* exist is a common ancestor of humans and our closest relatives, the chimpanzees and bonobos—and it did not look exactly like any of those modern species. Granted, we have reason to think that the common ancestor resembled a bonobo or chimp more than a modern human, but this is just because evolution happened to take place at a more rapid pace in hominids than in the apes. The apes are still modern species.

So what we *can* look for is that common ancestor. It is a "link" not in the sense of a chain, but in the sense of being that point where our two evolutionary lines converge. At the moment, that form is still missing. But as we find older and older fossils, we are closing in on our common ancestor.

What will it look like? It should have characteristics shared by both modern hominids and pongids, but it will look, on the whole, like neither. Genetic evidence suggests that our common ancestor is 5 to 7 million years old. So for the moment, the closest we've come to that elusive "missing link" are the fossils of *Ardipithecus* (see Figure 10.10), *Orrorin*, and *Sahelanthropus* (see Figure 10.18).

this may have put such pressure on the hominid adaptive responses that those groups less able to cope eventually became extinct. Unable to survive well enough to perpetuate themselves in the face of decreasing resources (this may have been the case for *Paranthropus,* who were specialized vegetarians), these now-extinct hominids were possibly outcompeted for space and resources by the better adapted, a phenomenon known as **competitive exclusion.** In this case, only the adaptive response that included an increase in brain size, with its concomitant increase in ability to understand and manipulate the environment, proved successful in the long run.

SUMMARY

The primates are one of the earliest of the existing mammal groups to evolve after the mass extinction of 65 mya. They appear to have evolved first in what are now North America and Europe, but the success of their adaptations allowed them to radiate over the Old World and into the New World.

About 23 mya, the hominoids appear in the form of primitive apes. This successful group has left fossils all over Africa, Europe, and Asia. It is from one of the African apes that our family, Hominidae, branched off 6 to 5 mya.

The evolution of habitual bipedalism marks the beginnings of our family and was the major distinguishing characteristic of this family for the first half of its time on earth. Bipedalism may have begun as part of one group's adaptation to the forests. We still see this trait—along with food sharing and sexual consciousness—in today's bonobos. However, these adaptations would also prove useful in Africa's increasingly variable environment, and the hominids soon were well established and radiated into three distinct groups, often classified as separate genera: *Australopithecus, Paranthropus,* and *Homo.*

The first two genera, *Australopithecus* and *Paranthropus,* with their chimp-sized brains, remained largely vegetarian and persisted until nearly 1 mya. They eventually lost out to a combination of environmental change and competition from the third hominid genus, *Homo,* with its bigger brain and ability to manipulate its environment. Our genus is the subject of the next chapter.

competitive exclusion: When one species outcompetes others for the resources of a particular area.

QUESTIONS FOR FURTHER THOUGHT

1. People often ask this logical question: If humans are descended from apes, then how come there are still apes? How would you respond to this?

2. Looking at the fossil record of the hominids, we see that the hominid line that survived after about 1 mya was the one with the big brain. From our perspective, this makes it seem as if our evolution was inevitable. Is this the case? Would the big-brained species have been successful in all circumstances? Once the evolution of hominids got started, were *we* a predictable result?

KEY TERMS

foramen magnum   sagittal crest   competitive exclusion

prognathism   knuckle walking

SUGGESTED READINGS

The primates and their evolution are covered in John G. Fleagle's *Primate Adaptation and Evolution*. The intriguing story of *Gigantopithecus* is told in *Other Origins: The Search for the Giant Ape in Human Prehistory*, by Russell Ciochon, John Olsen, and Jamie James. For a more technical account of early primate evolution, see R. D. Martin's article in the 20 May 1993 issue of *Nature*, "Primate Origins: Plugging the Gaps."

The story of the study of the human fossil record and of some of the major recent discoveries is told in *Lucy: The Beginnings of Humankind*, by Donald Johanson and Maitland Edey, and in a sequel, *Lucy's Child: The Discovery of a Human Ancestor*, by Donald Johanson and James Shreeve. Both of these books are somewhat outdated but still convey the excitement of paleoanthropology. A slightly different perspective on much of the same material is found in Richard Leakey and Roger Lewin's *Origins Reconsidered: In Search of What Makes Us Human*. A beautifully illustrated treatment of the subject, based on an exhibit at the American Museum of Natural History in New York, is Ian Tattersall's *The Human Odyssey: Four Million Years of Evolution*.

A *National Geographic* series, "The Dawn of Humans," covering the 6 million years of our evolution, appears in the following issues: September 1995; January and March 1996; February, May, July, and September 1997; August 1998; and May, July, and December 2000. The photographs and graphics are, as usual, superb. And see the October 2001 issue for photos of *Kenyanthropus*.

For more on the early apes and possible hominid ancestors, see David R. Begun's "Planet of the Apes" in the August 2003 *Scientific American*.

You might be interested in seeing what a primary report on an important fossil looks like. A good example is the first report on the discovery of *Sahelanthropus* by Brunet et al. in the 11 July 2002 issue of *Nature*, "A New Hominid from the Upper Miocene of Chad, Central Africa." And for a piece on all the new finds, see "An Ancestor to Call Our Own," by Kate Wong, in the January 2003 *Scientific American*.

For a nice summary of the different views on the possible climate-change influences on human evolution, see "Sunset on the Savanna," by James Shreeve, in the July 1996 issue of *Discover*. A nicely illustrated explanation of the Great Rift Valley, by Yves Coppens, appears in the May 1994 *Scientific American*, "East Side Story: The Origin of Humankind."

A review of two books on the bipedalism question, and a nice discussion of the topic in and of itself is Ian Tattersall's "Stand and Deliver" in the November 2003 *Natural History*.

THE EVOLUTION OF GENUS HOMO

The great tragedy of
Science—the slaying of
a beautiful hypothesis
by an ugly fact.
—Thomas Henry
Huxley

WilLiam of Ockham (c. 1285–1349), an English philosopher, is credited with the principle popularly known as *Ockham's razor*. The idea actually goes well back into human antiquity. Ockham said in effect that in logic, no more things should be presumed to exist than are absolutely necessary. In other words, "keep it simple."

Ockham's idea, also known as the **law of parsimony,** says that if several possible explanations exist to account for something in science or philosophy, *the simplest is the best,* at least as a starting point. It further means that explanations should be based on facts that are already known rather than on facts that *may* exist. Of course, as new facts come to light, explanations will change, and we may find that the simplest explanation is not the best one.

Applied to the interpretation of the human fossil record, Ockham's razor means that we should begin by creating a tree of relationships among fossil species that has the fewest evolutionary lines allowed by the data. It also means that we should not create new taxonomic categories unless the data support them. Moreover, we should not suggest evolutionary relationships that include a species or other taxonomic unit that may *someday* be discovered but for which no evidence exists at present.

Being simple, however, is not always so easy. There is no universal agreement on the dates of all the hominid fossils or on the interpretation of their phenotypic features or their taxonomic categories. There are, as noted, at least half a dozen different trees for the early hominids, each—according to whoever proposed it—the most parsimonious. The "correct" tree, if we can ever arrive at one, awaits more data from the fossil record.

If it is hard for us to agree on the fossils that represent the first 2.5 million years of the hominid record, it gets worse when we address the latest 2.5 million years. The reason is simple: this is the time during which our genus, *Homo,* evolved. The data from these fossils matter to us because they will tell us just who we are and where we came from.

There are widely different interpretations of the nature, dates, and taxonomic affiliations of the hominid fossils from this period, and there are several divergent schools of thought regarding just what the family tree of our genus looks like. At stake in these discussions is the very identity of the species to which we all belong. In this chapter, we will address the following questions:

How can we best go about describing and organizing the fossil evidence for the evolution of genus *Homo*?

What do we know about the dates, the distribution, and the physical appearance of the various groups of fossils assigned to genus *Homo*?

What can we say about their lives, particularly about their cultural behaviors?

LUMPERS AND SPLITTERS: AN ORGANIZING PLAN

Recall from Chapter 10 that there is disagreement over whether the early small-brained hominids all belong to one genus, *Australopithecus*, or to two genera, *Australopithecus* and *Paranthropus*. In this debate, those who support a single genus are "lumpers," and those who advocate two genera are "splitters."

Splitters tend to focus on differences among fossils and express those differences by assigning the fossils in question to different taxonomic categories—different species if the distinctions are small, different genera if they are more pronounced. Lumpers, emphasizing the extent of diversity present in living species and genera, consider differences among some fossil groups to reflect a similar degree of diversity. They believe that the most parsimonious course is to lump fossils into the same taxon unless there is clear evidence that they should be split.

Both these approaches are, of course, provisional starting points. All good scientists understand that hypotheses are open to testing and that new data may require new models—sometimes radically new ones. Time and again, someone's "beautiful hypothesis" is slayed by some new "ugly fact." Moreover, no researcher is always a splitter or a lumper. One scientist's approach can vary from group to group. I favor the two-genera classification of the early hominids (*Australopithecus* and *Paranthropus*), but as you will see, I favor a lumping model with regard to genus *Homo*.

The lumping and splitting factions are very much at odds regarding the evolution of genus *Homo*. At one extreme is the viewpoint that all members of *Homo* since the earliest members assigned to that genus (whom we will discuss in the next section) belong to a single species, *Homo sapiens*. The other extreme claims six species within genus *Homo* over that 2-million-year period. There are also versions of the splitter point of view that recognize two to five *Homo* species. Each model has evidence in its support, and each has opposition based on reasonable counterarguments. The issue is by no means even close to being settled. These models are the topic of Chapter 12.

law of parsimony: A principle that relies on using the simplest explanation in formulating a scientific hypothesis. Another name for Ockham's razor.

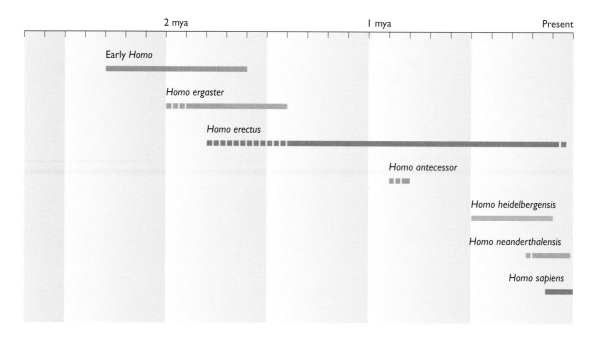

FIGURE 11.1

Timeline of species within genus *Homo* according to an extreme splitter model. Dashes indicate that some evidence exists for extending the time range of that species as shown. Each species, of course, may be extended in time either way as more fossil evidence is recovered. This model does not necessarily reflect the author's views but is used to clearly sort the fossils into named groups recognized by some authorities as separate species.

How, then, to begin discussing the fossil evidence for the evolution of our genus if authorities cannot even agree on the names? The simplest scheme would, of course, be the one that lumps nearly all the fossils into *Homo sapiens*—that would certainly cut down on the taxonomic categories. But such an approach would make it difficult to describe and discuss differences among groups of fossils that some authorities feel are enough to merit species distinction. And when these species names are used—regardless of one's point of view on the debate—there is usually no misunderstanding about which fossils are being referred to.

Thus, let's begin with an extreme splitter model—currently, the most complex organization, which divides all later *Homo* into six species (Figure 11.1). We will describe and discuss these species in terms of their phenotypic features, dates, geographic distributions, and behaviors. Then, in Chapter 12, we will discuss the various hypotheses for just how many species these groups represent and, most important, how they are related evolutionarily. *Understand that I am not necessarily advocating this model.* I just feel that organizing our discussion in this order will allow us to consider the other points of view (that is, lumping the species we have already named and defined) in Chapter 12. I like to think William of Ockham would have approved.

FIGURE 11.2
A sample of Oldowan tools. The two at the lower right are flake tools. The others are core tools.

THE FIRST MEMBERS OF GENUS *HOMO*

When the Leakeys found Zinjanthropus in 1959, they uncovered some simple stone tools at the same level of Olduvai Gorge (Figure 11.2). At first they thought Zinjanthropus had made the tools, but they began to feel that "Zinj" was too primitive to have made something so sophisticated.

These tools, called **Oldowan** after Olduvai Gorge, seem very simple to us. Also called *pebble tools*, they are nothing more than water-smoothed cobbles 3 to 4 inches across, modified by knocking off a few chips from one or two faces to make a sharp edge. But unlike the termite sticks of the chimpanzees, there is nothing in the raw material— the unmodified stone—that immediately suggests the tools that can be made from it or the method of manufacture. A stone tool requires that the maker be able to imagine within the stone the tool he wants to make and to picture the process needed to make it. Making even a simple Oldowan tool is also a far more complex technological feat than stripping the leaves off a branch to make it narrow enough to fit down the hole of a termite mound (Figure 11.3). (I can attest to the difficulty.) This leap of the imagination and increase in technological skill are what make the first evidence of stone toolmaking so important.

Authorities originally thought that the Oldowan tools were all **core tools** and that the flakes were the waste products of their manufacture. Recently, however, it has been shown that though some flaked cores may have been used as tools, the majority were the raw materials for the manufacture of **flake tools,** which were used for a variety of tasks, such as

Oldowan: A toolmaking tradition from Africa associated with early *Homo*.

core tools: Tools made by taking flakes off a stone nucleus.

flake tools: Tools made from the flakes removed from a stone core.

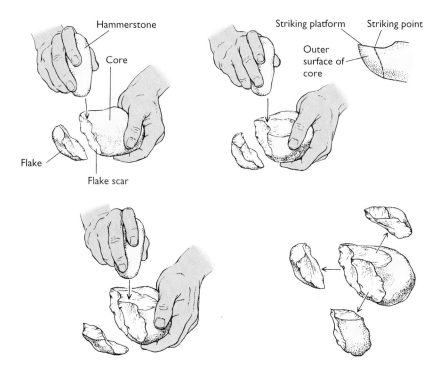

cutting meat and plant material, scraping meat off a bone, and sawing wood or bone (Schick and Toth 1993; Toth 1985). Under microscopic analysis, the edges of these flakes show a polish that is characteristic of these activities.

It also appears that the makers of the Oldowan tools may have traveled some distance to find a source of stone known to be superior for the production of sharp, durable tools. The cores themselves were probably carried around to wherever flakes were needed; it is common to find flakes at a site but not the cores from which they were struck. All this shows a high level of planning (Schick and Toth 1993).

Although there is some evidence for bone tool manufacture among the earlier hominids (Holden 2001b), no evidence of stone tool manufacture has been found. One study (Susman 1994) concluded that the thumbs of *Australopithecus* and *Paranthropus* had features that allowed the dexterity required to make stone tools—although this conclusion has been challenged (Gibbons 1997a). Furthermore, some simple stone tools have recently been found in Ethiopia that date to 2.6 mya, 300,000 years earlier than the earliest accepted fossils of *Homo* (Semaw et al. 1997). Still, no hard evidence links any hominid other than *Homo* with the manufacture of stone implements.

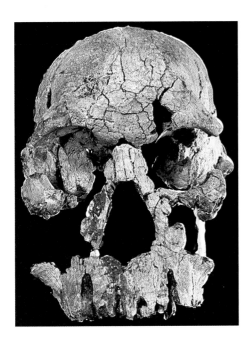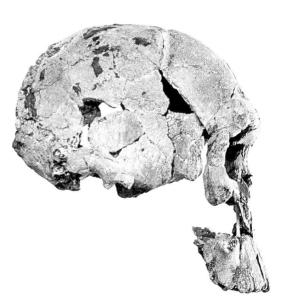

It appeared in 1959, and still does, that Zinjanthropus was not a good candidate for having been the maker of the pebble tools. Then in 1961 the Leakeys found a second hominid from the same time period. Actually, they had found fragmentary fossils of this form in the same year that they found Zinjanthropus, but they had not fully recognized them as something different. They named the new form *Homo habilis* ("handy man"; Figure 11.4).

The reasons for including these fossils in genus *Homo* are twofold. First, *H. habilis* shows a notable increase in brain size, from the average of about 480 ml for *Australopithecus* and *Paranthropus* to an average of 680 ml, with a possible maximum of 800 ml. Second, the presence of the stone tools indicates that those larger brains were capable of a complexity of thought not seen in the record of the other two hominid genera. Thus *H. habilis* seems to mark the beginning of a new trend in hominid evolution—toward bigger brains and greater intelligence. Fossils of *H. habilis* have now been found in Tanzania, Kenya, Ethiopia, and perhaps southern Africa and have been dated at 2.3 to 1.5 mya.

The exact taxonomic affiliations of this group of fossils, however, is far from agreed upon. The specimens from East Turkana, Kenya, are considered different enough by some to be placed in a new species, *Homo rudolfensis*. The specimen pictured in Figure 11.4 is an example. Differences include a larger body and brain size than in *H. habilis* and the lack of a continuous brow ridge over the eyes. (See Tattersall 1992 for a

FIGURE 11.4
The well-known skull 1470 from Lake Turkana, Kenya, front and side views. Note the flatter face, smoother contours, lack of a sagittal crest, and more rounded braincase as compared with *Australopithecus* and *Paranthropus*. This fossil was first classified as *Homo habilis* and still is by some authorities. Others consider it a separate species, *Homo rudolfensis*.

review of this argument.) Others (Blumenschine et al. 2003) believe that all these specimens belong in *H. habilis*. Still others (Wood and Collard 1999) feel that the fossils labeled *H. habilis* and *H. rudolfensis* are in important ways closer to *Australopithecus* than to *Homo* and should thus be lumped into the former genus. This assessment is based on similar body proportions, evidence of continued arboreal ability, and similarity of brain size *relative to body size* (rather than absolute differences in brain size). Still others (Sherwood 2000) agree that while *H. habilis* might be lumped into *Australopithecus*, *H. rudolfensis* should remain in *Homo*. For the remainder of this discussion, we will use the term "early *Homo*," in keeping with what is, at the moment, the majority view, and we will also consider all the fossils together. As more fossils that cover a broader span of time are found, the picture of hominid evolution during this period may become clearer. But the debate will probably never be fully resolved.

Finally, on the matter of evolutionary relationships, the arm-to-leg proportions of early *Homo* more closely resemble those of *Australopithecus africanus* (long arms, short legs) than they do *A. afarensis*. This argues for the former species being the direct ancestor of our genus (Berger 1998), even though later in our evolution the relative limb lengths became reversed (short arms, long legs).

What is it about the stone tools that may have given early *Homo* an edge? Paleoanthropologist Richard Leakey, the son of Louis and Mary, suggests that sharp stone tools allowed these hominids to more quickly cut meat and bones off a carcass, making the addition of meat to the diet through scavenging safer and more efficient. There is evidence for this suggestion.

Ten Olduvai sites from the early *Homo* period contain Oldowan tools, flakes, and animal bones. Once thought to be some sort of "home base," these areas are now considered "stone cache" sites (Potts 1984) where hominids left supplies of stones and to which they took scavenged animal remains for quick, safe processing and eating. Analysis indicates that these sites were used for short periods, but repeatedly, as one would expect of such places.

Archaeologist Lewis Binford (1985) has analyzed the animal bones from these sites and found that they are mostly the lower leg bones of antelopes. These bones carry little meat and, along with the skull, are about the only parts left after a large carnivore has finished eating. However, such bones are rich in marrow, so a major activity at the sites in question may have been to cut off what little meat remained on these bones and then to break them open for the nutritious marrow inside.

Finally, Pat Shipman has studied the taphonomy of these and other bones with a scanning electron microscope (1984, 1986). She found that

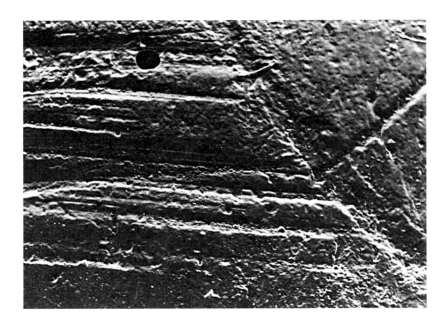

FIGURE 11.5
This micrograph of a fossil bone from Olduvai Gorge shows tool marks (the horizontal lines and the diagonal line beginning at the top of the photo) and a carnivore tooth mark (beginning on the right side and angled toward the center). In this case, the tooth mark overlaps the tool mark, indicating that the hominids sliced meat off this part of the bone *before* a scavenger began eating.

cut marks left stone tools were usually on the shafts of the bones as if pieces of meat were cut off, not near the joints as if an entire carcass had been butchered (Figure 11.5). Also, the hominid tool marks sometimes overlapped carnivore tooth marks, showing that the carnivores had gotten there first.

We may envision early *Homo* in small cooperative groups, maybe family groups, foraging in a mixed grassland/woodland area (Blumenschine et al. 2000) for plant foods and always on the lookout for the telltale signs of a carnivore kill—a group of scavengers gathered on the ground or a flock of vultures circling overhead. Their big brains allowed them to better understand their environment and to manipulate it, making imaginative and technologically advanced tools from stone. With these tools they may have cut apart the carcasses they found and taken the pieces back to a safe place, maybe where they had stored more tools. There they cut the remaining meat off the bones and, using large hammerstones, smashed open the bones for marrow. It was no doubt a harsh life, but it was successful. The adaptive themes of bipedalism, large brains, social organization, and tool technology set the stage for the rest of hominid evolution.

Fossils indicate that forms with the characteristics of early *Homo* were around for only about half a million years. Before they disappeared from the fossil record, a new hominid species came on the scene—one that continued and enhanced the trends of big brains and tool technology, adaptations that soon carried this hominid all over the Old World.

TABLE 11.1
Major Fossils of *Homo ergaster* and *Homo erectus*

Country	Locality	Fossils	Crania	Age (million years)	Est. Brain Size (ml)
Homo ergaster					
Kenya	East Turkana	Cranial and postcranial fragments including mandibles and pelvis and long bone fragments	KNM-ER 3733	1.78	850
			KNM-ER 3883	1.57	800
		Cranial fragments	KNM-ER 42700	1.55	—
	West Turkana	Nearly complete juvenile individual	KNM-WT 15000	1.6	880
Homo erectus					
Algeria	Ternifine	3 mandibles and a skull	—	0.5–0.7	—
China	Hexian (Lontandong)	Partial skull	"Hexian Man"	0.25–0.5	1,000
	Lantian (Gongwangling)	Cranial fragments and mandible	"Lantian Man"	>1	800
	Longgupo(?)*	Mandible fragments	—	1.8	—
	Yunxian	2 crania	—	>0.35	—
	Zhoukoudian	Cranial and postcranial remains of 40 individuals	II	<0.46	1,030
			III	<0.46	915
			VI	<0.46	850
			X	<0.46	1,225
			XI	<0.46	1,015
			XII	<0.46	1,030
			Locality 13	0.7	—
	Tangshan Cave	Fragments	—	0.58–0.62	—
Ethiopia	Bouri	Cranial and post-cranial fragments	BOU-VP-2/66	1.0	995
Georgia	Dmanisi	3 mandibles, 16 teeth, 3 crania	D2280	1.75	780
			D2282	1.75	650
			D2700(?)	1.75	600

TO NEW LANDS

Most of the fossils at the beginning of genus *Homo* (subsequent to the still-debated fossils of early *Homo*) are included in species *Homo erectus*. Some authorities split the fossils of this group from Kenya into a second species, *Homo ergaster* (Table 11.1 and Figure 11.6).

from the one discussed in class.

Country	Locality	Fossils	Crania	Age (million years)	Est. Brain Size (ml)
Homo erectus (continued)					
Israel	'Ubeidiya	Fragments	—	<1	—
Italy	Ceprano(?)	Cranium	—	0.8–0.9	—
Java	Modjokerto	Child's cranium	—	1.8(?)	—
	Ngandong	Cranial and postcranial	N-1	<0.1	1,170
		fragments from >12	N-6	<0.1	1,250
		invidiuals	N-11	<0.1	1,230
			N-12	<0.1	1,090
	Sambungmachan	Large cranial fragment	Sambungmachan	<0.1	1,000
	Sangiran	Cranial and postcranial	S-2	0.7–1.6	800
		fragments from ~40	S-4	0.7–1.6	900
		individuals	S–10	0.7–1.6	850
			S-12	0.7–1.6	1,050
			S-17	0.7–1.6	1,000
			1993 cranium	1.1–1.4	856
	Trinil	Skullcap and femur	"Java Man"	<1	940
Morocco	Salé	Cranium	Salé	0.4(?)	880
	Sidi Abderrahman	2 mandible fragments	—	—	—
	Thomas Quarry	Mandible and skull fragments	—	0.5	—
Tanzania	Olduvai(?)	Cranial and postcranial fragments, including mandibles and pelvis and long bone fragments	OH9	1.4	1,060
			OH12	0.6–0.8	700–800
				Mean	**984.79**

*The (?) indicates that the species identification or age of that fossil is in question.

The Dutch physician Eugene Dubois made the first finds ever of *H. erectus* in Java in 1891. Dubois chose Java to look for hominid fossils largely because he was already stationed there with the military. But the choice was also a logical one for the time, since most people thought that humans had first evolved in Asia, despite Darwin's clear suggestion that Africa was the hominid homeland. The idea that our evolutionary line was originally African apparently did not sit well with many Europeans.

FIGURE 11.6

Map of major *Homo erectus/ergaster* sites.

When Dubois found a skullcap and a diseased femur at the site of Trinil (Figure 11.7), he thought they represented the "missing link" between apes and humans, and he dubbed the specimens "Pithecanthropus erectus" (the "upright ape-man"), popularly known as "Java Man." Since Dubois's work, numerous other fossils have been located in Java (see Table 11.1) and are now recognized as fully hominid and assigned to our genus, *Homo*. The fossils found in Java are similar in phenotype to the African and other Asian specimens, although their average brain size is larger than in some of the earlier fossils, and many are over 1,000 ml.

FIGURE 11.7
Skullcap and femur of "Java Man" *Homo erectus.* The growth toward the top of the femur is the result of a pathological condition.

Perhaps the most famous *H. erectus* fossils are those from Zhoukoudian, a cave outside of Beijing, China. Starting in the 1920s, six nearly complete skulls, a couple dozen cranial and mandible fragments, over a hundred teeth, and a few postcranial pieces were recovered from the cave. Stone tools and animal bones, including those of horses and hyenas, were also recovered. The hominid remains are clearly similar to those of other specimens of *H. erectus.* Dating indicates that the cave was first occupied about 460,000 ya and was used until about 230,000 ya, although new evidence (Boaz and Ciochon 2001) suggests that most of the *H. erectus* bones in the cave were the remains of hyenas' meals.

The fame of the Zhoukoudian fossils, called "Peking Man" (from the old spelling of Beijing), lies mostly in the fact that they are missing. When Japan invaded China in 1937, U.S. Marines attempting to get the fossils out of the country were captured by Japanese troops. The fossils were never seen again. Their whereabouts remain one of the great mysteries in anthropology. Fortunately, extensive measurements had already been taken of the bones, and accurate casts had been made (Figure 11.8).

Since then, numerous fossils classified as *H. erectus* have been recovered, and we are filling in—although not without controversy—our knowledge of this important period in hominid evolution. Among the oldest

FIGURE 11.8
Cast of one of the missing "Peking Man" skulls.

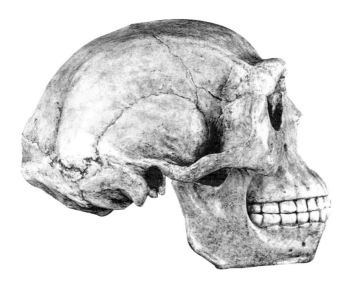

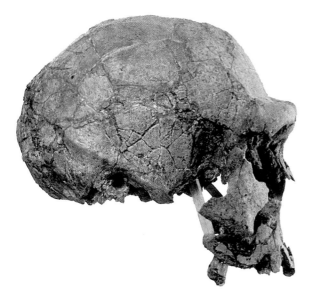

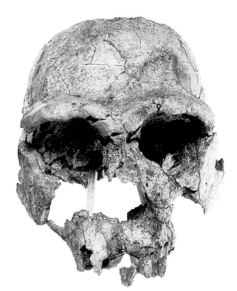

FIGURE 11.9
The *Homo erectus* (or *Homo ergaster*) skull of KNM-ER 3733 from Lake Turkana, Kenya, is fairly typical of this group.

fossils of this group are those that some authorities (see, for example, Tattersall 1997) place in a separate species, *H. ergaster* ("work man," a reference to stone tools found in association with the fossils). The oldest well-established find, from East Turkana in Kenya, is dated at 1.78 mya (Figure 11.9). In some ways it is typical of *H. erectus* crania. It has heavy brow ridges, a prognathous face, a sloping forehead, an elongated profile, a **sagittal keel,** a sharply angled occipital bone with a pronounced **torus,** and a

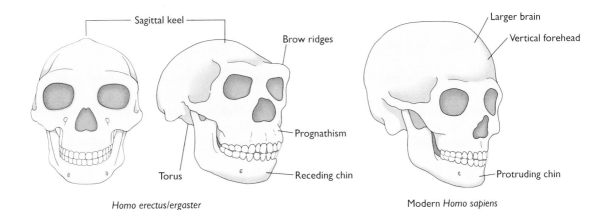

Sagittal keel — Larger brain
Brow ridges — Vertical forehead
Prognathism
Torus — Receding chin — Protruding chin

Homo erectus/ergaster   Modern *Homo sapiens*

cranial capacity of 850 ml (Figure 11.10). (The sagittal keel should not be confused with the sagittal crest. The crest is a ridge of bone for the attachment of chewing muscles. The keel is an aspect of the skull's shape). The average cranial capacity for this hominid group is about 980 ml, just slightly under the modern human minimum of 1,000 ml, but a considerable jump from the 680 ml average for early *Homo*. Some *H. erectus* fossils have cranial capacities within the modern human range (see Table 11.1).

In other ways, however, the Turkana skull differs from others labeled as *H. erectus*. It is thinner and higher in profile, with smaller facial bones. These modern-looking features are what have led to its placement in the species *H. ergaster*. The cranium is thought to have belonged to a female. A similar skull from East Turkana dated at 1.57 mya is more ruggedly constructed. It is thought to have belonged to a male.

From the neck up, then, *H. erectus/ergaster* is quite distinct from early *Homo* in overall size, ruggedness, and especially brain size. The skull still retains primitive features that distinguish it from modern *H. sapiens*. From the neck down, however, *H. erectus/ergaster* is essentially modern and apparently was so from its beginnings.

We know this because one of the oldest fossils of the group—also included in *H. ergaster*—is also the most complete. It is a nearly whole skeleton found at West Turkana in Kenya and is dated at 1.6 mya (Figure 11.11). The shape of the pelvis indicates that it was a male. Based on dental eruption and lack of any epiphyseal union, it is estimated that he was 12 years old when he died. "Turkana Boy," as he is commonly known, was about 5½ feet tall; he might have been 150 pounds and 6 feet tall had he lived to adulthood.

All other fossils from this group—including those from Africa outside Kenya—are assigned to *Homo erectus* (although a few are awaiting

FIGURE 11.10
Cranial features of *Homo erectus/ergaster* (side and front views) compared with those of modern *Homo sapiens*.

sagittal keel: A sloping of the sides of the skull toward the top, as viewed from the front.

torus: A bony ridge at the back of the skull, where the neck muscles attach.

FIGURE 11.11
The "Turkana Boy," *Homo ergaster* fossil KNM-WT 15000, is one of the most complete early hominid fossils ever found. The pelvis is clearly that of a male, and the epiphyses at the top of his left femur are obviously not fused (see Figure 9.3).

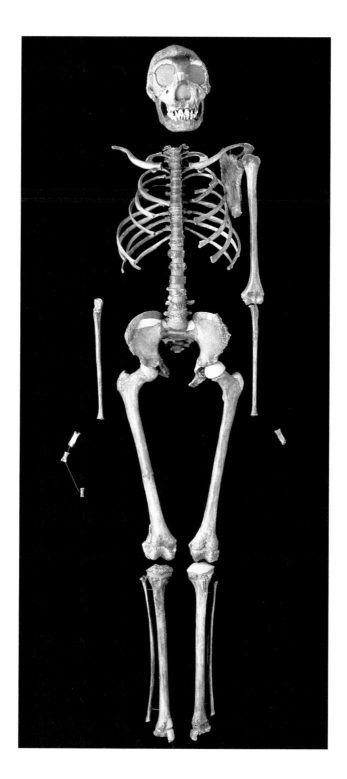

confirmation of their species affiliation). For the moment, we will treat them all as potentially *H. erectus*.

The *H. erectus* fossils from Africa—except for OH9 from Olduvai Gorge, dated at 1.4 mya, and a recent find from Ethiopia, dated at 1 mya (Asfaw et al. 2002)—are younger, from 400,000 to 800,000 years old. This means that *H. erectus* spread throughout the African continent and that populations of the species remained there for about a million years.

However, *H. erectus* did not remain only in Africa. According to recent data, members of the species had reached China and Southeast Asia by at least 1 mya. What prompted the people of this species to leave the savannas to which they were apparently so well adapted?

We can't know the answer for sure, but a good guess is that the spread of *H. erectus* was simply an outcome of their reproductive success. Their big brains enabled them to exploit the savannas to a greater extent than had the other hominids to date. They had better and more varied tools (which we'll discuss later), the ability to learn more about their environment and to reason out the problems that their habitat presented, and, no doubt, a more complex social organization. With these adaptations, *H. erectus* would have rapidly increased in population size.

Population increase, however, puts pressure on resources and, perhaps, on social harmony as well. So groups of *H. erectus* probably fissioned and moved outside of familiar areas in search of less competition over food, space, and two other resources that may have been even more important—water and shelter. Water can be scarce on the savannas. There are lakes, rivers, and waterholes, but many of these are seasonal and are dry for months on end. And *H. erectus* may have needed shelter as well. With bodies virtually the same as ours, they were no longer good tree climbers and so had to seek shelter on the ground, in groves of trees, or, if they could locate one, in a cave or rock shelter. But, of course, a leopard or other animal may have already taken up residence in the cave and had to be dealt with. They may also have been following migrations of animal herds.

In search of food, water, shelter, and perhaps space and social harmony, *H. erectus* wandered the Old World. Those wanderings eventually carried them as far from their African homeland as what is now Beijing, China, and the Indonesian island of Java, and perhaps to Europe as well. Not only did these journeys take them to new climates, but the travels also brought them into contact with the changeable environments of the ice ages, known technically as the **Pleistocene.**

Beginning about 1.6 mya and ending 10,000 ya, the Pleistocene was actually a complex series of extremely cold periods separated by warm phases, some warmer than today. There may have been as many as eighteen cold episodes during the Pleistocene, some lasting tens of thousands of years. We still don't know what caused these cold periods. Suggestions

Pleistocene: The geological time period, from 1.6 mya to 10,000 ya, characterized by a series of glacial advances and retreats.

FIGURE 11.12
A veritable river of ice, the Moreno Glacier is located in Patagonia, a region of Argentina.

range from increased volcanic activity, with dust and ash blocking the sun's rays, to changes in the earth's orbit.

When the average world temperature drops, ice and snow accumulate over the years at the poles and in higher elevations. The pressure of this accumulation forces the movement of great sheets and rivers of ice known as **glaciers** (Figure 11.12). During periods of glacial advances, much of

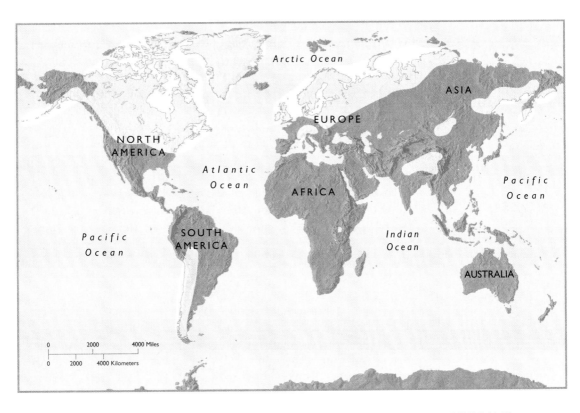

FIGURE 11.13
Maximum worldwide glacial expansion during the Pleistocene. The Antarctic ice cover, not shown here, also expanded during this epoch.

North America, Europe, and Asia were covered by ice, sometimes nearly a mile thick (Figure 11.13). Parts of the world not covered by the glaciers were nonetheless affected, having cooler summers and wetter winters. The advance of the glaciers also had the effect of condensing the world's climatic zones into smaller spaces. Several times during the Pleistocene, the temperate oak and pine forests of Connecticut, where I now live, were like the arctic **tundra** of Alaska and northern Canada. Moreover, with so much of the earth's water tied up in the great ice sheets, sea levels dropped as much as 400 feet, exposing large areas of land formerly under water. This allowed humans to migrate to areas previously inaccessible; for instance, modern *Homo sapiens* migrated to North America.

The world of the Pleistocene was the world through which *H. erectus* was able to migrate and establish themselves, and we find their remains in some of the far corners of the Old World. They undoubtedly also inhabited the areas in between, but we have yet to uncover fossils in these areas.

Redating of early finds from Java has posed interesting questions regarding the spread of *H. erectus* around the Old World. Using new

glaciers: Massive sheets of ice that expand and move.

tundra: A treeless area with low-growing vegetation and permanently frozen ground.

versions of the potassium/argon dating technique, researchers have redated the Sangiran *erectus* fossils to 1.6 mya and the Modjokerto remains to 1.8 mya—twice as old as previously thought and at least as old as the oldest African *erectus/ergaster* fossil. This could mean that *H. erectus* evolved somewhere other than Africa. But all previous hominid fossils come only from Africa, so it's unlikely that *erectus* evolved anywhere but there.

That leaves two plausible explanations. Perhaps *H. erectus* (or *ergaster*) actually first evolved in Africa earlier than any of the fossils we have—remember how rare fossilization is—and then spread. The other possibility is simply that their expansion began very shortly after they first evolved. Science writer James Shreeve (1994:86) notes that Java is 10,000 to 15,000 miles from Africa, depending on the route, and that parts of Indonesia were connected to Asia at the time due to lower sea levels during the Pleistocene. If *erectus* walked just a mile a year, it would only have taken about 15,000 years to reach Java. That's still pretty fast, considering that they did not necessarily move 1 mile every year *in the right direction*. I think that if the Java dates are correct, they probably mean that *H. erectus/ergaster* is older than we now assume based on existing fossils *and* that the species' expansion began early on.

New evidence for this interpretation comes from the Republic of Georgia and from Kenya. In 2002, a third cranium (D2700) from the Dmanisi site was discovered (Vekua et al. 2002). Dated at 1.75 mya, as were the previous Dmanisi fossils, this one was distinct in that it was smaller (an estimated 600 ml cranial capacity) and more "primitive" than the others, so much so that although it is provisionally assigned to *Homo erectus*, it has some features that resemble early *Homo* (Figure 11.14). In other words, hominids may have ventured out of Africa sooner and at an earlier evolutionary stage than we had previously assumed (Balter and Gibbons 2002). (In late 2003, anthropologists announced the discovery of some leg and ankles bones at the Dmanisi site, but details and technical reports are still forthcoming.)

Then in 2003, Meave Leakey (Leakey et al. 2003) announced the discovery of a skull in Kenya, dated at 1.55 mya, that bears a resemblance to the new Dmanisi skull in its size and some detailed features. The skull is assigned to *H. erectus*, but like the Dmanisi skull, it shows that early *H. erectus* had a transitional or intermediary stage—as compared with early *Homo*—and it was at this stage that the species first left Africa.

Moreover, new dating on a site in northern China shows the stone tools there to be 1.36 million years old, by far the oldest evidence of human presence in that region (Zhu et al. 2001) This is further evidence for an earlier initial migration of some populations from African than previously thought.

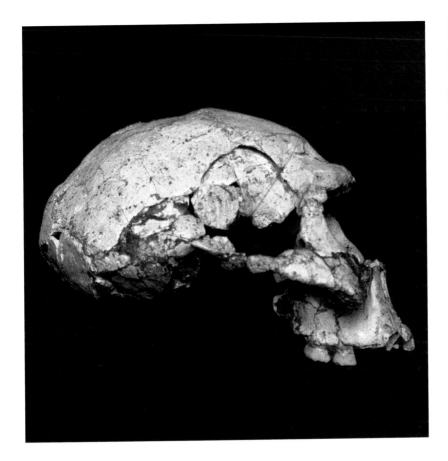

FIGURE 11.14
One of the previously discovered crania from Dmanisi, Georgia, dated 1.75 mya and provisionally assigned to *Homo erectus*. The skulls from this site show a remarkable degree of variation and some have traits that resemble early *Homo* from Africa.

Another important date concerns the Java site of Ngandong. There is evidence that some *erectus* fossils there may be younger than 100,000 years—perhaps as young as 27,000 to 53,000 years old. If so, there were populations of *erectus* still around well after modern *Homo sapiens* had evolved. (We'll discuss the meanings of this in the next chapter.)

It should be noted that with the exception of the Ceprano find (see Table 11.1), the European evidence of *H. erectus* comes in the form of cultural artifacts dated at times that have been associated with that species from other locations. At the site of Soleihac in France are tools and animal remains dated at 800,000 ya. Another French site, Terra Amata on the Riviera, has been proposed as a site where *H. erectus* built shelters and established a village around 400,000 ya. This interpretation has recently been called into question, however. Some individuals lived there, but probably not in a village of huts. In Spain, at two adjacent sites called Torralba and Ambrona, dated at 400,000 ya, are the remains

FIGURE 11.15

Bifacially flaked hand axes became one of history's most popular tools and were found in a variety of sizes showing varying degrees of quality. The hand axe on the far right is from the French site of St. Acheul, which lent its name to this toolmaking tradition.

of some large mammals, including elephants, along with some stone tools that suggest a hunting or, more probably, a scavenging site. Until, however, we locate definite fossils of *H. erectus* from Europe—other than the cranium from Ceprano, Italy—we can only conclude that the species was there but was not widespread or, perhaps, that these sites are associated with another hominid species.

What do we know about the lives of *Homo erectus/ergaster*? Like early *Homo*, early *H. ergaster* made stone tools by taking a few flakes off a core, just enough to make the "business end." (They also, of course, used the flakes as tools.) But beginning about 1.4 mya, *H. erectus/ergaster* elaborated on this stone toolmaking technique by flaking the entire stone, controlling the shape of the whole core tool. This toolmaking tradition is called the **Acheulian technique,** after the site in France where it was first identified. The core tool produced by the Acheulian technique is the **hand axe.** It is symmetrical, edged and pointed, and **bifacial** (flaked on both sides; Figure 11.15). It was the all-purpose tool of its time, used for any number of tasks, from butchering to cutting wood. My colleague, archaeologist Ken Feder, calls it the "Swiss Army rock."

In addition to hand axes, *H. erectus/ergaster* also made tools with straight, sharp edges called *cleavers.* Moreover, making a hand axe or cleaver produces a great many flakes—as many as fifty usable ones by one estimate—and *H. erectus/ergaster* also made flake tools, used either unmodified or further worked to produce a desired shape.

Hand axes appeared in Africa about 1.4 mya and lasted for over a million years. They spread throughout Africa and into Europe. They are,

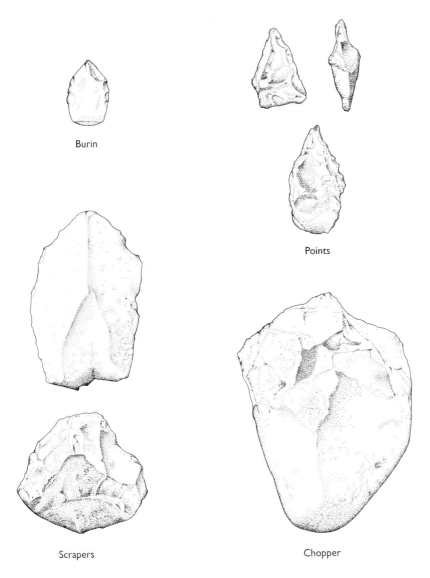

Burin

Points

Scrapers

Chopper

FIGURE 11.16
Flake and chopper tools
associated with *Homo
erectus* from the cave at
Zhoukoudian. Although the
functions of these tools are
uncertain, some are named
for inferred use. Burins may
have been used to etch out
thin slivers of antler or bone,
which were then further
modified into awls or needles. Points may have served
as cutting tools for fine work.
Scrapers may have helped remove flesh from animal hides.
And choppers chopped wood
and perhaps broke open
bones to extract marrow.

however, rarely found in Asia. Instead, Asian *erectus* populations, like those at Zhoukoudian, made what are called *choppers*, with flakes removed from one side, and a few other tools with flakes removed from both sides (Figure 11.16). But these tool types, unlike the Acheulian hand axe, were asymmetrical and not flaked over the whole surface.

On the subject of hand axes, some new evidence from Tanzania (Schuster 2001) includes hand axes dated at 1.5 mya that bear traces of acacia wood on their blades. One interpretation suggests that the

Acheulian technique: A
toolmaking tradition associated with *Homo erectus/
ergaster* in Africa and Europe.

hand axe: A bifacial, all-
purpose stone tool, shaped
somewhat like an axe head.

bifacial: Refers to a stone
tool that has been worked
on both sides.

toolmakers used these stone tools for woodworking. No actual wooden artifacts were recovered, however.

Perhaps the most striking behavioral advance associated with *Homo erectus* is the purposeful use of fire. There is some evidence, though it is disputed, for the use of fire in Africa at 1.5 mya and France at 750,000 ya. A rock shelter in Thailand has yielded evidence of fire dated at 700,000 ya. The earliest well-accepted date (although even it is not without its skeptics) is from the cave at Zhoukoudian sometime after 500,000 ya (Binford and Chuan 1985; Binford and Stone 1986).

Fire, of course, provides heat, and so it is not surprising that some of the earliest evidence of fire comes from cold northern areas. Fire also provides protection from animals and can be used for cooking, making meat easier to chew and digest. But in the long run, perhaps its most important use is as a source of light. Science writer John Pfeiffer (1969) suggests that fire could extend the hours of activity into the night and provide a social focus for group interaction. Sitting around the campfire at night was when people experimented, created, talked, and socialized. Fire serves these functions in human cultures today. Moreover, the use of fire may well have given people a psychological advantage—a sense of mastery and control over a force of nature—and a source of energy. As Pfeiffer (1966) says in the title of his article, "When *Homo erectus* Tamed Fire, He Tamed Himself."

Was *Homo erectus* a hunter of big game, as often portrayed, or did this species continue to scavenge for most of the meat in its diet? At the 400,000-year-old Spanish sites of Torralba and Ambrona, located on two hills on either side of a mountain pass, scientists found the remains of fifty elephants and over sixty other game animals (see Figure 9.10). The traditional interpretation is a rather elaborate reconstruction of a cooperative hunt, indeed, of several seasons of cooperative hunting (see, for example, Time-Life Books 1973). In this scenario the animals were stampeded, possibly with the use of fire, into a bog where they were killed and butchered. The pieces of the carcasses were then taken to a campsite where they were further cut up, cooked, and eaten. There are also some tools at the sites.

Is there evidence for this interpretation? A taphonomic analysis of 3,000 bones from these sites found that 95 percent of them were so damaged that the search for specific evidence of human activity was impossible (Shipman and Rose 1983). Scratches on many of the bones, once thought to be stone tool cut marks, turn out on examination under a scanning electron microscope to be merely the results of soil abrasion and root growth. Of the fifty-five bones that could be analyzed, the microscope showed only sixteen cut marks on fourteen bones. The pattern of the marks does not indicate systematic butchering. There is even little evidence of carnivore tooth marks. Furthermore, the tools found at the site are not associated with the elephants but with the leg bones and mandibles of horses, deer, and wild cattle—the very parts of the animals that would be gathered by scavenging. At best, it appears that H. erectus was present at these sites and cut some meat off animal carcasses found there. There is no compelling evidence for cooperative big-game hunting.

Two other alleged kill sites, at Olduvai Gorge and Olorgesailie in Africa, similarly give rise to elaborate interpretations of cooperative big-game hunting, but they too are based on questionable evidence. The bones found at these sites are more indicative of scavenging than of large-scale hunting. (For a good, detailed discussion, see Johanson and Shreeve 1989, chap. 8.)

So, we may probably conclude that Homo erectus was a forager, collecting plant foods and scavenging for meat, who also hunted at least smaller animals when the opportunity or necessity presented itself (see Ragir 2000 for a detailed discussion of early hominid diet and foraging behavior).

Finally, what about the intellectual and linguistic skills of H. erectus/ergaster? As noted, their average cranial capacity was just a little short of the modern human minimum, and individual erectus remains fall within the modern human range. It's difficult to be certain what this fact means. After all, the modern range of 1,000 to 2,000 ml means that some people have brains twice the volume of others, but there is no solid evidence that within this range brain size has anything to do with intelligence. Was H. erectus, then, just a little bit less intelligent than we are?

Because the inside of the skull reflects, rather specifically, some of the features of the brain it once held, anthropologist Ralph Holloway (1980, 1981) has been able to look at the structure of H. erectus brains. By making **endocasts** of the inside surfaces of fossil crania, Holloway has produced images of the very brains of our ancestors (Figure 11.17). One intriguing find is that the brains of H. erectus were asymmetrical—the right and left halves of the brain weren't the same shape. This is found to some extent in apes but to a greater extent in modern humans, because the halves of our brains perform different functions. Language and the ability to use symbols, for example, are functions of our left hemispheres, while spatial reasoning (such as the hand-eye coordination needed to make complex tools) is performed in the right hemisphere. This hints that H. erectus also had hemisphere specialization, perhaps even including the ability to communicate through a symbolic language.

Further evidence of language use by H. erectus is suggested by the reconstruction of the vocal apparatus based on the anatomy of the cranial base. Even though the vocal apparatus is made up of soft parts, those

endocasts: Natural or human-made casts of the inside of a skull.

FIGURE 11.17
Natural endocasts from South African australopithecines. Notice the degree of detail, particularly the blood vessels of the upper right cast. Such casts may also be made artificially and allow us to compare the brains of our ancestors with those of modern humans.

parts are connected to bone, and so the shape of the bone is correlated with the shape of the larynx, pharynx, and other features (Figure 11.18).

Reconstruction work on australopithecines indicates that their vocal tract was basically like that of apes, with the larynx and pharynx high up in the throat. While this would have allowed them to drink and breathe at the same time (as human infants can do up to 18 months), it would not have allowed for the precise manipulation of air that is required for modern human languages. The early hominids could make sounds, but they would have been more like those of chimpanzees.

Homo erectus, on the other hand, had vocal tracts more like those of modern humans, positioned lower in the throat and allowing for a greater range and speed of sound production. Thus, *erectus* could have produced vocal communication that involved many sounds with precise differences. Whether or not they did so is another question. But given their ability to manufacture fairly complex tools, to control fire, and to survive in different and changing environmental circumstances, *erectus*

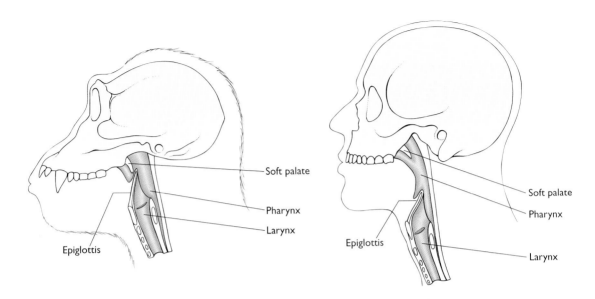

Soft palate

Pharynx

Larynx

Epiglottis

Soft palate

Pharynx

Epiglottis

Larynx

FIGURE 11.18

Vocal tract of a chimp compared with a modern human's. The high placement of the chimp's vocal tract makes it impossible for it to produce all of the sounds that are part of modern human languages.

certainly had complex things to talk *about*. It is not out of the question that *erectus* had a communication system that was itself complex, although there are authorities who feel that a communication system with the attributes of modern human language is associated only with the sophisticated behavior of modern *Homo sapiens* (See Holden 1998 for a detailed discussion).

If we can consider it a separate species, *H. erectus*—although now extinct—was a smashing success by any standards. The species evolved nearly 2 mya in Africa, possibly from an earlier species, *H. ergaster*, and by perhaps 1.8 mya had spread as far as Java. By 500,000 ya, they had reached northern China and Europe. They lasted as an identifiable group in Africa and China until 250,000 ya and may have persisted in Java until less than 100,000 ya. Their adaptations—now focused on learning, technology, and the cultural transmission of information— allowed them to exploit a number of different environments.

There is some debate over just how much *H. erectus* changed during its tenure on earth. There is a small increase in average cranial capacity over this time (about 180 ml), as well as some refinement in their hand axe–making technique and variation in their flake tool production. These changes, however, are small and slow, so the overall impression is one of stability—not a bad thing in evolutionary terms.

Perhaps as early as 800,000 ya, there was another sudden surge in brain size, to an average matching our own. This marks the beginning of perhaps the most complex part of our story.

BIG BRAINS, ARCHAIC SKULLS

The next three hominid species—using the six-species model—are marked by brain sizes within the modern human range that, indeed, match or approximate the modern human average; nonetheless, they have other features, especially of the cranium, that retain primitive characteristics. These hominid groups are sometimes collectively referred to as "archaic." The most recent of these, *Homo neanderthalensis*, will be considered separately in the next section. Here we will discuss the earlier *H. heidelbergensis* and the even earlier *H. antecessor* (Table 11.2 and Figure 11.19).

The newest suggested hominid species, named in mid-1997, is *Homo antecessor* ("advance guard" or "explorer"). Many authorities do not recognize the fossils involved as a separate species, but the discoverers see sufficient distinctions to warrant the new name (Bermúdez de Castro et al. 1997). Fossils have been discovered at the site of Gran Dolina cave in the Atapuerca hills in northern Spain. They consist of more than eighty fragments, including skulls, jaws, teeth, and other portions of the skeleton. There are also associated tools. Using paleomagnetism (see Table 9.1), the site has been dated at more than 780,000 ya. If that date is correct, these would be the oldest well-accepted fossil humans found in Europe.

The most striking fossil is the partial face of an 11-year-old boy (Figure 11.20). His features, described by the researchers as "fully modern," include a projecting nose region with a sharp lower margin, hollowed cheekbones (technically, the *canine fossae*), and several details of the dentition. Analysis of the specimens indicates a cranial capacity of greater than 1,000 ml.

On the other hand, other fossils from this site show primitive features such as prominent brow ridges and premolars with multiple roots (modern human premolars have a single root). This unique mix of traits, especially the very modern appearance of the face, is what led the investigators to assign the new species name—and to further suggest that this species is the direct ancestor both of modern humans and of *H. heidelbergensis* and *H. neanderthalensis* (see Chapter 12).

A logical objection to the analysis of the Gran Dolina boy is that the modern-looking traits seen so clearly in the boy's face might be juvenile features, not present in adults of his group and, therefore, not of diagnostic value for species assignment. The investigators, however, report that some of the other fragmentary facial bones from the site also show these modern traits and that *later* fossils from a nearby site, Sima de los Huesos, do not (Gibbons 1997b).

The fossil bones from Gran Dolina are striking for their antiquity, but some of the 200 tools found at the site are even older, dating back

TABLE 11.2
Major Fossils of *Homo antecessor* and *Homo heidelbergensis*

Country	Locality	Fossils	Age	Est. Brain Size (ml)
Homo antecessor				
Spain	Gran Dolina	More than 80 fragments	>780,000	>1,000
Homo heidelbergensis				
China	Dali	Cranium	200,000	1,120
	Jinniushan(?)*	Nearly complete skeleton	200,000	1,350
	Maba(?)	Cranium	130,000–170,000	—
	Xujiayao(?)	Fragments of 11 individuals	100,000–125,000	—
England	Swanscombe	Occipital and parietals	276,000–426,000	1,325
	Boxgrove	Tibia, teeth	362,000–423,000	—
Ethiopia	Bodo	Cranium	600,000(?)	1,250
France	Arago	Cranium and fragmentary remains of 7 individuals	250,000	1,200
Germany	Bilzingsleben(?)	Cranial fragments and tooth	320,000–412,000	—
	Mauer	Mandible	500,000	—
	Steinheim(?)	Cranium	200,000–240,000	1,200
Greece	Petralona	Cranium	160,000–240,000	1,200
Hungary	Vértesszöllös	Occipital fragment	250,000–475,000	1,250
India	Narmada	Cranium	200,000	1,300
Spain	Sima de los Huesos	2,500 fragments from at least 33 individuals	300,000	—
				1,390
Tanzania	Ndutu (Olduvai)(?)	Cranium	400,000–700,000	1,100
Zambia	Kabwe (Broken Hill)	Cranium and additional cranial and postcranial remains of several individuals	400,000–700,000	1,280
			Mean	**1,247.00**

*The (?) indicates that the species identification of that fossil is in question.

to 1 mya. These early tools resemble pre–hand axe tools from Africa, such as cores and simple cutting flakes. Later tools found in the same strata as the human remains are more sophisticated. One long flake has a sharp edge on one side and a dulled flat edge on the other. It was

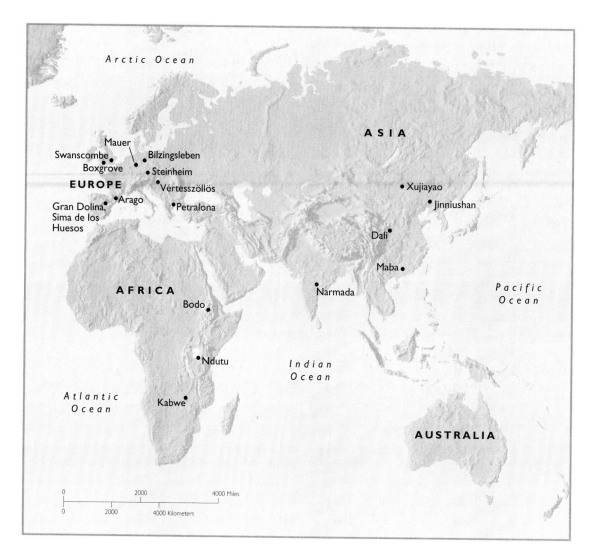

FIGURE 11.19

Map of major *Homo antecessor* and *Homo heidelbergensis* sites.

presumably formed to be used as a knife. None of the tools at the site, however, are as complex as some of the Acheulian tools being made by *H. erectus* and *H. ergaster* at the same time period or earlier.

Finally, there is some intriguing evidence of the diet of the Gran Dolina people. Bison and deer bones, as well as some from other species, have been found that show stone tool cut marks, implying that the people hunted. According to the investigators, there are also cut marks on some of the human bones that were mixed in with animal bones, suggesting cannibalism (Kunzig 1997).

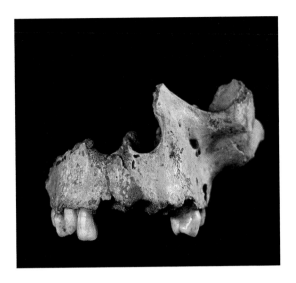

FIGURE 11.20
Fossil ATD6-69 from Gran Dolina cave, Atapuerca, Spain. This partial face of an 11-year-old boy who died perhaps more than 780,000 ya is fully modern in many features, including the hollowed cheekbone easily seen here.

It should also be noted that there is a site in southeastern Spain, called Orce, that some contend is even older than Gran Dolina—900,000 years old or even older. It contains simple stone tools and alleged hominid bones. Other authorities, however, have identified the fragmentary bones as those of wild horses, and the dating is still contested (Bower 1997a). More study is clearly needed at this location.

Table 11.2 and Figure 11.19 show that the fossils assigned to *Homo heidelbergensis* are geographically widespread and range over about 275,000 years in time (longer if one includes *H. antecessor*). The species was first named for a mandible found in 1907 at Mauer, near Heidelberg, Germany. Note that the inclusion of several of the fossils is questioned by those who recognize this group as a species.

Members of this group show an average brain size of nearly 1,300 ml, a more than 30 percent increase over the average for *H. erectus*. The brains are also differently proportioned than those of *H. erectus*, with greater emphasis on the forebrain, reflected by steeper foreheads. This may be important because the frontal lobes of the human brain are the areas thought to be most involved in the control of voluntary movements, speech, attention, social behavior, planning, and reasoning (see Figure 7.8).

The bones of the cranium, compared with those of *H. erectus*, are thinner; the overall size of the face is reduced; the profile is less prognathous; the brow ridges, though still present, are less pronounced; and the **postorbital constriction,** characteristic of *erectus*, is lessened (Figure 11.21). The postcranial skeletons, essentially modern in overall shape, are more rugged and muscular than in modern humans. The 500,000-year-old

postorbital constriction: A narrowing of the skull behind the eyes, as viewed from above.

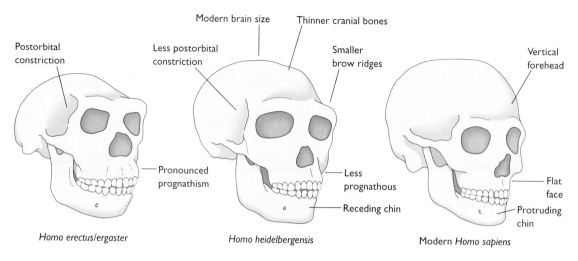

FIGURE 11.21
Cranial features of *Homo erectus/ergaster, Homo heidelbergensis,* and modern *Homo sapiens.*

tibia from Boxgrove in southeast England, for example, is strikingly thicker in cross section than the tibia of a modern person. Figures 11.22 and 11.23 show two of the more complete examples of *H. heidelbergensis* crania.

Given the fragmentary remains of many of these fossils, the fact that some were found early in the history of anthropology or by nonscientists, and the widespread range of the species, fairly little can be specifically said about the lifestyle of these early humans. We do know, however, some things about their tools. For example, we have evidence from Boxgrove that the hand axe was in use by 500,000 ya. And by about 200,000 ya, people included in *H. heidelbergensis* invented a new and imaginative way to make stone tools. The method appears first in Africa and later in Europe. Called the *prepared core,* or **Levallois technique** (after the suburb of Paris where it was first recognized), it involved the careful preparation of the rough stone core so that a number of flakes of a desired shape (up to four or five) could be taken off. The flakes could then be used for cutting, scraping, or piercing. Figure 11.24 shows the steps involved and a replica of such a tool. There is also evidence of other materials used for manufacturing tools, such as some wooden spears from the 400,000-year-old site of Schöningen in Germany. The size and characteristics of these approximately 6-foot-long weapons suggest that they were meant to be thrown at fairly large animals (Thieme 1997).

Levallois technique: A tool technology involving striking uniform flakes from a prepared core.

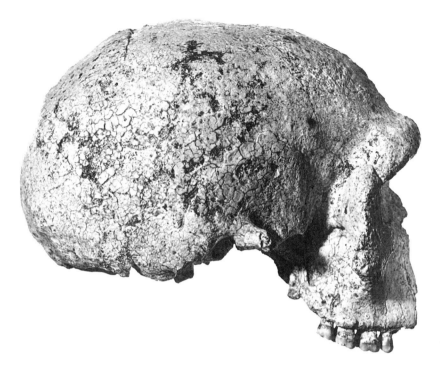

FIGURE 11.22
Skull of *Homo heidelbergensis* from Steinheim, Germany. Note the more rounded shape and higher forehead as compared with *H. erectus*. At the same time, note the retention of heavy brow ridges.

FIGURE 11.23
The Kabwe (formerly called Broken Hill) specimen is one of the best-known examples of a premodern *Homo sapiens* from Africa. Note the extremely large brow ridges on this skull, which has a cranial capacity of 1,280 ml, quite close to the modern mean.

FIGURE 11.24

The Levallois technique step-by-step: (*a*) produce a margin along the edge of the core, (*b*) shape the surface of the core, (*c, d*) prepare the surface to be struck (the "striking platform"), (*e*) remove the flake, and return to step (*b*) for additional flake removal. Shown below is a replica of a Levallois core and tool.

Side Views

Top Views

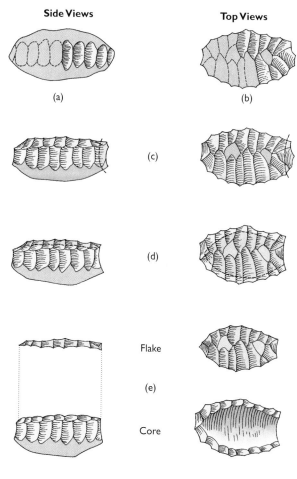

(a)

(b)

(c)

(d)

Flake

(e)

Core

Finally, an intriguing but still dim glimpse into the lives of the people of this era comes from another site in Atapuerca, near Gran Dolina (Kunzig 1997). Known as Sima de los Huesos ("pit of bones"), it is a shaft inside a cave, dated by electron spin resonance (see Chapter 9) at about 300,000 ya. It contains the bones of animals and the remains of at least thirty-three humans—many so well preserved that they include even fingertips and small inner ear bones. Most of the bones are from teenagers and young adults, both male and female. Although the bones show signs of chewing by a carnivore, it is unlikely that some predator would have selected just that age group, and the nonhuman remains in the pit are not those of prey animals but those of foxes and bears, which may have fallen in and chewed on the human bones before dying. Investigators think the bodies were thrown into the pit after death (one seems to have died from a massive infection), probably not as part of a formal funeral ritual (no artifacts were found) but more likely for simple disposal purposes. Perhaps they all died together in some catastrophe or at least over a short period of time. Many of the bones show signs of childhood malnourishment.

No doubt the peoples labeled *H. antecessor* and *H. heidelbergensis* had other mental, cultural, and perhaps physical adaptations to help them deal with the various and changeable environments they encountered as the Pleistocene continued. We certainly know this was true for one famous group of humans from Europe and the Near East. Some crania from Sima de los Huesos are said to show traits that might be ancestral to this next group, the Neandertals.

THE NEANDERTALS

The Neandertals—*Homo neanderthalensis* in the six-species model—were named after one of the first human fossils found and recognized as a human fossil, a skullcap from the Neander Valley in Germany recovered in 1856 (Figure 11.25). This was before Darwin wrote *Origin of Species*. (In German, *thal* means "valley" and is always pronounced *tal*. Recent spelling drops the silent *h*, but some still use it. The formal species name retains its original spelling.) Table 11.3 and Figure 11.26 show the basic data for fossils of this species and the locations of these finds.

The Neandertals have had an interesting history in anthropology. At one time they were considered brutish, hunched-over, dim-witted members of a dead-end side branch of human evolution. At other times they have been thought of as just an ancient, slightly different-looking form

FIGURE 11.25
The original Neandertal
skullcap from Germany. The
cranial vault held a very large
brain, but the brow ridges indicate an obvious difference
from modern humans.

FIGURE 11.25
The original Neandertal skullcap from Germany. The cranial vault held a very large brain, but the brow ridges indicate an obvious difference from modern humans.

of modern *Homo sapiens* (Figure 11.27). These are both exaggerations. We now recognize the sophistication of the Neandertals' intellectual and cultural achievements. They were certainly similar to modern humans physically but still different in significant ways. So debate at present centers on whether the similarities place them within our species or whether the differences make them a separate species (see Chapter 12). Figures 11.28 and 11.29 compare the skulls and skeletons of a Neandertal and a modern *Homo sapiens*.

The crania of the Neandertals are striking in appearance. They had, essentially, more pronounced versions of the cranial features of *Homo heidelbergensis*. Their cranial capacities ranged from about 1,300 ml to 1,740 ml, well within the modern range, but their foreheads were still sloped, the backs of their skulls broad, and the sides bulging. The brow ridges were still large, but smaller at the sides than in *H. erectus*, and they were filled with air spaces (called the *frontal sinuses*), unlike the solid ridges of *H. erectus*. The brow ridges of the Neandertals were also rounded over each eye, rather than forming a straight line, as in earlier archaics. The face was large and prognathous, with a broad nasal opening and wide-set eyes. The chin was receding.

From the neck down, there were striking features. The bones of the Neandertals, even the finger bones, were more robust and had heavier muscle markings than their modern counterparts. The Neandertals were stocky, muscular, powerful people. This is seen even in the bones of Neandertal children, so it is assumed to be a result of inheritance, not simply of a hard-working lifestyle.

TABLE 11.3
Major Fossils of *Homo neanderthalensis*

Country	Locality	Fossils	Age	Est. Brain Size (ml)
Belgium	Spy	2 skeletons	—	—
Croatia	Krapina	Cranial and postcranial fragments of >45 individuals	130,000	1,200–1,450
	Vindija	52 fossil fragments	28,000–42,000	—
France	Biache St. Vaast	2 crania	150,000–175,000	—
	Fontechévade	Cranial fragments of several individuals	100,000	1,500
	La Chaise	Cranium	126,000	—
	La Chapelle-aux-Saints	Skeleton	—	1,620
	La Ferrassie	8 skeletons	>38,000	1,680
	St. Césaire	Skeleton	36,000	—
Germany	Neandertal	Skullcap	—	>1,250
	Ehringsdorf	Cranial fragment	225,000	—
Gibraltar	Forbe's Quarry	Cranium	50,000	—
Iraq	Shanidar	9 partial skeletons	70,000	1,600
Israel	Amud	Skeleton	70,000	1,740
	Kebara Cave	Postcranial skeleton	60,000	—
	Tabun	Skeleton, mandible, postcranial fragments	100,000	1,270
Italy	Monte Circeo	Cranium	—	—
	Saccopastore	Cranium	—	—
			Mean	**1,478.89**

Although very strong and stocky, the Neandertals were relatively short. Estimates put the average for males at 5 feet 6 inches and for females at 5 feet 3 inches. Their short stature was partially a result of relatively short lower legs. The lower arms were short as well. All these physical features hint at adaptations to a strenuous lifestyle and to cold climates. Shorter, heavier bodies with short limbs conserve heat better than narrow, long-limbed bodies (Holliday 1997, and see Chapter 13). As evidence, the limbs of the Neandertals from warmer Southwest Asia are relatively longer than the limbs of those living in ice-age Europe, who faced some of the extreme climates of the glacial advances.

Another possible adaptation to cold has been suggested by several investigators (see Menon 1997). In eight Neandertal skulls, they found

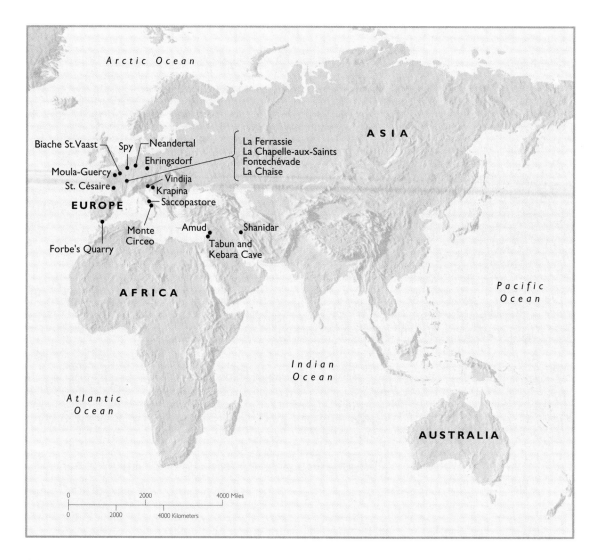

FIGURE 11.26
Map of major Neandertal
sites.

Mousterian technique: A
toolmaking tradition associated with the European
Neandertals.

triangular bony projections in the nasal cavity unlike anything seen in
modern humans or in any other human ancestors. These projections are
thought to have provided increased surface area for the nasal mucous
membranes, which would have helped warm and moisten the cold, dry
air of Europe during the Pleistocene glaciations. It has also been suggested that the large sinus cavities served a similar function. Moreover,
it is thought that the larynx of the Neandertals was higher in the throat
than in modern humans (see Figure 11.18), which would have prevented
them from gulping in cold, dry air through the mouth.

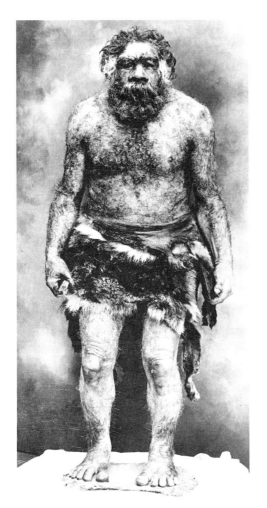

FIGURE 11.27
An old reconstruction from
the Field Museum in Chicago
(*left*) reinforces stereotypes
of Neandertals as brutish,
hairy, stooped-over distant
cousins. In contrast, anthropologist Milford Wolpoff
poses with a reconstructed
Neandertal in modern dress
to show that the differences
between us and them were
not that extreme.

Neandertal fossils date from 225,000 to as recently as 28,000 ya (see Table 11.3). During this time, it has been proposed, Neandertals were responsible for a number of important cultural achievements. What do we know about their behavior?

Among the well-established accomplishments of the Neandertals is an elaboration on the Levallois stone toolmaking technique. Called the **Mousterian technique,** after the site of Le Moustier in France, it involved the careful retouching of flakes taken off cores. These flakes were sharpened and shaped by precise additional flaking, on one side or both, to make specialized tools (Figure 11.30). One authority has identified no less than sixty-three tool types (Bordes 1972).

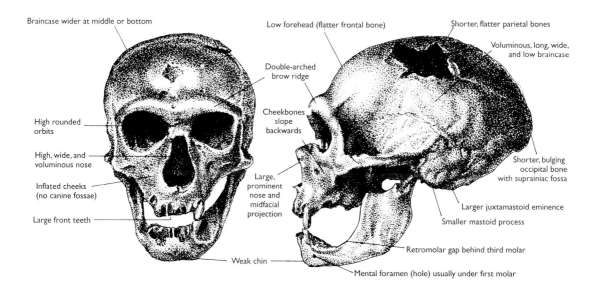

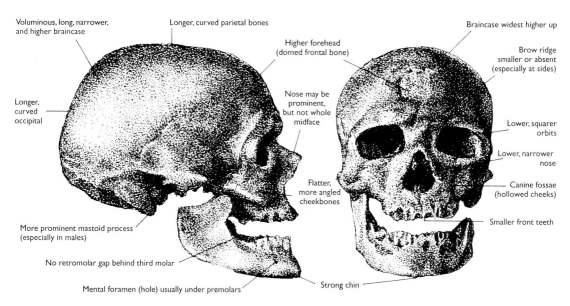

FIGURE 11.28

Cranial features of the La Chapelle specimen of Neandertal (*above*) compared with modern *Homo sapiens*.

Several specific uses of Mousterian tools have been inferred from microscopic wear-pattern analysis on specimens from the Kebara Cave site in Israel. Archaeologist John Shea (1989) notes wear patterns that indicate animal butchering, woodworking, bone and antler carving, and working of animal hides. There are also wear patterns like those

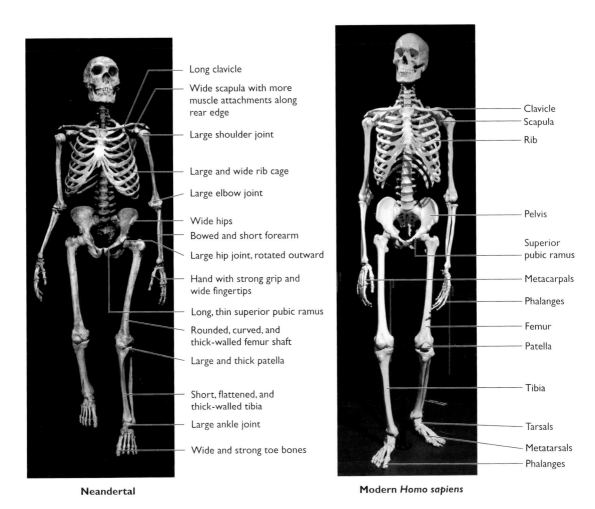

Long clavicle

Wide scapula with more muscle attachments along rear edge

Large shoulder joint

Large and wide rib cage

Large elbow joint

Wide hips
Bowed and short forearm

Large hip joint, rotated outward

Hand with strong grip and wide fingertips

Long, thin superior pubic ramus

Rounded, curved, and thick-walled femur shaft

Large and thick patella

Short, flattened, and thick-walled tibia

Large ankle joint

Wide and strong toe bones

Neandertal

Clavicle
Scapula
Rib

Pelvis

Superior pubic ramus

Metacarpals

Phalanges

Femur

Patella

Tibia

Tarsals

Metatarsals

Phalanges

Modern *Homo sapiens*

produced by the friction of a wooden shaft against a stone spear point. The Neandertals may have been the first to **haft** a stone point.

Although there is still debate about whether the Neandertals were big-game hunters or mostly scavengers, there is no doubt that they were dependent on the animals that abounded during the Pleistocene—animals such as reindeer, deer, ibex (wild goats), aurochs (wild oxen), horses, woolly rhinoceroses, bison, bear, and elk. Bones of these creatures have been found in association with Neandertal remains.

While we now have earlier evidence of intentional human burials (discussed in the next section), the first and most famous evidence comes from the Neandertals. Although many of these "burials" have now been attributed to natural causes, at least thirty-six Neandertal sites show

FIGURE 11.29
Skeletal features of Neandertal compared with modern *Homo sapiens*.

haft: To attach a wooden handle or shaft to a stone or bone point.

FIGURE 11.30
Unifacially retouched Mousterian flakes from the original site, Le Moustier, France.

evidence of intentional interment of the dead, and in some graves there were remains of offerings—stone tools, animal bones, and, possibly, flowers (Figure 11.31).

There is some debate, however, over whether or not these Neandertal burials had ritual significance. Did they represent belief in an afterlife or reverence for the physical remains of the deceased, or were the people simply disposing of a corpse, as seems to have been the case much earlier at Sima de los Huesos? Were animal bones present in the graves as offerings, or did scavengers and predators drag them there, along with Neandertal bones, where they were subsequently buried by natural processes? The pollen found in a Neandertal grave at Shanidar, Iraq, may not have been from flowers placed in the grave but may have been brought in by burrowing rodents, carried in by water, or blown in by wind at the time of burial. The jury is still out on this issue. But we know the Neandertals did sometimes bury their dead, for whatever reason.

FIGURE 11.31
Neandertal burial from La
Ferrassie, France. This body
was interred in the flexed
position, with the knees
drawn up to the chest, perhaps to mimic sleep. (The
basket belongs to the
excavators.)

Along the same lines, evidence has traditionally been cited for
a Neandertal cave bear "cult" in Europe. The cave bear, now extinct,
was a huge, impressive species, about 12 feet tall when standing upright.
Caves in Switzerland and France are supposed to contain a number of
cave bear skulls placed in special stone chests or in niches in the cave
walls. But these interpretations were apparently wishful thinking on the
part of early investigators. Reanalysis of the site descriptions indicates

FIGURE 11.32
The famous "Old Man" of La
Chapelle-aux-Saints, France.
(See front view and labels in
Figure 11.28.)

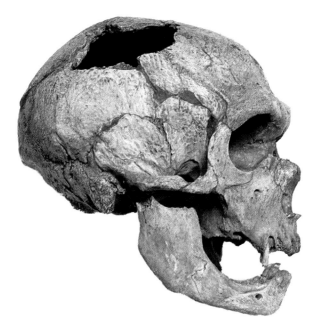

that the placement of the skulls was the result of natural processes such as cave-ins. Moreover, none of the bear bones show any signs of cut marks. This intriguing story has fallen to scientific investigation.

It has also been suggested that Neandertals were among the first to care for their elderly, ill, and injured. According to an early interpretation, the famous "Old Man" of La Chapelle-aux-Saints in France (Figure 11.32) was aged, lacked most of his teeth, and had a debilitating case of arthritis. That he survived for a time with these infirmities, according to the interpretation, indicates that he was cared for by his group.

Recent reexamination, though, shows that much of his tooth loss was after death and that his arthritis may not have been quite as debilitating as previously thought. Nor was he really old. He died when he was less than 40, probably rather quickly, as did the vast majority of Neandertals. Care of the elderly was probably not something they had to contend with very often.

On the other hand, there is a skeleton of a man from Shanidar, Iraq, that shows signs of injuries that may have resulted in blindness and the loss of one arm. He lived with this condition for some time and, therefore, was obviously cared for by his comrades.

But things may not have been completely peaceful among Neandertal populations. There is evidence of cannibalism from the Neandertal sites of Moula-Guercy in France (Defleur et al. 1999) and Krapina and

Vindija in Croatia (White 2001). Fragmentary bones from at least six individuals show stone tool cut marks in the same anatomical locations as those found on bones of wild goats and deer at the site. Some of the human long bones also show signs of having been smashed, in the way that would have allowed access to the rich bone marrow. Whether the inferred cannibalism was ritual (ingesting part of, or ashes of, a group member at a funeral ceremony) or gustatory (eating the flesh as food) cannot be determined.

Finally, we have the question of the linguistic abilities of the Neandertals. Some investigators have reconstructed the vocal tract of Neandertals based on the structure of the underside of the cranium. They have concluded that because of the higher larynx noted before, Neandertals were not capable of making all the vowel sounds of modern humans. However, a recently found hyoid bone—a horseshoe-shaped bone in the throat—from the Neandertal site of Kebara in Israel appears fully modern. This would mean that the vocal tract of the Neandertals *was* like ours and that they *could* make all the sounds of which we are capable. The point, of course, is—as we said for *Homo erectus*—that the Neandertals had sufficiently complex things to talk *about*, and just how they did so is less important than the fact that they did talk.

Archaic members of genus *Homo* were successful in adapting to different environments and, in the case of the Neandertals, harsh and demanding climates. They were clearly intelligent. We will no doubt find more fossils of archaics in new areas in the future. But the archaics differed in their complex of physical features from humans alive today. To begin the story of anatomically modern *Homo sapiens*, we once again return to Africa.

MODERN HUMANS

Beginning perhaps as early as 300,000 ya, fossils with what are considered to be near-modern or modern features appear, earliest in Africa and later in Southwest Asia, Europe, and East Asia. Later still, modern humans migrated to Australia, the islands of the Pacific, and North and South America. Under the six-species model, fossil forms with modern features are the only ones placed in *Homo sapiens*. There is no general agreement among proponents of this model about the exact species affiliation of some transitional forms—fossils with a mix of archaic and modern traits. Table 11.4 and Figure 11.33 give the basic information and locations of some of the more important fossils of early *H. sapiens*, as well as transitional forms.

TABLE 11.4
Some Important Fossils of Early *Homo sapiens*

Country	Location	Age
Kenya	Ileret	270,000–300,000 (trans.)*
South Africa	Florisbad	100,000–200,000 (trans.)
Ethiopia	Omo	130,000 (trans.)
Tanzania	Ngaloba	120,000 (trans.)
Morocco	Jebel Irhoud	100,000 (trans.)
Ethiopia	Herto	154,000–160,000
South Africa	Klasies River Mouth Langebaan Lagoon (footprints) Border Cave	84,000–120,000 117,000 62,000–115,000
Israel	Qafzeh Skhul	92,000–120,000 81,000–101,000
Germany	Stetten	36,000
France	Cro-Magnon Abri Pataud	<30,000 >27,000
China	Zhoukoudian	10,000–18,000
Australia	Lake Mungo	40,000
United States	Midland, Texas	11,600

*The abbreviation *trans.* indicates those fossils that are considered transitional between archaic and modern *Homo*.

We call these fossils "anatomically modern" because they lack some features characteristic of earlier hominids and possess features common in humans today. Gone is the prognathous profile. The modern human face is essentially flat. There are no heavy brow ridges. The skull is globular rather than elongated, and the forehead is more nearly vertical. The face is smaller and narrower, and there is a protruding chin. The postcranial skeleton is less robust. Refer back to Figures 11.28 and 11.29, and then look in the mirror.

Note in Table 11.4 that the earliest fossils are all from eastern and southern Africa and that they are considered, at least by some authorities,

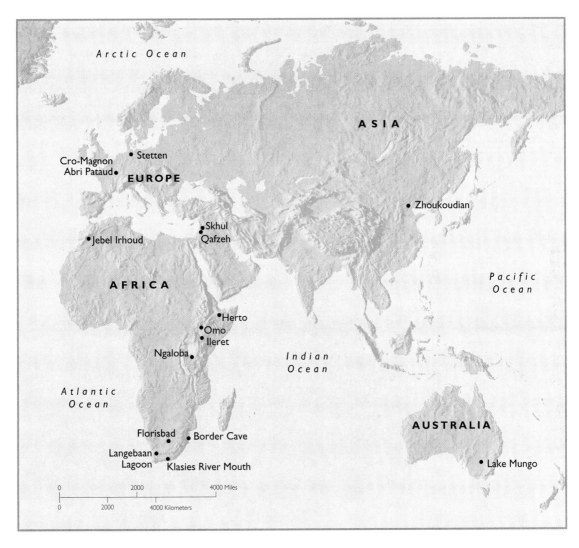

FIGURE 11.33
Map of major early *Homo sapiens* sites in Africa, Asia, Australia, and Europe.

as transitional between archaic and modern *Homo*. There is also a transitional form from Morocco (Figure 11.34). The implication is that modern humans—whether a new species or just the modern form of an existing species—arose in Africa. Until recently, the earliest dates for the appearance of transitional forms was about 200,000 ya from South Africa, but recent finds from Kenya (Bräuer et al. 1997), dated by several methods that appear to correspond well, have pushed this date back to perhaps 300,000 ya.

By around 160,000 ya, we begin to find fossils that represent humans of fully modern appearance relative to their geographic area. The earliest

FIGURE 11.34
Cranium from Jebel Irhoud, Morocco. This skull, dated at about 100,000 ya, is considered by some to be transitional between archaic and modern *Homo*. The braincase is low, the face is relatively large, and it has distinct brow ridges. Otherwise, its features are modern.

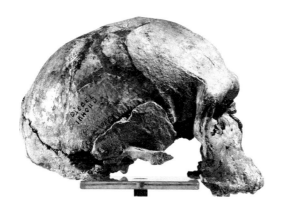

FIGURE 11.35
The most complete early *Homo sapiens* skull from Herto, Ethiopia, dated at 160,000 ya. The wide upper face, rounded forehead, divided brow ridge, flat midface, and large cranial capacity are all modern traits.

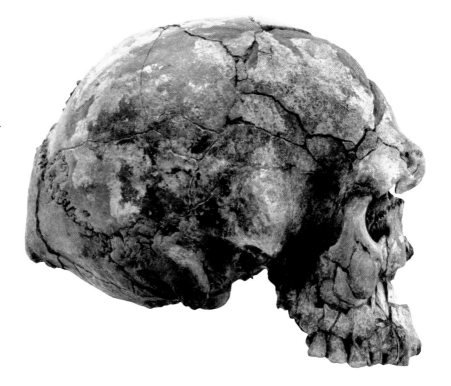

of these at present are recent finds from Ethiopia (Clark et al. 2003; White et al. 2003). Three partial skulls, one fairly complete (Figure 11.35), show very modern features, including a large cranial capacity of up to 1,450 ml. They are thought to constitute the "oldest definite record of what we currently think of as modern *Homo sapiens*" (Stringer 2003). These remains are associated with a mix of primitive and more sophisticated stone tools,

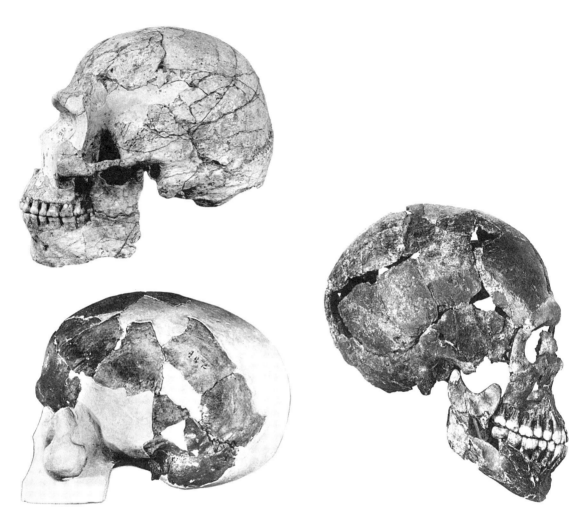

FIGURE 11.36

Examples of early modern *Homo sapiens* from (*counterlockwise from top*) Skhul, Israel; Border Cave, South Africa; and Qafzeh, Israel. Note the higher foreheads, protruding chins, and flatter faces compared with archaic *Homo*. Despite the rather prominent brow ridges in the Skhul specimen, it is still considered fully modern due to its other features.

and the skulls show some signs of postmortem manipulation, possibly for ritual purposes.

Slightly more recent fossils are from South Africa and Israel (Figure 11.36). At the South African site of Langebaan Lagoon, a small human, possibly a female, left her footprints in rock claimed to be dated 117,000 ya —a moment frozen in time reminiscent of the Laetoli footprints from Tanzania (see Chapter 10). As we move farther away from Africa and Southwest Asia, the dates for the early appearance of modern *H. sapiens* get more recent, a further indication that Africa is the birthplace of modern humans.

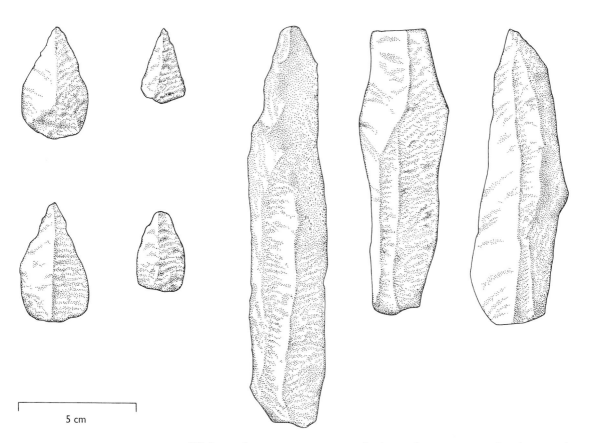

FIGURE 11.37
Blade tools from Klasies
River Mouth, South Africa.

5 cm

With modern anatomy came further advances in technology and expressions of modern behavior patterns. Although much of the tool technology of early moderns resembles that of archaics, artifacts from one of the oldest anatomically modern sites do show an important advance. From Klasies River Mouth in South Africa, dated at perhaps 120,000 ya, come long, bifacially worked spear points made from stone blades. These were flaked from cores by the *punch technique* (Figure 11.37). Here a pointed punch, usually made from an antler, is placed on the core and then struck with a stone hammer. This method directs the force of the blow more precisely so that longer, narrower, thinner flakes of predictable shape may be taken off. The same technique shows up later in Europe.

The Klasies River site also provides evidence that the people there may have hunted adults of such large animals as cape buffalo and eland (a large antelope); both these animals can weigh up to a ton. The site contains a spear point lodged in a buffalo vertebra. Certainly these people also scavenged and may have hunted only weak or old individuals of these dangerous species. But there is good evidence of at least limited

FIGURE 11.38
These bifacially flaked Upper Paleolithic spear points represent some of the finest stonework ever seen.

big-game hunting. That behavior, it seems, can be associated with the appearance of anatomically modern humans.

Although the Neandertal burials are perhaps the most famous examples of early human symbolic behavior, it is at two of the early *Homo sapiens* sites that we find the earliest established examples. At Qafzeh and Skhul, there are graves, dated at between 120,000 and 80,000 ya, with bodies and grave goods carefully laid out. In one grave at Qafzeh, a child was buried with a deer antler. Another grave at the same site contained the body of a young woman with that of an infant, possibly hers, at her feet. At Skhul, a skeleton was found holding the jawbone of a wild boar.

By the time the Neandertals disappeared, about 30,000 ya, modern *H. sapiens* had spread all over the Old World, even as far as Australia, and we enter a cultural period called the Upper Paleolithic, known first through finds in Europe. This period is marked by several important cultural innovations. Blades struck off cores become so precisely and beautifully made as to be virtual works of art—in fact, some blades are so thin and delicate we think they may have been just that (Figure 11.38).

Tools in the Upper Paleolithic were also made from bone, antler, and ivory. Some are practical, such as harpoons, spear points, and shaft straighteners. Some have symbolic significance. Even some of the utilitarian items are decorated (Figure 11.39). Indeed, art is seen in the Upper Paleolithic in some of its most striking and beautiful forms. Over a hundred cave sites, mostly in France and Spain, have yielded paintings as aesthetically

FIGURE 11.39
Upper Paleolithic artifacts. Among the artifacts shown here are a shaft straightener with carved animals (*top*), a harpoon carved from antler (*upper left*), and an example of the famous Venus figurines (*lower right*) that may have served as fertility symbols.

pleasing as anything produced today (Figure 11.40). There are also carvings in stone, bone, antler, and ivory, among the most famous of which are the so-called Venus figurines, often thought to be fertility symbols (see Figure 11.39, lower right). Some Venus figurines even depict clothing styles such as woven caps (Wong 2000a). An ivory "lion man" figurine from Germany, dated at 30,000 ya, may be the oldest figurative art in the world. There is also an engraved antler from France dated at about 32,000 ya, that may have been a calendar based on phases of the moon.

There is some evidence of even older art from northern Australia. A hematite "crayon"—used to produce red ocher, a pigment—has been dated at almost 60,000 ya at the site of Malakunanja II, and painted ocher figures and carved holes at a rock shelter site called Jinmium may date to between 176,000 and 116,000 ya. Both sites, however, were dated using luminescence dating (see Chapter 9), which is still somewhat experimental. There is other evidence that the Jinmium site may be only about 10,000 years old (Gibbons 1997c).

FIGURE 11.40
One of many beautiful paintings from the cave of Lascaux in southern France, this mural depicts an aurochs (an ancient ox) and several horses. There is an antlered animal, probably a deer, in the lower right. Notice that the left front leg of the red horse is separated from the body, adding a three-dimensional appearance. This photograph is really from Lascaux II, a replica near the actual cave, created because of damage to the original from bacteria and carbon dioxide given off by too many visitors. The walls of the replica cave are reproduced to within 5 mm of the contours of the original cave, and many of the pigments in the paintings are the same as those used by the original artists perhaps 17,000 ya.

As the Upper Paleolithic continued, big-game hunting became a way of life, especially for people living in glacial climates with limited plant resources. People no longer relied on caves or rock shelters for places of habitation but began manufacturing shelters. At Mal'ta, for example, an 18,000-year-old site in south-central Russia, scientists found the remains of a hut built on a wood frame supported by woolly mammoth bones and reindeer antlers and covered with animal hides.

Contemporary Reflections

What Do We Mean by "Human"?

Back in Linnaeus's time, when species were thought to have been separately created, the answer was an easy one. People were human, and everything else wasn't. Then fossils representing the history of other organisms began to appear and to be recognized as the intermediate evolutionary steps from previous states to present ones. And then Charles Darwin explained how this all happened. As anthropologist Ian Tattersall puts it, by the end of the nineteenth century, when it had become clear that we too had a fossil record and had evolved like other creatures, the issue of humanness became far more complex (1994).

We use the word *human* all the time in different contexts and with different meanings—and we usually communicate and understand those meanings with little ambiguity. Even in a biological context, it is perfectly clear which present-day species the term refers to. We use *human* as precisely as we use *ape* or *monkey*. But how about a more scientific definition that takes into account what we know about our evolutionary history and, thus, about our place in nature in a broader context? Put another way, although it's clear that *human* refers to us, who *else* might it refer to?

Human could be used as a synonym for *hominid*. In the traditional (and still most common) taxonomic sense of this category, *human*, then, would refer to any habitually bipedal primate and so would include *Australopithecus* and *Paranthropus*, who share few specific traits—other than upright walking—with modern peoples. One cladistic taxonomy (see Chapter 7) includes our sister species—chimpanzees, bonobos, and gorillas—in family Hominidae. Using *human* as a synonym for *hominid* here would be so broad as to be fairly meaningless.

A seemingly more realistic approach is to limit the use of *human* to just *Homo sapiens* (for splitters) or just anatomically modern *Homo sapiens* (for lumpers). No one would deny that

Around 20,000 ya, and probably earlier, humans moved into North America, coming across a land bridge between Siberia and Alaska that was exposed when the sea level dropped during glacial periods. They soon moved throughout the continent and into South America. Modern *Homo sapiens* had populated every landmass on the planet except Antarctica.

SUMMARY

The record of the latest 2.5 million years of hominid evolution is complex. The fossils from the first 99 percent of this period are scarce, often fragmentary, scattered geographically, physically variable, and, in some cases, questionably dated. Not surprisingly, the interpretations of these fossils vary as greatly as do the fossils themselves. Our survey uses as a starting point an elaborate model for classifying and naming these modern *H. sapiens* falls into that classification, which could include the criteria of "high intelligence, language, aesthetic sensibilities, and the mastery of complex technologies" (Tattersall 1994:114)—all those things we know define, delineate, and differentiate our species today. Under this use, the other species of *Homo* (*H. neanderthalensis*, for instance) "possessed [almost nothing] even remotely resembling the restless spirit of innovation and inventiveness that informed the lives of Upper Paleolithic peoples. . . . It is only with the Upper Paleolithic that we find evidence for behaviors that would allow us to characterize their possessors as fully human" (115).

But anthropologist Milford Wolpoff (in a 1994 rebuttal to the Tattersall piece cited above) argues that this definition is too limited. While older forms of *Homo* may have had less complex cultural behaviors than ours, they nonetheless *had* culture. The makers of the Oldowan tools some 2 mya were the first stone toolmakers and the first hominoids to show a trend toward larger brains. Even with our far more complex cultural expressions, we share with these other members of our genus—and *only* with them—these large brains and the abilities they facilitate. It would seem, then, that to limit the use of *human* to just modern *Homo sapiens* would necessarily require recognizing *degrees* of humanness to account for the behaviors of premodern peoples. Indeed, Tattersall says that despite his limited definition, he finds "great difficulty in denying Neanderthals human status" (1994:115).

All this may seem rather a matter of philosophical point of view—and on some levels it is. But scientifically, if we link being human to being included in certain taxonomic categories, then just how we classify groups of hominids will make a difference. If, for instance, we limit humanness to members of *Homo sapiens*, then it matters a great deal whether we accept a six-species or a one-species model for the evolution of our genus. This is the real issue of the Tattersall and Wolpoff pieces cited, and it leads directly to the discussion in Chapter 12.

---

fossils—the recognition of six species within genus *Homo* after the early *Homo* stage. I do not necessarily endorse this model but begin with it for the purpose of clearly organizing our discussion of a fairly complex topic.

The earliest species, *H. ergaster*, is found only in Kenya, but a possible branch of this group, *H. erectus*, spread through the rest of Africa and into Asia and possibly southern Europe. These two species are characterized by virtually modern postcranial skeletons, brain sizes close to and even overlapping the modern human range, and the invention of more sophisticated stone tools and other cultural innovations, including the use of fire. In Java, *H. erectus* may have persisted until as recently as 27,000 ya.

A geographically and chronologically scattered species, *Homo heidelbergensis*, appears next. The earliest examples of this group, from Spain, are placed by some authorities into a new species, *H. antecessor*. Located from England to South Africa to China, *H. heidelbergensis* displays brain sizes within the modern human range and at the modern human average, though their crania retain primitive features, giving them the label "archaic." They are known, starting about 200,000 ya, for the invention of the Levallois stone toolmaking technique—a sophisticated way of "mass producing" flake tools. They may have done some hunting as well.

The most famous of the "archaic" humans are the Neandertals, a separate species, *Homo neanderthalensis*, according to many. Living in Europe and Southwest Asia from 200,000 to 28,000 ya, this group exhibits traits that distinguish it from both *H. heidelbergensis* and later *H. sapiens*. These traits include large, prognathous faces, ruggedly built skulls, and robust, muscular bodies—possibly adaptations to the cold glacial conditions many of their populations encountered. Neandertals are known for their retouched flake tools, which may have been used to carve bone and work wood, and for abstract cultural achievements such as burial of the dead and care of the elderly and infirm. They may also have been the first to haft stone points on wooden shafts.

Fossils transitional between archaic and modern *Homo* appear in Africa perhaps as early as 300,000 ya, and the first fully modern *Homo sapiens* are found in Africa and Southwest Asia beginning around 160,000 ya. From there, modern-appearing humans spread throughout the Old World and eventually to the islands of the Pacific and to the Americas. Archaic peoples—or archaic traits—disappear. During this time, big-game hunting develops, tool technology advances, sophisticated shelters are built, and humans create art.

This leads us to the following questions, which we will discuss in the next chapter: Just how many species of genus *Homo* are we actually dealing with? And, how are all these groups related evolutionarily?

QUESTIONS FOR FURTHER THOUGHT

1. We will discuss the debate over the evolution of genus *Homo* in greater detail in the next chapter. For now, however, does it matter to *you* how many species of our genus have existed? Why or why not? Why do you think it matters so much to professional scientists?

2. The issue of whether groups of organisms are separate species within one genus or are variable populations within a single species has ramifications for living things other than hominids. One related topic is the Endangered Species Act. Why might this issue matter with regard to the implementation of that legislation?

3. As a lead-in to the discussion in the next chapter, consider what the arguments might be in favor of lumping the Neandertals into *Homo sapiens*. What arguments might be made for splitting them into a separate species?

KEY TERMS

law of parsimony	Pleistocene	endocasts
Oldowan	glaciers	postorbital
core tools	tundra	constriction
flake tools	Acheulian technique	Levallois technique
sagittal keel	hand axe	Mousterian technique
torus	bifacial	haft

SUGGESTED READINGS

For more on the new Dmanisi find, see a typically well-illustrated article in the August 2002 *National Geographic,* "New Find." For more on the Atapuerca finds from Spain, see the also well-illustrated book *The First Europeans: Treasures from the Hills of Atapuerca,* published by Junta de Castilla y León.

An interesting article linking an increase in human brain size with dietary change is "Food for Thought," by William R. Leonard, in the December 2002 *Scientific American.* And for more on ancient cannibalism see Tim D. White's "Once We Were Cannibals" in the August 2001 *Scientific American.*

For summaries of human evolution, see *The Last Neanderthal,* by Ian Tattersall, and *Extinct Humans,* by Ian Tattersall and Jeffrey Schwarz. Be aware that these authors are splitters, who advocate a maximum number of separate species for *Homo* and the other hominid genera. The books, however, are accurate, up-to-date, and beautifully illustrated.

For the fascinating story of Eugene Dubois and the discovery of "Java Man," see Pat Shipman's *The Man Who Found the Missing Link: Eugene Dubois and His Lifelong Quest to Prove Darwin Right.* The story of the missing "Peking Man" fossils is the topic of *The Search for Peking Man,* by C. Janus.

More detailed discussion on the fossil and archaeological records of the genus *Homo* can be found in Kenneth Feder's and my *Human Antiquity: An Introduction to Physical Anthropology and Archaeology,* fourth edition.

Computer tomography (CT) scans have recently been used in paleoanthropology in the reconstruction of fossils of the Neandertals. See www.ifi.unizh.ch/~zolli/Neanderthals.htm.

Another interesting Neandertal Web site is www.neanderthal-modern.com. For still more on Atapuerca, try www.ucm.es/info/paleo/ata/english. And for some Paleolithic art from Chauvet Cave, see www.culture.fr/culture/arcnat/chauvet/en.

THE DEBATE OVER MODERN HUMAN ORIGINS

We carry within us the
wonders we seek
without us; There is all
Africa and her
prodigies in us.
—Sir Thomas Browne

Many of the current great debates in science involve, not surprisingly, the distant past. Scientists argue about the origin and early history of the universe, about the formation of our solar system and its planets, about the origin of life on earth, and about the causes and effects of mass extinctions seen in the fossil record. There are, of course, also debates about the early evolution of the hominids—the number of early hominid genera, for example, or the exact relationships among the groups of early hominids.

But no point in the history of our evolution is as contentious as the latest chapter—the origin of modern *Homo sapiens*. An astounding number of articles and books advocate one point of view or another, summarize and evaluate the various hypotheses, or analyze and interpret the debate itself. And this debate is far from peaceful. Arguments get heated at times, with some accusing others of poor scholarship or hidden agendas. Comments can get downright nasty.

Moreover, some investigators see, in the choice of hypotheses, implications that are not necessarily directly relevant to the issues being discussed (see the "Contemporary Reflections" box in this chapter.) These connections are picked up by the popular media and passed on to the public, who get the wrong impression of what the debate is really about. None of this helps us sort out, examine, and evaluate an issue that is already complicated enough. There are large amounts of data about the possible origin of modern *H. sapiens*, much of it interpreted quite differently by various specialists. Even impartial and dispassionate accounts can still be detailed and confusing.

At the risk of adding yet another version, with yet another set of diagrams and names, I will try in this chapter to reduce the competing hypotheses (or models) down to their essential elements in a way that relates them directly to the material we have covered so far, at a level of detail appropriate to this book. I hope that this approach will make sense in terms of the themes and data we have been dealing with and that it will provide you with a basic framework to which you can add further information.

As confusing as the issue might be, it is a good example of science in action, as both a scholarly and a very human endeavor. Even summarizing the debate—with its different interpretations, different theoretical points of view, related agendas, and sometimes rancorous rhetoric—is to catch scientific progress "in the act."

The origin of modern *H. sapiens* is a fascinating topic and an understandably important debate because, as I pointed out in Chapter 11, at stake is our very identity—our specific place in nature, our relationships to the other hominids, and our nature as products of the processes of evolution. We will address the following questions in this chapter:

What are the major competing hypotheses regarding the origin of modern *Homo sapiens*?

What evidence has been offered—from the fossil record, from genetics, and from evolutionary theory—for and against each model?

Is there an alternative model?

THE TWO MAJOR MODELS

It would appear based on current available evidence (see Table 11.4) that fully modern-*looking* people first appeared about 160,000 ya, with transitional forms showing the beginnings of modern traits as far back as 300,000 ya. It also appears that these traits first evolved in Africa. But at issue is the question, Do these traits accurately define and distinguish a new species of hominid, *Homo sapiens,* or is the collection of traits we think of as modern just the latest set of variable features in the evolution of a much older species? You should recognize these points of view as another way of stating the lumper-splitter debate introduced in Chapter 11 between the single-species model of the evolution of genus *Homo* and the five- or six-species model.

If we focus on these two schools of thought, we can define two models for the origin of our species. The single-species model is known formally as the **Multiregional Evolution (MRE) model.** Models that recognize *H. sapiens* as only the most recent of multiple species of *Homo* are called by a number of names, most commonly the **Out-of-Africa model.** However, the MRE model also acknowledges that our species arose in and expanded out of Africa—just a lot earlier—so I prefer to call the latter model the **Recent African Origin (RAO) model.** Figure 12.1 has generalized diagrams that depict these two models. Once you have grasped the arguments for and against these well-known and quite opposite models as a basis, we'll examine an alternative, the **Mostly-Out-of-Africa model.**

The Recent African Origin (RAO) Model

Major proponents of the Recent African Origin model are Christopher Stringer of the Natural History Museum in London (Stringer and McKie

Multiregional Evolution (MRE) model: The hypothesis that *Homo sapiens* is about 2 million years old and that modern human traits evolved in geographically diverse locations and then spread through the species.

Out-of-Africa model: Another name for the Recent African Origin model.

Recent African Origin (RAO) model: The hypothesis that *Homo sapiens* evolved recently as a separate species in Africa and then spread to replace more archaic populations.

Mostly-Out-of-Africa model: The hypothesis that *Homo sapiens* is about 2 million years old as a species but that most of the genetic variation and phenotypic features of modern humans have an African origin.

FIGURE 12.1
Generalized models for the
origin of *Homo sapiens*.

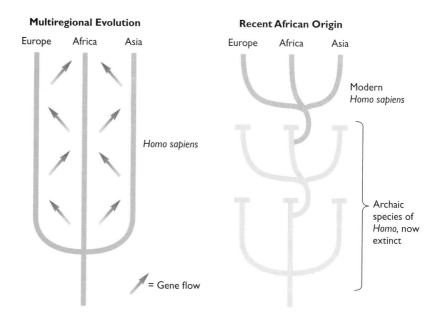

FIGURE 12.1
Generalized models for the
origin of *Homo sapiens*.

1996) and Ian Tattersall of the American Museum of Natural History in
New York (Tattersall 2001; Tattersall and Schwarz 2000). Although various supporters of this model recognize different numbers of species
within genus *Homo,* they all share the view that modern *Homo sapiens*
is a separate species that branched from a preexisting archaic *Homo*
species in Africa around 200,000 to 150,000 ya. This new species then
spread over the Old World, replacing archaic populations when they
came in contact, presumably because *H. sapiens* was a better-adapted
species. (This model is sometimes called the *Replacement model.*)

If this model is correct, we must be able to find distinctions between
our modern species and premodern (or archaic) humans that clearly distinguish us *as separate species.* There must be an anatomical definition of
modernity; in other words, there must be traits that all *Homo sapiens*
share that are not found in premoderns, and traits found in premoderns
that are lacking in modern humans. We would also expect to find genetic
distinctions of a degree that would indicate separate species.

If we can anatomically define and distinguish premodern from modern humans, then we can deduce that fossils transitional between premodern and modern humans should occur only in the single region in
which moderns evolved. Elsewhere, there should be evidence of anatomical premoderns and anatomical moderns coexisting in the same regions,
once the latter spread out from their initial source area. Eventually, the

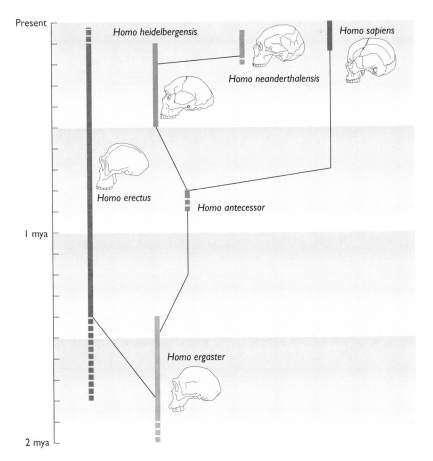

Present

Homo heidelbergensis

Homo sapiens

Homo neanderthalensis

Homo erectus

Homo antecessor

1 mya

Homo ergaster

2 mya

FIGURE 12.2
One possible set of relationships for the six proposed species of *Homo*, according to the RAO model. The data are the same as in Figure 11.1.

premodern human forms would have become extinct, unable to compete with their anatomically modern cousins. Figure 12.2 shows one way this model interprets the relationships among the six species of *Homo* described in Chapter 11.

The Multiregional Evolution (MRE) Model

The names most often associated with the Multiregional Evolution model are Milford Wolpoff and Rachel Caspari of the University of Michigan (Wolpoff and Caspari 1997). This model—a bit more complicated than the RAO model—also claims that *Homo sapiens* arose in Africa, but it pushes back the date of *H. sapiens*'s appearance to as much as 2 mya. Members of this new species (traditionally called *Homo erectus*) spread throughout the Old World, evolving genetic and phenotypic regional differences in response to the wide variety of environmental circumstances they encountered and the complex population movements, isolations, mergings, and fissionings that must have taken place. The degree of species mobility resulted in sufficient gene flow to maintain a single species, as no population was isolated long enough or to a great enough degree for speciation to occur. As successful advantageous adaptive features arose, they were dispersed across the species through gene flow. Ideas and technologies spread and were exchanged as well (Wolpoff et al. 2001). Physical features we associate with modern humans appeared everywhere but may have been manifested in different ways in different populations and in different environments. Thus, we are today and have always been a variable species—but a single species.

It is important to understand that this does *not* mean that *every* population within this long-lived and widespread species survived to contribute genes to modern humans. Certainly, individual isolated populations could have become extinct with few or none of their genes passed down. Nor does this deny the distinctive sets of traits that characterize some of the premodern (archaic) populations such as the Neandertals. The MRE model simply says that these populations were not separate species, that *Homo sapiens* did not arise in the recent past, and, thus, that it did not spread and become dominant by replacing other species of *Homo*.

If the MRE model is correct, we should find no clear evidence that modern *H. sapiens* is a separate species from any of the so-called premodern groups. In other words, there should be no biologically meaningful definition of modernity—no set of traits that is found among all populations classified as modern that is lacking among all premodern populations. However, populations with transitional sets of traits should be found in many locations. Ideally, there should be some evidence of interbreeding in the form of a mix of traits in fossils from those areas where groups coexisted. Finally, there should be regional continuity of traits—features characteristic of geographic areas that appear not only in modern populations but premodern ones as well.

One conclusion of this model is that if premodern groups are in fact members of our species, then the rules of taxonomy dictate that the earliest name used for any of them must be applied to them all. Thus, if all six species of *Homo* are indeed the same species, they would all be *Homo sapiens*, the name first used by Linnaeus in 1758 (see Chapters 7 and 14). Figure 12.3 shows how the MRE model views the interrelationships among the various regional fossil populations discussed in Chapter 11.

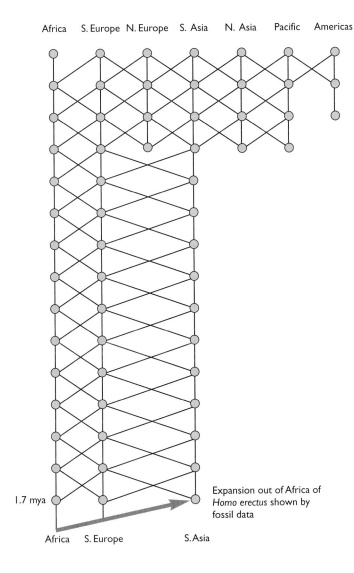

Africa S. Europe N. Europe S. Asia N. Asia Pacific Americas

1.7 mya

Africa   S. Europe   S. Asia

Expansion out of Africa of
Homo erectus shown by
fossil data

FIGURE 12.3
Diagram of the MRE model.
The red arrow represents
the initial expansion out of
Africa nearly 2 mya. Vertical
lines represent direct regional descent. Diagonal lines
represent gene flow among
regional populations. (See
Figure 12.8 for a more complete diagram representing a
somewhat different model.)

(Adapted from Templeton 2002:48)

The Key Requirements of Each Model

As we evaluate the evidence in this debate, here are the main points to
keep in mind about each model:

RAO

- Requires an anatomical definition of modernity that clearly distinguishes modern humans from premodern species

- Requires genetic distinctions of a degree that indicates modern humans are a separate species
- Requires that transitional forms appear only in the single region in which modern humans evolved

MRE

- Requires that there be no biologically meaningful definition of modernity; that is, no set of "modern" traits that is lacking among all premodern populations
- Requires that populations with transitional sets of traits be found in many locations
- Requires a regional continuity of traits; that is, features characteristic of a given geographic area should appear in premodern and modern populations within that region

THE EVIDENCE

Clearly, the evidence for the past 2 million years of our evolution is limited. Fossils exist, but they are often fragmentary, and they are scattered across space and time. The same can be said for archaeological evidence of our ancestors' cultural activities. Genetic data are available, but only from fully modern populations alive today—or at least recently. And evolutionary theory is still being debated, both in general terms and more specifically when applied to the history of a specific group.

Thus, in reviewing the extensive literature on modern human origins, we find that different authorities have very different interpretations of the same data. Indeed, the same general data have been convincingly used to support both the MRE and RAO models, but proponents differ in which specific pieces of data they emphasize. It can become, as anthropologist David Pilbeam once said in another context (1984, 1986), like "peering" too closely at a pointillist painting or trying to look at a newspaper photo with a magnifying glass. The details become a bunch of "meaningless dots." Following, then, is a general summary of the available evidence and interpretations by both the MRE and RAO "camps."

The Fossil Record

In using the multiple-species model as an organizing format for our previous discussion of genus *Homo,* we have already presented the fossil evidence as interpreted by the Recent African Origin proponents. Look again at the tables and maps in Chapter 11.

As suggested by the RAO model, forms transitional between archaic species (*H. heidelbergensis* and *H. neanderthalensis*) and *H. sapiens* are found only in Africa. Modern forms appear first in Africa (see Figure 11.35) and then show up at increasingly recent dates as one moves away from that continent. And archaics and moderns overlap in time in some areas. Note, for example, that the modern fossils from Skhul and Qafzeh in Israel actually predate the Neandertals in the same country and that the two groups shared the area for a time (see Tables 11.3 and 11.4).

In stark contrast, Wolpoff and Caspari assert that the variation seen within the fossil record of *Homo* does not warrant division into separate species. They claim, for example, that in broad perspective "just about every way *H. erectus* differs from its australopithecine ancestors also characterizes *H. sapiens*: virtually no features are unique to *H. erectus*" (1997:256). In other words, *H. sapiens* and *H. erectus* are the same species. They also contend that modern traits did not all arise in one location but in many and that they spread throughout the species through gene flow, to be expressed differently in different geographic locations. As required by the MRE model, transitional forms are found in many locations.

Moreover, Wolpoff and Caspari feel that "it has proved impossible to provide an acceptable [physical] definition of modernity" in the first place (1997:313). Some features proposed to define modern humans *do not* include all recent or living peoples. For example, it has been suggested that Neandertals' large, continuous brow ridges are a major diagnostic feature helping to distinguish them from modern humans. But some living indigenous people of Australia—fully modern biological humans in every sense of the word—also have large, continuous brow ridges (Figure 12.4). There is sufficient variation among modern humans, says Wolpoff, that modernity must be defined regionally, as no general definition includes all clearly modern humans and excludes all other proposed species.

A study (Pearson 2000) on postcranial remains and the question of modern human origins notes that defining modernity is also difficult for that area of the skeleton: "Any definition of what constitutes anatomically modern form should take into consideration the fact that some populations of living humans have evolved a body form that is substantially different from that of early modern humans" (241). In other words, through time, populations labeled "modern human" have undergone notable change, thus making it hard to list the phenotypic criteria for modernity.

FIGURE 12.4
Two Tiwi from Melville Island, northern Australia. Note their large, continuous brow ridges—a trait associated with archaic humans yet present here in fully modern *Homo sapiens*. The man on the right is in mourning, which requires that he paint his body and not feed himself, so he is receiving water from a friend.

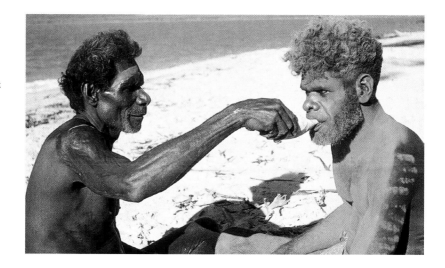

Pearson also notes that the Neandertals are frequently used to establish a definition of modern, based on the assumption that they are a "good approximation of generalized archaic human morphology." This assumption, he says, is "partially in error" since the characteristic Neandertal features are very different from those of earlier archaics such as *H. heidelbergensis*, who in fact "more closely approximated modern human morphology" (2000:231) for many postcranial traits. To use the Neandertals in a comparison with modern populations, then, is sort of "stacking the deck," since they are *more* different from moderns in some ways than are other archaics. Moreover, the Neandertals were a small population, isolated by distance and ecology in an Old World backwater. Even if most of their populations, and thus their phenotypes, became extinct, that does not preclude their being members of our species, nor does it negate the MRE model. A physical definition of modernity thus seems to be in the eye of the beholder, based on one's interpretation and choice of populations and characteristics.

Wolpoff and supporters also see continuity of individual traits in certain areas, especially Asia and Australia. He also says some features show continuity between Neandertal and modern populations in Europe. Especially important are nonadaptive traits, which would not be affected by environmental changes over time but *would* be affected by large-scale population replacement. An example is an opening for a nerve on the inside of the mandible (the mandibular foramen). A form of this opening (of no apparent adaptive significance) found only in European Neandertals is also found in high frequency in early moderns from

Europe—and in *no* Asian or African populations—suggesting a direct evolutionary relationship.

In another study, Wolpoff and colleagues (2001) compared anatomical features of skulls from both moderns and archaics from different parts of Europe, Africa, and Asia. The study and its results are complex, but essentially what these researchers found were a series of similarities and differences that pointed to a mixed ancestry of the modern populations. In some cases the modern skulls were closer to the archaics from their geographic regions than they were to the African archaics or to those skulls considered to represent the first modern humans out of Africa (such as those from Skhul and Qafzeh in Israel.) In other words, archaic populations, rather than being separate species (as in the RAO model) and becoming extinct, contributed to the ancestry of moderns. This study appears to support the MRE model.

As further potential evidence of the MRE model, we have a 1998 find from Portugal of a 3½- to 5-year-old child who lived 24,500 ya (Duarte et al. 1999). The child's mandible displays a protruding chin and proportionately small front teeth, diagnostic of moderns. The postcranial bones, however, are robust, with proportionately short lower arms and legs, diagnostic of Neandertals. The investigators' interpretation is that the boy represents a hybrid, the result of an interbreeding between a Neandertal and a modern human—making those two groups, by definition, members of the same species. Not unexpectedly, of course, RAO proponents reject this claim. Ian Tattersall suggests that the child was simply a "chunky" anatomically modern human (Holden 1999).

I think that in regard to this debate, the fossil record is ambiguous. It can clearly be interpreted to support either point of view, and there is wide disagreement between those points of view. Note that even splitters cannot agree on the exact number of premodern species of *Homo*. They only agree that *Homo sapiens* is a recent, separate species. The fossils that do exist are usually incomplete, not necessarily representative of the populations from which they came, and often of questionable age. Moreover, many of the morphological features being used for these analyses are of unknown heritability; that is, we don't know how much they tell us about actual genetic distinctions (Minugh-Purvis 1995).

Finally, it is hard to translate physical features into species classification. As we saw in Chapters 4 and 5, some separate species look nearly identical, while other species can exhibit an amazing amount of phenotypic variation (see Figure 2.7). The RAO people see the variation in the fossil record as being outside the range of modern human diversity. The MRE people feel that the fossil variation is well within the potential range of our species, just different in specifics at different points in time from modern variation.

Along with fossil evidence, archaeological data have also been cited in support of the two models. Recent African Origin supporters note the appearance of sophisticated toolmaking techniques and art (Henshilwood et al. 2002) earlier in Africa than elsewhere (see Figure 11.37 for an example). They also see evidence of the fairly rapid replacement in Europe of tools associated with Neandertals by those associated with modern *Homo sapiens*.

In contrast, MRE advocates claim that these early African tool forms are not all that different from the tools of Neandertals and that artifacts associated with modern fossils from Skhul and Qafzeh are virtually identical to those associated with nearby Neandertal finds. At Grotte XVI, in the French Dordogne Valley, investigators see a gradual change in cultural behavior over the course of many thousands of years, from Neandertal to moderns, with a great degree of similarity in behavior between these two supposedly different groups. Based on analyses of tools and other archaeological evidence from these populations, researchers conclude that both moderns and Neandertals hunted, fished, and apparently even smoked their catch to preserve it (Wong 2000b). In other words, tool type is not necessarily diagnostic of species, and the variation, scattered nature, and questionable dating of some archaeological data present the same problems as does the paleontological record.

Genetics

We mentioned genetic evidence in Chapter 9 regarding the relationship between humans and the nonhuman primates. Genetic data can also be used to compare living human populations and examine the question of modern human origins. Genetic lines of inquiry have usually been interpreted to support the Recent African Origin model, that is, a recent African source for modern humanity. As we will see, there are other possible interpretations.

In general, living human beings exhibit very little genetic variation—in fact, less than that seen within ape species (Stringer and Andrews 1988:1264). Indeed, some chimpanzee DNA exhibits ten times the amount of variation as does human DNA (Wilson and Cann 1992:71). This suggests a relatively recent, common source for all living humans, which is consistent with the RAO hypothesis. In other words, if there is little genetic diversity, not much time has elapsed since the species first evolved.

On the other hand, the Multiregional Evolution model can also account for this genetic homogeneity. As a mobile species with a network of constant genetic exchange among populations, regional genetic differences (although they *do* exist in terms of genetic details) would become increasingly lessened as the species increased its population and improved its ability to move around. In such a species, even a very old one, we would also expect relatively little *modern* genetic variation. Thus, our species' genetic homogeneity does not help us distinguish between the two models.

Although overall genetic variation is low in modern human beings, when some details of our DNA are compared across geographic populations, using the techniques discussed in Chapter 9, some potentially interesting patterns emerge. There are three basic types of DNA that are used in this regard. We may look at the DNA in the nucleus of our cells, the **nuclear DNA.** Most nuclear DNA is noncoding, and this noncoding DNA is especially useful because it appears to be selectively neutral. Thus, mutations that accumulate in it are neither selected against, resulting in their disappearance, nor selected for, resulting in an increase in their frequency. Therefore, nuclear DNA may provide a more accurate record of the genetic history of two or more divergent lineages.

Of special interest to us is **mitochondrial DNA (mtDNA).** Mitochondria are the energy factories within the cells of plants and animals. They possess their own distinct DNA, which, in complex interaction with the nuclear DNA, codes for the mitochondria's function of producing the biological fuel that energizes the cell. Most human cells contain hundreds or thousands of mitochondria. At some point in early cellular evolution, the ancestors of mitochondria were separate organisms. Through what may be the first example of **symbiosis,** they became functional elements within larger cells, maintaining their own genetic code. This code is particularly useful for some genetic studies because mtDNA accumulates mutations at a rate five to ten times faster than nuclear DNA, and there is evidence that the mutation rate is fairly constant. In addition, the entire mtDNA genome is known; that is, all the base pairs have been identified, and there are large noncoding sequences. Finally, mtDNA is inherited only through the female line; although both human eggs and sperm contain mitochondria, the 50 to 100 mitochondria from the sperm disappear from the egg shortly after fertilization. Thus, one's mtDNA is not a combination of the mtDNA from two parents, as is nuclear DNA.

The third type of DNA used is that on the Y chromosome. Analogously to mtDNA, Y-chromosome DNA is inherited only from one's father and is passed on only by males. Moreover, since the X and Y chromosomes

nuclear DNA: The genetic material in the nucleus of a cell.

mitochondrial DNA (mtDNA): The genetic material found in the cell's mitochondria rather than in the cell's nucleus.

symbiosis: An adaptive relationship between two different species, often, but not necessarily, of mutual benefit.

are not paired, they don't exchange sections like the other paired chromosomes, a process called *recombination* (see Chapter 3), except at their tips. Thus Y-chromosome analysis allows us to trace inheritance through one parental line with little or no influence from the other.

How are data from these types of DNA used to study the question at hand? The basic idea is that with our ability to sequence DNA, we can specifically compare species and populations within a species at the most basic genetic level. Since at that level evolution is the accumulation of genetic variation through mutation, the genetic differences among populations tell us how many mutations have taken place since they were a single population. We get a measure of relative evolutionary relationships, which allows us to construct "family trees."

Moreover, if we can estimate the mutation rate for a given type of DNA, we can turn these data into a "molecular clock." We ask how long it would take for a certain degree of difference to accumulate between two groups. This, we assume, is how long they have been evolving separately (if two species) or relatively separately (if populations within a species). Then, we may add dates to the family tee.

So what have the studies based on this reasoning told us about the question of modern human origins? Two conclusions from many of these studies are that (1) the world's peoples tend to cluster into two genetic groups, those from sub-Saharan Africa and those from everywhere else, and (2) Africa is more genetically diverse than the rest of the world put together (Figure 12.5). This evidence seems to support the RAO model and a recent African origin of modern humanity. If people have been evolving in Africa longer than elsewhere and only recently spread to the rest of the world, then the African population should be distinct from those of Europe and Asia and should show greater genetic diversity.

The data from these studies could, however, also result if the species were an old, single evolving lineage. Since most of hominid evolution occurred strictly in Africa, that continent has had the largest population for most of human history. A large population on a large and environmentally diverse continent would be expected to have a great deal of genetic diversity and thus be genetically different from all the rest of humanity, which (whether 2 million or 200,000 years old) is more recent (Relethford and Harpending 1995). Moreover, it might be the case that given the geography of the continents, there was more gene flow within Africa and within populations in the rest of the world than *between* Africa and the rest of the world. This would also contribute to a genetic distinction.

All these studies have used DNA from living populations. What about DNA from ancient remains? DNA is not a very stable molecule,

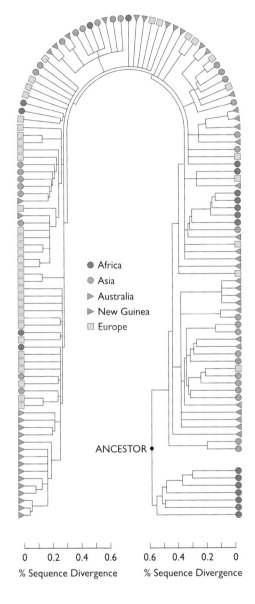

FIGURE 12.5
This computer-generated tree is from an early, limited study (Cann et al. 1987) but demonstrates how such studies work. It shows the lines of descent of 147 women. The diagram is drawn as a horseshoe simply to fit on the page; mentally straighten it out, and you have a more familiar-looking family tree. The higher the percentage figure at the point of divergence (measured against the scale at the bottom of each end), the more different were the women's mtDNA and so the longer ago the divergence took place. Note the cluster of African women at the lower right. They are distinct from other African women and all others (0.6 percent on the scale). They also show greater diversity in their mtDNA, as seen by the fact that their lines of descent converge closer to the center of the diagram, that is, in the more distant past.

and scientists at one time doubted that it could be recovered from old bones. But this has proved possible. Perhaps the most famous ancient DNA samples have come from four Neandertal specimens. The first, from the original Neandertal (see Figure 11.25), consisted of a short sequence of 379 base pairs of mtDNA (out of a total of about 16,500 for human mtDNA). When compared with the same sequence in modern humans, there were more than three times the number of differences between the Neandertal and the moderns than between any two groups of moderns (Krings et al. 1997). Moreover the sample showed no special similarity to modern Europeans, being equally distinct from all modern populations. The investigators concluded from this that the Neandertals made no contribution to modern human mtDNA and that our two lines diverged 690,000 to 550,000 ya. A follow-up study from the same sample on another section of mtDNA, this time with about 600 base pairs, came to a similar conclusion (Krings et al. 1999). Three more Neandertal samples (Ovchinnikov et al. 2000; Scholz et al. 2000) showed similar results.

MRE proponents have questioned these conclusions. The DNA sequences are short, they note. And, says geneticist Simon Easteal, the fact that chimpanzees have much more mtDNA diversity than do humans shows that "the amount of diversity between Neanderthals and living humans is not exceptional" (Wong 1998). Moreover, one would expect there to be more genetic diversity in the human species in the past, before the larger populations, less isolation, and extensive gene flow of more recent times increased our genetic homogeneity. Clearly, more and larger ancient DNA samples will have to be obtained and studied.

Moreover, in 2000 mtDNA was extracted from ten skeletons in Australia dated at 60,000 to 2,000 ya (Holden 2001a). The oldest skeleton had an mtDNA sequence that differed both from that of similarly dated fossils from other regions and from modern peoples as well. This sequence is, in fact, now extinct in modern mtDNA. This means that an anatomically modern individual with very old, very different DNA lived thousands of miles away from where modern humans are supposed to have originated, supporting the idea that moderns are the result of a multiregional ancestry.

Yet another conclusion from the early mtDNA studies is that the origin of all modern mtDNA can be traced—based on the degree of diversity and the estimated mutation rate—back to somewhere around 150,000 ya. This has been supported by a study (Ingman et al. 2000) that used, for the first time, the entire mtDNA sequence of approximately 16,500 base pairs in a comparison of fifty-three individuals of diverse geographic origins. The study shows a tree rooted in Africa with the most recent common ancestor of all modern humans dated at 171,500 ya, plus or minus 50,000 years. This general age has also been supported by some studies on Y-chromosome DNA (Gibbons 1997d; Ke et al. 2001). One of these studies also found two important variants on the Y chromosome that are shared by other primates and in humans are found today only among Africans—mostly among Khoisan peoples.

FIGURE 12.6
Recent studies have indicated that the oldest versions of certain genes on the male-inherited Y chromosome are found among Khoisan men, like this !Kung San hunter from the Kalahari Desert in southern Africa (the "!" indicates a click sound). These data are taken to mean that Khoisan may be the closest living populations, genetically, to the earliest modern humans.

These, then, could be considered the oldest versions of the genes and those populations the closest, genetically, to the first modern humans (Figure 12.6). This seems strong support for the RAO model.

Other studies on repeating segments of nuclear DNA (Bower 1995b) and segments of chromosome 12 (Tishkoff et al. 1996) provide similar dates. But all these dates have been called into question. Additional studies, particularly those of Y-chromosome genes, have given widely divergent dates, some as old as 500,000 ya and some as recent as 135,000 ya (Donnelly et al. 1996; Fu and Li 1996; Rogers et al. 1996; Weiss and von Haesler 1996), showing there is less than complete consistency and agreement.

A more general problem is the fact that the history of mtDNA or any other gene "does *not* reflect population history" (Wolpoff and Caspari 1997:302). Rather, it reflects the history of a specific genetic system, in the same way the history of "a single Scottish name might be different from the history of the Scottish people" (304). The evolutionary history of a population involves the histories of many genes. If there was a recent origin of a separate modern human species, then all genetic systems should have similar histories, which does not seem to be the case. Wolpoff suggests that there were genetic bottlenecks in the past—different periods when in regional populations genetic diversity was greatly limited because of some event that decreased the population size or limited lines of descent. These bottlenecks, then, would have differentially affected the present diversity in genetic systems, limiting the diversity of some more than others. Thus, the great homogeneity of modern mtDNA (as well as the genes of the Y chromosome) might reflect a severe bottleneck in the past that had the effect of making the last common ancestor of mtDNA lines a recent one, while our actual common ancestor could be much older.

Templeton (1997:353) also suggests that because mtDNA is inherited only through females, it may show a more recent time of origin for all existing mtDNA than does nuclear DNA. Calculations based on certain features of the two forms of DNA suggest, says Templeton, that if all our current mtDNA can be traced to 200,000 ya, it is likely that all our nuclear genes—which we inherit from both parents—have their point of origin at more than 1 or 2 mya—coincident with the MRE model (Figure 12.7).

Here's an analogy: The earliest occurrence of my last name does not indicate my earliest ancestor, nor does the history of my last name tell my whole family history. There are lots of different last names and, thus, family lines involved in my genealogy, each with its own history. My last name is *Park* because it is my father's last name and because in our society last names are inherited through males. My mother's last name did not get passed on to me, so her contribution to my family history would not be noted if I just looked at the history of *Park*. Similarly, mtDNA and Y-chromosome DNA are specific genetic systems, passed down through only one sex, whose histories may be quite different from the history of an entire genome.

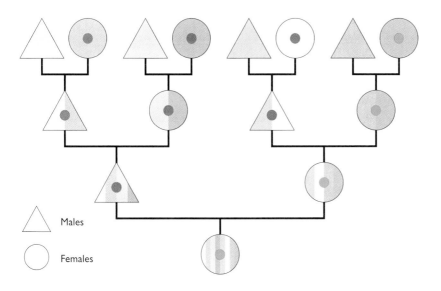

FIGURE 12.7

The different inheritance patterns of mitochondrial DNA and nuclear DNA. The four couples at the top each have one child. These children pair off, and each pair has a child. These children then mate and produce the individual at the bottom. The colored dot in the center of each figure represents the mtDNA. The other colors represent nuclear DNA. Notice that the person at the bottom has inherited her mtDNA through only one line. The other mtDNA lines have become extinct because the matings produced a male, who could not pass on his mtDNA. The nuclear DNA of the individual at the bottom, however, is a combination of the genes of *all* her ancestors. Her nuclear DNA, therefore, is much older than is her mtDNA. Similarly, all modern humans could have inherited their mtDNA from a recent common ancestor while tracing their nuclear DNA to a common ancestor back much further in time.

(Adapted from Hammer and Zegura 1996:122; after Jobling and Tyler-Smith 1995)

Finally, the variety of the histories of different genetic systems is being demonstrated by ongoing studies of new systems, especially within nuclear DNA. Rosalind Harding of Oxford University, for example (Wong 1998), found a lineage for the betaglobin gene (the gene for the beta chain of hemoglobin, a mutation of which causes sickle cell anemia), which has been dated to 200,000 ya. It is found in high frequency in Asia but is rare in Africa, suggesting that premodern populations in Asia contributed to the modern gene pool.

As with fossils and artifacts, the genetic evidence is ambiguous. While most of the analyses appear to support an RAO model, there are serious questions due to the fact that we have so far been able to look at only portions of specific genetic systems. Now, however, with our ever-increasing knowledge of the entirety of the human genome, we should see more extensive research and, eventually, better results. Still, with such a huge amount of data, analytical techniques will have to be refined. For example, even for the data shown in the tree in Figure 12.5, there are millions of different versions, with significantly different results, depending on just how those data are analyzed (Barinaga 1992; Hedges et al. 1992). Genetics may hold the key to resolving this debate, but not yet.

Evolutionary Theory

From the preceding discussion, it is clear that much of the haggling over these two major hypotheses focuses on details of the data. What about some of the broader considerations of evolutionary theory? What happens when we step back and look at the bigger picture? A major issue from this perspective is the plausibility of the gene flow required by the Multiregional Evolution model. Could such gene flow have taken place, and if so, how?

Christopher Stringer (Stringer and McKie 1996:142), representing the Recent African Origin view, thinks that such gene flow is unlikely at best, for three reasons. First, he says, until recent times hominid populations were too thinly spread across the three continents of the Old World to be so connected by gene flow. The gaps between groups were too large for genes to move around as much as MRE requires.

Second, there were too many geographic barriers. There were mountain, desert, and water barriers, and over the past million years or so, large portions of the world were in the grip of the Pleistocene ice ages, which caused extreme climatic disruptions and fluctuations. The flow of genes would have been severely limited by these geographic obstacles.

Third, even supposing that different human groups were potentially interfertile, would they have *wanted* to share their genes? Science writer James Shreeve (1995) offers the possibility that Neandertals and moderns in Southwest Asia never interbred because they looked so different they didn't even recognize members of the other group as potential mates. Quoting geneticist L. L. Cavalli-Sforza (Cavalli-Sforza et al. 1994), Stringer suggests that cultural and social barriers to fertility may have been very powerful, and interbreeding might have been considered "taboo."

There are—as you must suspect by now—responses to these issues from the MRE point of view. On the issue of population density, one estimate that Stringer quotes (Stringer and McKie 1996:144) uses mtDNA variation to calculate the number of females present in our species in its early evolution. The figure derived is 7,000 females, too few to have allowed much gene flow. But the use of mtDNA assumes the conclusion from other studies of that genetic system—that our species arose very recently from a localized group. The reasoning seems circular.

In addition, the apparently thin spread of early human populations across the Old World may be in part attributable to the nature of the fossil record. Remember that most individual hominids who ever lived did not leave fossilized remains, nor have we found but a fraction of all the fossil hominid remains that *were* left. The actual distribution of early populations may have been quite different from the distribution of the fossils recovered.

Moreover, there are two processes involved in gene flow. One is the kind of genetic exchange Stringer cites, where "populations essentially sat still while genes passed through them" (144), that is, exchanged between neighboring groups. But genes also flow as a result of migration. For the past 2 million years, we humans have been a migratory genus. In a short period of time, members of *Homo erectus* got all the way from Africa to Java. There is no reason why humans, having once arrived in these far-flung areas, would necessarily all stay put. They moved because they were following needed resources or looking for better conditions— and the Pleistocene climatic changes may have required a great deal of moving. As Templeton puts it, "all that is needed is to have humans distributed throughout the Old World and able to disperse a little bit in any direction every generation" (1997:357).

In response to the second issue, geographic barriers to human habitation and movement certainly existed and still do. They did not, however, prevent the spread of human populations. Even if there were six different species of *Homo*, the fossil record shows that most managed to move around a bit (see the tables and maps in Chapter 11). And the climatic disruptions of the Pleistocene fluctuated. Barriers changed in severity and location. Sea levels rose and isolated some land areas but then dropped again. Dry periods followed wet periods. Glaciers covered huge masses of land but then retreated. Spread over a 2-million-year period, such temporary and changeable barriers might not have presented severe limitations to gene flow.

Regarding the third issue, what can we say about behavioral barriers to interbreeding? Without a time machine, we obviously cannot conduct a conclusive test. We do know, however, that different physical appearances have not been absolute barriers to interbreeding in modern humans. For example, despite claims by slave owners in this country that Africans were at best less civilized and at worst virtually a different species, genetic exchange (usually forced by the slave owners) still took place. Even cultural barriers that enforce **endogamy** (marriage within one's group) are temporary over long periods of time as rules and group

endogamy: Restricting marriage to members of the same culturally defined group.

Contemporary Reflections

Is There a Connection between Modern Human Origins and Race?

"The Out-of-Africa model makes mincemeat of racial difference" reads a quote on the back of Christopher Stringer and Robin McKie's *African Exodus: The Origins of Modern Humanity* (1996). The title of Milford Wolpoff and Rachel Caspari's (1997) book is *Race and Human Evolution: A Fatal Attraction.* What is the connection between race and the models we have been examining?

We will cover the topic of human biodiversity and the issue of race in detail in Chapter 14. For the moment, let me give away the punch line of that chapter and state that in the view of modern biological anthropology, the human species *is not* and *cannot* be divided into any number of clearly defined biological subgroups that warrant the title *race.* To be sure, we display phenotypic variation—in everything from skin color to relative frequencies of blood types—and this variation sometimes has geographic correlations. We can often accurately identify people's regional backgrounds from their visible physical features. But those correlations are merely the result of different frequencies of alleles that have accumulated in different areas in response to some combination of environmental circumstances and population dynamics (in other words, in response to the operations of natural selection, gene flow, and genetic drift). Genetically, the whole species is remarkably homogeneous, and the genetic variation is relatively evenly spread. Nonetheless, it is these outward physical similarities and differences that cultures use to divide humans into races. Race is a cultural construct.

The biological unity of our species is now a well-documented fact, and it leads to certain socially relevant ideas and ideals—namely, that although individual humans vary in many ways, there exist no profound inherent differences *among human groups* that would warrant differential treatment in social and cultural environments. Skin color, for example, is no predictor of intellectual capabilities.

A majority of anthropologists have leaned toward the Recent African Origin model not only because many believe the data support it but also because it neatly explains our species' current homogeneity. If our species is very young—only a few hundred thousand years at most—and if it arose from one localized population, then it could not possibly display deep and profound variations among its populations. There simply hasn't been enough time. If the RAO model is correct, human races could not exist. This makes the RAO model attractive indeed.

definitions change, and such rules are not always adhered to anyway. So *our* assessment of physical differences among ancient human groups and *our* assumptions about their behavioral taboos can't really tell us much about how they were really behaving.

Furthermore, we must consider the evidence of possible hybridization between archaics and moderns. We've already discussed the young child from Portugal with both modern and Neandertal features. While some supporters of the RAO model insist the child must be one species

Moreover, it has been stated by some RAO supporters that one fatal problem with the Multiregional Evolution model is that it does "suggest, at face value, that modern humanity's constituent races are divided by fundamental and deep-rooted differences" (Stringer and McKie 1996:60). If, such arguments go, local populations show continuity of features into the distant past, that implies that modern racial groups are themselves very ancient and profoundly different. Such a suggestion goes against current social ideals, not to mention the scientific facts regarding our relative homogeneity.

There were, to be sure, earlier models of a multiregional perspective that did make such suggestions. In his 1962 book *The Origin of Races*, anthropologist Carleton Coon proposed that five subspecies, or races, of *Homo erectus* independently evolved into five major races of *Homo sapiens*, crossing "a critical threshold from a more brutal to a more *sapient* state" (658). To make matters worse, he claimed that the different races crossed the "sapiens threshold" at different times and that this accounted for some of the differences we see today in levels of cultural complexity. "If all races had a recent common origin," he asked, "why were the Tasmanians and many of the Australian aborigines still living during the nineteenth century in a manner comparable to that of Europeans of over 100,000 years ago?" (4). It is clear who Coon thought crossed the threshold first and last. Such ideas may well have sensitized anthropologists against any model of our evolution that included great time depth for the species and regional continuity of traits.

The modern MRE model, however, is quite different from Coon's and other early ideas. The MRE model does not claim that *populations* show continuity but that some regional *traits* do, especially traits that are found in fairly isolated areas, such as Australia and other places on the margins of the human geographic range. So-called racial groups are not now, nor were they ever, completely isolated. Rather, the species has displayed continual gene flow, enough to maintain species identity and spread physical features and their genes all over the world.

But this is all really a nonissue. Even if the extreme single-species MRE model proves correct, today's human species is *still* genetically and physically homogeneous. We know this because of well-established scientific studies of genetics and morphology. How we got to be this way doesn't change how we are, and either major model under debate could account for our current nature. As anthropologist Matt Cartmill puts it, "We are what we are, not what our ancestors were. . . . The truth of racial egalitarianism hinges on the facts about living people. Their genealogies are irrelevant" (1997:62).

or the other, Christopher Stringer, a major RAO proponent, has said that even if this child was a hybrid, hybridization between moderns and Neandertals was rare and had little impact on evolution (Bower 1999). Elsewhere, Stringer (1994) has claimed that interbreeding may have taken place between archaics and moderns in Eurasia but that it was limited and left no genetic or physical results in modern populations. In a later article, G. Bräuer and Stringer (1997) indicate they think interbreeding did occur, and O. M. Pearson (2000), writing on postcranial remains, admits the possibility of some admixture between moderns and Neandertals.

The problem here is that if there was *any* interbreeding between Neandertals and moderns that led to hybrid individuals, then, by definition, they were members of the same species. This is true even if few or no Neandertal genes or morphological features are still present in modern humans (a debatable point itself). Gene flow between archaics and moderns, no matter how limited, refutes the RAO model and is, rather, basic to the MRE model (Wolpoff et al. 2001:296, n. 3).

Another relevant aspect of evolutionary theory involves the process of speciation (see Chapter 5). New species evolve when a portion of an existing species is completely isolated from the parent species long enough that subsequent genetic and phenotypic change eventually creates an absolute barrier to reproduction. Humans are and have been a mobile species, and our big brains have allowed our genus to experience increasing control over our environments and adaptations to those environments. It would seem to be a rare event for any individual group of such a genus to be isolated long enough to evolve sufficient differences in reproductive behavior or biology to become a technically separate species. The most extreme RAO model (Tattersall and Schwarz 2000) recognizes as many as *eight* species of *Homo* (including *H. habilis* and *H. rudolfensis*). In terms of how new species evolve, and the nature of genus *Homo*, this appears highly unlikely indeed.

Perhaps we have been misled because we have examined every available minute genetic and phenotypic variation in living humans and our fossil ancestors through a microscope—literally and figuratively. A single species, as it responds to the processes of evolution through time, may change, of course, and it certainly may show regional variation. But over the long haul, the temporal changes and regional variation within a species occur around some central adaptive theme that defines that species. Our central adaptive theme is our big brains and the resultant behaviors, especially culture, that those brains make possible. Evidence of this theme is found in all accepted members of genus *Homo*—and is absent in all other hominids.

MOSTLY-OUT-OF-AFRICA: AN ALTERNATIVE MODEL

The data from the fossil and archaeological records, genetics, and evolutionary theory are incapable of unambiguously supporting either the

Multiregional Evolution model or the Recent African Origin model. The debate over these models, then, seems to be without solution. But there is now another model that nicely reconciles the existing data. Forms of this model have been expressed by, among others, biologist Alan Templeton, who titles his article "Out of Africa Again and Again" (Templeton 2002), and bioanthropologist John Relethford (2001, 2003b). Relethford calls it the "Mostly-Out-of-Africa" model.

The basic idea is straightforward enough: that while *most* of the ancestors of modern humans are from Africa, not *all* are. The Mostly-Out-of-Africa model agrees that our species is an old one, perhaps as old as almost 2 million years, and that a network of gene flow maintained that species' identity across all geographic regions. Thus, it is a multi-regional model.

But it also acknowledges the evidence from the fossil record that modern human anatomy, for the most part, seems to have originated in Africa. And it acknowledges the evidence from genetics that tends to point to greater genetic diversity in Africa and a degree of differentiation between African DNA and that of every other regional population, in the sense that all other populations are really subsets of the genome of Africans. How can these ideas work together?

Perhaps there were at least two major expansions out of Africa, the first being in *Homo erectus* times and the latest around the time suggested as the origin of modern *Homo sapiens* (Figure 12.8). There may well have been other expansions, not all necessarily "out of Africa." These expansions would have spread collections of genes and traits across geographic space. Thus, the evolution of at least some features of modern human anatomy, and the genes that coded for them, could have occurred first in Africa, but their spread around the world would not necessarily have resulted in the replacement of one species by a new one. Rather, the features spread via gene flow among existing populations that descended from the first and subsequent expansions. Indeed, Templeton's study (2002), using seven types of genetic data and a sophisticated statistical analytic procedure, has suggested times and directions of some of the expansions, both out of Africa and elsewhere.

Moreover, the genetic data can be explained, because Africa—being the homeland of the hominids and the only place hominid evolution took place for millions of years—would have had for a long time a larger human population than the rest of the world. Thus, the contribution of African genes and traits would have been disproportionately large. As a result, African DNA is the most diverse (being the oldest), with the DNA of other populations being a subset of the African genome.

FIGURE 12.8
The multiple expansion, or Mostly-Out-of-Africa, model. Vertical lines represent direct regional descent, that is, regional continuity. Diagonal lines represent a network of recurrent gene flow among regional populations. (Actual gene flow, of course, would not have been this regular or even.) The red arrows represent major population expansions. In the original diagram, Templeton indicates that there is genetic evidence for the timing and direction of each of these expansions, as well as for certain sections of the network of gene flow. Note that, at least early on, Africa made major contributions to the gene pool and, thus, to the traits of the rest of the world. Also note that none of the expansions is a replacement or a speciation event, just the spread of a sample of genes among an existing, widespread species.
(Adapted from Templeton 2002:48)

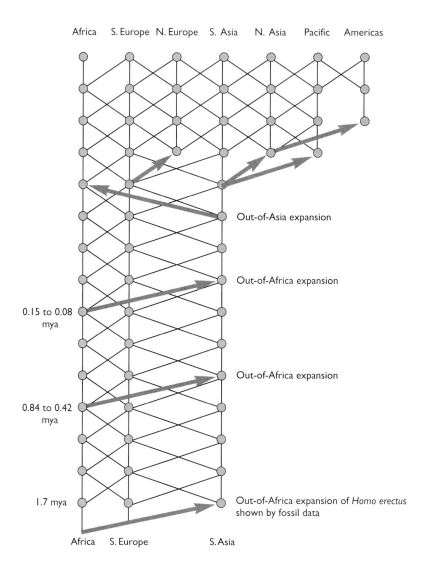

Africa   S. Europe   N. Europe   S. Asia   N. Asia   Pacific   Americas

Out-of-Asia expansion

Out-of-Africa expansion

0.15 to 0.08 mya

Out-of-Africa expansion

0.84 to 0.42 mya

1.7 mya

Out-of-Africa expansion of *Homo erectus* shown by fossil data

Africa   S. Europe   S. Asia

Although further research obviously needs to and will be done, at the moment this model seems reasonable in that it accounts for the seeming ambiguity of the fossil and genetic data, as well as the arguments from evolutionary theory. In fact, the data only seem ambiguous if viewed in the context of the two competing major models, which are really quite the opposite of one another. The Mostly-Out-of-Africa model makes all the data seem less ambiguous and, in fact, quite mutually supportive.

▽   ▽   ▽

SUMMARY

The "hottest" current debate in bioanthropology is over the origin of modern *Homo sapiens*. Many, if not most, authorities support either of two major models. One, the Recent African Origin (RAO) model, proposes that modern humans evolved as a separate species 200,000 to 150,000 ya in Africa, having a set of characteristics that made them distinctly different from their ancestor, and other contemporary, species. They then spread throughout the Old World, replacing populations of archaic humans because of their better-adapted traits.

The other model, the Multiregional Evolution (MRE) model, claims that our species is as much as 2 million years old and incorporates other previously recognized species of genus *Homo* possibly back through *H. erectus*. After first evolving in Africa, the species spread throughout the Old World, developing regional differences but always maintaining species identity through gene flow. As new and successful adaptations arose in different areas, they were shared across the species. Thus, "modern" humans are those of us—all 6 billion living today—who share a collection of traits that is the latest set of physical features in a very ancient species.

The data from paleontology, archaeology, and genetics are ambiguous on this issue. Either model may be supported by the same basic facts. But now a newer model, the Mostly-Out-of-Africa model, or multiple expansion model, seems to reconcile all the evidence into a more satisfying scheme. It says that after an initial expansion out of Africa, nearly 2 mya, there were several other major expansions out of that more heavily populated continent that spread genes and traits across other geographic areas, already populated by descendants of earlier migrations and characterized by a network of recurrent gene flow. So most of our ancestors are African, but not all of them, and our species is an old one.

QUESTIONS FOR FURTHER THOUGHT

1. Having read about the debate over the evolution of genus *Homo,* go back to question 1 from Chapter 11. Now what are your thoughts on the issue? Is this debate interesting and important to you? Why or why not?

2. Aside from the alleged race implications, why do you think professionals are so emotional about this debate? Do you see any issues other than purely scientific ones—philosophical ones, perhaps—that could be involved?

3. Some claim that the Multiregional Evolution model is potentially "racist." (Someone said it to me.) How would you respond to such an accusation?

KEY TERMS

Multiregional
    Evolution (MRE)
    model

Out-of-Africa model

Recent African
    Origin (RAO)
    model

nuclear DNA

mitochondrial DNA
    (mtDNA)

symbiosis

endogamy

SUGGESTED READINGS

There is extensive literature about the RAO/MRE debate. I would especially recommend the two books by the major proponents of each point of view: *Race and Human Evolution: A Fatal Attraction*, by Milford Wolpoff and Rachel Caspari, in support of the MRE model, and *African Exodus: The Origins of Modern Humanity*, by Christopher Stringer and Robin McKie, in support of the RAO model. The Wolpoff and Caspari book includes a good historical review of the issue. For the newer Mostly-out-of-Africa model, see Alan Templeton's "Out of Africa Again and Again" in the 7 March 2002 *Nature* and John Relethford's two highly readable books, the more technical *Genetics and the Search for Modern Human Origins* and the more popular and broader *Reflections of Our Past: How Human History Is Revealed in Our Genes*.

On the fascinating topic of mitochondria, see "Symbionts and Assassins," by Guy C. Brown, in the July/August 2000 issue of *Natural History*.

A good description of some of the genetic research and the analogy to human family names can be found in "After You, Eve," by Carl Zimmer, in the March 2001 *Natural History*.

On the topic of the race connection, see Matt Cartmill's "The Third Man" in the September 1997 issue of *Discover,* and have a look at Carleton Coon's *The Origin of Races* to see why that book caused such a furor.

For a collection of twenty-nine articles on all aspects of the debate, see *Conceptual Issues in Modern Human Origins Research*, edited by G. A. Clark and C. M. Willermet. And for a more recent collection, see *The Speciation of Modern* Homo sapiens, edited by T. J. Crow.

CHAPTER

13

THE STUDY
OF LIVING
PEOPLES

From distant climes,
o'er widespread seas
we come.
—George Barrington

We have followed the evolutionary history of the hominids up to *Homo sapiens* in its anatomically modern biological state. But the story of hominid evolution doesn't end just because we finally arrive at modern humans. The processes of evolution within a species, including our own, are continuous. A species undergoes change over time, even as it remains a single species. Remember Darwin's finches from Chapter 4.

Ever since the basic nature of our species was established, all the processes of evolution have continued to operate, acting on the human "theme" and changing us over time and across geographic space. As we divided ourselves into groups based on ethnic identity, nationality, language, and religion, we provided those evolutionary processes with new and varying breeding populations. Because evolution takes place within populations, the nature of those cultural groups also affected the further evolution of our species as a whole. So did the behaviors—the cultural systems—of the people in those populations. In other words, our biology and our culture are interrelated and affect one another.

As biological anthropologists, then, we are interested not only in how we evolved but also in what we evolved into, how we continued to evolve over the recent past, and how we are evolving even today. In this chapter, we will look at some of the ways bioanthropologists study living peoples in terms of evolution within populations, the nature of our populations, the adaptive differences among populations, the influence of disease, and, finally, our individual life histories. We will address these questions:

How do we recognize evolutionary changes in populations and identify and study their causes?

What basic data do we gather in order to describe human populations?

What sorts of trends can we see in populations within our species?

In what ways have we humans adapted to the varying environments in which we live?

How have diseases influenced human populations?

What are the results of our species' evolution on the life histories—the "personal evolution"—of the human individual?

EVOLUTION WITHIN POPULATIONS

Today, with the technologies discussed earlier, we are able to characterize populations and study their evolution at the most basic genetic level of the individual letters (the four bases) of the genetic code (see Chapter 3). A variation in these letters is known as a **single nucleotide polymorphism** (or **SNP,** pronounced *snip*). Of the 3.1 billion nucleotides in the human genome, only about 10 million are SNPs; that is, only 10 million nucleotides show regular variation. These account for about 90 percent of human genetic variation (International HapMap Consortium 2003). But because many of these variations are relatively rare, *any two* humans differ on average by only 3 million SNPs—1 in every 1,000 nucleotides, or about 0.1 percent.

These differences in letters of the code are what distinguish alleles of a gene. Thus, we have the basis for eventually understanding our biological diversity (the topic of the next chapter). In addition, because SNPs reflect past mutations, we can use them to estimate evolutionary relationships among individuals and populations (as we discussed in Chapters 9 and 12).

These exciting new technologies make one aspect of my study of the Hutterites (see Chapter 1) rather obsolete. If I were conducting my research today, I'd collect genetic instead of phenotypic data. But the research model would remain the same, and so I'll use my old study as an example of how we might examine evolution within a living population, regardless of the data used.

When I conducted my study of evolutionary processes among the Hutterites, I used **dermatoglyphics**, the study of the parallel ridges on the skin of the fingers, palms, toes, and soles of the feet. I focused on those of the fingers—in a word, fingerprints. I was not collecting data about the small features that make each individual's fingerprints absolutely unique from everyone else's. Rather, I was looking for the frequencies of various types of fingerprint patterns and for data about the size, or *ridge count*, of the patterns. The ridge count is measured by counting the number of ridges between a reference point, the *triradius*, and the center of the pattern (Figure 13.1).

We know that one's fingerprints are under some genetic control since certain features, especially the ridge count, are similar among members of a family line. Moreover, certain unusual dermatoglyphic traits or characteristic frequencies of some traits have been correlated with abnormalities of known or suspected genetic origin. We also know, however,

single nucleotide polymorphism (SNP): A single base pair of the genetic code that displays variable expressions among individuals.

dermatoglyphics: The study of the parallel ridges and furrows on the fingers, palms, toes, and soles of the feet.

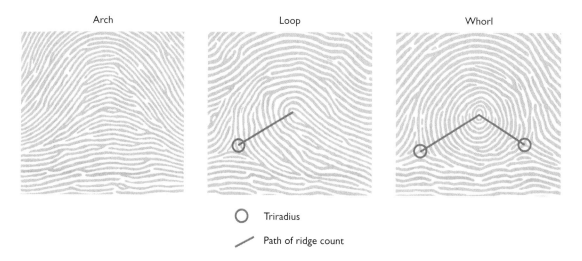

Arch   Loop   Whorl

○   Triradius

╱   Path of ridge count

FIGURE 13.1

Fingerprint features used as anthropological data. Arches have no triradius and, therefore, no ridge count. Loops have one ridge count. Whorls have two ridge counts; the largest is used as data. The ridge count of the loop is 13 and that of the whorl is 14.

that other fingerprint traits are affected by prenatal environmental factors or simply by chance. Not knowing what genes were involved in my study, I obviously couldn't calculate allele frequencies and use population genetics calculations (see Appendix), so how did I use these features?

In 1973 I collected fingerprint data from two Hutterite colonies that resulted from the splitting of an original colony in 1958 (Figure 13.2). As you recall from Chapter 1, I was interested in examining the effects of gene flow and genetic drift. I examined 133 sets of fingerprints for pattern type, pattern size, and a few other variables (about 1,330 individual prints—although many of the men in this farming society had fewer than ten fingers). I then statistically compared the fingerprint data of various subgroups to get a numerical *approximation* of the genetic distances among them. I used different methods of analysis to see if some dermatoglyphic data were better than others for estimating genetic distance.

First, I was specifically interested in seeing how much genetic change was brought about by splitting (fissioning) the population. This would measure the form of genetic drift known as the founder effect (see Chapter 4). Second, I wondered how much change had occurred between generations and how much of that change was the result of the fact that about half of the mothers of the second generation had moved into the two colonies after marriage (gene flow). Natural selection was ruled out as a cause of change since there is no evidence that it makes any difference in reproductive success what ridge patterns you have and how big they are. Nor do people choose mates based on their fingerprints.

I felt I could apply what I found to a broader perspective on human evolution. The Hutterites nicely mirror the nature of many human

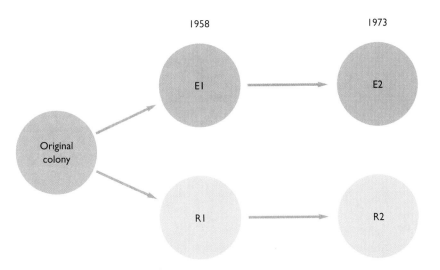

FIGURE 13.2
Hutterite colonies in the study described. E and R are code letters I used to identify each colony to maintain my subjects' anonymity. The original colony, in Alberta, Canada, split in 1958. Half of the families stayed in the Alberta colony (R1), and half founded a new colony in Saskatchewan (E1). By 1973, when I conducted my study of the two colonies, a second generation (R2 and E2) had been born.

populations throughout much of our history—small groups of interrelated families that split and merged in various ways as they moved about in search of resources.

I proposed and tested two hypotheses (Figure 13.3). First, I guessed that there would be a founder effect after the original population split in 1958 to create two new populations. That is, I hypothesized that the new populations would be genetically different from one another as a result of being founded by nonrepresentative samples of the original. I did not think the effect would be particularly extensive, however, since splitting a sample into two nearly equal halves lessens the chance of a major difference between them. In addition, all the families involved were descended from seven brothers, so there would not be a whole lot of genetic variation to begin with.

As a second hypothesis, I expected some effect from genetic drift and a significant effect from gene flow, making the next generations after the split (E2 and R2 in Figures 13.2 and 13.3) different from their parental generations (E1 and R1). I expected the second generations of the two colonies to be even more different from one another than were the two founded colonies. As noted in Chapter 4, nearly three-quarters of the mothers of the second generation "flowed" into the colonies of their husbands at marriage, and families with one of these women accounted for over half the children of the second generation. A lot of new genes were brought into each colony, and all of the women carrying those genes became parents. By reasoning, then, the parents should have been distinctly genetically different from the nonparents.

FIGURE 13.3
Diagram of tests run. (1) Founded colonies were compared. These were re-constructed by using only those individuals still alive in 1973 who were involved in the split. (Most were still living.) (2) The members of the founded colonies (those present in 1958) were compared with all the offspring born since 1958. (3) All members of the 1973 colonies were compared.

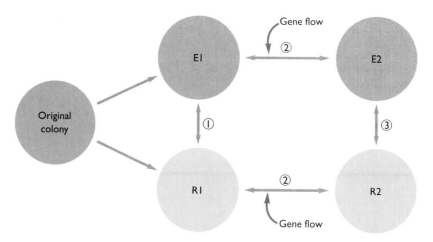

Comparisons for genetic distance ◄──────►
① Founder effect
② Difference between generations
③ Difference after one generation

What did I find? For the first hypothesis, the data showed evidence of a founder effect, but there was more difference between the two founded populations than I expected. You obviously can't base a whole conclusion on one limited study, but my results did suggest that fission and the founder effect could be important processes not only within the Hutterites but in the small, interrelated human populations that they represent.

My second hypothesis was not supported by the evidence. The two second-generation populations were *more* similar to one another than were the founder populations. This was surprising at first, but then the reason became clear.

The colonies from which the flow-group women came belonged to the same subgroup of Hutterites. The Hutterites are divided into three subgroups. Since World War I, these groups have been endogamous— members marry only within their group. Thus, the women were more closely related than if they had come from the Hutterite population in general.

Moreover, since the two colonies I studied were geographically close, the colonies from which the women came were also geographically close. Hutterites often find their mates in colonies they regularly visit. This increased the chances that the flow-group women were themselves closely related to each other. The genes flowing into the two colonies were similar, so the differences between the colonies were lessened over time, even over a single generation. Differences among populations, then, can increase and decrease, back and forth, depending on how the memberships of those populations are organized and exactly who marries whom. Culture, in other words, influences biology—one premise of the biocultural perspective.

Finally, I observed which statistical tests most closely matched the predicted results (once I had figured out that gene flow *decreased* the genetic distance). I was able to suggest that ridge count (the size of the fingerprint patterns) was the best dermatoglyphic feature to use in such a study.

This dermatoglyphic research on the Hutterites is just one of many examples of a population genetic study—and a somewhat outdated one in terms of the data used. It does, however, show the ways in which we can make real or approximated genetic comparisons among various populations and then analyze the evolutionary processes behind the differences we find.

This example also points out the importance of collecting and organizing data, including cultural factors, about the populations we study. How do we do this, and what can we learn from such data about the nature of the human species as a whole and of the groups into which we have divided ourselves?

DESCRIBING POPULATIONS

The statistical study of the size and makeup of human populations, and of changes in those measures, is called **demography.** Normally examined in detail by those who study human or cultural geography, demographic data are also important to biological anthropologists. Populations are, after all, the units of evolutionary change, and so the nature of the groups we study cannot be separated from the evolutionary processes that affect those groups. The Hutterite example clearly shows this.

The most obvious thing we need to know about a population is its size—how many people there are. Since we're interested in change over time, we also want to know to what extent and in what direction the size of a population has changed during a given period. For example, we know that the population of Europe dropped from about 70 million in 1347 to 45 million by 1352—a 35 percent decrease over a mere 5 years. It then took 118 years (until 1470) for Europe to once again achieve a population of 70 million. By contrast, the number of Hutterites in North America has increased from about 300 in 1875 to about 35,000 at present. This is more than a hundredfold increase over 126 years.

demography: The study of the size and makeup of populations.

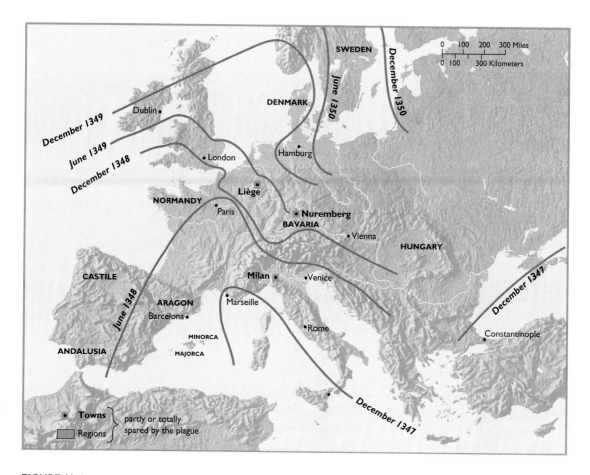

FIGURE 13.4

This map shows the progression of the Black Death across Europe in the fourteenth century, an event that killed over one-third of Europe's people in only 5 years.

In bioanthropology, we are interested in the causes of population changes, in these and other cases. Clearly, there are three variables involved: births, deaths, and migration into or out of the population. When the birth rate exceeds the death rate, the population size increases. It decreases when the death rate is greater. Only in rare cases is migration a major factor, though it certainly may play a significant role.

In the case of fourteenth-century Europe, we know that the drop in population was the result of plague, mostly bubonic plague, a fatal bacterial disease carried by fleas, which are in turn transported by rats. A major outbreak began in Italy in 1347 and spread rapidly across Europe over the next 5 years, killing 25 million people, including William of Ockham (see Chapter 11). The period came to be known as the Black Death (Figure 13.4). No birth rate could have made up for this rate of death. The fact that it took longer to replace the 25 million than to kill them off results from two facts. First, there were further, though smaller, outbreaks of plague over the next century that kept the death rates high. Second, a phenomenal growth rate of around 100 persons per thousand would have been required each year to restore the population in only 5 years. (*Growth rate* is birth rate minus death rate.) By comparison, the U.S. growth rate for 1970 was only about 9 persons per thousand.

Bubonic plague appeared earlier than the fourteenth century and is still around today. It spread so quickly through Europe during those years because of the dense populations of its cities and the extensive trade networks that linked them. Rats that carried the fleas moved easily from place to place, and the bacteria easily moved from person to person. Culture affected a biological event—and vice versa. Many aspects of European culture were affected by the Black Death—everything from economy to art to religious dissent and reform movements.

The increase in the Hutterite population in North America can be attributed to the high birth rate among this group. They have, on average, 10.4 children per family, one of the highest recorded rates for any population. This results in a birth rate of about 46 per thousand. The death rate is about 4 per thousand, yielding a growth rate of 42 per thousand. This amounts to a doubling time of a mere 16.6 years. This high growth rate is the result of Hutterite religious beliefs—their firm adherence to the biblical injunction to "be fruitful and multiply"—and, most likely, the healthy rural lifestyle they lead, which entails hard work and excludes drugs and all but occasional alcohol.

Biological anthropologists are also interested in the composition of populations. How many people are there of each sex, in each age group, and in various other ethnic, occupational, economic, and religious groups? We can display these data with a pyramid diagram. Figure 13.5 shows the age-sex structure of the Hutterite colonies I studied, but the data are typical for all Hutterites.

As you might expect for a group with such a high birth rate, the graph is wider on the bottom, showing that there are more children than adults. The fact that there are many more children between ages 5 and 9 than between 0 and 4 may indicate that the growth rate is slowing, at least in these colonies.

That females outnumber males (79 to 54) may indicate any number of factors that would have to be examined more closely. Perhaps male death rates are higher—they are in the general population. It could also be that despite what I was told and what I calculated, I *did not* get to see everyone in the colonies. Maybe some of the men did not want to participate and, thus, I never knew they existed.

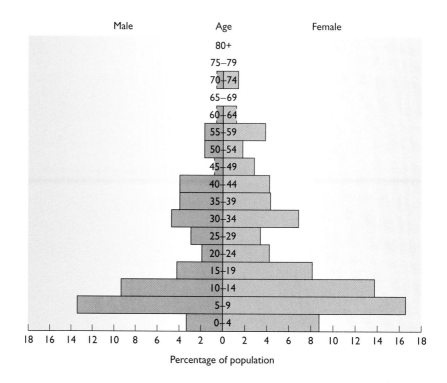

Now, compare the graph for the Hutterites with one representing developing nations, such as Mexico, where industrialization is fairly recent (Figure 13.6). This age-sex graph also shows larger numbers of children, but unlike the Hutterite graph, the numbers of adults rapidly decrease with age. This second graph reflects higher death rates, especially in the higher age ranges.

For adults, the Hutterite graph more closely resembles a graph for developed nations, such as the United States, that have been industrialized for some time (Figure 13.7). Here the numbers of adults do not decrease as quickly with age, indicating that people in developed countries live longer in general. Regarding children, however, developed nations differ from Hutterite populations in having lower birth rates.

What are the cultural connections here? As we noted, the Hutterites are responding to their religious beliefs by having many children. Their communal, self-sufficient lifestyle can accommodate large families, and their practice of splitting colonies prevents local overpopulation.

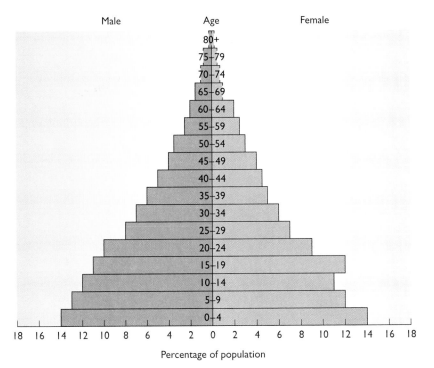

Male   Age   Female

80+
75–79
70–74
65–69
60–64
55–59
50–54
45–49
40–44
35–39
30–34
25–29
20–24
15–19
10–14
5–9
0–4

18 16 14 12 10 8 6 4 2 0 2 4 6 8 10 12 14 16 18

Percentage of population

FIGURE 13.6
Age-sex graph for a typical developing nation showing large numbers of children.

Developing nations have high mortality rates. This provides one incentive to produce as many children as possible—simply to try to offset the deaths. In addition, birth control technology is not always available, and there may be cultural rules against it. But although the bottom of the pyramid diagram is wide for such populations, it narrows quickly. Poor medical care and poor nutrition and sanitation lower people's chances of living into the next age group. Recent data have shown, however, that family size is decreasing in many developing countries. This may eventually narrow the bottom of the graph for such countries (see Figure 13.6) and may lead to better living conditions that would, in turn, widen the top of the graph, as people's chances of longevity increase.

In developed countries, there is increasing motivation to limit population, and there is greater access to the means of birth control than in developing nations. Moreover, the quality of medical care and diet in general allows people to live longer—thus, the nearly vertical shape of the diagram.

FIGURE 13.7

Age-sex graph for typical developed nations showing fewer children and longer life expectancy.

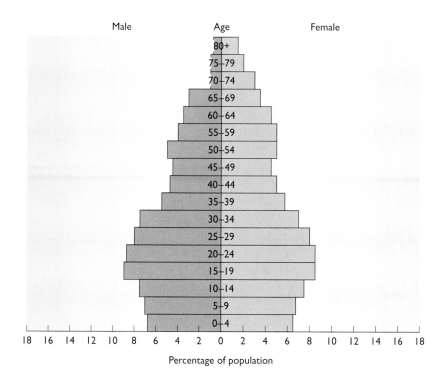

Finally, what can we say from demographic statistics about the human species in general? One thing is certain—our total population is going to increase. Since the beginning of farming and animal domestication some 12,000 ya, the rate of increase of the human population has accelerated, jumping sharply with the Industrial Revolution of the eighteenth century (Figure 13.8). As of May 5, 2004, at 2:09 p.m. EST, the U.S. Census Bureau estimated the world population at 6,366,501,025. At the current growth rate of about 1.2 percent, the world population will double in 58 years.

In addition to a growing population, the structure of the population over this century will change. As birth rates and death rates continue to drop in developed nations and, perhaps, as other nations become increasingly developed, the age-sex pyramids will become top-heavy. There will be more older people than younger people. This will radically change the social and economic nature of such cultures.

Both of these changes carry implications that are beyond the scope of this book. Clearly, though, they will require responses that will put a very different face on the world of the next generation and that will

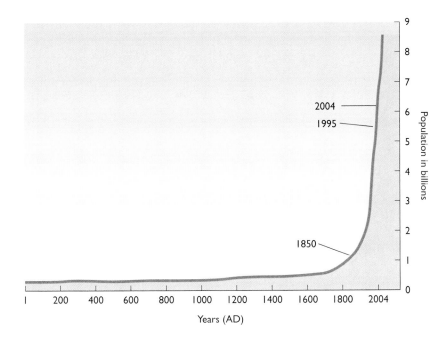

FIGURE 13.8
World population curve.

profoundly affect *Homo sapiens* of the twenty-first century (see the "Contemporary Reflections" box in this chapter).

HUMAN ADAPTATIONS

Living human populations inhabit every continent except Antarctica (though there are small, temporary groups of people who live there, mostly doing scientific research). Humans have to deal with nearly every imaginable set of environmental circumstances the earth presents, and we have been doing this for just about as long as modern *Homo sapiens* has existed. Indeed, even back in *H. erectus* times, humans successfully moved into a wide range of environments.

One would expect, therefore, that different populations of our species would be differently adapted to those various environments. Obviously, most of our adaptations are cultural. We build shelters, manufacture clothing, make tools, and invent various technological devices that are specifically geared to the environmental conditions with which we have to contend (Figure 13.9).

FIGURE 13.9
Cultural adaptation. The famous igloo of the Inuit has
many ingenious features that
make it remarkably adapted
to life in a harsh climate.

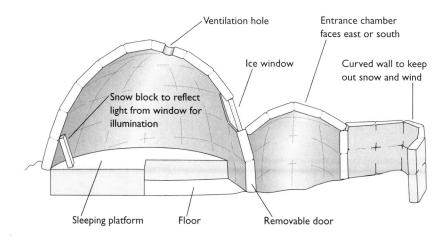

Human populations also differ in their physical appearance and in features of their physiology. Our species displays variations in phenotypic traits
that are the results of genetic variation. Most of this genetic variation can
be explained by the single nucleotide polymorphisms, discussed earlier, that
produce different alleles of a gene, but other **polymorphisms**—any variations in the genetic code—contribute to this variation as well. Are some
of these variable traits adaptive responses to different environments?

Species Adaptations

As members of the same species, all humans certainly share many adaptations to variable conditions (see Beall and Steegmann 2000 for a
detailed discussion). One important environmental variable is temperature. All humans sweat as a means of dissipating heat from the body. In
addition, heat causes surface blood vessels to widen. As noted in Chapter 10, our relative hairlessness may be an adaptation to promote the
quick evaporation of sweat. Alternatively, when it becomes too cold, we
shiver, our metabolic rate increases, and our blood vessels alternately
widen and narrow to increase or decrease the flow of blood to warm various body parts as needed.

Similarly, we are all exposed to ultraviolet radiation from the sun.
An excess of UV radiation can damage skin cells, alter the cells' DNA
(thereby causing skin cancer), and adversely affect the body's immune
system. Excess UV radiation can also break down folate, a chemical necessary for embryo development. To protect tissues from UV damage, specialized skin cells called **melanocytes** produce the pigment **melanin,** a
protein, and deliver it to the upper layer of skin, where it absorbs UV

radiation. Melanocytes respond to increased UV levels by increasing their melanin production and darkening the skin. This, of course, is tanning. Even dark-skinned individuals can exhibit a tanning response.

Humans are also exposed to varying levels of oxygen. At high altitudes, low oxygen levels can have damaging, even deadly, effects on the human body. All humans, however, have some ability to respond biologically to this condition. After a time at higher-than-normal altitudes, a person's respiratory and heart rates will increase, as will one's red blood cell count. Hemoglobin concentration may go up as well. All this helps the body better acquire and use what oxygen is available.

Humans, however, live in such a variety of conditions—including those related to temperature, UV radiation, and oxygen level—that these species-wide responses may not be sufficient to adapt all populations to their environments.

Variation in Adaptations

Humans have settled in places from the hottest deserts and rain forests to the coldest reaches above the Arctic Circle. No matter how much we may sweat, shiver, increase our metabolic rate, and change the shape of our blood vessels, it may not be enough to deal with some environmental extremes. For example, there is no difference in the number of sweat glands among human populations, regardless of regional temperature. There are, however, other adaptations to temperature that do vary with location.

Populations that inhabit hot climates tend to be linear in build, and those in cold areas tend to be stockier (Figure 13.10). This is because the linear individual has a greater surface area and so loses heat more rapidly, whereas the stockier person has a smaller surface area and so retains heat better. People in cold climates also tend to be bigger in general than those in hot climates since, obviously, the larger person would have more body mass away from the surface and so retain heat more efficiently.

Ultraviolet radiation varies with latitude. Sunlight strikes the earth more directly at the equator; it strikes at an increasingly greater angle the farther one gets from the equator. The greater the angle, the more atmosphere the solar radiation must travel through. Thus, more UV radiation is absorbed by the ozone in northern latitudes. Not only do humans have the ability to tan in response to increased UV levels, but, as is obvious to us all, populations are genetically programmed for differences in skin color, and these differences also vary by latitude. In general, populations closer to the equator have darker skin, and those farther away from the equator have lighter skin (Figure 13.11). It is generally agreed that the relationship between dark skin and high levels of UV radiation is an example of

polymorphisms: Variations in the genetic code within a species.

melanocytes: Specialized skin cells that produce the pigment melanin.

melanin: The pigment largely responsible for human skin color.

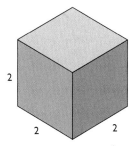

Volume = $2 \times 2 \times 2 = 8$ in.^{3}
Surface area = $(2 \times 2)(6$ sides$)$
          $= 24$ in.^{2}
(Numbers in inches)

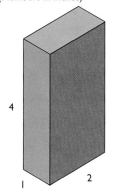

Volume = $1 \times 2 \times 4 = 8$ in.^{3}
Surface area = (1×2) (2)
          $+ (1 \times 4)$ (2)
          $+ (2 \times 4)$ (2)
          $= 28$ in.^{2}

FIGURE 13.10
The body build of the Inuit (*center*) is adapted to heat retention, while that of the Masai cattle herder from Kenya (*right*) is built to promote heat loss. The relationship between surface area and shape for two solids of equal volume (*left*) explains the adaptations of the two men pictured.

an adaptive response (Beall and Steegmann 2000; Jablonski and Chaplin 2000b, 2002). Because of the damaging effects of UV radiation, peoples at or near the equator have undergone selection for permanently higher levels of melanin production. Darker-skinned people do not have more melanocytes than lighter-skinned ones, just more melanin production. An implication of this, of course, is that dark skin was the original human skin color, since—at least according to all the evidence—our species first evolved in equatorial Africa. Moreover, the African great apes, our closest relatives, have darkly pigmented skin, so it could be a shared trait inherited from a common ancestor. The adaptation would have become even more important when hominids lost their protective covering of hair (as noted before, an adaptation to promote more efficient heat loss.)

The question then becomes, Why did populations who moved away from the equator evolve lower melanin production and therefore lighter skin? It is easiest to say that since dark skin was no longer needed, it became light. Evolution, however, doesn't really work this way. More likely, there was an adaptive reason why lighter skin was actively selected *for*.

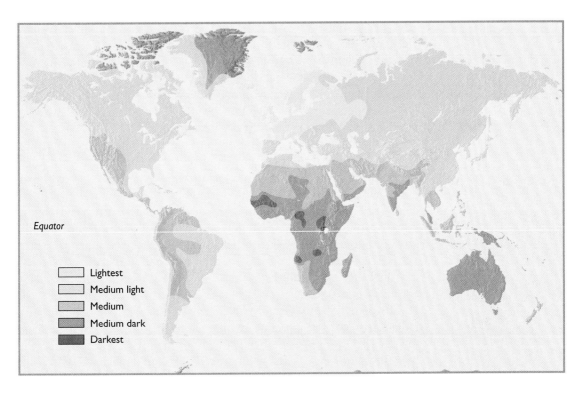

FIGURE 13.11
Skin color distribution (using five categories). Darker skin is concentrated in equatorial regions. (The categories are, of course, arbitrary; there could be more or fewer. Skin color varies gradually across geographic space, a topic we'll take up in detail in Chapter 14.)

Within the map: *Equator*

Legend:
- Lightest
- Medium light
- Medium
- Medium dark
- Darkest

One common explanation has to do with vitamin D production. Vitamin D can be synthesized by the body in the lower layers of skin when a precursor of the vitamin is activated by UV radiation. This vitamin is important in regulating the absorption of calcium and its inclusion in the manufacture of bone. This is especially important during pregnancy and lactation, possibly accounting for the fact that in all populations females tend to be more lightly pigmented than males (Jablonski and Chaplin 2000b, 2002). Deficiency in vitamin D can lead to a condition of skeletal deformity in children known as rickets. (There is an adult version of the abnormality as well.) Bones with rickets are also more prone to breakage, and the disease can cause a deformity of the pelvis that can make childbirth difficult.

It has been thought that as populations moved away from the equator, those with darker skin could not manufacture sufficient vitamin D for normal bone growth and maintenance. Those with lighter skin, therefore, were at an adaptive and, thus, a reproductive advantage. Over time, lighter skin became the normal, inherited condition in these groups. Skin color was thus seen as a balancing act—dark enough to protect from the damaging effects of UV radiation and light enough to allow the beneficial effects.

The vitamin D explanation has been questioned, however (Robins 1991). Rickets is associated with recent urban populations (in narrow city streets, children get little direct sunlight) and is seldom found in rural areas. There is little evidence for it in the fossil record. Moreover, although dark skin does slow down the production of vitamin D, it can still allow for sufficient synthesis to maintain healthy levels. Vitamin D synthesis, therefore, may not have been a selective factor for our ancestors.

Now, of course, we can also obtain vitamin D through vitamin supplements and by drinking vitamin D–fortified milk. It is also found in fish liver oils and egg yolks. A correlation between dark-skinned urban populations and rickets—once proposed as evidence for the adaptive connection—may be based more on socioeconomic matters resulting in poor diet than on skin color differences (see Beall and Steegmann 2000 for a detailed discussion of this debate).

Researchers have proposed another explanation for an active selective factor for light skin. Data from the military suggest that darker skin is more prone to damage from frostbite than is lighter skin (Post et al. 1975; Robins 1991). Selection for lighter skin may not be related to UV radiation but to temperature, while selection for darker skin remains related to UV radiation. Beall and Steegmann (2000) discredit this hypothesis, however. The evolution of light skin pigmentation, it would seem, remains a matter of some debate.

As these examples of body build and skin color demonstrate, our species, despite its ability to adapt through culture to a wide array of environments, has still undergone natural selection for and against certain features in response to those environments. The adaptation of sickle cell anemia in malarial areas is another example. Although we might like to think we have buffered ourselves against this process of evolution, natural selection has occurred in modern *Homo sapiens*, and it continues to affect populations of our species.

Are All Polymorphisms Adaptively Important?

We can see in the distribution of body build and skin color some obvious correlations with environmental factors that lead us rather directly to our conclusions about the adaptive significance of these polymorphic traits. Other variable traits, on the other hand, seem distributed among our populations in such a way that there is no obvious relationship to environmental circumstances.

The distribution of blood types in the ABO system (see Chapter 3) is a perfect example of a polymorphism with no obvious relationship to the environment (Figure 13.12). There seems to be no rhyme or reason to

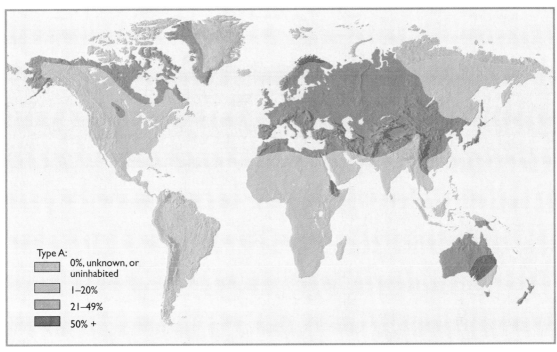

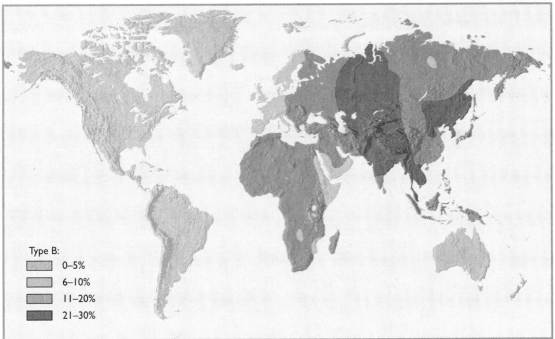

FIGURE 13.12

These maps show the approximate frequency distributions of type A and type B blood, demonstrating the lack of an obvious pattern in the distribution of this polymorphism. (As with skin color in Figure 13.11, the categories here are arbitrary. The blood group frequencies in reality vary gradually across geographic space.)

TABLE 13.1
ABO Blood Group Phenotypes and Antibodies

Genotypes	Phenotypes	Antigens	Antibodies
AA AO	A	A	anti-B
BB BO	B	B	anti-A
AB	AB	A, B	none
OO	O	none	anti-A, anti-B

how the various frequencies of the phenotypes are dispersed around the world. Type A, for example, is totally absent among some native South American groups but is found in frequencies of over 50 percent in parts of Europe and native Australia. Type B, although found in moderate to high frequencies in Asia, is nearly absent among Native Americans, who originated from Asian migrants. Type B is also nearly totally absent in Australia but is found in moderate frequencies in New Guinea. Type O, the most common in the species, still ranges from 40 percent in parts of Asia to 100 percent among some native South Americans.

Are the variations of this genetic trait adaptively neutral? Scientists believe this to be the case for some other blood group systems. (There are about thirty different blood group systems besides the ABO system, that is, different chemical phenotypes in the blood that are the results of different genes with multiple alleles.)

The actual phenotypic trait involved in the ABO system is the presence or absence of certain proteins, called **antigens**, on the surface of the red blood cells. In addition, from shortly after birth your blood plasma contains other proteins, or **antibodies,** that react against the alternate version of your antigen. For example, the alternate version of antigen A is antigen B. Table 13.1 shows how these are expressed in the ABO system.

The reactions between antigens and antibodies are the reason that blood used for transfusions must match the blood type of the recipient. As a type A person, if I received a transfusion of type B blood, my anti-B antibodies would recognize the B antigen of the transfused blood as foreign to my system. My antibodies would bind with the antigens on the transfused red blood cells and destroy the cells by causing them to burst (*hemolyze*). If extensive enough, this reaction could lead to shock or kidney failure. In emergencies, however (as we all know from TV medical dramas), a person of any blood type may receive type O, since O has no antigens and therefore would stimulate no reaction.

Since antibodies of various sorts are important components of our bodies' immunological system, disease is one obvious factor to examine for an adaptive significance of the ABO polymorphism. Some microorganisms possess antigens that are similar to the A and B antigens, so perhaps certain blood types are predisposed to fight off certain infectious diseases. At the same time, if an infecting microorganism possesses antigens that are similar to your own, then your system may not be stimulated to produce the proper antibodies against the organism, making you more susceptible to that disease.

Some correlations between blood type and susceptibility to diseases have been suggested. Type A has been statistically associated with bronchial pneumonia, smallpox, and typhoid; type O has shown correlations with bubonic plague. Among the data that support some connections among these factors is the low frequency of type O in India, where there is a long history of frequent plague epidemics.

It should also be noted that there is some evidence that mosquitoes are more attracted to type O persons. If so, then diseases carried by mosquitoes, such as malaria, would also be influenced, although indirectly, by blood type.

There are correlations as well between blood types and noninfectious gastrointestinal diseases. Type O persons appear to have a greater chance of duodenal and stomach ulcers and type A persons of stomach cancer. Most people have blood group antigens in their body fluids, including their gastric juices, as well as in their blood, and so there may well be some reactions between these antigens and chemicals in the food one eats. The reactions may have a positive or negative effect on the digestive process itself, or they may lead to some irritation of the digestive tract. Thus, certain blood types may have been selected for, and others against, depending on what foods were typically consumed in certain areas by certain populations.

Along the same lines, there may also be reactions between blood antigens in the digestive tract and some intestinal bacteria. Individuals of certain blood types may be more or less affected by bacterial ailments such as infant diarrhea. Such ailments are major factors in infant mortality in many parts of the world. Thus, they are important selective factors, and any polymorphism that influences the severity of these problems could be selected for or against.

What do blood-type correlations tell us? Certainly these data indicate that a selective role for the ABO system is possible, especially with diseases that affect people during or before their reproductive years. We

antigens: Substances, such as proteins, that can trigger an immune response, for example, the production of an antibody.

antibodies: Proteins in the immune system that react to foreign antigens.

must demonstrate, however, that selection is, in fact, taking place. The fact that we have gained control over some of the diseases in question limits our ability to study them in the present, and so we have to rely, as with the plague connection, on historical records.

Moreover, we must establish a cause-and-effect relationship between antigen and disease, and we must also show if, and under what conditions, this would make enough of a difference to affect reproductive success. The ABO system is also found in chimps and gorillas, so the origin of the polymorphism itself may be hidden in our evolutionary past. Some of the more important connections are with diseases of dense urban populations. Thus, selection for certain blood types, and their distribution, may be a fairly recent phenomenon.

As this single example shows, the topic is a complex one. We asked at the beginning of this section, Are all polymorphisms adaptively important? The answer is, We don't know for sure. Human polymorphisms need to be examined for their selective contributions to populations within the species. We may find, however, that some of our variable traits make no difference at all—or at least make no difference now.

DISEASE AND HUMAN POPULATIONS

We tend to think of diseases as abnormalities—and for individuals suffering from them, they are. But diseases are as much a part of life as any other aspect of our biological world. Since many diseases are caused by other living organisms—viruses, bacteria, and protozoa—and are carried by other species, they are really perfectly natural. Disease-causing species have adapted to the biology of their hosts, and the hosts at least attempt to adapt to the disease-causing species. Diseases are thus excellent examples of evolutionary processes.

We also tend to think that our species, especially in modern times, has removed itself from many, if not most, such relationships. After all, those of us in developed countries virtually ignore some diseases that a generation ago were serious threats. Polio (still a problem during my childhood) has been virtually eliminated from the United States and Europe. Tuberculosis is rare in the United States, as are mumps and measles. In 1980 smallpox was declared eradicated worldwide. In the United States, only one of the ten most common causes of death (pneumonia/influenza) is an infectious disease (Figure 13.13).

But there are still diseases that disable and kill us, and new diseases or new strains of old diseases are even now emerging as the species that

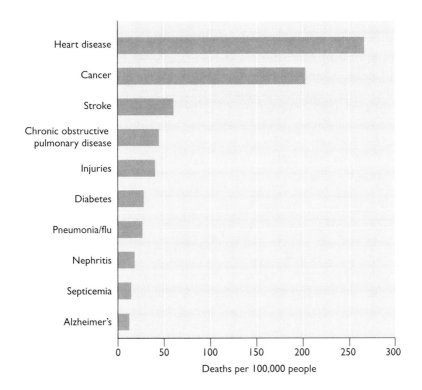

FIGURE 13.13
The ten leading causes of death in the United States in 1999. Note that only one (pneumonia/flu) is infectious.
(From Relethford 2003a:436)

cause them continue to undergo the processes of evolution. We have already discussed the examples of sickle cell anemia, malaria, and plague, and there may well be evolutionary relationships between our blood types and certain diseases. These examples all show diseases as significant factors of natural selection.

Evolutionary relationships among human and animal viruses (based on some of the same genetic techniques and analyses we've discussed) suggest that some viruses have even played a role in hominid evolution (Van Blerkom 2003). As major causes of illness and death, viruses can be agents of selection within populations—for example, selecting for and maintaining general diversity in the all-important human immune system.

Viruses can also be involved in competition between populations. Because some viruses are carried by insects and other animals, affected populations do not even have to be in close contact with one another. The fact that viruses are often more infectious and deadly in a new host could account for the extinction of individual populations within our species. Perhaps early migrants out of Africa—where populations had a long time to develop immunities to certain diseases—carried pathogens to hosts who lacked immunity. An analogous phenomenon occurred, for example, when the Spaniards conquered the Aztecs of Mexico in 1521. European diseases—smallpox, measles, and influenza—to which the Aztecs had no prior exposure and thus no immunity, probably did more to lead to their downfall than did the military actions of the Spanish soldiers.

Finally, since viruses operate by commandeering host cell machinery for their own purposes, some may also have played a more direct role in altering the human genome and thus, perhaps, in accounting for some of the evolutionary changes seen in hominid history (Van Blerkom 2003). Remnants of ancient viruses make up about 1 percent of the human genome. Some of these viral sequences may cause pathological conditions, but others, after millions of years of evolution, may be involved in such normal processes as placental formation and fetal development. An evolutionary tree of certain related virus types mirrors the evolutionary tree of their host species. This is evidence of a long-term coevolution.

Looked at from the biocultural perspective we have used throughout this book, we may see general trends in the relationship between diseases and the human species. Anthropologist George Armelagos (1998; Armelagos et al. 1996) has outlined these trends and refers to them as three "**epidemiological** transitions."

For most of our species' history, we lived in small, widely dispersed, nomadic foraging groups. Our ancestors certainly experienced diseases of various sorts and would have come into contact with new diseases as they migrated to new environments. But infectious diseases may not have had serious effects on large numbers of people or many different populations since they would have had little chance of being passed on to many other humans.

When some people began to settle down and produce their food through farming and animal domestication—starting about 10,000 ya—the first epidemiological transition occurred. Infectious diseases increased in impact, as larger and denser concentrations of people provided the disease vectors with greater opportunity to be passed from host to host. Animal domestication may have brought people into contact with new diseases previously limited to other species. Working the soil would have exposed farmers to insects and other pathogens. We have already seen how irrigation in some areas provided breeding places for mosquitoes, increasing the incidence of malaria. Sanitation problems caused by larger, more sedentary populations would have helped transmit parasitic diseases in human waste, as would the use of animal dung for fertilizer.

In addition, agriculture also led to a narrowing of food sources as compared with the varied diets of foragers. This could have resulted in nutritional deficiencies; moreover, the storage of food surpluses attracted new disease carriers such as insects and rats. Trade between settled communities, as we saw in the case of the Black Death in Europe, helped spread diseases over large geographic areas. Epidemics, in the sense of diseases that affect a large number of populations at the same time, were essentially nonexistent until the agricultural revolution.

Beginning in the last years of the nineteenth century and continuing into the twentieth, we experienced the second epidemiological transition. With modern medical science providing immunizations and antibiotics and with better public health measures and improved nutrition, many infectious diseases were brought under control or even, as with smallpox, eliminated. In terms of what ailed and killed us, there was a shift to chronic, degenerative diseases such as cancers, heart and circulatory diseases, and pulmonary disease. The increase in many of these came not only from the fact that fewer people were dying from infectious diseases and were living longer but also from the results of modern lifestyles in developed countries and among the upper classes of developing countries—a more sedentary life leading to less physical activity; more stress; environmental pollution; diets contributing to obesity, clogged arteries, and diabetes; and smoking and alcohol consumption. But at least, we thought, many of these problems were things we could potentially control; all those infectious epidemics were things of the past (or, at least, of developing countries).

But on the heels of the second transition has come the third epidemiological transition, and we are in it now. New diseases are emerging, and old ones are returning. Both of these phenomena can be understood in terms of evolutionary theory.

The return of old diseases is the result of the fact that microorganisms are evolving species themselves. For example, new and serious antibiotic-resistant strains of tuberculosis have recently appeared. This evolution may have been encouraged by what some authorities consider our overuse of antibiotics, giving microorganisms a greater chance to evolve resistance by exposing them to a constant barrage of selective challenges. Remember, some bacteria reproduce *hourly*, and so the processes of mutation and natural selection are speeded up in these species.

The emerging diseases are also the results of human activity in the modern world, which brings more people into contact with more diseases, some of which were unheard of even a few decades ago. As people and their products become more mobile, and as our populations

epidemiological: Pertaining to the study of disease outbreaks and epidemics.

spread into previously little-inhabited areas, cutting down forests and otherwise altering ecological conditions, we contact other species that may carry diseases to which they are immune but that prove deadly to us. HIV-1, the virus that is the most common cause of AIDS, crossed over to humans from chimpanzees in West Africa as early as 1931 (Hahn et al. 2000; Korber et al. 2000). (Another virus, HIV-2, came from the sooty mangabey monkey.) Hunting, butchering, and the consumption of undercooked contaminated meat probably accounted for the contact that initially allowed the virus to be transmitted to humans from the nonhuman primates that had evolved the ability to carry the virus with no adverse effects. Early cases were isolated, so the disease didn't spread, even though the virus easily moves from host to host through the exchange of bodily fluids during sexual activity or as the result of using unsterilized hypodermic needles. AIDS reached epidemic proportions later in the twentieth century and continues in the present century (Figure 13.14) as a result of social factors, including but not limited to our increased mobility. In addition, the virus itself has evolved since its transmission to humans, producing strains that might be drug resistant, more virulent, and hard to detect (Hahn et al. 2000).

We have long known of another deadly virus, rabies, that is successful because it can jump from species to species (Mills 1997). Hantavirus from rodents, Ebola virus from an as yet unknown source (which is decimating the apes in West Africa; see Chapter 6), and campylobacter, a bacterium from chickens, are some other examples of pathogens that have recently jumped from other species to ours, with serious consequences.

Finally, and perhaps most frightening, are the *prion* proteins. Not living organisms, prions begin as normal proteins (of as yet unknown function) in the nervous tissue of humans, other animals, and birds; these prions, however, sometimes rearrange themselves into an abnormal configuration. In this abnormal form the prions trigger the same rearrangement of the normally configured proteins and then build up in brain tissue, which they eventually destroy. The condition is called *spongiform encephalopathy*. "Mad cow" disease in cattle, Creutzfeldt-Jakob disease in humans, and kuru, a disease described among the Fore people of highland New Guinea, are some examples of this condition, as are other manifestations in sheep, goats, minks, and possibly elk and mule deer. Although the trigger for the abnormal shape of the protein may come, not surprisingly, from a genetic mutation (since, as you recall, genes code for the synthesis of proteins), the frightening thing about prions is that they can easily be transmitted across species. Moreover, they are very hard to destroy. Mad cow disease may have spread as the result

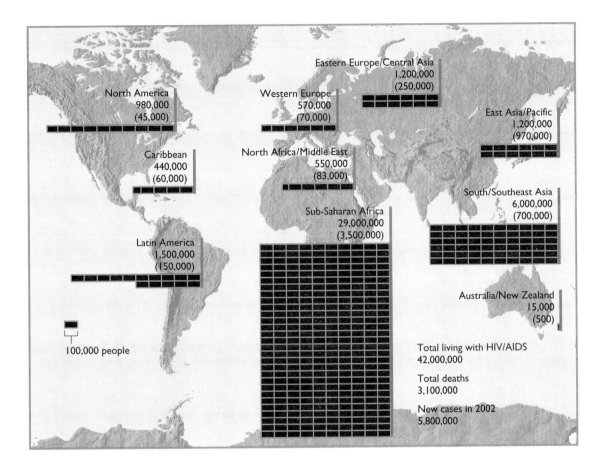

FIGURE 13.14

HIV/AIDS in the year 2002. This map shows the number of people, by region, living with HIV/AIDS as of December 2002. The number of new cases in each region in 2002 is in parentheses. (Since 2000, the number of people living with HIV/AIDS has gone up 6 million; deaths, up 100,000; and new cases, up 500,000.) It is estimated that since the beginning of the epidemic (generally, the late 1970s) 14 million children have been orphaned as a result of the disease.

of cattle being fed meal that contained the remains of other infected domestic animals. Even though these remains were rendered (cooked and processed into meal), the prions survived and passed to other cows through ingestion (Rhodes 1997). As of December 2000, there were nearly 180,000 reported cases of mad cow disease (bovine spongiform encephalopathy, or BSE) from Europe, mostly from the United Kingdom but with some cases from eleven other countries as well (Donnelly 2000). As of the same date, there were 91 confirmed and probable cases of the form of Creutzfeldt-Jakob that is caused by human consumption of contaminated beef, most from Britain and a few from France and Ireland (Aldhous and Abbot 2000). In December 2003 the first case of BSE was recorded in the United States.

So, the evolution of our species has been, and is still being, affected by diseases caused by, originating in, and carried by other species that are themselves evolving. An important area for understanding these diseases, then, is evolutionary theory, which explains important factors about their source and transmission. In fact, this approach has been given the name "Darwinian medicine" (Nesse and Williams 1998; Oliwenstein 1995), and I imagine it will become increasingly important in the future.

THE BIOANTHROPOLOGY OF INDIVIDUALS

Individuals don't evolve, at least not in the sense that we are using the term here. And yet bioanthropologists are interested in growth rates, developmental rates, and the timing of important events in the lives of individual members of our species. Why is this information important to bioanthropology?

First of all, we are interested in these topics simply because they are part of our species' makeup. Studying just the adults of a species does not tell us everything about that species. We need to know such things as how developed an individual is at birth, how fast it reaches certain levels of growth, when it becomes sexually and physically mature, how long its reproductive span lasts, and how long it lives. We also look at rates at which certain components of the body grow and compare them with one another, and we compare all these data for different populations within a species and for different groups within populations—such as males and females.

For example, we may plot a curve that shows the height of the members of a human population at certain ages (Figure 13.15). This type of curve is called a **distance curve.** We see from such a curve that change in height as people mature does not occur at a steady rate but alters at different stages. The sudden increase in height in early adolescence is obviously related to puberty and is called, in fact, the *adolescent growth spurt*.

We all remember from our teens that the adolescent growth spurt did not occur at the same time for boys and girls. This and other differences in growth rate can be seen by comparing distance curves for males and females (Figure 13.16). These differences will be discussed in the next chapter.

distance curve: A graph that compares some variable at different points in time.

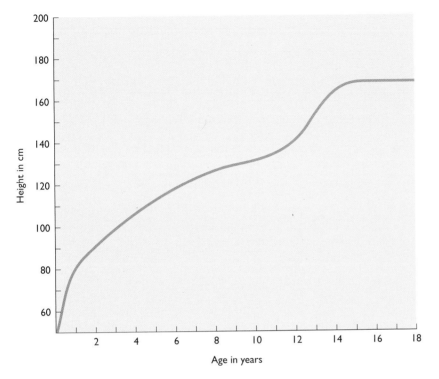

FIGURE 13.15
Distance curve for height and age.

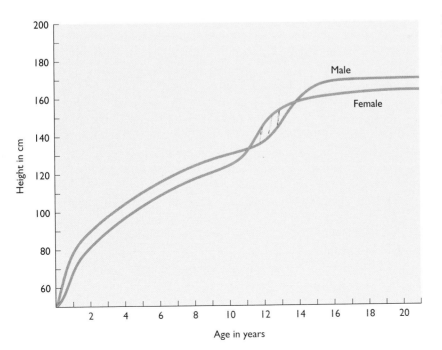

FIGURE 13.16
Distance curves for height and age in males and females. Note the gender difference in timing of the adolescent growth spurt and the result-ant differences in relative average stature.

FIGURE 13.17
Velocity curve for data in
Figure 13.15.

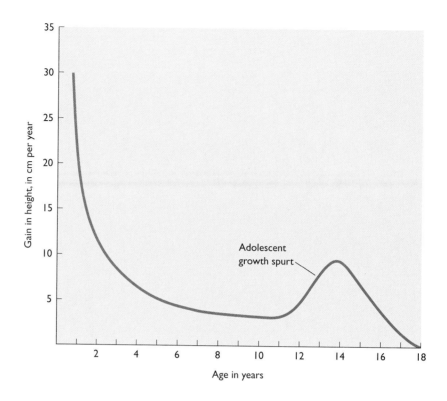

These changes can be seen in another way by plotting the rate of change for different ages. This is called a **velocity curve,** and it measures how *fast* changes are taking place, in this case, how many centimeters per year the plotted individual is growing (Figure 13.17). Note the increase (acceleration) of the growth rate at early adolescence, which follows a basic trend of decreasing growth rate since birth.

Not every part of the body, of course, grows at the same rate. Figure 13.18 compares height with brain size, using the percentage of final adult size as a scale. Note that, unlike the increase in height, the fastest brain growth occurs in the first few years of life.

These and many other analyses show us the patterns of growth of our species in general and of different populations and groups within the species. Observing these patterns leads to other areas of interest.

First, we want to know what factors influence the differences we see between populations of our species and the changes within populations at different points in time (see Stinson 2000 for a good, detailed discussion). Different populations, of course, have different average statures and body sizes (see, as an example, Figure 14.1). Some of these differences can

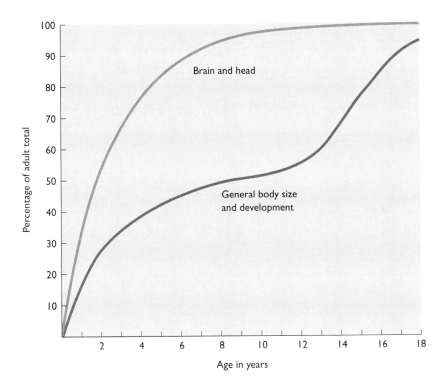

FIGURE 13.18
Distance curves for height compared with brain growth.

be traced to natural selection, for example, with regard to heat loss and retention (see Figure 13.10); these differences may work through such immediate factors as differences in hormone production and utilization.

Environmental factors are also at work. Socioeconomic status (income, education, occupation, possessions), which affects nutrition, disease rate, and access to quality medical care, is an obviously important factor. And there may be feedback in terms of cultural values. Stinson (2000:430) points out that because tallness is valued in many societies (nearly all U.S. presidents have been taller than average), taller individuals may find it easier to improve their socioeconomic status. Of course, they may have come from privileged backgrounds in the first place.

Differences in environmental factors between urban and rural areas also influence growth, as do other influences such as time period. In the nineteenth century, for example, when cities were relatively unhealthy places to live, rural children were larger and healthier in general than their urban counterparts. As conditions in cities improved, urban children on the whole became larger than their rural counterparts; in the most affluent societies, however (such as the United States), there are

velocity curve: A graph that compares the rate of change in some variable at different points in time.

Contemporary Reflections

Where Is the Population Crisis?

A major influence on Darwin's thinking was the English economist Thomas Malthus (1766–1834). In *An Essay on the Principle of Population,* he wrote, "Population, when unchecked, increases in a geometrical ratio. Subsistence increases only in an arithmetical ratio. . . . I can see no way by which man can escape from the weight of this law which pervades all animate nature" (1789:1). Malthus predicted famine and war if humans continued reproducing at the rate current in his day. If he only knew.

Since Malthus's time, the human population has increased nearly sixfold (see Figure 13.8). Given the war, famine, and environmental degradation we see around us, we have every reason to believe that Malthus was right and that with our current annual growth rate of 1.2 percent, we will eventually run out of something—food, water, land, clean air, patience with one another— and our species and its world will be in for some very bad times indeed. The human species has even been likened to a cancer—growing uncontrolled, spreading, and eventually destroying its environment (Hern 1993, who even compares photos of malignant brain cancers with diagrams of the spread of London from 1800 to 1955 and with aerial photos of American cities!).

It is tempting to those of us in the developed West to place the blame for rampant growth on the developing countries of Latin America, Africa, and Asia, where some total fertility rates (loosely, the average number of births per woman) have been as high as 8. We tend to see no evidence of a population problem here in the United States and comfortably see the Malthusian predictions as affecting *other* countries. If only *they* would change, the problem could be solved.

In fact, many *are* changing. In some undeveloped and developing nations, frequent birth was traditionally practiced in order to make up for high infant mortality and high mortality rates in general. But many developing countries are experiencing a fairly rapid decline in birth rates (Robey et al. 1993), and this is the result not of becoming more like the West but of having better education about and access to contraceptive technology. People in many of these countries realized the problems inherent in overpopulation but lacked the means to address it. In Thailand, to give

no such differences between rural and urban populations. Family size (with children in smaller families tending to be larger) and exposure to toxins (such as cigarette smoke) are additional factors that affect growth.

We may also plot changes over time, known as *secular trends.* Over the past century, better nutrition and medical care have resulted in increased adult height and earlier sexual maturity in the United States and other industrialized countries. There are still differences in age of **menarche** between poor women and those of more affluent means within such countries. At the same time, however, age of **menopause** is no different in populations of different nutritional and medical levels. Nor has better nutrition and health expanded the maximum human lifespan,

just one example, fertility rates dropped by 50 percent from 1975 to 1987 (1993:61). On the other hand, some countries may find it hard to overcome years of rapid growth. The population has grown so rapidly across Africa that it will continue to increase, more than doubling by the year 2050—this in spite of the predicted millions of future deaths from the AIDS epidemic. (South Africa, which has lowered its fertility rate and has a high frequency of AIDS, is the exception and may experience a decrease in growth; Crossette 2001.)

Further, it is rather arrogant to think that *we* are not part of the problem. We do live, as the cliché says, in a global village. All parts of the world are now interrelated in every way imaginable. Global ecological effects are well known. Politics and economics are no different. *Every* new human, no matter where he or she lives, will help use up world food, water, and energy resources and will contribute to the buildup of waste products. *Every* new human adds to the population density of the world and encourages the further spread of people, with its resultant alteration of environments (and also, as we have seen, possible contact with new pathogens).

Moreover, to think that there is no population problem in the United States is simply incorrect. The United States is the most fertile of the developed nations, just above the replacement rate of 2.0 (two children to replace two parents), and by 2050 this country will be the only developed nation among the world's top twenty most populated (Crossette 2001). Although we might in theory be able to feed, clothe, and house all the people of the United States, the fact is we don't. Resources here are unevenly distributed, as they are in the rest of the world. Many of the children born in this most affluent of societies are unwanted. One survey concluded that of the 5.4 million pregnancies among American women in 1987, 57 percent were unintended (Cohen 1996).

To be sure, aspects of the population problem are still being debated. There are arguments as to how many people the planet could ideally support, as well as arguments as to how best to (or if it is even possible to) bring about those ideal conditions (see Smail 1999 for a good discussion of these issues). But, that there *is* a population problem is undeniable. And to think that it is not *everyone's* concern is complacent at best.

which remains about a hundred years (Hill 1993), or the average life expectancy, which is unlikely to rise above 85 years without major scientific and medical advances (Olshansky et al. 2001). Culture can affect some aspects of our stages of life, but not others.

The second reason we are interested in life course data is that it may help explain how we evolved. An approach called **life history** collects such data and compares it within and between groups of organisms to try to draw some general rules about the life histories of living things and therefore explain their evolution. For example, humans have a shorter infancy (the period of dependency on the mother for survival, largely coincident with weaning) but a longer juvenile stage (the period

menarche: A woman's first menstrual period.

menopause: The end of a woman's reproductive cycle.

life history: The study of the timing of life cycle events such as fertility, growth, and death.

between infancy and adulthood) than other mammals, even the other primates (Bogin and Smith 2000). Among other things, the length of the juvenile period is correlated with the degree of environmental variation (in climate, food, predators, disease, and so on) that a species experiences. A longer developmental period allows for more plasticity, that is, more experience with environmental variation and, thus, more behavioral flexibility for coping with that variation when an adult. Perhaps this is connected with the need for "variability selection" (see Chapter 10) among the early hominids, a need that might also explain the early hominids' mix of arboreal and bipedal adaptations.

The shortened infancy period means that mothers may give birth more often since they don't nurse as long (lactation interrupts the fertility cycle). The relatively long juvenile stage means that children are not competing as much with adults for food resources. Young children still need food, of course, but it is often provided by members of the group other than the mother. Again, recall the hypothesized importance of social cohesion and cooperation in early hominid evolution. Clearly, recent and future research into life histories promises to shed a great deal of light on human evolution.

▽   ▽   ▽

SUMMARY

While a major focus of bioanthropology is on the evolutionary history of the hominids, the study of the current product of that evolution—modern *Homo sapiens*—is also important. We study living populations of our species from several different yet interrelated approaches.

We may use a trait, such as dermatoglyphics, to study processes of evolution, provided it is under some genetic control. By statistically comparing populations, or groups within a population, for such a trait, we may estimate their genetic distances. In this way, we can hypothesize what sorts of evolutionary changes are taking place. Now, of course, we may compare individuals and populations at the most specific genetic level, the sequence of base pairs in the DNA. When we analyze such data, we see that the biology of demographic changes is intimately linked to cultural variables of the studied populations.

Since humans live in such a wide range of environmental circumstances, it stands to reason that human groups would have different adaptations to those environments. Most adaptations of our species are cultural, but we still exhibit a number of variable traits based on genetic polymorphisms. There is evidence that our variation in these traits is the result of natural selection at some point in our evolution to climatic and other environmental variables.

Among the environmental factors to which humans respond evolutionarily are diseases. Many diseases are caused by or carried by other species, so evolutionary theory may be applied to our understanding of their epidemiology. Viewed from this perspective, we may see some general trends in the relationship between our species and other disease-causing species, in the past and in the present.

Finally, we understand that we need to study not only adult members of our species but also the growth and development of immature members, who are in the process of becoming adults. The timing of certain changes and the pace at which they occur are part of our species' characteristics. Understanding how these changes and rates of change differ from those of other species is beginning to shed more light on the nature and course of our evolution.

QUESTIONS FOR FURTHER THOUGHT

1. We mentioned in the text that the shape of age-sex pyramids will change over this century, becoming top-heavy as birth rates and death rates continue to drop in developed nations. In this country, for example, members of the "baby boom" generation (those born between 1946 and 1964, a total of 76 million) are now in or reaching middle age and will soon greatly increase the rolls of the elderly. What effects will this have on social and economic factors in the United States? What measures might we take to adjust to this change? Will the effects be different in other nations undergoing similar changes?

2. The AIDS epidemic (with over 25 million deaths so far) could be compared to the Black Death of the fourteenth century (with an estimated 25 million deaths). How do the two epidemics compare? In what ways are they similar or different? Do the effects of the plague of fourteenth-century Europe give us any indication of how the HIV/AIDS epidemic might affect Africa or other regions where its frequency is now on the rise? What sorts of steps should we take to deal with this modern "plague" in this country? in other nations? (To find out what life was like during the Black Death, read chapter 5 of Barbara W. Tuchman's marvelous book, *A Distant Mirror*.)

3.   The population crisis is a controversial topic. Do you think, as do some, that overpopulation is a key problem in the world today, precipitating many other major problems? Or do you think that the world can sustain the current population and the even larger population that will surely inhabit the world in the future? If the latter, how will we deal with such numbers of people in terms of food and water, space, pollution, and intercultural conflict?

KEY TERMS

single nucleotide polymorphism (SNP)

dermatoglyphics

demography

polymorphisms

melanocytes

melanin

antigens

antibodies

epidemiological

distance curve

velocity curve

menarche

menopause

life history

SUGGESTED READINGS

If you would like to know more about dermatoglyphics, the standard work is *Finger Prints, Palms, and Soles*, by Harold Cummins and Charles Midlo.

Again, for details on human genome research and its applications, see the February 2001 issues of *Nature* and of *Science*. Particularly relevant to this chapter is the article in *Nature* by Mark Stoneking, "From the Evolutionary Past. . . ."

A very useful and well-done book is *Human Biology: An Evolutionary and Biocultural Perspective*, edited by Sara Stinson, Barry Bogin, Rebecca Huss-Ashmore, and Dennis O'Rourke. It covers in detail many of the topics of this chapter: genetics, adaptation, disease, nutrition, the life cycle, and demography and population. I highly recommend it.

A nice review article on skin color is "Skin Deep" by Nina Jablonski and George Chaplin in the October 2002 *Scientific American*.

On the topic of the emerging diseases, see Frank Ryan's *Virus X: Tracking the New Killer Plagues out of the Present and into the Future* for a general treatment, Jaap Goudsmit's *Viral Sex: The Nature of AIDS* for a discussion on AIDS, and Richard Rhodes's *Deadly Feasts* for more on prion protein diseases. The perspective of Darwinian medicine is described by Lori Oliwenstein in "Dr. Darwin" in the October 1995 issue of *Discover* and by Randolph Nesse and George Williams in "Evolution and the Origins of Disease" in the November 1998 *Scientific American*.

For information on world population, check out the United States Census Bureau's Web site, www.census.gov. It has all the latest statistics and some population clocks that show the world population as it increases. Very scary. For more on the nature of the population crisis and some proposals for addressing it, see the roundtable discussion, "World Population Policy," in the September 1997 issue of *Politics and Life Sciences*.

CHAPTER

14

HUMAN BIOLOGICAL DIVERSITY

Scrutiny of the actual
facts shows that there
are only *three primary
colors peculiar to the
human body;* . . . ruddy,
black and brown.
—John Clark Ridpath
(1894)

In the previous chapter we discussed some human variable traits. The distribution of some traits, such as skin color, points fairly clearly to an explanation involving natural selection to varying environmental conditions. Other traits, such as blood type, are distributed in such a way as to make them seem adaptively neutral or at least with an adaptive significance that is complex and not immediately obvious.

If our interest in phenotypic variation among modern humans were limited to describing and explaining the distribution of variable traits, we would still have a challenging task. But our biological variation has further meaning to us. Some of our variable traits—whether they have adaptive significance or not—are distributed with some geographic regularity, enough so that one can very often tell from what part of the world a person comes.

People look European or Asian or African or Native American. But we can often be more specific: People from Japan don't on average look like people from China. Swedes don't look like Italians. Masai from East Africa don't look like the Khoisan from the Kalahari. Inuit don't look like Maya.

Look at Figure 14.1. The photographer in the center and his highland New Guinea subjects are about as different looking as humans could be, though all are demonstrably members of the same species, *Homo sapiens*. Even if you had not been told where these people were from, even without the cultural cues of clothing and other artifacts, you could still probably venture a good guess as to their geographic origin. We seem to have evidence, in other words, that our species is divided into some number of fairly distinct subgroups. The term usually applied to such groups is *race*. It seems, on the surface, a logical assumption. Indeed, throughout much of its history, anthropology focused on discovering just how many human races there are and on listing their identifying characteristics.

However—as noted in Chapter 12—races, on a biological level, don't exist within the human species. Races *are* real, but they are *cultural* categories. Every culture responds to and interprets objective reality—in this case human biological and cultural diversity—and creates subjective categories that have meaning to its members. A good example of this process, and a somewhat more clear-cut one, is the way in which different cultures translate the biological categories of sex into the cultural categories of gender.

These ideas require more detailed examination, and such an examination is, perhaps, one of the more important contributions of biological anthropology. Let's look at the following questions:

How are the two human sexes interpreted differently by different cultures, and how can we use this as a model for examining "racial" variation?

Is race a valid biological concept?

What is the scientific evidence for our statement that there are no biological human races?

What, then, *are* human races?

How can bioanthropology contribute to understanding some of the problems surrounding the idea of race?

FIGURE 14.1

A European American photographer (6 feet 2 inches tall) stands among a group of Yali men from the highlands of Irian Jaya (the western half of New Guinea). There is little doubt as to who is who—or that members of our species can display a striking degree of phenotypic variation. The major question then becomes, Does this degree of variation mean that there are distinguishable human races?

SEX AND GENDER

Most human beings are unambiguously either biologically male or female. As noted in Chapter 9, with regard to skeletal features we exhibit sexual dimorphism—varying phenotypic traits that distinguish the two sexes. In living humans there are still more clearly dimorphic traits—hair distribution, for example.

Human males, on average, are larger and more heavily muscled than females. They have relatively larger hearts and lungs, a faster recovery time from muscle fatigue, higher blood pressure, and greater oxygen-carrying capacity. Males are more susceptible than females to disease and death at all stages of life. During the first year of life, one-third more males die, mostly from infectious disease. Males are also more likely to have speech disorders, vision and hearing problems, ulcers, and skin disorders.

Females have a greater proportion of body fat than do males. They mature faster at almost all stages of life, most notably exhibiting earlier puberty and the adolescent growth spurt. They are less likely than males to be thrown off their normal growth curve (see Figure 13.16) by disease or other factors and, if they are, will recover more quickly than males. Although females appear to have a greater tendency than males to become obese, males suffer more from the effects of obesity—strokes, for example. Females seem to be more sensitive to touch and pain and perhaps to higher sound frequencies, and they are said to be better at locating the sources of sounds. Smell sensitivity is about the same in both sexes, but females seem better at identifying smells. (For more detail, see Barfield 1976.)

Not all of these dimorphic features are understood, and there is a good deal of overlap in the range of variation of these traits—for example, there are some females who are more heavily muscled than some males. But the tendencies do suggest an adaptive explanation. Many of the characteristics of the human male are aimed at sustained, stressful physical action at the expense, however, of overall health. Females' overall better health, earlier maturity, and greater sensitivity to stimulation of the senses might be geared toward their reproductive and child-rearing roles. Perhaps some basic themes of primate dimorphism (we find these size and strength differences in apes as well) were retained and some others selected for in our early ancestors as their small, cooperative bands (described in Chapter 10) confronted the challenges of life in the changing environments of Africa.

Although there is some individual and regional variation in the degree and nature of our sexually dimorphic traits, in general we rarely have any difficulty telling the **sex** of another human being. Male and female are two biological categories that are objectively real and are common to all human groups.

The biological differences between male and female begin at the genetic level. Two of the human chromosomes are sex chromosomes, X

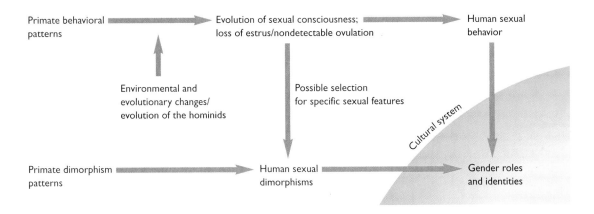

FIGURE 14.2
The evolved sexual identities and roles common to all members of the human species are translated by individual cultural systems into gender identities and roles.

and Y. Females have two X chromosomes; males have an X and a Y. Although the Y chromosome is smaller than the X and carries far fewer genes (several dozen compared with the X's 2,000 to 3,000), it apparently carries a single gene that determines maleness. This gene codes for a protein that triggers the formation of the testes by activating genes on other chromosomes. Products of the testes, including testosterone, then make the developing embryo a male. Some interesting recent research indicates that the X and Y chromosomes were once a pair—like the other 22 pairs of human chromosomes (see Figure 3.6)—that diverged an estimated 300 million years ago through various processes of mutation to take on different versions of their original biological roles (see Jegalian and Lahn 2001 for more detail about the evolution of and relationship between these chromosomes).

As these two real categories of sex—male and female—are incorporated into various cultural systems, however, differences arise. The identity, place, and role of males and females under different cultural systems vary according to the nature of those systems—their economies, politics, family organizations, and abstract beliefs. Thus, *males* and *females* of the human species become the *men* and *women* of a particular society practicing a particular culture. We refer to the cultural interpretation of biological sex categories as **gender** (Figure 14.2).

From cultural anthropology we acquire data about the incredible range of variation in gender identity and gender roles among the world's cultures. The variable factors include the roles of genders in economic activities, differences in political and other decision-making power and influence, and expected norms of behavior. All these may change over time within a single culture.

sex: The biological categories and characteristics of males and females.

gender: The cultural categories and characteristics of men and women.

For example, in the United States only a century ago, men were educated because they were seen as the gender that properly had political, economic, and social power. Women were far less likely to receive a college education, seldom held any sort of management position (if they did any work outside the home at all), and until 1920 were not even allowed to vote. Women were sometimes thought of as "the weaker sex." Obviously things are different now, at least to a degree. As our culture has changed over the past hundred years, our gender roles and identities have changed to fit our evolving cultural system.

We refer to culturally defined categories as **folk taxonomies,** or cultural classifications. A society of people orders its world in ways that reflect objective reality, as its people see and understand that reality, and that also meet its particular cultural needs and fit the totality of its cultural system.

To take an example from a different area, Western society considers the causes of disease from a scientific viewpoint. We understand that diseases are the results of natural processes, and one way we classify them is by the nature of their cause. Diseases are genetic, bacterial, viral, parasitic, environmental (drugs, radiation, pollutants), nutritional, congenital (where the development of the embryo is disrupted), emotional, and so on. The Fore, a farming people of Papua New Guinea (Lindenbaum 1979), also classify disease by cause, but the causes are very different. The Fore believe that all disease results from the malicious intent of either sorcerers or spirits and that life-threatening diseases are caused by sorcery—the malevolent action of one person against another. These beliefs are reflected in the political and economic tensions, rivalries, and jealousies that have become prevalent aspects of the Fore lifestyle. Less-severe diseases are caused by nature spirits inhabiting important places or by the ghosts of the recently deceased. These diseases are punishments for violating important norms with regard to nature or the dead. Minor illnesses are attributed to a person's having violated some social rule among the living. The Fore folk taxonomy for disease, though it differs a great deal from our own, makes sense within the context of the Fore cultural system.

Similarly, folk taxonomies for gender differ to a great degree among the cultures of the world, even though we all accept that there are basically two sexes and two gender categories. We need to note, however, that biological sex is not always unambiguous. There are people born with underdeveloped sexual characteristics, sometimes as a result of having too many or too few of the sex chromosomes. For example, about 1 in every 3,000 female births has a missing or defective X chromosome, and 1 in 500 male births has one or more extra X chromosomes. An estimated 2 percent of humans are *intersexes*, born with characteristics (including genitalia) of both sexes (Fausto-Sterling 2000.)

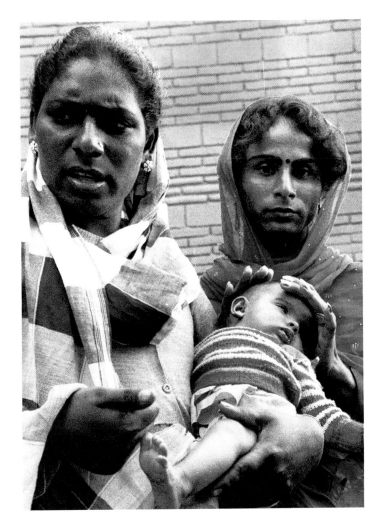

FIGURE 14.3

Hijras, emasculated men who dress and behave like women, make up a third gender category in India. These hijras are blessing a child, one of the important ritual functions they perform.

In addition, there are those who are ambivalent toward their own sexual identity. As a result, some cultures recognize more than two genders. A striking example is the *hijras* of India (Nanda 1990). The word means "not men," and, indeed, hijras are men who have been voluntarily surgically emasculated. They make up a third gender and have very specific identities and roles within the culture of Hindu India. Although often mocked and ridiculed because of their exaggerated feminine expressions and gestures, they are also in demand as performers at important rituals such as marriages and births (Figure 14.3).

folk taxonomies: Cultural categories for important items and ideas.

A less-extreme example comes from a number of traditional Native American cultures in which some men dressed as women and assumed the occupations and behaviors of women. Such men have been referred to by the term *berdache* (a French term with derogatory implications but still in common use). In some cases, they engaged in sexual relations with other men, and certain rituals could be performed only by them. Within their respective cultures, berdaches were not considered abnormal but were thought of as another gender.

It appears, then, that various societies acknowledge that some of their members are, or think of themselves as, ambiguous with regard to the two standard sex categories. These societies have evolved third or even fourth gender classifications to accommodate them, and these classifications have assumed defined places, identities, and roles within these societies' cultures. Sex is biological. Gender is a folk taxonomy; so, as we will see, is race in humans.

⚲ RACE AS A BIOLOGICAL CONCEPT

The processes of evolution ensure that each species of living thing possesses genetic variation and displays some degree of phenotypic variation. Some species are more variable than others, depending on the nature of the species' geographic distribution and the variety of specific environments to which its members are adapted.

As noted in Chapter 5, some species are said to be *specialized*. They inhabit a relatively small geographic area or are adapted to a highly specific set of ecological circumstances—a narrow niche. Such species, of course, tend to be relatively homogeneous genetically and phenotypically. Natural selection has selected for essentially the same characteristics in all members of specialized species. A classic example is the koala, which lives only in Australia and eats primarily the leaves of the eucalyptus tree. We would not expect koalas to show a whole lot of variation, and, relatively speaking, they don't.

A species that inhabits a wide geographic range and is adapted to many niches is said to be *generalized*. Selection will promote variations in the species' basic traits in response to the environments found in different parts of its range. Such species tend to be more variable.

To remain a single species, of course, all males and females of the group must be capable of interbreeding. Furthermore, there must be sufficient gene flow to prevent one or more groups from becoming completely isolated. Gene flow, however, is not always even. Members of a species may be clustered into breeding populations (see Chapter 4). More genes are exchanged within a single breeding population than between different breeding populations, often because some geographic barrier prevents extensive gene flow or because the environments to which the species are adapted come in clusters themselves with gaps between them that limit steady genetic exchange (see Figure 4.5).

Breeding populations may be thought of as important factors in many cases of speciation. If a breeding population becomes so isolated that virtually no genes are exchanged with another breeding population, if its environment is different enough to cause selection for a distinct set of traits, and if enough time elapses, the breeding population may eventually become a separate species, unable to interbreed with what were formerly other breeding populations of the same species.

If, however, isolation is not complete or the preceding conditions have not been in operation for a long enough time, the breeding populations may represent phenotypically distinguishable regional populations within the same species. Such a species is said to be **polytypic** ("many types"), and such breeding populations may be referred to as **subspecies,** or **races.**

For example, the reindeer of Europe and Asia and the caribou of North America are classified as a single species, *Rangifer tarandus* (Figure 14.4). Now isolated from one another in separate hemispheres, the reindeer and caribou were no doubt able to interbreed when Alaska and Siberia were joined during the Pleistocene, connecting the Old and New Worlds. Reindeer and caribou, then, have been separated for only 10,000 years, not long in terms of speciation in a large mammal. Enough time has elapsed, however, for the two populations to become physically distinguishable. They might legitimately be considered subspecies, or races, of a single species—or, better, as **semispecies,** populations at an intermediate state between being a single interbreeding group and being separate species (Mettler et al. 1988). They still *can* interbreed (it has been done under artificial conditions), but in the wild they *don't*.

The North American population of *R. tarandus* has been further classified into at least four subspecies as a result of their distribution in different environments of Alaska, Canada, and Greenland. These subspecies, some woodland dwellers and some tundra dwellers, are distinguishable by such features as size, antler shape, and coat color (Figure 14.5). There are, then, five named subspecies, or races, of *Rangifer tarandus,* one in the Old World and four in the New World.

But the four North American subspecies pose a problem. Since all the populations are members of a single species that maintains its species

polytypic: A species with physically distinguishable regional populations.

subspecies: Physically distinguishable populations within a species.

races: In biology, the same as subspecies. In culture, cultural categories to classify and account for human physical diversity.

semispecies: Populations of a species that are completely isolated from one another but have not yet become truly different species.

FIGURE 14.4

The caribou, *Rangifer tarandus*. This woodland caribou of Alaska and Canada is sometimes classified as subspecies *Rangifer tarandus caribou*. Well adapted to a wide range of environments, the caribou has such traits as hollow outer guard hair that gives it extra bouyancy for swimming and extra insulation for warmth. This feature makes caribou hides a favorite material among the Inuit for making parkas.

identity through the flow of genes among those populations, these subspecies distinctions are artificial. In reality, the dividing lines on the map in Figure 14.5 don't exist. The caribou at the extremes of the ranges may look quite different, but one doesn't step over one of these geographic lines and find the caribou suddenly looking completely different. Rather, their variable traits grade into one another over geographic space. This gradual variation is known as a **cline,** a continuum of change from one area to another, as opposed to a sudden and distinct change (Figure 14.6).

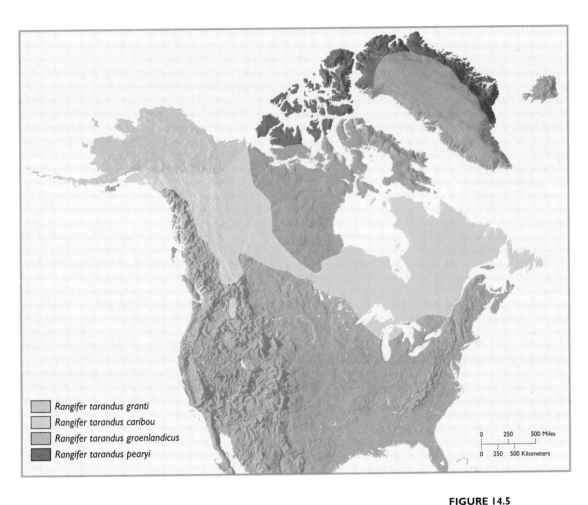

Rangifer tarandus granti
Rangifer tarandus caribou
Rangifer tarandus groenlandicus
Rangifer tarandus pearyi

0   250   500 Miles
0   250   500 Kilometers

FIGURE 14.5
North American populations of caribou are considered by some to represent subspecies, or races.

Recent books on evolutionary biology, in fact, indicate that the concept of *race* or *subspecies* is generally falling into disfavor. In Mark Ridley's *Evolution* (1996), for example, neither term appears in the index or glossary, nor is either used formally in the discussions of species variation or formation. In *Population Genetics and Evolution*, by Lawrence Mettler and colleagues (1988), the term *race* is said to be "a subjective convenience," and the authors favor, as just noted, the recognition of only semispecies as important and definable groups within species. Now, with this general biological background in mind, we can address the question of human races.

cline: A geographic continuum in the variation of a particular trait.

FIGURE 14.6
Distribution of size variation in male house sparrows, (determined by sixteen skeletal measurements). The numbers in the key correspond to size: the larger the number, the larger the sparrow. The classes, however, are arbitrary. If a line is drawn from Atlanta to St. Paul or from St. Paul to San Francisco, the size variation in the sparrows is distributed as a cline. (Notice also that the birds tend to be larger in the north, another example of a trait adaptation to the cold; see Chapter 13.)

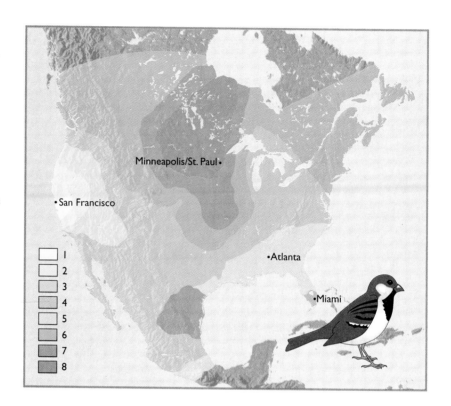

WHY ARE THERE NO BIOLOGICAL RACES WITHIN THE HUMAN SPECIES?

It is all too easy to agree that there are no human biological races because we don't *want* them to exist. The nonexistence of definable racial groups coincides with and reinforces our ethical ideas of human equality. But wishful thinking cannot take the place of scientific rigor. We must be able to say *why* there are no races. It's not enough to be sure it's the case or to assume it is because it makes us feel good. We need to present sound scientific evidence for it.

This evidence comes from three intersecting, interrelated areas. As we discuss them, we need to be as objective as possible, to try not to argue toward a predetermined conclusion. In the end, this will make our affirmation of the nonexistence of human races all the more meaningful.

Human Phenotypic Variation

Given the perceived wide range of human phenotypic variation (see Figures 14.1 and 13.10), could it be that, like the caribou and reindeer, at least some of our populations were isolated enough and have become distinct enough to warrant semispecies status? What do our variable traits indicate?

To address this question, we need to go back to Figures 13.11 and 13.12. Although skin color varies by latitude and ranges from very dark to very light, in no way does this variation assort itself into distinct geographic groups. My categories ("lightest," "medium light," and so on) are arbitrary, as are my geographic dividing lines. I could have demonstrated the relationship between skin color and latitude with any number of different schemes, with actual numbers for color (we can measure skin color quantitatively) and more categories, which would have required more geographic boundaries. Human skin color variation, like size variation in the sparrow (see Figure 14.6), is distributed as a cline—gradually going from dark to light or light to dark across geographic space—and is not limited to any one traditional racial population. Dark skin, for example, usually conceptually associated with Africa, is an equatorial trait that is also found almost halfway around the world in New Guinea. Clearly, skin color is of no use in defining subgroups within the human species that have any biological meaning.

Skin color, of course, doesn't come in nice, neat categories. It is said to be a continuous trait. So how about traits that do come in discrete, either/or categories? Maybe these would better describe discrete biological populations. Blood type is a good example, since, as discussed in Chapter 13, everyone on earth falls into one of four groups for the ABO system. There are no intermediates.

But look at Figure 13.12. Again, the percentage categories on the maps are arbitrary. I could have divided them into more groups or fewer. Each category is a range and, thus, a generalization. For instance, across Africa, type A is shown to appear in 1 to 20 percent of the population in some areas and 21 to 49 percent of the population in other areas. With more detail, in fact, we would see the distribution of blood group frequencies as clinal, just as we would with skin color. And notice that the distribution of type A is very different from that of type B. In other words, blood-group frequencies are of no more use than is skin color in pointing out and defining discrete subspecific human groups.

No matter what phenotypic trait one uses, the human species simply cannot be divided into distinct subgroups based on biological differences.

FIGURE 14.7

Diagram of discordant variation. Each layer represents the geographic variation in one variable trait. Each "core," or cylinder, represents a sample of individuals from a particular area. Notice that each core is different and that any other four cores are very likely to be different as well. The expression of one trait does not predict a particular expression of another. There are no natural racial divisions based on specific combinations of traits.

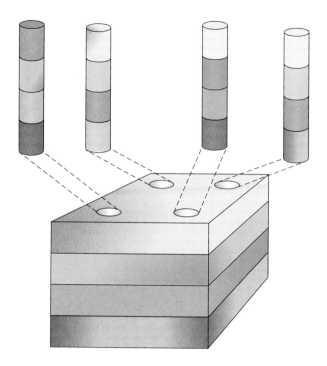

Nor will such a division show up if we use combinations of traits, because the distributions of traits are discordant—that is, a particular expression of one trait does not necessarily predict a particular expression of another (Figure 14.7). The nature and distribution of human variable traits, then, is like that of most other species—varying as clines with no clear-cut boundaries. Clearly defined biological groups below the species level are not scientifically supported for *Homo sapiens* by these data.

Genetic Variation

Phenotypic features, as we pointed out in Chapter 4, can be deceptive, influenced as they are by multiple genes, environmental factors, and natural selection (see Figure 2.7). For the past several decades, we have had the ability to look at aspects of the genetic code itself. Some have thought that perhaps this type of research could provide better data for determining the identity of subspecific groups of *Homo sapiens*.

From the beginning, however, it was clear that genetic data did more to refute the concept of biological race than did phenotypic data. When scientists genetically compared samples from traditional racial groups, they determined that the groupings accounted for only a small percentage of genetic diversity; in other words, there was actually little genetic difference among the groups (see Brown and Armelagos 2001 for a review of these studies). Most diversity in genes, 93 to 95 percent (Rosenberg et al. 2002), was found between *individuals*, even individuals within the same "racial" affiliation. In other words, only around 5 percent of genetic variation exists between major population groups.

This means that diversity on the genetic level is not clustered into any definable subspecies divisions but is, rather, fairly evenly distributed. As an expression of this conclusion, population geneticist Richard Lewontin (1982:123) calculated that if some great cataclysm left only Africans alive, the remaining members of the human species would still retain 93 percent of the variable genes of the former species, although, of course, some of the variations would be found in different frequencies from the previous average (a higher frequency of alleles that increase melanin production, for example).

As discussed previously, new technologies now allow us access to the most basic genetic level. We are quickly gathering data about the extent of diversity at that level—the single nucleotide polymorphisms (SNPs) that account for most human genetic variation and, of course, phenotypic variation. As noted in Chapter 13, while there are about 10 million SNPs (nucleotides that show regular variation) in the human population, any two people differ, on average, by only 3 million SNPs (International HapMap Consortium 2003; Stoneking 2001). This means that, on average, any two humans are more than 99 percent genetically identical at the most basic genetic level. Moreover, because most of the genome is noncoding, most of those SNPs are in noncoding regions. Only an estimated 60,000 are in actual genes (International SNP Map Working Group 2001), and many of those may be involved in the differences between the two sexes. All the phenotypic variation that we try to assort into race is the result of a virtual handful of alleles.

Finally, the nature of the genetic variation that influences phenotype is such that the variation may well show a geographic pattern due to the processes of evolution. We see this in skin color, blood type, and other physical features that are characteristic of certain areas. But these patterns are no indication of the distribution of variation in *other* parts of the genome. Thus, two people from the same part of the world who look alike superficially may actually be less genetically similar than either is to people from different parts of the world who look distinctly different (Pääbo 2001.) The genetic data also indicate that modern humans cannot be divided into discrete biological subspecific groups.

Does this all mean, however, that there is *no* pattern to our genetic diversity or that genes are useless for learning about population history? We have already discussed the application of genetics to the question of modern human origins (see Chapter 12). Similarly, we can find patterns of genetic differences that may help us trace relationships, migrations, and histories of human populations.

In one study, researchers focused on **microsatellites,** repetitive sequences of noncoding DNA (Rosenberg et al. 2002). They collected sequences with over 4,000 alleles from more than 1,000 individuals from around the world. Without using knowledge of the individuals' origins, a statistical program clustered the individuals into groups that corresponded to major geographic regions and into subclusters that corresponded to actual individual populations (Figure 14.8). Furthermore, the major clusters corresponded geographically to what scientists thought were ancient migration routes; these clusters further corresponded to major physical barriers such as oceans, mountains, and deserts (Rosenberg et al. 2002:2384).

Interestingly, only a few alleles (about 7 percent) were unique to any one population, and these alleles were rare in those populations. This means that they were in no way *characteristic* of those populations. Moreover, although some clusters that were geographically distant or isolated by a barrier were statistically different for the studied alleles, the frequencies of those alleles changed gradually across space; in other words, they were distributed as clines. As with phenotypic features, variation and regional differences in gene frequencies do not translate into support for racial groups.

Studies such as these can also be combined with archaeological and linguistic research to try to trace the migrations of groups across geographic space. The settling of the islands of the Pacific, for example, is now the subject of research that focuses on similarities and differences in artifacts (such as pottery), features of languages, and the distribution of genetic markers—unique features characteristic of certain populations (Gibbons 2001).

Evolutionary Theory

Let's look at the question from a more general perspective. Given the nature of our species and what we know of the workings of evolution, we could ask whether groups distinct enough to be semispecies *could* exist within *Homo sapiens*. After all, semispecies have developed over 10,000 years in *Rangifer tarandus* (reindeer and caribou), and even by the most

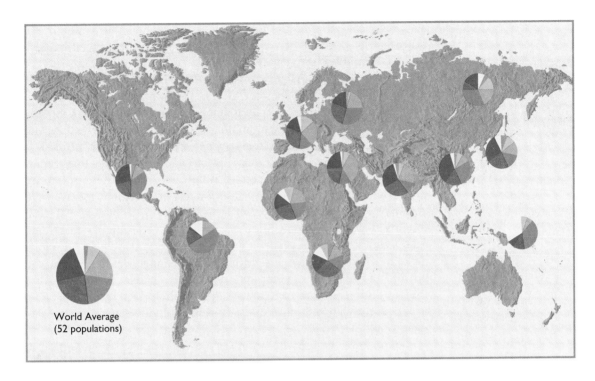

World Average
(52 populations)

FIGURE 14.8

Worldwide genetic variation at a neutral marker. Allele frequencies of one randomly chosen microsatellite marker reveal common alleles shared in all populations and the gradual and arbitrary differences in allele frequencies across geographic regions. Populations shown in this example are Yoruba and Bantu (Africa); French, Russians, Palestinians, and Pakistani Brahui (Eurasia); Han Chinese, Japanese, and Yakut (East Asia); New Guineans (Oceania); and Maya and Karitianans (America). Each color on the diagram represents one of nine alleles of GGAA29H03 (D13S1493), which range in length from 219 to 255 base pairs. By accumulating small differences in allele frequencies from hundreds of such highly variable markers and hundreds of people, statistical methods reveal genetic clusters of Africans, Eurasians, East Asians, Pacific Islanders, and Americans, corresponding to major ancient human migrations.

(Caption and figure from King and Molutsky 2002:2343)

conservative estimates, our species is ten times as old. Moreover, we are a populous species; we live in widely varied environmental conditions, sometimes in fairly isolated regions; and we further isolate our populations through cultural boundaries. These would seem to be the perfect circumstances for creating definable groups.

However, one noteworthy feature of our species for its entire biological history has been mobility. We evolved first in Africa—whether that was 2 mya or 200,000 ya (see Chapter 12)—and then spread with

microsatellites: Long repetitious strings of noncoding DNA. Their length and the fact that they are not influenced by selection make them good genetic landmarks for DNA comparisons.

amazing speed all over the Old World, despite mountains, water, and other barriers. And when we reached the far corners of Africa and Eurasia, we did not stay put. We continued to move around in search of resources and space. As we evolved, we acquired increasing ability to move around (with the domestication of the horse and with inventions such as boats and navigation instruments), and we found increasing motivation for doing so. Such mobility leads to extensive gene flow, and it's fair to say we tend to exchange genes at nearly every opportunity.

But what about our cultural rules of endogamy? Don't they genetically isolate populations at certain times? To answer these questions, recall the Hutterites, who have been largely endogamous for over 470 years. The Hutterites' nearly half a millennium history is not all that long in evolutionary terms; not much genetic variation can arise over such a short period, especially in a species such as our own with a long generation time. Moreover, cultural rules change, and the political, ethnic, and religious populations they define change over time. Also, rules of endogamy are not always fully upheld. As such, biological isolation through the cultural institution of endogamy is a temporary condition.

Gene flow, then, is the norm for our species, and as widespread as we are, we still manage to exchange enough genes—through intermediary populations—to prevent any group of humans from being isolated long enough to evolve the differences sufficient for semispecies status.

Finally, what about all the different environments our species inhabits? Couldn't natural selection have led to differentiation of some populations? Certainly, the variation and distribution of some of our traits— skin color, for example—can be attributed to natural selection. But our major adaptive mechanism is culture, with its values, social systems, and, especially, its technologies that, to a great extent, have increasingly buffered us against the constant editing of natural selection. Adaptively, we change less biologically than we do culturally. Culture and the big brains that make culture possible are species characteristics, shared by all humans. They are the basis of our modern identity. Culture, in a sense, *is* our environment, and we may say that, for some time, our species has experienced little of the kind of environmental variation that would lead to the development of distinct, isolated subpopulations. As anthropologist C. Loring Brace puts it, we all have undergone the "same selective pressures" leading to essentially the "same lifeway," (personal communication).

If this reasoning sounds familiar, that's because it is basically the same argument supporters of the Multiregional Evolution model use to explain why genus *Homo* did not branch into multiple species. If an organism with our characteristic network of genetic (and cultural) exchange has not divided into definable *subspecific* groups, how likely is it to have split into different related *species*? Thus, aside from what we *want* to think about human biological diversity, sound scientific evidence and reasoning make it clear that there is no basis for the recognition of biologically meaningful groups within the species *Homo sapiens*. Human *variation* exists, to be sure, and some of it shows patterns of geographic distribution. But human *races*—in a biological sense—do not exist.

WHAT, THEN, *ARE* HUMAN RACES?

Like gender categories, human races are folk taxonomies. Several years ago I gave one of my classes a weekend assignment to pose two questions to ten people, preferably from different backgrounds and of different ages and both sexes: How many races are there? What are they?

Nearly all the responses were versions of a familiar set of categories: "white," "black," and "yellow"; or "Caucasian," "Negro," and "Oriental"; or some other terms that varied by individual. The similarity of most responses is an indication that some basic taxonomy is shared among members of our culture.

However, there was some interesting variation in the responses as well. One respondent said there were three races: "black," "white," and "Polish." Jews were considered a race by some, as were Hispanics. A few people added Native Americans and native Australians to the usual three. This showed that despite the similarities, there was no universally agreed-upon classification, as there would be for some scientific categories, such as the atomic weights of the elements. Specific responses, though variations on a theme, were as different as the individual backgrounds of the respondents.

Cultures classify other people relative to themselves. Isolated societies with some knowledge that others exist will have a very simple racial classification: us and them. Among more mobile or cosmopolitan groups, as the relations among people become more varied, the classifications become more complex. These classifications reflect a knowledge about other groups' cultural practices, their relations with our group, and their physical appearance. Thus, a racial taxonomy also carries implications about a society's attitude toward others. In short, race—which differs from society to society—is a folk taxonomy used by a particular society at a particular time for particular culturally based reasons.

FIGURE 14.9

Columbus's first contact with natives of the New World. To the Europeans, the Indians were so strikingly different physically and culturally that it was natural to consider them as a distinct category of human. Notice the men planting the cross to claim the land as theirs.

(From a seventeenth-century Spanish version of a 1594 engraving by de Bry. The Granger Collection.)

The categories of race that we in North America recognize are no exception. The categories' origins can be traced to European knowledge and attitudes first acquired during the Age of Exploration. European explorers, using mostly water transportation, could observe only a limited range and distribution of human variation. They sampled points along the continuum of human variation. Because points along a continuum can differ greatly from one another, depending on how far apart they are, it appeared to these explorers that human variation fell into a number of relatively discrete categories (Figure 14.9, and see again Figure 14.1).

In addition, the peoples contacted were not seen as simply different human beings; instead, they were compared to and ranked against European peoples, usually unfavorably. They had, after all, a different appearance, different cultures, often less complex technologies, and—most important to the Europeans—non-Judeo-Christian beliefs. Furthermore, the motivation for the explorers' voyages was less to acquire knowledge than to find new territories, sources of labor, spices, and gold. An attitude of dominance was built in to the Europeans' relationships with these new peoples. Witness the way Europeans would claim new lands "in the name of the crown," entirely ignoring the fact that there were already people to whom the lands belonged. Obviously, it was thought, the indigenous people were too primitive to really have laws of ownership.

The racial folk taxonomy that resulted from these cultural events was formalized, and thus made more real, by Linnaeus. In the final edition of his taxonomy in 1758, he included *Homo sapiens* and divided the species into "varieties," or races. Actually, he recognized a second species, *Homo monstrosus*, to accommodate explorers' yarns of wild "half-men" covered with hair and sporting tails, and a variety of *Homo sapiens* he called *ferus* ("wild man") for the probably retarded and abandoned children who were sometimes found wandering in the woods and were said to have been raised by wolves and other animals. His main races were American, European, Asiatic, and African, and his descriptions of these races were a blend of biological generalizations and, as Stephen Molnar says, "personality profiles" based on European perspectives (1992:10). Here is Linnaeus's taxonomy for humans (based on translations in Gould 1996b and Kennedy 1976):

Class: Mammalia
  Order: Primates
    Genus: *Homo*
      Species: *monstrosus*　　Varying by climate or art
              sapiens　　Diurnal; varying by education and situation
          Varieties:
              ferus　　Four-footed, mute, hairy
              americanus　　Red, choleric [angry], upright. Hair black, straight, thick; nostrils wide; face harsh; beard scanty; obstinate, content free. Paints himself with fine red lines. Ruled by habit.
              europeaus　　White, sanguine [cheerful], muscular. Hair yellow, brown flowing; eyes blue; gentle, acute, inventive. Covered with cloth vestments. Ruled by custom [or law].

| *asiaticus* | Pale-yellow, melancholy, stiff. Hair black; eyes dark; severe, haughty, covetous. Covered with loose garments. Ruled by belief [or opinions]. |
| *afer* | Black, phlegmatic [sluggish], relaxed. Hair black, frizzled; skin silky; nose flat; lips tumid [swollen]; crafty, indolent, negligent. Anoints himself with grease. Ruled by caprice [impulse]. |

Because the history of the United States has been so influenced by European cultures, it makes sense that these basic categories and attitudes would be carried over to this country and altered by its subsequent history. For example, the reason we distinguish Hispanics from other European Americans is, in part, because of the conflicts between Spain and other European countries over territory in the New World and later between Mexico, a former Spanish colony, and the United States. Notice, too, that in some lists of race, Puerto Rican has been separated from Hispanic. It's not that some new group of people has arisen but rather that, for certain purposes, we choose to distinguish people from that U.S. territory—people who previously and still in other lists are categorized as Hispanic.

Our racial categories are real. They may not reflect universal biological reality on the species level, but they do have meaning within our cultural system, for better or for worse.

RACE, BIOANTHROPOLOGY, AND SOCIAL ISSUES

The issue of race in the human species is not just a matter of whether to apply the biological concept of subspecies or semispecies. If only it were. Rather, the idea of race can be, and is, used to make prejudgments about people and to determine their place in society, often without regard for their individual characteristics. This is **racism.** The moral dimension of this problem should be important to everyone, but it is not something we can or should deal with in a brief book about bioanthropology. We may, however, show how bioanthropology, through the use of science, can examine some claimed connections between racial categories and biological traits. In so doing, we can inform ourselves more fully about just what race is and what it is not.

Let's briefly look at one topic. If a group of people were interested in limiting the social position and power of another group, they could argue that the other group possessed some unalterable biological difference that inherently limited their abilities and therefore justified their lower social status. The practice of slavery in the United States was often justified by the claim that the African slaves were biologically less intelligent than the whites and therefore could never hope to attain the dominant race's social, political, and intellectual level. Claims like this have been quite common, even during the past century (Gould 1996b).

Such broad statements about race and intelligence, or even race and evolutionary level, are so clearly motivated by social and economic aims as to be at least questionable, if not obviously false. Perhaps more dangerous, however, are the more subtle correlations whose propositions are based on scientific investigation. Ideas that sound scientific are often treated more seriously, especially because, even today, many people feel that science is something so complex and obscure that only a handful can really understand it. Many people take the position that if something sounds scientific and they don't get it, it must be valid.

Such is the case for the claimed connection between the American black and white races and IQ (intelligence quotient). The most famous (or infamous) example is educational psychologist Arthur Jensen's 1969 article in the *Harvard Educational Review* titled "How Much Can We Boost IQ and Scholastic Achievement?" The article is 123 pages long and quite scientific in its wording, logic, and methodology, and it includes a lengthy mathematical formula or two. As a result, many people, both supporters and critics of Jensen's work, have never bothered to actually read it. A more recent and perhaps better-known work, *The Bell Curve* by Richard Herrnstein and Charles Murray (1994), repeats and greatly expands the same essential argument (see Gould 1996b for a detailed critique).

A focus of Jensen's article was the documented fact that American black children score, on average, fifteen points lower on IQ tests than American white children. Jensen wondered why programs aimed at the obvious solution of culturally enriching children's lives had basically failed at eliminating the fifteen-point IQ difference. Hence, the title of his article (emphasis mine for the right intonation): "How Much *Can* We Boost IQ and Scholastic Achievement?"

Jensen embarked on a scientific investigation. His first conclusion was that IQ tests measure something called g, or general intelligence—a biological, inherited entity. This entity, g, has a **heritability** of .80 (80 percent). This means that 80 percent of the variation in intelligence within a population is explained by genetic differences. Only 20 percent is the result of environment—that is, having been brought up under different cultural conditions. (It bears restating that heritability measures

racism: Judging an individual based solely on his or her racial affiliation.

heritability: The amount of variation of a particular trait within a population that is caused by genetic, as opposed to environmental, differences.

the amount of variation *within a group* that is due to genetic differences. It does not measure the amount of genetic control of a trait in an individual. It does not say that 80 percent of my intelligence is genetically determined.)

The obvious conclusion, then, is that the difference in intelligence between these two racial groups must be largely the result of some genetic difference and, thus, that all the cultural enrichment programs in the world can have only a limited effect. In response to his own question—How much can we boost IQ and scholastic achievement?—Jensen concluded, Not much. He stated, "No one has yet produced any evidence based on a properly controlled study to show that representative samples of Negro and white children can be equalized in intellectual ability through statistical control of environment and education" (1969:82–83).

Jensen went further, however. He compared scores from different parts of IQ tests and concluded that the different IQs of blacks and whites are the result of their having different kinds of intellectual abilities: whites are better at problem solving and abstract reasoning, while the abilities of blacks are focused on memorization, rote learning, and trial-and-error experience. His ultimate conclusion was that education should be as individualized as possible, taking into account not only individual differences in ability and skill but these racially based differences as well.

As you can imagine, Jensen's article caused a great deal of controversy. He was labeled a racist, and, certainly, those with racist leanings embraced his work enthusiastically. I don't know what Jensen's social attitudes were, but we can look at his article from a scientific point of view, drawing especially on what we have learned from anthropology.

First, the idea that IQ tests measure some innate mental ability is fraught with problems. It has been said that IQ tests measure the ability to take IQ tests. This is not, as it sounds, just a sarcastic remark. IQ tests, in fact, measure particular knowledge and abilities that are largely learned through one's culture. IQ tests can be a valuable tool, however. They may, for example, point out some learning disability that could be biologically based. Moreover, because they measure the kinds of skills required by education in our culture as well as by many occupations, they do have predictive value as to one's success within those realms of our cultural system.

But we don't even really know what intelligence is. How, then, can we apply a single number to such a complex and multifaceted concept through a test given in a cultural language, in a cultural setting, with cultural problems? When we do this, we commit the logical error called **reification.** With IQ scores we have reified intelligence—translated a complex idea into a single entity, in this case a number, which we then use to divide people into groups such as different learning tracks in schools.

Let's put this another way. As anthropologist Jonathan Marks suggests, there is a difference between *ability* and *performance* (1995:240 ff.). One's score on an IQ test is a score of one's performance. Certainly some internal factor—one's innate intellectual abilities, whatever those are—plays a part in one's performance on an IQ test. But that performance is also affected by all sorts of external factors. In test taking, for example, your cultural background, quality of education, personality, home life, even your mood on the day of the test can all affect your performance. We cannot, therefore, infer innate abilities from the test score, any more than we can, say, infer a person's athletic abilities from his or her performance in one game. We cannot do so, in part, because there *are* so many external influences; and we have no way of accounting for them, controlling them, or even knowing what they are. More importantly, though, to make such an inference from IQ is to reify intelligence—to take the measurement of performance on a test and assume that it is also a measurement of an innate ability. As Marks puts it, "We can't measure ability; we can only measure performance" (1995:241).

But what about the claimed heritability of IQ? This is a complicated issue (see Gould 1996b for the best discussion), but there is one major problem we can point out here. Heritability studies—estimating the genetic and environmental components of the phenotypic variation in a population—are done regularly, but these studies are done on organisms such as fruit flies, whose genetic mechanisms for phenotypic traits are well known (and can even be manipulated) and whose environmental variables can be controlled in detail. Numbers may be placed on these genetic and environmental variables that may then be plugged into the heritability formula. This is the formula that Jensen reproduces in his article.

To apply the heritability formula to humans, however, is virtually impossible. What numbers can we place on the external environmental variables that affect us? How, in other words, can we reify culture? What number is applied to having a culturally enriched childhood? to being a member of a minority group? to having a poor early education?

Heritability has been *estimated* for humans based on twin studies. Because identical twins have no genetic variation between them, any phenotypic difference, including intelligence, must be the result of environmental differences. IQ scores of identical twins are generally very similar, even in twins raised separately, and this seems to indicate that environment has little effect on intelligence. We must remember,

reification: Translating a complex set of phenomena into a single entity such as a number.

Contemporary Reflections

Are There Racial Differences in Athletic Ability?

Nearly 80 percent of players in the National Basketball Association are African American. The figure is 70 percent for professional women's basketball. The National Football League is 65 percent black. In track and field, nearly every men's world record belongs to an African or someone of African descent. In the 2003 New York City Marathon, seven of the top ten male finishers were from Kenya (including the top four), as were five of the top ten female finishers (including the top three). These statistics pose an obvious question, which we may address by focusing on a controversial book by journalist and TV producer Jon Entine called *Taboo: Why Black Athletes Dominate Sports and Why We're Afraid to Talk About It*. This complex book nicely covers many aspects of the topic of sports and race. Entine wrote it, he says, because "sport remains a haven for some of our most virulent stereotypes" and because he believes "that open debate beats backroom scuttlebutt"(8). And open debate it does.

Our immediate explanation for the disproportionate representation of athletes of African descent in some sports is what might be called "social selection." This is the idea that in this country and others, sports—particularly those not requiring specialized and often expensive equipment—became an outlet for members of minority groups, an achievable goal when access to numerous opportunities such as higher education and careers were limited by social prejudices, poor primary and secondary education, and lower socioeconomic status.

Entine points out that this, in fact, was the case with Jews and basketball in the first half of the twentieth century; basketball (as well as boxing) was a way out of the ghetto and ethnic prejudice. So stereotyped did the association between Jews and basketball become that one 1930s sportswriter made a semibiological connection, claiming that Jews were better at the game because of their "alert, scheming mind" and "flashy trickiness" (quoted in Entine 2000:203).

But Entine also claims that there are biological explanations and that these are, in some cases, more influential. Specifically, he documents evidence that three regions of Africa—the west coast, North Africa, and East Africa—have populations with physical attributes more common to them than to other populations that make them innately better at sports involving endurance, sprinting, and jumping. These traits include such things as a lower percentage of body fat, a higher proportion of certain muscle fibers, and physiological features related to the efficiency of oxygen use. He says that the reason these traits—of obvious adaptive utility—are more common in Africa is that "while people of African descent have spent most of their evolutionary history near to where they originated, the rest of the world's populations have had to modify their African adaptations after migrating to far different regions and climates" (18).

The arguments in Entine's book and in reviews of it (Bogin 2001; DiPietro 2000; Malik 2000, for example) are complex and require further discussion and examination, but for our purposes here we can address two issues. First, is it possible that there are variable human phenotypic traits, even ones showing patterns of geographic distribution, that might relate to athletic ability? Of course it is. How many heavyweight boxers could hail from the highlands of New Guinea (see

Figure 14.1), where indigenous people are, on average, much smaller than the average European or African? Could the average Inuit compete successfully in a 400-meter sprint against someone built like the Masai in Figure 13.10?

And why couldn't physiological differences that have an impact on athleticism exist? Some performance-enhancing drugs are versions of natural human biological products; anabolic steroids, for example, are synthesized versions of testosterone. Recent experiments have used gene therapy on mice and rats to produce increased level of IGF-1, a protein that promotes muscle growth and repair, resulting in bigger, stronger rodents (Sokolove 2004). In theory, genetic variation in humans, some of which could show a geographic pattern, might lead to such phenotypic variation. Moreover, social factors, motivation, and practice can explain only so much. As sports writer Michael Sokolove puts it (2004:32), "You cannot will yourself into an elite athlete, or get there through punishing workouts, without starting out way ahead of the rest of the human race."

But, second, the problem with Entine's overall argument is that he uses individuals who are exceptional (for whatever reason) to make generalizations not only about particular populations (such as the Kenyan runners) but about whole "racial" groups. He starts with the assumption that these groups exist and have some degree of temporal depth, definition, and internal homogeneity. He says, for example, that "although there is considerable disagreement, the *three major racial groupings—Caucasian, Mongoloid, Negroid*—split from 100,000 years ago to as recently as the beginning of the last ice age [emphasis mine]" (113); he even espouses a minority view that "different races [may not be] modifications of *Homo sapiens*, they were in existence before the emergence of *Homo sapiens*" (116). In other words, he assumes that the populations he is examining *are* races in the traditional, biological sense of that word. This, then, is the basis for his explanation of the dominance of African Americans in some sports, namely as a result of their African heritage. According to Entine, Africans are on average innately better athletes for some skills and so a great number of African Americans have inherited these innate skills.

These are logical leaps with little if any validity. We understand that variation exists and some is geographically patterned. But clear-cut racial groups do not exist. While a small Kenyan population just might have some features that make them better runners (and this still needs, I think, to be seriously studied), that in no way means that those features are necessarily more common on the African continent, because this assumes that Africa is synonymous with a racial group. And it certainly doesn't explain the sports phenomenon in the United States. Among other problems with Entine's conclusions is the fact that the average African American can trace a fair percentage of his or her genes to Europe. This should mean that African Americans would be expected to be worse athletes than West Africans, but this is not the case (Malik 2000).

This is a complex issue. Obviously, *both* biological and sociocultural components contribute in different degrees to various aspects of sports. We should not be afraid to examine this issue. But doing so in terms of the demonstrably nonexistent biological races only serves to detract from an accurate understanding of the topic and might further reinforce those "virulent stereotypes" that Entine justly seeks to refute.

however, that IQ does not measure intelligence but rather one's performance on an exam. Therefore, IQ is measuring, to a great extent, the results of environmental influences in the first place and not just the results of genetic endowment. Even in twins raised apart, it may well be that they are raised in homes of similar socioeconomic level and so receive educations of similar quality. It cannot be denied that identical twins are probably similar in whatever those innate abilities are that we call intelligence, but studies based on the IQ scores of such twins reflect a whole lot more than those innate abilities.

To further claim that two races have different kinds of intellectual abilities is to ignore the very nature of the modern human species. This claim says that there is a major degree of difference in the very abilities—to solve problems or to formulate abstractions and generalizations—that are a hallmark of our species' evolution. Certainly, we express individual variation in some of these abilities, and some of this variation may well be based on some sort of biological difference. I have no doubt that Beethoven and Einstein had some fundamental innate processes going on in their brains that I don't. But to think that natural selection would promote, in two different groups, profoundly different expressions of the major adaptive mechanism of a species makes little sense in light of what we know about the workings of adaptive evolution.

Finally, if you are looking to make biological comparisons between two groups, the groups need to be biologically defined. American whites and American blacks are decidedly not biological groups. We have already established that race is not a biological concept for the human species (or, perhaps, for any other species). What variation does exist is distributed in such a way as to make discrete groups of *Homo sapiens* nonexistent. We perceive differences in these two groups—average skin color, major geographic area of origin, frequency of diseases such as hypertension, and even frequency of some genes such as that for sickle cell anemia—but the groups themselves are cultural. There's simply not much genetic difference, certainly not on the level of genes for different intellectual abilities. Indeed, it has been estimated that about 15 percent of African American genes are of European American origin as a result of gene flow between the two populations over the past several hundred years (Lewontin 1982).

So, the difference in performance on IQ tests can be seen as heavily influenced by the socioeconomic limitations imposed on African Americans over the past several centuries, limitations that have resulted in separate and often poor-quality education, limited access to various forms of cultural enrichment, and even the psychological effects of being identified as members of a minority group. These are all intangible factors that are impossible to fully control or even identify. Scores on IQ tests certainly involve some aspect of a person's innate intellectual abilities, but again, because of all these external factors, we cannot infer those abilities from the results of test performance. And we certainly cannot make a biological generalization about a culturally defined group of people based on those performance results.

Our folk taxonomies are powerful and influential. We respond to them often without realizing that they are *our* culture's way of ordering *our* world and are not necessarily scientific universals. The influence of the American folk taxonomy for race can easily be seen in Jensen's work. By understanding what race is, and what it's not, and by applying what we know about the workings of genetics and evolution, we may see the fallacies of this and similar research. This perspective is an important one for helping us deal with the other issues of race that confront us almost daily.

▽   ▽   ▽

SUMMARY

Human societies need to find order in and make sense of the environments in which they live. Cultural systems, therefore, translate objective reality into categories that have meaning to them. We call these categories folk taxonomies.

So important are the relationships between the sexes and the relative places in society of males and females that different cultural systems have evolved very different folk taxonomies for sex. These are gender roles and identities, and in some societies they may even comprise more than two genders if those societies formally classify persons of ambiguous sex or sexuality.

That humans in general display variable traits is obvious, on some level, to all societies, and so all cultural systems also include folk taxonomies for race. On a biological level, however, races (or subspecies) do not exist for our species. Indeed, the concept of race is falling from use in biology in general. But even if we attempt to apply the race concept to humans, we find that the biological nature of our species does not lend itself to division into clear-cut, discrete units.

So powerful is the folk taxonomy for race that our categories take on a reality beyond that which is warranted, and we find that we use them as cues to tell us how to think about other groups of people and how to treat them. We can all too easily confuse culture and biology, and this effect can even be seen in scientific investigations, such as those that look for some biological racial difference in the cultural measure of intelligence called IQ.

QUESTIONS FOR FURTHER THOUGHT

1.   Expand upon the brief discussion in the text concerning the identities and roles of the two genders in this culture. How would you characterize them? How have they changed during your lifetime? Do you see a need for further change? Why? How would it come about?

2.   Still looking at your own culture, think about gender categories. Are there just two? Should there be more in light of what we know about the frequency of intersexes? Are more categories possible within this culture? Where does homosexuality fit into this discussion?

3.   Discuss further the North American categories of race. What specific historical events or sequences may have influenced our commonly understood racial groups? If you are familiar with the racial taxonomy of another culture, similarly analyze it.

4.   Apply the race and athleticism argument to a specific sterotype: "White men can't jump." Watching an NBA game, it sure can appear to be true. What *is* true about it? Why does it appear so?

5.   On a practical level: Suppose it was shown that some populations in Kenya have a disproportionate number of members who possess physical and physiological features that make them better runners. How should we accommodate this in organized sporting competitions such as the Olympics?

KEY TERMS

sex	subspecies	microsatellites
gender	races	racism
folk taxonomies	semispecies	heritability
polytypic	cline	reification

SUGGESTED READINGS

A good book on sex and gender from an anthropological perspective is *Female of the Species*, by M. Kay Martin and Barbara Voorhies. Despite the title, it is really about both sexes and all the gender categories found in various cultural systems. The fascinating case of India's hijras

is documented in *Neither Man Nor Woman: The Hijras of India*, by
Serena Nanda. I cover the topic of sex and gender in more detail,
with more on the cultural dimension, in my *Introducing Anthropology:
An Integrated Approach*.

On race, I highly recommend Stephen Molnar's *Human Variation: Races,
Types, and Ethnic Groups;* this text covers the entire issue of race from
an anthropological viewpoint. It includes detailed sections on our
variable traits. Another treatment of the same subject, but from a biologist, is Richard Lewontin's *Human Diversity*. A book on the subject,
and one that includes an extended discussion of race and athletic ability, is Jonathan Marks's *Human Biodiversity: Genes, Race, and History*.

For a collection of articles on the nonexistence of human biological
races, see *The Concept of Race*, edited by Ashley Montagu, and for a
nice treatment of the history of race studies, try Kenneth A. R.
Kennedy's *Human Variation in Space and Time*. Also, see the chapters
on race in Jonathan Marks's *What It Means to Be 98% Chimpanzee*.

The analysis of human genetic differences and what they tell us about
the history of human groups is nicely covered by Luigi Luca Cavalli-
Sforza and Francesco Cavalli-Sforza in *The Great Human Diasporas:
The History of Diversity and Evolution*.

The best book on racism, emphasizing an examination of scientific
attempts to find correlations between race (and sex) and intelligence
is Stephen Jay Gould's *The Mismeasure of Man*.

I do recommend Jon Entine's *Taboo*. Even though I disagree with major
aspects of his analysis, his thought-provoking book succeeds very well
in its goal of stimulating "open debate" on the subject.

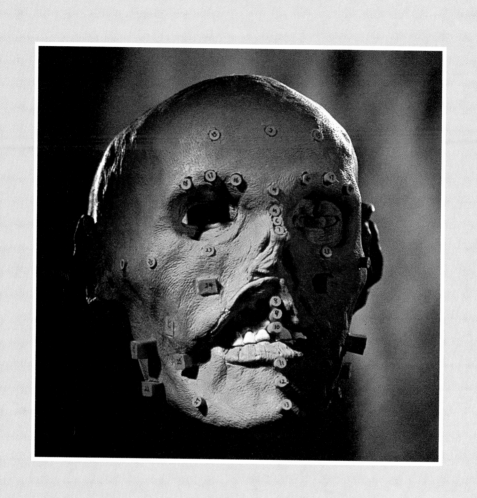

CHAPTER

15

BIOLOGICAL ANTHROPOLOGY AND TODAY'S WORLD

We too are part of
history's seamless web.
—Reinhold Niebuhr

On September 11, 2001, Amy Zelson Mundorff, a forensic anthropologist, was at her job at the New York City medical examiner's office. When news broke of the attacks on the World Trade Center, she and three coworkers rushed to the site to lend their aid. Shortly after they arrived, the South Tower collapsed and Mundorff narrowly escaped with her life. She nursed her injuries for two days before returning to her job as one of the first to examine the more than 16,000 human remains from Ground Zero. In 2002, she was among those cited by New York Mayor Michael Bloomberg for her courage on that day and her leadership afterward in identifying some of the victims.

Although certainly not to everyone's taste, such work is one of the ways that biological anthropology makes a tangible contribution to our lives. It is, of course, unfortunate that such services are needed. But they are, and the work of identifying human remains and, sometimes, of identifying the cause of death is an important one, bringing some comfort to the survivors and perhaps justice to the slain.

Although the work of all biological anthropologists is useful in its contribution to knowledge, there are some practical ways in which our field can be applied and some lessons all people can learn from biological anthropologists' unique perspective on our species. In this last chapter, we will address the simple question:

What are some of the applications and lessons of biological anthropology?

FORENSIC ANTHROPOLOGY: READING THE BONES

One meaning of the term *forensics* is "the application of science to legal matters." The skills anthropologists use to retrieve information from ancient skeletons (see Chapter 9) have also proved useful in retrieving information from more modern ones—the victims of violent crimes and accidents. Forensic anthropology is increasingly called upon to examine skeletal remains and the conditions under which they were found to determine identity, time and cause of death, and any other information that may prove helpful to law enforcement agencies. In turn, some of the methods developed by forensic anthropologists have been applied to older remains that are of scientific, rather than legal, interest.

Perhaps the best-known case of the latter is the well-publicized "Ice Man," or "Ötzi." He was found by hikers in September 1991, at over 10,000 feet in the Ötztaler Alps, on the Italian side of the border with Austria. He had been naturally mummified by the dehydrating action of the cold and the wind and was in a remarkable state of preservation. The

FIGURE 15.1
The Ice Man's body, pre-
served for over 5,000 years
in the Italian Alps, was naturally mummified by cold and
wind. Pressure from the ice
disfigured his nose and lip
and pushed his left arm into
this odd position. We are still
learning about his life and
death from his preserved
body, which includes his
brain and internal organs.

find became all the more remarkable when carbon-14 dating of the body itself, and of grass with which he had stuffed his boots, provided a date of 3300 BC. The body was over 5,000 years old.

The Ice Man was found with a fascinating array of artifacts, including much of his clothing and some tools. Details on these may be found in the readings listed at the end of the chapter. Here, we'll concentrate on the body itself (Figure 15.1).

Investigators X-rayed the body and, using techniques we discussed in Chapter 9, determined that it was that of a male about 5 feet 2 inches tall. Initially, he was thought to have been in his late 20s or early 30s when he died, but more recent analysis has indicated he was around 46. Oddly, he has only eleven pairs of ribs, instead of the usual twelve, and his seventh and eighth left ribs had been broken at one time or another but were healed at the time of his death. There is some evidence of hardening of the arteries, and his lungs were blackened, probably by smoke from open fires.

There are sets of parallel lines on the Ice Man's lower back, left thigh, and right ankle that are charcoal-dust tattoos. An early hypothesis is that these tattoos, near Chinese acupuncture points, were therapeutic measures to relieve arthritis (Stone 2000), but recent X-rays have revealed little or no evidence of that condition (Dickson et al. 2003).

The Ice Man's teeth show considerable wear, some of which can be clearly seen on his upper incisors. This probably indicates that he used his teeth as tools, perhaps for leatherworking, and that he ate a tough diet including dried meat and the products of flour from grains that had been mixed with sand to aid in grinding. Both practices are known from the archaeological record.

His diet, however, may not have been particularly good. Patterns on a fingernail recovered later (the others had fallen off) suggest periods of reduced nail growth from disease or malnutrition. And eggs found in his stomach show that the Ice Man suffered from an intestinal parasite called a whipworm. The parasite causes diarrhea and acute stomach pains.

When and how did Ötzi die? For years, the assumption was that he had died of exposure, caught in rapidly deteriorating conditions in the mountains in early fall. But more recent studies of food residue in his colon revealed pollen from a tree that flowers in late spring and early summer. And in 2001, an X-ray showed an arrowhead embedded in his left shoulder that might have been the cause of his death. Moreover, his right hand shows a deep stab wound, and DNA analysis suggests that his clothing and tools had the blood of four other persons on them (*Science* 2003). The plot thickens.

Finally, in part to put to rest the inevitable questions about possible fraud, scientists performed mitochondrial DNA analysis. It indicated that the Ice Man was a European and that he was related to living populations from the northern Alps. Techniques of reconstruction have even given us an idea of what he looked like (Figure 15.2). And some new research (Müller et al. 2003) using isotope comparisons of soil and water samples with samples from Ötzi's teeth and bones, and argon/argon dating of mica pieces in his intestine, has even pinpointed where he lived—a valley about 60 kilometers south of where his body was discovered.

All the preceding information and more can be gleaned from a mummified corpse over fifty centuries old. When the Ice Man died, writing was just being invented in Mesopotamia, the great pyramids of Egypt had yet to be built, and the lives of Julius Caesar and Jesus were over 3,000 years in the future.

As famous as the Ice Man is, we do not, of course, know his name. Forensic studies, however, have provided us with new information about some famous people whose names we do know. For example, the late forensic anthropologist William Maples (Maples and Browning 1994) helped identify the skeletal remains of the assassinated Russian czar Nicholas II and his family. (The bones did not, by the way, include those of Anastasia, the czar's daughter, said to have survived and escaped to the West.) Maples also examined the remains of U.S. president Zachary Taylor to prove that he was not murdered by arsenic poisoning. He also helped identify the true remains of Spanish conquistador Francisco Pizarro and proved that a mummy reported to be Pizarro's was actually someone else's.

Clyde Snow, another well-known forensic anthropologist, identified a skeleton found in Brazil as that of Nazi war criminal Josef Mengele. The standard information about the skeleton fit what was known about Mengele, but Snow clinched it by superimposing images of the skull over photographs of the man known as the "Angel of Death." They matched, and the identification was verified shortly thereafter, when Mengele's dental records were discovered. Snow has also been involved in a review of the assassination of John F. Kennedy and has, as mentioned in Chapter 1, searched in Bolivia for the remains of the famous outlaws Butch Cassidy and the Sundance Kid, so far without success.

More important, however, than these cases of the rich or famous are those involving the remains of common, everyday people who, for one reason or another, need to be identified and who, perhaps, require justice. Clyde Snow has, for example, examined and tried to identify the remains of some of the more than 10,000 people who "disappeared" during the military rule in Argentina from 1976 to 1983. His evidence has been used to help prosecute some of those responsible. He has done similar work in the Philippines and in Southwest Asia, and he has helped identify the victims of airline crashes, including one that took place in Chicago in 1979 that killed 273 people. And we've already mentioned Amy Mundorff's work at the World Trade Center.

Investigating smaller tragedies, however, is not outside the activities of the forensic anthropologist. For a typical example, we can look at one

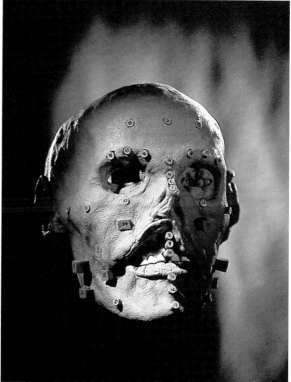

of Clyde Snow's cases (Snow and Luke 1970). In the summer of 1967, two young girls, ages 5 and 6, disappeared in the Oklahoma City area within a few weeks of one another. In November of that year, two hunters found some bones, including a human cranium, in a rural area outside the city. The bones were scattered on the surface of the ground. Further investigation, however, revealed a crude grave that contained more bones and children's clothing. An extensive excavation was conducted. Among the several hundred bones eventually recovered—most of which belonged to various nonhumans—were those of a young child. Snow investigated further to see if the bones could reveal a specific identity and perhaps a cause of death. There was a good chance that these were the bones of one of the missing girls, and perhaps even both.

Snow determined that the bones had been buried fairly recently. They still had the greasy texture of fresh bone, and there were no signs of weathering that would indicate they had been there over winter. Although the bones had been damaged by scavengers, there were no rodent gnaw marks on them (rodents gnaw well-weathered bones for minerals and protein). The bones were recent, but how recent?

They were completely skeletonized, but this could certainly have happened during the previous summer. It was shown that in Oklahoma's

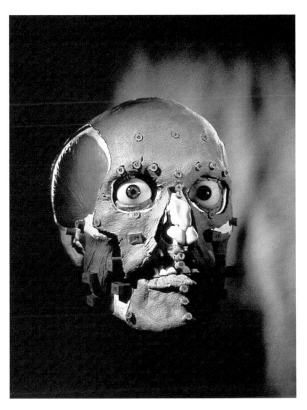

FIGURE 15.2

Artist John Gurche reconstructed the face of the Ice Man. He began with measurements, computer images, X-rays, and CAT scans and produced a model of the Ice Man's skull. Next, he added clay to resemble the mummified face and then, like a plastic surgeon, rebuilt the face, reconstructing the nose and adding fatty tissue and muscles (represented by the red pegs) using anatomical data and his own interpretation from anthropological training.

climate, a child's body would be reduced to bone within 2 to 6 weeks. There were spider webs and other signs of insect activity in the skull, so it was determined that the bones had been completely exposed before cold weather set in and those creatures became inactive. Burial had occurred in early September at the latest.

Soon, the possibility that more than one human was represented was ruled out. The cause of death was a problem, though. Much of the skeleton was missing, and the bones that remained were found scattered about. Some bones were damaged, and some teeth were missing. None of this, however, could be clearly attributed to trauma before death or purposeful dismemberment afterward. More likely, it was the result of decomposition and the work of carnivorous scavengers that dug up the grave, scattered the bones, and carried off those with fleshy parts.

Determining the sex of the skeleton was difficult. No pelvis was found, nor was there enough of the remainder of the skeleton to make a good assessment for a preadolescent. The clothing found was that of a little girl, however.

Both the missing girls were white, and the presence of a Carabelli's cusp on one of the remaining teeth pointed to that population. Carabelli's cusp is a small dental feature found in about 50 percent of white Americans, 34 percent of black Americans, and only 5 to 20 percent of Native Americans. The incisors were not shovel-shaped, a form found in over 80 percent of Native Americans. It was important to rule out Native Americans since Oklahoma has a high Native American population. Some remaining hair verified the assessment, as its color and shape were those common to white populations.

Age was determined through cranial sutures, epiphyseal union, and dental eruption and development (see Chapter 9). In addition to the four separate bones of the cranial vault, each bone itself grows in separate pieces. The occipital, at birth, is in four pieces, which fuse together at 4 or 5 years of age. The occipital found was completely fused with no trace of sutures.

The epiphyses at the proximal (closest to the torso) femur and radius and the distal (farthest from the torso) humerus were all open. These close at 17, 14, and 14 years respectively. Taken with the evidence from the occipital, an age range of 4 to about 15 was determined. This was narrowed to 5 to 12 years by looking at further sites of bone union in the vertebral column.

Both first permanent molars were fully erupted. The central incisors were missing, but the size and form of the sockets indicated that they too had erupted. Taking into account the range of variation at which eruption occurs among individuals, these data provided an age range of about 5½ to 8 years. In addition, X-rays of unerupted teeth below the gum line further narrowed the age range to about 6 to 8 years. The evidence, then, favored the skeleton being that of the older missing girl. Finally, stature was estimated using formulas that compare the length of various long bones to total height. The skeleton was estimated to have belonged to someone about 50 inches tall. The older missing girl was about that height, while the younger was 8 inches shorter.

Snow concluded that the remains probably belonged to one of the two missing girls. There had been no other unsolved cases of missing girls of that age from the area in several years. The bones most likely were those of the 6-year-old. Sadly, the remains of the other girl have not been found, and no suspect has been identified. But Snow's forensic work helped strengthen the identification, which would have been little more than a good guess without the precise information he was able to extract by reading the bones.

LESSONS FROM THE PAST

Besides applying the skills of the biological anthropologist to legal matters, we may also apply the perspective of our discipline to areas of modern life. Our evolutionary perspective tells us that we are not a species that suddenly appeared a few million years ago, nor are we, as modern humans, what evolution was somehow directed toward all along.

Rather, humans evolved from previous primate species. We are variations on the primate theme. We retain many of the major primate characteristics, and our unique features are still based on them. Moreover, in no way can we say that the modern manifestation of our species is the culmination or the best-adapted form of our evolutionary line. We have manipulated our environment, our very biology, and our behavior through culture, so our present environment may not be the one to which our species was biologically adapted. We may well learn a few valuable lessons by taking a closer look at what we were like in the past, before culture played so great a part in our lives.

For instance, anthropologists Marcia Thompson and David Harsha (1984) have looked at the daily routines of people in modern industrial societies and compared them with those of people in nonindustrial cultures and nonhumans living in the tropics. They conclude that in the common structure of our workdays, we are violating a pattern that evolved in our tropical ancestors and cousins that programs us for a two-peaked rhythm of daily activity, one peak in the late morning and another in the late afternoon, with a lull in between. That period of tiredness we often feel after lunch may have nothing to do with eating.

Tropical animals and people in many human societies take an afternoon break. Originally, this break may have been a response to the heat of the midafternoon sun, but as we are coming to understand it, this behavior may reflect a real biological decrease in human activity level. After all, other bodily functions—more than a hundred physiological and performance variables—fluctuate in predictable cycles during the twenty-four hours of our day. Thus, the afternoon nap is a natural phenomenon. (I knew it!)

Thompson and Harsha suggest that the best way to respond to this fluctuation—given that most of us can't nap, at least during weekdays—would be to move lunch back a few hours to correspond to the afternoon lull. As it is, we often take lunch during one of our peak activity periods. By taking into account a possible biological pattern, we might make ourselves more productive in our modern cultural environment.

Another anthropologist, James McKenna (in Small 1992), has looked at the sleep behavior of other primate groups and of people in cultures in which it is common for young babies to sleep with their parents. In the West, we have long been advised that babies should sleep by themselves, probably as a response to our emphasis on independence and the idea that the parents' lives, perhaps especially in bed, are separate from those of their children.

McKenna suggests that, in fact, infant nonhuman primates and human babies seem better off psychologically and physically if they sleep with their parents. In humans, this may even extend to learning to breathe properly. For humans, speech is so important that we have two kinds of breathing—automatic and controlled—and we need to learn to switch between kinds. In addition, remember that the vocal tract of human infants is initially higher than that of adult humans and similar to that of chimpanzees. As the vocal tract begins to drop early in life, the baby goes through a great physical change.

These two facts—the development of the two kinds of breathing and the physical change in the vocal tract—may explain sudden infant death syndrome (SIDS), when babies inexplicably die in their sleep. It is thought that miscues in regulating breathing cause these babies to stop breathing and prevent them from waking themselves up so they can start breathing again. Sleeping with a parent, McKenna argues, may help prevent SIDS, because the parent's movement causes the baby to wake up periodically, and so the infant learns better how to jump between kinds of breathing. McKenna notes that SIDS is twice as common in the United States as in Japan, where infants normally sleep with their parents. A more recent study (Mosko et al. 1997) has also suggested that close proximity to the mother while sleeping, especially sleeping face-to-face, may also provide the infant with increased levels of CO_2 from the mother's respiration, which might help stimulate its breathing.

From bioanthropology we may also learn more about disease. For example, the evolutionary perspective that sheds light on the nature of sickle cell anemia may also be applied to other diseases, especially those associated with particular populations. Biologist Jared Diamond (1991) offers an intriguing evolutionary explanation for the high frequency of Tay-Sachs disease among Eastern European (Ashkenazic) Jews and their descendants. Tay-Sachs is a lethal disease caused by a recessive gene. In homozygotes, it results in the body's inability to produce an enzyme that breaks down a particular fatty substance. This substance accumulates in nerve cells and literally destroys the victim's nervous system. Most sufferers die by age 4. The disease is incurable and cannot be prevented.

Tay-Sachs has a frequency of about 1 in 400,000 worldwide but is found in 1 of every 3,600 Ashkenazim. In other Jewish populations, Tay-Sachs is no more common than in the general population. The usual explanation for this incredibly high frequency among the Ashkenazim is the founder effect. The founders of the Ashkenazic populations happened to have a high frequency of the gene, which then persisted through genetic drift, aided by the fact that it was usually hidden from natural selection as a recessive. Some of the other ten diseases that are overrepresented among Ashkenazim have been explained in this way (Glausiusz 1995), as has the high frequency of Tay-Sachs in a Pennsylvania Dutch population (see Chapter 4).

But Diamond contends that the founders of the Ashkenazim were large populations and that their communities in Eastern Europe were widespread. The founder effect has significant results only in small populations. In the numerous and widespread communities, drift would have increased the frequency of the gene in some but decreased it in others. In addition, since these communities were first founded almost a thousand years ago, one would expect natural selection to have had sufficient time to decrease the frequency of this lethal gene to that found in the general population.

Moreover, it seems as if there are several different mutations along the same segment of DNA that can cause Tay-Sachs and that two of them are overrepresented among the Ashkenazim. It is unlikely that the same random evolutionary events could have happened twice. In addition, two of the other diseases that are more common in Eastern European Jews than in the general population also result from the excess accumulation of fatty substances.

Diamond suggests that, as with sickle cell, the heterozygous condition for Tay-Sachs must confer some selective advantage. He notes that Ashkenazic Jews were confined to towns for much of the past two thousand years. They were forbidden to own land and so lived as businessmen in confined, urban areas known as ghettos (this is the origin of the term *ghetto*). A common ailment in such towns was TB (tuberculosis). In the early twentieth century, for example, TB caused up to 20 percent of all deaths in Eastern Europe. One study, however, indicates that relatively few Jews died from TB (1 in 306 people for whom data were available, a far cry from 20 percent). Thus, a reasonable hypothesis is that heterozygotes for Tay-Sachs, who do not exhibit symptoms of the disease, nevertheless have slightly elevated levels of the fatty substance, and this—for reasons that are still unknown—may provide some immunity to TB. Although the cause-and-effect relationship has not been established, this hypothesis provides a basis for further investigation and is an example of how our knowledge of evolutionary processes can provide a possible answer to a question involving modern human populations.

Finally, S. Boyd Eaton and Melvin Konner propose that the major chronic illnesses that we in the industrialized West suffer from are caused by a "mismatch between our genetic constitution" and various factors in our modern lifestyles, including diet, exercise, and exposure to such things as alcohol and tobacco. Our genes, they suggest, "must now function in a foreign and, in many ways, hostile Atomic Age [environment]" (1985:1).

They note that some studies indicate that our ancestors who lived before the advent of farming, about 12,000 ya, were taller and more heavily muscled than we are. Their teeth also showed a much smaller percentage of dental caries (tooth decay). The authors suggest that by looking at the lives of recent hunter-gatherer groups, we may have a "window" into the world of our Stone Age ancestors (Figure 15.3). (They are careful, of course, to caution that recent hunter-gatherer groups are fully modern humans with technologies, such as the bow and arrow, that were not available until about 15,000 ya.) One thing we note right away is that such people have a lower incidence of coronary disease, emphysema, hypertension (high blood pressure), and cancer of the breast, prostate, colon, and lung.

When the diets of fifty hunter-gatherer groups were analyzed, it was seen that, on average, they ate more red meat than we do now. This doesn't sound like a healthy diet at first, until we understand that wild game has much less saturated fat than do domestic animals and that most of that is "structural" fat (rather than "storage" fat), which is largely polyunsaturated—not the harmful kind. Thus, our ancestors ate about three times the protein we do but only about half the fat.

FIGURE 15.3
The Ju/'hoansi, a population of Khoisan peoples from the Kalahari Desert in Namibia, Botswana, and South Africa, are, of course, fully modern humans. Yet their way of life, until recently that of hunters and gatherers, can give us a window into the lives of our ancestors before the invention of farming and animal domestication. Here, members of a Ju/'hoansi family are on the move, carrying with them their children, tools, weapons, and other possessions. The lives of the Ju/'hoansi, and of all Khoisan, have been changed forever by political and military events in southern Africa since this photo was taken over forty years ago (See also Figure 12.6.)

Because most of the plant foods eaten were wild and unprocessed, they had a higher nutritional value, fewer calories, more complex carbohydrates (rather than simple ones that turn to fat), more fiber, and less salt (a contributor to hypertension). Furthermore, our ancestors drank mostly water and seldom were exposed to alcohol and tobacco.

Additionally, rather than concentrating on one sort of exercise, our ancestors were more like "decathlon athletes," responding to the harsh physical demands of their lives with a varied "exercise program" that changed daily and seasonally.

As an example of this, a study (Cooper et al. 1999) compared rates of hypertension in subjects from Nigeria (7 percent), Jamaica (26 percent), and Chicago (33 percent; all of the subjects from Chicago were African American). The subjects sampled shared, on average, 75 percent of their genes (probably more; this study was done before the genome was sequenced), so major genetic differences were ruled out. Rather, differences in lifestyle, diet, and exercise were suggested as accounting for 40 to 50 percent of the increased risk for hypertension characteristic of African Americans over Nigerians. Specifically, by comparison, African

Contemporary Reflections

What Can One Do with a Degree in Bioanthropology?

It's safe to say that most people who work as professional biological anthropologists (or, for that matter, any sort of professional anthropologist) have at least a master's degree and, more likely, a PhD. The majority of these do what I do—teach in a college or university while researching and writing. Although acquiring a PhD requires, on average, four additional years of university class-work and a variable number of years after that to complete a doctoral dissertation (I took six years), it is a career I can highly recommend. Essentially, you get paid to learn about and think about the subject you're most interested in and then to impart that knowledge to your students and apply it to science and society. It entails a good deal of (often inconsequential) committee work and other related activities, but all in all it's a very rewarding life.

Unfortunately, at the moment there are more PhD's and near PhD's in anthropology than there are university faculty jobs. The job market, however, has improved and worsened several times in the thirty years I've worked at my university, and the situation could improve again. You shouldn't let current conditions dissuade you if a PhD and a university position are your goal.

Some bioanthropology PhD's work in other departments of universities. It is not uncommon to find them in medical, dental, and nursing programs, or in biology, genetics, psychology, public health, or physical therapy departments. Others work outside academia. I glanced through the list of current members of the American Association of Physical Anthropologists and found people who work for museums, medical research and forensics institutes, the armed forces, and government agencies such as the Bureau of Land Management. As I mentioned, the Connecticut State Archaeologist is a former student of mine who has his PhD in bioanthropology.

Americans were more prone to being overweight, getting little exercise, and having a poor diet that included a high level of salt.

The lessons from this research are obvious and are, indeed, suggestions we hear all the time. We know we're supposed to eat low-fat foods, cut down on salt, get plenty of fiber, and exercise regularly. Evolution, though, provides an explanation and rationale for following those suggestions.

BIOANTHROPOLOGY AND GLOBAL ISSUES

Global issues are global in two senses: (1) they impact a wide geographic range and large number of people and (2) they involve many different aspects in a complex set of interrelationships. Biological anthropology

Most of you reading this book, however—if you are working toward a degree in anthropology—will get a BA. It has been said that one bachelor's degree is as good as another in terms of finding jobs that require a college education. On a practical level, that may well be true. What a four-year degree means is that you have shown mastery of a certain core curriculum at a certain level with a focus on a particular discipline and that you have the skills, dedication, and persistence to achieve that degree. In terms of specific skills needed for a certain job, the college degree essentially tells an employer that you will have the ability to learn and use those skills.

But *what* degree you get may have deeper meaning, and—although I'm clearly biased—I think a degree in biological anthropology is a good choice. The breadth of knowledge inherent in the field is wide. There is the focus on scientific methodology but with the need—because it *is* anthropology—to understand other areas of knowledge and other cultures. The central theme of evolution necessarily involves a deep understanding of biology in general and of the biology of other species in particular. Genetics, anatomy, physiology, behavior, ecology, chemistry and physics (for dating techniques), geology, paleontology, and medical topics are all integral parts of the field. The number of careers to which such topics, such a breadth of knowledge, and such a perspective could be applied is huge—limited only by your imagination.

The only barrier might be the fact that many people have little understanding of what bioanthropology is and so might not at first think such a degree would be appropriate for certain jobs. I tell my students that in such instances they must be prepared to make their case, to explain to potential employers what bioanthropology is and why that background would be ideal for their job.

For some sound practical advice, read *Careers in Anthropology,* by John T. Omohundro (2001). In the meantime, the answer to the question about what you can do with a degree in bioanthropology is, just about anything you want.

can neither address in detail all those aspects nor hope to solve any of these problems alone. But the perspective of bioanthropology—its evolutionary and holistic point of view—can help us gain insight into some of these issues and can certainly make a contribution as we seek responses and possible solutions.

In Chapter 13 we examined in some detail two global issues: overpopulation and emerging diseases. Each of these encompasses other problems and leads to still others. Another issue of major concern is global warming. Although there is still some debate on the existence of this phenomenon, most dissent is economically or politically motivated. People, corporations, and governments don't *want* global warming to be acknowledged because having to deal with it will adversely affect them. Few scientists today, however, doubt that global warming is a real trend (Epstein 2000).

Even in these areas of practical concern, however, anthropology in general can play a role. We humans will have to make adjustments if we are to slow, much less reverse, the warming trend. Changes in energy use, consumption of resources, waste disposal, and transportation habits will affect everyone—from the individual consumer to the largest multinational corporation. And even changes brought about initially by one nation will have effects on other nations, because we truly live in a global economy and a global environment. Anthropology can help predict what ramifications such changes will have on individual cultural systems and on the relationships among different cultural systems.

Some of the potential results of global warming relate directly to the subjects we've covered in this book. Climatic change is a major category. Genus *Homo* certainly has dealt with climatic change since first appearing on the planet, but global warming threatens to produce changes at a much more rapid rate than before. Furthermore, it must be understood that the modern world we know has come about in just the past few hundred years; during this time we have not seen climatic change of the scale predicted. In other words, modern cultures have adapted to a relatively unchanging set of environments and could be severely disrupted by the more sudden changes that computer models of global warming project.

For example, if warming continues, ocean temperatures will increase and polar ice caps and glaciers will melt. This will cause sea levels to rise and thus flood coastal areas, where populations tend to be concentrated. As a result, large numbers of people will have to move. The influx of salt water will destroy crops and natural plants and render land unusable for agriculture. There will be severe heat waves, which will produce droughts, heat-related deaths, and an increase in smog production.

Global warming will also have an impact on disease. As climates warm, disease-causing and disease-carrying organisms will expand their ranges. Already there have been cases of West Nile virus in New England and malaria in Toronto, as the associated mosquito species move into regions formerly inhospitable to them. Rodent-borne disease will also increase as those highly adaptable mammals expand their ranges, aided by decreases in predator populations as climates change. Dryness will cause major fires, which will add to pollution-caused ailments.

The risks are many and multifaceted. The perspective of biological anthropology—looking for connections, seeing our species as a biological/cultural system adapted to environmental systems—is a valuable one for understanding the causes and ramifications of global warming and for suggesting and implementing ways of dealing with them.

While the theoretical issues covered in this book are interesting in and of themselves, I believe they also make anthropology uniquely qualified to play a role in these and other global concerns. Indeed, I think we as anthropologists are obligated to do so.

▽   ▽   ▽

SUMMARY

Biological anthropology studies the human species, past and present, from the perspective of evolutionary processes, change, and adaptation. To understand how these forces affected our ancestors, we have developed technologies that allow us to squeeze an amazing amount of information out of the meager skeletal remains that those ancestors left us. These skills are now being increasingly recognized and used by law enforcement agencies in the identification and analysis of skeletal remains of missing persons and accident and murder victims. Forensic anthropology is a fast-growing specialty within our field.

Our evolutionary perspective can also be useful in more abstract ways. By understanding the nature of our adaptations as a species, we may evaluate some of our behaviors and practices in light of the recent cultural environment we have made for ourselves. We find that some of our cultural adaptations may be out of step with our biological ones. Using the evolutionary viewpoint to look at daily biological rhythms, sleep patterns, the nature of our breathing, diseases that affect us, our diet, and our exercise habits—among other aspects of our lives—may enable us to adopt behaviors that are more in line with how our species is actually adapted and, in so doing, improve our lives.

Biological anthropology may also be applied to modern global issues such as overpopulation and emerging diseases (see Chapter 13.) Even something as seemingly removed from anthropology as global warming can be examined from anthropology's holistic and evolutionary perspectives.

In the end, however, it must be noted that to be useful and important, knowledge need not have a practical, concrete application. There is nothing wrong with the idea of knowledge for its own sake, and, certainly, learning about our species—where we came from, what processes brought about our evolution, who we are, and where we fit in the natural world—should be important to us as individuals and as members of our own society and the society of all the world's peoples.

QUESTIONS FOR FURTHER THOUGHT

1. What other issues of personal health and lifestyle do you think bioanthropology could address? How might the perspective of this discipline add something that other fields might have missed?

2. Within or resulting from the major issues of population, emerging diseases, and global warming are other matters of concern: pollution, deforestation and other examples of environmental destruction, and warfare between nations, religions, and ethnic groups. How might anthropology, especially biological anthropology, shed some light on these issues? What avenues of research would be opened up by applying bioanthropology to these cases?

3. In Chapter 14, we concluded that biological races do not exist for the human species. But on page 426 of this chapter, I describe the use of racial categories and biological traits in the identification of the two missing girls from Oklahoma. Is this contradictory? If not, why?

4. Finally, a real challenge. As noted back in Chapter 1, science and belief systems are two very different areas of inquiry and knowledge. And yet the nature of the real world certainly influences religious, philosophical, and ethical ideas. Consider some current ethical debates—abortion, euthanasia, stem cell research, for example—and ask whether the perspective of bioanthropology and the facts about the real world that our science has discerned might contribute to the direction and possible resolution of these debates.

SUGGESTED READINGS

The June 1993 issue of *National Geographic* includes an article, "The Ice Man," by David Roberts, that covers the Ice Man as well as some of the related archaeology of his time and place. For the very latest on Ötzi, see "The Iceman Reconsidered," by James Dickson, Klaus Oeggl, and Linda Handley in the May 2003 *Scientific American.*

Two finds of mummified bodies have been reported from western China and from Peru. See "The Silk Road's Lost World," by Thomas B. Allen, in the March 1996 *National Geographic* and three articles by Johan Reinhard in the June 1996, January 1997, and November 1999 issues of the same magazine.

More on the reconstruction of ancient faces can be found in John Prag and Richard Neave's *Making Faces.*

On forensic anthropology, see *Dead Men Do Tell Tales*, by William R. Maples and Michael Browning; *Bones: A Forensic Detective's Casebook*, by Douglas Ubelaker and Henry Scammell; *Flesh and Bone*, by Myriam Nafte; *Bone Voyage*, by Stanley Rhine; and *No Bone Unturned: The Adventures of a Top Smithsonian Forensic Scientist and the Legal Battle for America's Oldest Skeletons*, by Jeff Benedict. The latter is about anthropologist Doug Owsley and includes an update on the Kennewick Man story. See also two articles in the 11 August 2000 issue of *Science*: "A New Breed of High-Tech Detectives," by Andrew Watson, and "Where Dead Men Really Do Tell Tales," by Robert Service.

The Clyde Snow case covered in this chapter is recounted in detail in "The Oklahoma City Child Disappearances," by Snow and James Luke, in Aaron Podolefsky and Peter Brown's, *Applying Anthropology*. A profile of Snow appears in the December 1988 issue of *Discover* in a piece by Patrick Huyghe, "No Bone Unturned."

The global warming situation is nicely discussed in "Is Global Warming Harmful to Health?" by Paul R. Epstein in the August 2000 *Scientific American*.

Appendix

Genes in Populations

In Chapter 4, I introduced the concept of allele frequency. The genetic definition of evolution is *change in allele frequency over time*. Therefore, evolution entails any process that alters the frequencies with which alleles of genes appear in a population. We can use the concept of allele frequency more specifically by applying actual allele frequency numbers in our study of human evolution.

The example of evolution we focused on in Chapter 4 was sickle cell anemia. Let's continue with that example. Suppose we can test a population for the sickle cell genotypes at two points in time. Our first test gives the following numbers (based on an example in Relethford 2003a):

AA (normal hemoglobin)	50 people
AS (sickle cell trait)	100 people
SS (sickle cell anemia)	50 people
Total	200 people

(A and S are *alleles of a single gene*, the *Hb* gene for hemoglobin.)

Now, when we return to test the population at some point in the future, we find the following numbers:

AA	35 people
AS	100 people
SS	10 people
Total	145 people

Obviously, some change has taken place in the frequency of the genotypes and in the total population size. Have allele frequencies changed as well? In other words, has evolution, by the genetic definition, taken place? To calculate the allele frequencies, we add up the total number of each allele and divide by the number of alleles in the population, which would be twice the number of people since each person has two alleles at each locus. Thus, for the first test, the number of A alleles is:

$(50 \times 2) + 100 = 200$ (since each AA person has two A alleles and each AS heterozygote has one)

The frequency of A alleles in the population is thus:

200/400 (since each of the 200 people has two alleles) = .50 (50%)

Using the same reasoning, the frequency of the S allele is also .50 (50%).

Now, let's calculate the allele frequencies in the second test, after the obvious changes in genotype frequency and number of people have taken place. Using the same procedure:

frequency of A = ([35 × 2] + 100) / (145 × 2) = .59 (59%)
frequency of S = ([10 × 2] + 100) / (145 × 2) = .41 (41%)

(The results are rounded for simplicity.) Thus, the frequency of the A allele has increased and that of the S allele has decreased. Evolution, by technical definition, is taking place.

The reason for this change is obvious, because we understand sickle cell anemia. Those individuals with the SS genotype have a fatal disease, so only 20 percent (10 out of 50) of them survived between the two tests. Those with the AA genotype don't have sickle cell, but some may have succumbed to malaria; here there was a 70 percent survival rate (35 out of 50) for the AA genotype. All of the heterozygotes survived since they have nonfatal symptoms of sickle cell and also possess an immunity to malaria.

If, however, we did not already understand the situation, the calculation of these figures would show that *something* was happening and would indicate in which direction the change was taking place. It would be clear in this case that one allele is increasing in frequency because both homozygote genotypes are decreasing in number, but to different degrees. As a result of *this*, the heterozygote genotype is becoming more common. We would then try to figure out why.

Suppose, however, we could only examine the population once, as is often the case. How could we possibly see evidence for change over time? There is a formula, known as the Hardy-Weinberg equilibrium, that provides us with a tool to do this. The formula is an example of a *null hypothesis*, a condition where nothing occurs. If you can state the conditions of *no* change, you can then compare them to a real situation and see whether change is taking place and, if it is, state the nature and direction of that change. The Hardy-Weinberg formula assumes that the genotype frequencies in a population will remain the same under certain conditions: (1) if mating is random (that is, everyone stands an equal chance of mating with anyone else of the opposite sex), and (2) if there is no gene flow, no drift, no mutation, and no natural selection for any allele over another. In other words, none of the processes of evolution are taking place.

For example, using our two alleles for hemoglobin, A and S, we designate the frequency of A as p and the frequency of S as q. (These letters, although they may make it a bit confusing at first, are used because of a mathematical convention.) So, for our population in the second test above:

$p = .59$ and $q = .41$

Now, we calculate the probability (the chance) of creating each of the three possible genotypes *based solely on the percentages of the two alleles*. The probability is the product (the result of multiplication) of the frequencies of the alleles that make up each genotype. How often a genotype is produced depends on how often the alleles of that genotype appear in the first place. Thus, the following applies:

GENOTYPE	PRODUCT OF FREQUENCIES
AA	$p \times p = p^2$
AS	$p \times q = pq$
SA	$q \times p = qp$ $\Big\} = 2pq$
SS	$q \times q = q^2$

The heterozygote is counted twice because there are two ways of producing it, depending on which allele comes from which parent. Because all genotypes are now accounted for,

$p^2 + 2pq + q^2 = 1$ (or 100 percent)

This is the Hardy-Weinberg formula for a two-allele gene.

We can now return to our population and see what its genotype frequencies would be if they were based only on the frequencies of the alleles, that is, if there were no evolutionary processes taking place and the percentages of the genotypes were strictly a matter of chance. For the AA genotype, for example, we calculate p^2 as $.59 \times .59 = .3481$. Next, we multiply this by the population size, 145, to show how many people would be *expected* to have this genotype if no evolution were taking place: $145 \times .3481 = 50$. Looking back, however, we observe that only 35 people actually possessed this genotype. We can do the rest of the calculations, producing the following results:

GENOTYPE	EXPECTED FREQUENCY	EXPECTED NUMBER	OBSERVED NUMBER
AA	$p^2 = .59^2 = .3481$	$.3481 \times 145 = 50$	35
AS	$2pq = 2 \times .59 \times .41$ $= .4838$	$.4838 \times 145 = 70$	100
SS	$q^2 = .41^2 = .1681$	$.1681 \times 145 = 24$	10

(The "expected number" and "observed number" columns should each add up to 145 but don't exactly because of rounding.)

The results are based on chance alone: the observed number of people possessing each genotype is not the same as the expected number. In evolutionary terms, then, our sample population is not in Hardy-Weinberg equilibrium. Something else is going on; namely, some evolutionary processes are in action.

In real life, we would still have to run certain statistical tests on our results, because the fact that the expected and observed numbers do not match could still be the result of chance. For the record, I ran a chi-square (a test of statistical significance) and found that the above results are not a matter of chance. They are, therefore, in mathematical terms, statistically significant.

At any rate, we can note the direction of the differences. Again, comparing expected with observed frequencies, we see that there are large drops in the numbers of people with the AA and SS genotypes and a large increase in those with the AS genotype. This hints that the heterozygote is being selected for and that the two homozygotes are being selected against. We know, of course, that this is the case with sickle cell anemia in malarial areas.

The other processes of evolution may also be quantified and studied in a similar fashion—by observing changes in allele frequencies over time or by calculating deviations from Hardy-Weinberg equilibrium—and then by noting the direction of change and determining the probable causes of that change. (For practice, see the exercise on population genetics in the following section.)

Exercises

Exercises in Biological Anthropology

Some of the ideas covered in this text can be better understood when applied to specific situations. Here are four brief exercises to increase your grasp of important areas of bioanthropology. These can be done individually but would also be useful as a focus for study groups. A discussion of the answers follows.

Exercise 1   MENDELIAN GENETICS

Understanding the basic features of genetic inheritance described by Mendel is important for grasping larger-scale processes of evolution. Answer the following questions using the Punnett square (as shown in Figure 3.8) to help visualize your reasoning.

1. Suppose two people who are both heterozygous for the taster trait produce offspring. What are the possible genotypes and phenotypes of their offspring? In what proportions will they be produced; that is, what are the chances (ratios or percentages) of producing each genotype and each phenotype?

2. For this example, we will add a second simple (Mendelian) trait. We'll use earlobes. These are either free (where the lobe extends downward from its point of connection to the side of the head) or attached (where the lobe slopes upward from the point of connection). Free is the dominant condition (F); attached is the recessive (f). The gene for earlobes and that for the taster trait are on different chromosomes, so they assort independently. Now, if two nontasters with attached earlobes produce offspring, what can you predict about the phenotypes of their offspring? Why?

3. If two people who are both heterozygous for the taste and earlobe traits produce offspring, what possible genotypes and phenotypes can they produce? In what proportions? (Remember, these traits assort independently.)

4. Blood type for the ABO system (see Table 13.1) is determined by a single gene with three alleles: A, B, and O. A and B are codominant,

and both are dominant over O. Suppose a type B woman has given birth to a type O child and has identified a type A man as the father. Could he possibly be the father? Why or why not?

Exercise 2 TAXONOMY

The difference between phenetic and cladistic taxonomies (Chapter 7) can be further appreciated by applying the two methods to categorize some nonbiological items. Consider the seven items pictured below and on page 444: (a) a laser pointer, (b) portable CD player, (c) portable tape recorder, (d) digital watch, (e) self-winding analog watch, (f) electric analog watch, and (g) cell phone.

1. Categorize the items phenetically, that is, by phenotypic features and adaptive functions. Your scheme should consist of sets of nested categories. Now, construct a family tree based on your classification (see Table 7.1 and Figure 7.2).

2. Using shared derived characteristics, construct a cladistic diagram of the items (see Figures 7.3 and 7.4). You may have a hard time sorting out the relative importance of the shared derived characteristics and thus the "branching order" of the cladogram. There may be several equally reasonable trees. This exercise illustrates one of the difficulties inherent in the cladistic method.

(a)

(b)

(c)

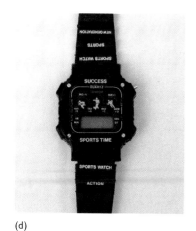

(d)

(e)

(f)

(g)

Exercise 3   SKELETAL IDENTIFICATION

Practice analyzing skeletal remains with the following examples. Refer to Figures 9.1, 9.2, and 9.3. (You may want to consult additional sources, such as those listed in Chapter 9, for more information.)

1. A human mandible was recovered from a burned building. Muscle markings were not pronounced, the chin was rounded, and the gonial angle (the angle at the back of the jaw) was about 110°. All the teeth were permanent. The first molar, the central and lateral incisors, and the first premolar (bicuspid) were all fully erupted. The canine and second premolar were just starting to break through the gum line.

   Sex: _____   Age at death: _____

2. A set of postcranial bones was uncovered at a construction site. All epiphyses were fused except for the medial clavicle (the end of the clavicle nearest the middle of the body). The pelvis was badly damaged, but the subpubic angle appeared to be about 90°.

    Sex: _____   Age at death: _____

3. After all other victims of an airline accident had been positively identified, all that remained were one skull and one pelvis. There was little question that they came from the same person, yet initial analysis seemed contradictory. The skull showed slight muscle markings, the gonial angle was large, and the forehead was fairly vertical with no brow ridges. The pelvis, however, had a narrow sciatic notch and small subpubic angle, with vertical ilia. What do you think is the sex of this individual? How were you able to resolve the seeming contradiction?

Exercise 4   **POPULATION GENETICS**

Following are some examples that will ask you to apply the basic population genetics concepts discussed in the Appendix. First, we need some numbers: suppose in a class of eight students we have five tasters and three nontasters. (If you have access to PTC [phenylthiocarbamide] paper—which is either extremely bitter or tasteless, depending on a person's phenotype for the taster trait—you could test the members of your class and use those data.)

1. For the taster trait, calculate the *phenotype* frequencies for the class. (A frequency is a percentage: divide the number of people with each expression by the total number in the class.)

2. Now, calculate the *genotype* and *allele* frequencies for the class for the taster trait. You should immediately see a problem: Unlike the case with sickle cell anemia, where we could distinguish the three genotypes (see page 438), here we can't distinguish homozygous tasters from heterozygotes (because of the complete dominance of the taster allele). There is, however, one piece of information we *do* know and can use to estimate the frequencies. (*Hint:* Assume the class is in Hardy-Weinberg equilibrium for these traits.)

3. Let's say we could distinguish the three genotypes for the taster trait. A population of 208 people presents us with the following data: there are 119 homozygous tasters, 76 heterozygous tasters, and 13 nontasters. Is this population in Hardy-Weinberg equilibrium for the taster trait?

Discussion and Answers

Exercise I   MENDELIAN GENETICS

1. A heterozygote produces gametes with the dominant allele (*T*) and the recessive allele (*t*) in equal numbers. The Punnett square for a mating between two heterozygotes is like that in Figure 3.8.

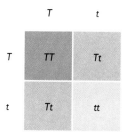

The chances of producing the two phenotypes are 75 percent for the taster trait and 25 percent for the nontaster trait. Genotype frequencies are 25 percent *TT*, 50 percent *Tt*, and 25 percent *tt*.

2. Since nontasters are homozygous recessive, they produce only gametes with the recessive allele. Similarly, those with attached earlobes only pass on the recessive allele. Thus, all the offspring from a mating between two nontasters with attached earlobes will also be nontasters with attached earlobes.

(To fill in this Punnett square with two traits, simply combine the individual gamete alleles of each gene into genotypic pairs. Thus, the taster alleles, *t* for both gametes, combine to make a *tt* genotype And the same holds true for the earlobe alleles, which combine to form the *ff* genotype.)

3. Since these traits assort independently, each double heterozygote person can produce four different types of gametes with regard to these alleles: *TF*, *Tf*, *tF*, and *tf*. Thus, all genotypic and phenotypic combinations are possible.

	TF	Tf	tF	tf
TF	TT FF	TT Ff	Tt FF	Tt Ff
Tf	TT Ff	TT ff	Tt Ff	Tt ff
tF	Tt FF	Tt Ff	tt FF	tt Ff
tf	Tt Ff	Tt ff	tt Ff	tt ff

(This Punnett square works the same way as the one in the preceding question, only there are more boxes since there are more possible gametes. Again, simply combine the individual gametic alleles from the vertical and horizontal margins and fill each genotype pair in the corresponding intersecting box. *Note:* For computing purposes, begin each allele combination with the dominant trait, where applicable— for example *Ff*, not *fF*.)

Phenotypically, there are nine tasters with free earlobes, three tasters with attached earlobes, three nontasters with free earlobes, and one nontaster with attached earlobes.

Genotypically, the numbers are as follows:

TTFF	1
TTFf	2
TTff	1
TtFF	2
TtFf	4
Ttff	2
ttFF	1
ttFf	2
ttff	1

4. If both the man and woman were heterozygotes (*AO* and *BO*), then there's a one-quarter chance the child could be type O (*OO*).

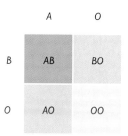

Exercise 2   TAXONOMY

1. As with classifications of living organisms, there are probably several taxonomies that could be imposed on these items, all with different-looking family trees. The following tree is based on function. All the watches, of course, serve to tell time. The digital and electric analog watches both use batteries and so are more closely related, like "species" of watches. The tape recorder and CD player play sound, but the tape recorder can also record it. Thus, I have chosen to separate these two items at the same level as the two general types of watches (requiring batteries or not). The cell phone and laser pointer each serve a separate function.

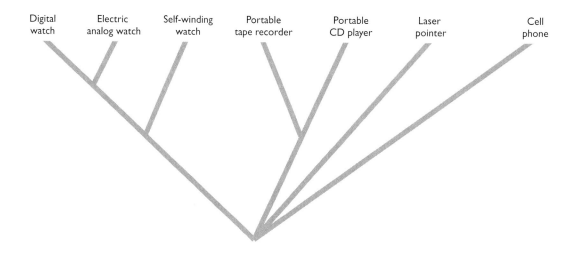

2. Following is a taxonomy based on shared derived characteristics: All of the items but the self-winding watch use electricity. The electric analog watch and the tape recorder are fairly simple mechanisms, but all the others require a microchip. The laser pointer and the CD player share the use of laser beam technology.

   As an example of another approach to this taxonomy, notice that the cell phone, digital watch, and CD player all feature LCDs (liquid crystal displays) or LEDs (light-emitting diode displays). Using this as a shared derived characteristic would result in a different-looking tree. Can you think of any other schemes?

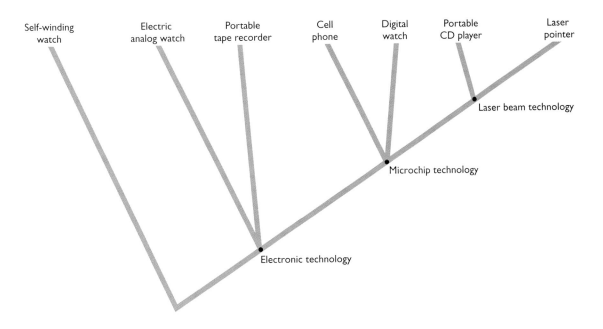

Exercise 3   SKELETAL IDENTIFICATION

1. All indications suggest the skull of a female. Keeping in mind that all the teeth were permanent, or adult teeth, we note that if the first premolar had erupted, the person would have to be older than 10 years. The canine and second premolar erupt at 11 years. Since they had not yet fully erupted in this individual, we can set the age of death at between 10 and 11 years.

2. The subpubic angle of 90° indicates a male. Because all epiphyses except the medial clavicle were fused, we know that the lateral clavicle (the end of the clavicle at the shoulder) was fused. The lateral

clavicle fuses at 20 years, and the medial clavicle fuses at 28 years. Thus, this man died at between 20 and 28 years of age.

3. The features of this skull were characteristically female, yet the pelvis had male features. If these came from the same person, it is likely the person was a male. While the features of the skull, even those related to sex, can show some degree of variation, those of the pelvis are less ambiguous because of their relationship to childbearing. Everything about the female pelvis is wider than in the male pelvis.

Exercise 4   POPULATION GENETICS

1. Of the eight students in the class, five are tasters. To arrive at the phenotype frequency for tasters, we divide 5 by 8 to get 62.5 percent, or, stated as a decimal (which is easier to work with), .625. The frequency of nontasters is everyone else: 1.00 (100 percent) − .625 = .375.

2. We don't know how many tasters are homozygous dominant and how many are heterozygotes. But we do know that all three nontasters must be homozygous recessives. Here's where the Hardy-Weinberg equilibrium comes in (refer to pages 440–441 in the Appendix). Remember that it states that

    $$p^2 + 2pq + q^2 = 1 \text{ (or 100 percent)}$$

    where each factor to the left of the equation is the frequency of each genotype ($p = T$, $pq = Tt$, and $q = t$).

    As calculated in the preceding example, we know that q^2, the frequency of the homozygous recessive genotype (tt), is .375. Thus, q (the frequency of the t allele) is the square root of .375, or .612.

    Now, to find the value of p (the frequency of the T allele), we subtract .612 from 1.00 to get .388.

    We can now calculate the other genotype frequencies:

    p^2 (the frequency of TT) is $.388^2 = .150$

    $2pq$ (the frequency of the heterozygote Tt) is $2(.388)(.612) = .475$

    Summarizing, the frequency of

    $TT = .150$
    $Tt = .475$
    $tt = .375$

    Added together, these equal 1.00 (100 percent).

3. As discussed in the Appendix, the Hardy-Weinberg equilibrium compares observed numbers with expected numbers. First, we calculate allele frequencies assuming Hardy-Weinberg equilibrium. We know that q^2, the frequency of nontasters (tt), is 13 divided by 208, or .062. Thus, q (the frequency of the t allele) is the square root of that, or .25. Then p (the frequency of the T allele) must be .75. Thus, we have expected genotype frequencies as follows:

TT $(p^2) = .75^2 = .563$
Tt $(2pq) = 2(.75)(.25) = .375$
tt $(q^2) = 25^2 = .062$

Now we multiply the expected frequencies by the total population (208) to get the expected numbers for each genotype:

TT $.563 \times 208 = 117$
Tt $.375 \times 208 = 78$
tt $.062 \times 208 = 13$

These numbers, however, don't match exactly the observed numbers of the population—119, 76, and 13. Thus, based on a comparison of the observed and expected numbers, this population is not in Hardy-Weinberg equilibrium. Some processes of evolution are occurring. (Actually, we would have to run a statistical test such as a chi-square test to see if the deviation from Hardy-Weinberg expectations is statistically significant and, thus, meaningful. In this case, it is not. This example, however, illustrates how the process works.)

Glossary of Human and Nonhuman Primates

Adapidae (*ah-da'-pih-day*) A group of early primates from the previously connected landmass of North America and Europe, dating to more than 50 mya and thought to be ancestral to prosimians such as lemurs and lorises.

Aegyptopithecus (*ee-gyp'-tow-pith'-ah-cuss*) An extinct monkey genus with several apelike traits. Discovered in Egypt and dated at approximately 34 mya, it may represent a form of primate ancestral to Old World monkeys and apes.

Ankarapithecus (*ahn-kah-rah-pith'-ah-cuss*) A fossil ape genus from Turkey dated at 9.8 mya. Shows similarities to *Sivapithecus*.

Anthropoidea (*an-throw-poy'-dee-ah*) According to the traditional taxonomic system, one of the two suborders of order Primates (the other is Prosimii). Means "humanlike" and includes monkeys, apes, and humans.

Ardipithecus kadabba (*ar-di-pith'-ah-cuss kah-dah'-bah*) An earlier species of *Ardipithecus* from Ethiopia and dated at 5.2 to 5.8 mya; interpreted by some as bipedal. The subspecies name means "base family ancestor" in the Afar language.

Ardipithecus ramidus (*ar-di-pith'-ah-cuss rah'-mi-dus*) A hominid species from Ethiopia and dated at about 4.4 mya, based on skeletal fragments and teeth. Not yet fully documented or accepted, it is thought by its discoverers to represent one of the earliest species in the hominid line; thus the species name, which means "root" in the local language.

Australopithecus afarensis (*os-trail-oh-pith'-ah-cuss ah-far-en'-sis*) A fossil species from East Africa, the oldest well-established species in the hominid line. Dated at 3.9 to 3 mya, *afarensis* had a small, chimp-sized brain but walked fully upright.

Australopithecus africanus (*os-trail-oh-pith'-ah-cuss ah-frih-cane'-us*) A fossil hominid species from South Africa dated from about 3 to 2.3 mya. It is similar to *A. afarensis* and may well be a direct evolutionary descendant of the earlier species. It retained the chimp-sized brain and was fully bipedal.

Australopithecus anamensis (*os-trail-oh-pith'-ah-cuss ana-men'-sis*) The earliest well-documented fully bipedal hominid, found in Kenya and dating from 4.2 to 3.8 mya.

Australopithecus bahrelghazalia (*os-trail-oh-pith'-ah-cuss bar-el-gah-zahl'-ya*) A new species of this genus, based on a jaw and several teeth found in Chad and dated at 3.5 to 3 mya. The species name is derived from an Arabic name for a nearby riverbed. It is noteworthy as the only early hominid found outside of East Africa or southern Africa.

Australopithecus garhi (*os-trail-oh-pith'-ah-cuss gar'-hee*) Recently discovered fossils from Ethiopia, dated at 2.5 mya, that display resemblances to both *Australopithecus afarensis* and early *Homo*, leading some authorities to consider them a new species and a direct ancestor of *Homo*.

Catarrhini (*cat-ah-rine'-eye*) One of two infraorders of suborder Anthropoidea (the other is infraorder Platyrrhini, the New World monkeys). Catarrhini is the infraorder of the Old World monkeys, apes, and hominids. Along with their geographic distinction, catarrhines can be distinguished from platyrrhines by their narrow nose shape, fewer premolar teeth, and lack of a prehensile tail.

Cercopithecidae (*sir-co-pih-thee'-sih-day*) The family that includes all the Old World monkeys.

Cercopithecoidea (*sir-co-pith-ah-coy'-dee-ah*) The superfamily of all monkeys of Europe, Africa, and Asia.

Eosimiidae (*ee-oh-sim-ee'-ih-day*) A group of early primates from Asia, dated at around 45 mya, that may represent direct ancestors of monkeys, apes, and hominids.

Equatorius (*ee-kwa-tor'-ee-us*)   A fossil genus from East Africa dated at 15 mya and showing similarities in arm and ankle structure to the modern chimpanzee. Lumped by some authorities into *Kenyapithecus*.

Gigantopithecus (*ji-gan-tow-pith'-ah-cuss*)   A genus of fossil apes, dated at 7 mya to perhaps as recently as 300,000 ya, found in China, India, and Vietnam. It may have reached a height of 12 feet when standing erect and weighed 1,200 pounds, making it the largest primate known.

Gorilla gorilla (*guh-ril'-ah guh-ril'-ah*)   The gorilla (well, duh!), one of the three great ape species from Africa and the largest living primate.

Gorillinae (*guh-ril'-ih-nay*)   In a cladistic taxonomy, the subfamily for the gorilla, as distinct from Homininae.

Haplorhini (*hap-low-rine'-eye*)   According to the cladistic taxonomic system, one of two suborders of order Primates (the other is Strepsirhini). Haplorhini are primates lacking a moist nose and other primitive features. Includes the tarsier and all primates traditionally included in suborder Anthropoidea.

Hominidae (*ho-mih'-nih-day*)   In a traditional taxonomy, the family of modern and extinct human species, defined as the primates that are habitually bipedal. Members of this group are called hominids.

Homininae (*ho-mih'-nih-nay*)   In a cladistic taxonomy, a subfamily that includes chimpanzees, bonobos, and humans. (In such a taxonomy, Hominidae would include the African great apes and humans.)

Hominini (*ho-mih-nih'-nee*)   In a cladistic taxonomy, the tribe for humans.

Hominoidea (*ho-min-oy'-dee-ah*)   The superfamily that includes the large, tailless primates: apes and hominids, living and extinct.

Homo antecessor (*ho'-mow an-tee-sess'-or*)   A recently proposed species from Spain and dated at 780,000 ya or more. The fossils show a mix of primitive and modern human features and are interpreted by their discoverers as possibly ancestral to *H. heidelbergensis* and *H. neanderthalensis*. This species is not widely recognized at present.

Homo erectus (*ho'-mow ee-reck'-tuss*)   A fossil hominid species dating from at least 1.8 mya to 100,000 ya or so. First appearing in Africa, *H. erectus* was the first hominid species to expand beyond that continent. Fossils are found throughout Africa and Asia, and there is possible evidence in Europe. Members of this species, with an average brain size about two-thirds that of modern humans, made advances in stone tool technology and were able to control fire late in their existence.

Homo ergaster (*ho'-mow er-gas'-ter*)   The earliest *H. erectus* fossils from Kenya, said by some researchers to be sufficiently different that they represent a separate species that was ancestral to both *H. erectus* and, later, *H. sapiens*.

Homo habilis (*ho'-mow hah'-bill-us*)   Fossil hominid species dating from about 2.3 to 1.5 mya and found in East Africa and perhaps southern Africa. Fully bipedal and with an average brain size of 680 ml, *H. habilis* was the first confirmed hominid stone toolmaker. Because this was the first hominid with a brain larger than that of a chimpanzee, and because of the species' association with stone tools, *H. habilis* is thought to be the earliest member of our genus, *Homo*.

Homo heidelbergensis (*ho'-mow high-del-berg-en'-sis*)   A proposed species from Africa, Asia, and Europe, dated at between 475,000 and 200,000 ya. They had a modern human brain size but retained primitive features such as brow ridges, prognathism, and postorbital constriction.

Homo neanderthalensis (*ho'-mow nee-an-dir-tall-en'-sis*)   A proposed species from Europe and Southwest Asia, dated at between 225,000 and 36,000 ya. They had more pronounced versions of some of the cranial features of *H. heidelbergensis*, such as brow ridges and prognathism. The postcranial skeletons were robust and heavy, with short arms and legs, possibly adaptations to cold climates.

Homo rudolfensis (*ho'-mow rue-dolf-en'-sis*)   Thought by some authorities to be a separate species made up of the East Turkana, Kenya, specimens traditionally placed in *H. habilis*.

Homo sapiens (*ho'-mow say'-pee-ens*)   The taxonomic name for modern humans. There is debate as to whether or not this name covers certain other species, including *H. erectus, ergaster, antecessor, heidelbergensis,* and *neanderthalensis.*

Hylobatidae (*high-low-bat'-ah-day*) The family that includes the gibbons and siamangs, the arboreal so-called lesser apes of Southeast Asia. They are highly efficient brachiators.

Kenyanthropus platyops (*ken-yan'-throw-pus plat'-ee-ops*) A new fossil genus from Kenya, dated at 3.5 mya and suggested by some authorities, because of its flat face and other features, to represent a better human ancestor than any species of *Australopithecus.* Thus far, it is based on only two specimens.

Kenyapithecus (*ken-ya-pith'-ah-cuss*) A fossil genus from East Africa dated at 14 mya. A possible candidate for the first hominoid.

Lufengpithecus (*lew-feng-pith'-ah-cuss*) A fossil pongid from Thailand, dated at 10 to 14.8 mya, suggested by some as an ancestor of modern orangutans.

Morotopithecus (*more-row-tow-pith'-ah-cuss*) A fossil genus from Uganda dated at 20 mya. A possible candidate for the first hominoid, it may have been capable of occasional upright walking.

Omomyidae (*oh-mow-me'-ah-day*) A group of early primates that lived in the previously connected landmass of North America and Europe. Dating to more than 50 mya, they are thought to be ancestral to tarsiers and may have been ancestral to Anthropoidea as well.

Orrorin tugenensis (*or-or'-in too-gen-en'-sis*) A new fossil genus from Kenya, based on thirteen specimens and dated at 5.6 to 6.2 mya. Its purported bipedal features have led some to suggest it represents the ancestor of all later hominids. The identity and features of this form are still a matter of much debate.

Ouranopithecus (*oo-ran-oh-pith'-ah-cuss*) An ape from Greece dated at 9 to 10 mya. Based on some hominidlike features, it is thought by some to be a member of the ape line that led to the hominids.

Panini (*pan'-ih-nee*) In a cladistic taxonomy, the tribe that includes chimpanzees and bonobos.

Pan paniscus (*pan pan-iss'-cuss*) The bonobo, sometimes called the pygmy chimpanzee. One of the three great ape species from Africa.

Pan troglodytes (*pan trog-low-dye'-tees*) The chimpanzee. One of the three great ape species from Africa.

Papio (*pah'-pee-oh*) A genus within superfamily Cercopithecoidea (the Old World monkeys) that comprises several species of baboons, large monkeys living in social groups on the African savannas.

Paranthropus aethiopicus (*par-an'-throw-puss ee-thee-oh'-pih-cuss*) A species from East Africa dating from 2.8 to 2.2 mya. They were the first members of the so-called robust early hominids, having large, rugged features associated with chewing, although other features, including their brain size, were very similar to those of genus *Australopithecus.* Many authorities still include it in that genus. It is thought they were adapted to tough, gritty, hard vegetable foods. The most famous, and first, specimen of this species was the "Black Skull."

Paranthropus boisei (*par-an'-throw-puss boys'-ee-eye*) The East African robust hominid, dated at 2.2 to 1 mya. It had large features associated with chewing, although less pronounced than in *P. aethiopicus.* The first specimen was "Zinjanthropus." Sometimes included in genus *Australopithecus.*

Paranthropus robustus (*par-an'-throw-puss row-bus'-tus*) The southern African robust hominid, dated at 2.2 to 1.5 mya. It was marked by robust chewing features, although they were less robust than in either *P. aethiopicus* or *P. boisei.* The postcranial skeleton and the brain size remained similar to those of *Australopithecus.* It is sometimes included in that genus.

Platyrrhini (*plat-ee-rine'-eye*) One of two infra-orders of suborder Anthropoidea (the other is infraorder Catarrhini, the Old World monkeys, apes, and hominids). Platyrrhines comprise the New World monkeys. Members of this group can be told apart from the catarrhines by their broad nose shape, greater number of premolar teeth, and the fact that several species have prehensile tails.

Plesiadapiformes (*pleez-ee-ah-dah'-pih-form-ees*) A branch of archaic primates from sites in present-day North America that became extinct about 55 mya.

Pongidae (*pon'-jih-day*)   The family of the so-called great apes: the orangutans of Southeast Asia and the gorillas, chimpanzees, and bonobos of Africa.

Pongo pygmaeus (*pon'-go pig-may'-us*)   The orangutan. The only great ape from Southeast Asia.

Primates (*pry-mate'-ees*)   An order within class Mammalia. Large-brained arboreal mammals with stereoscopic color vision and grasping hands (and sometimes feet). Includes prosimians, monkeys, apes, and hominids.

Prosimii (*pro-sim'-ee-eye*)   According to the traditional taxonomic system, one of two suborders of order Primates (the other suborder is Anthropoidea). Prosimians are the more primitive of the two suborders in that they retain features of some of the oldest primate fossils. Many lack color vision, are nocturnal, and have limited opposability of the thumb.

Sahelanthropus tchadensis (*sah-hale-an'-throw-puss chad-en'-sis*)   A possible fossil hominid from Chad, dated at 7 to 6 mya. Despite some apelike features, it has other cranial features that some claim make it the earliest hominid.

Sivapithecus (*she-vah-pith'-ah-cuss*)   Genus of fossil ape from India and Pakistan, dated at 15 to 12 mya. Thought to be ancestral to the orangutan.

Strepsirhini (*strep-sir-rine'-eye*)   According to the cladistic taxonomic system, one of two suborders of order Primates (the other is Haplorhini). These primates have a moist nose and other primitive features. Includes all primates traditionally in suborder Prosimii except the tarsier.

Glossary of Terms

absolute dating technique A dating method that gives a specific age, year, or range of years for an object or site. Compare with **relative dating technique.**

Acheulian technique A toolmaking tradition associated with *Homo erectus/ergaster* in Africa and Europe. Includes hand axes, cleavers, and flake tools.

adaptation The state in which an organism is adjusted to and can survive in its environment through its physical traits and behaviors. Also, the process by which an organism develops this state through natural processes.

adaptive radiation The evolution and spreading out of related species into new niches.

allele frequency The percentage of times a particular allele appears in a population. Another name, and the preferred term, for gene frequency.

alleles Variants of a gene. Most genes possess more than one possible allele, the different alleles conveying different instructions for the development of a certain phenotype (for example, different blood types).

altruistic Benefiting others without regard for one's own needs or safety.

amino acids The chief components of proteins. Each "word" in the genetic code stands for a specific amino acid.

analogies Traits shared by two or more species that are similar in function but unrelated evolutionarily, for example, the wings of a bird and of an insect. Compare with **homologies.**

anthropology The holistic study of the human species. Anthropology includes the study of human biology, human physical evolution, human cultural evolution, and human adaptation.

antibodies Proteins in the immune system that react to foreign antigens.

antigens Substances, such as proteins, that can trigger an immune response, for example, the production of an antibody. The antigens of the ABO blood group system are examples.

applied anthropology Anthropology used to address current practical problems and concerns.

arboreal Adapted to life in the trees.

archaeology A subfield of anthropology that studies the human cultural past and the reconstruction of past cultural systems.

argon/argon dating A radiometric dating technique that uses the decay of radioactive argon into stable argon gas. Can be used to date smaller samples and volcanic rock with greater accuracy than potassium/argon dating. See also **potassium/argon dating.**

asexually Reproducing without sex, by fissioning or budding. Compare with **sexually.**

behavioral ecology Another name for sociobiology.

belief systems Ideas that are taken on faith and cannot be scientifically tested. Examples are religions, philosophies, and ethical and moral beliefs. Compare with **scientific method.**

bifacial A stone tool that has been worked on both sides.

bioanthropology Another name for biological anthropology.

biocultural Focusing on the interaction of biology and culture.

biological anthropology A subfield of anthropology that studies humans as a biocultural species.

biostratigraphy The study of fossils in their stratigraphic context. Used as a relative dating technique.

bipedal Walking on two legs.

bottleneck A severe reduction in the size of a population or the founding of a new population by a small percentage of the parent population that results in only some genes surviving and characterizing the descendant population.

brachiation Locomotion by swinging arm-over-arm.

breeding populations Populations within a species that are genetically isolated to some degree from other populations.

carnivore An organism adapted to a diet of mostly meat. Compare with **omnivore.**

catastrophists Those who believe the history of the earth is explained by a series of global catastrophes, either natural or divine in origin. See also **uniformitarianism.**

chromosomal mutations Mutations of a whole chromosome or a large portion of a chromosome. Compare with **point mutations.**

chromosomes Strands of DNA in the nucleus of a cell.

chronometric techniques Another name for absolute dating techniques.

cladistics A classification system based on order of evolutionary branching rather than on present similarities and differences. Compare with **phenetic taxonomy.**

cline A geographic continuum in the variation of a particular trait.

codominant When both alleles of a pair are expressed in the phenotype.

codon The three-base sequence that codes for a specific amino acid. Technically, the sequence on the mRNA.

comparative anatomy Comparing the anatomical features of various species. Used to reconstruct a fossil species from fragmentary remains.

competitive exclusion When one species outcompetes others for the resources of a particular area.

core tools Tools made by taking flakes off a stone nucleus. See also **flake tools.**

crossing over When sections of chromosomes switch between chromosome pairs during meiosis. See also **recombination.**

cultural anthropology A subfield of anthropology that focuses on human cultural behavior and cultural systems and the variation in cultural expression among human groups.

culture Ideas and behaviors that are learned and shared. Also, the system made up of the sum total of these ideas and behaviors that is unique to a particular society of people. Nonbiological means of adaptation.

Darwinian gradualism The view, held by Darwin, that evolution is slow and steady with cumulative change. Compare with **punctuated equilibrium.**

deduction Suggesting specific data that would be found if a hypothesis were true, a step in the scientific method involving the testing of hypotheses. See also **induction.**

demography The study of the size and makeup of populations.

deoxyribonucleic acid (DNA) The molecule that carries the genetic code.

dermatoglyphics The study of the parallel ridges and furrows on the fingers, palms, toes, and soles of the feet, commonly referred to as fingerprints, palm prints, and so on.

distance curve A graph that compares some variable at different points in time, for example, height and age. Compare with **velocity curve.**

diurnal Active during the day. Compare with **nocturnal.**

DNA See **deoxyribonucleic acid.**

dominance hierarchy A social pattern among animal species where there are recognized individual differences in power, influence, and access to resources and mating. Found in many primate species.

dominant The allele of a heterozygous pair that is expressed in the phenotype. Compare with **recessive.**

electron spin resonance (ESR) dating An absolute dating technique that measures the number of electrons excited to higher energy levels by natural radiation and trapped at those levels. Can be used to date tooth enamel, shells, corals, mineral cave deposits, and volcanic rock, but does not work well on bone.

endocasts Natural or human-made casts of the inside of a skull. The cast reflects the surface of the brain and allows us to study the brains of even extinct species.

endogamy   Restricting marriage to members of the same culturally defined group.

environmental   Any nongenetic influence on the phenotype. Also refers to the conditions under which an organism exists, such as climate, altitude, other species, food sources, and so on.

enzymes   Proteins that control chemical processes.

epidemiological   Pertaining to the study of disease outbreaks and epidemics.

estrus   The period of female fertility or the signals indicating this condition.

ethology   The study of the natural behavior of animals under natural conditions.

evolution   Change through time, usually with reference to biological species, but may also refer to changes within cultural systems.

evolutionary psychology   Another name for sociobiology.

fission   A process of evolution that involves the splitting up of a population to form new populations.

fitness   The relative adaptiveness of an individual organism, measured ultimately by reproductive success.

flake tools   Tools made from the flakes removed from a stone core. See also **core tools.**

folk taxonomies   Cultural categories for important items and ideas. Gender and race are examples of folk taxonomies.

foramen magnum   The hole in the base of the skull through which the spinal cord emerges and around the outside of which the top vertebra articulates.

forensic anthropologist   A scientist who applies anthropology to legal matters. Usually used with reference to the identification of skeletal remains and the assessment of time and cause of death.

fossils   Remains of life-forms of the past.

founder effect   A process of evolution. Genetic differences between populations produced by the fact that genetically different individuals established (founded) those populations.

gametes   The cells of sexual reproduction, commonly sperm and egg, which contain only half the chromosomes of a normal cell.

gamete sampling   A process of evolution. The genetic change caused when genes are passed to new generations in frequencies unrepresentative of those of the parental generation. An example of sampling error.

gender   The cultural categories and characteristics of men and women. The translation of sex into a folk taxonomy. Compare with **sex.**

gene flow   A process of evolution that involves the exchange of genes among populations through interbreeding.

gene frequency   See **allele frequency.**

gene pool   All the alleles in a population.

generalized   Species that are adapted to a wide range of environmental niches. Such species tend to be genetically and physically variable. Compare with **specialized.**

genes   Those portions of the DNA molecule that code for a functional product, usually a protein.

genome   The total genetic endowment of an organism.

genotypes   The alleles possessed by an organism. See also **phenotype.**

glaciers   Massive sheets of ice that expand and move. Found on the polar ice caps and in mountains.

grooming   Cleaning the fur of another animal, which promotes social cohesion. Common among primate groups.

haft   To attach a wooden handle or shaft to a stone or bone point.

half-life   The time needed for one-half of a given amount of a radioactive substance to decay.

hand axe   A bifacial, all-purpose stone tool, shaped somewhat like an axe head. First invented by *Homo erectus* and usually associated with that species.

heritability   The amount of variation of a particular trait within a population that is caused by genetic, as opposed to environmental, differences.

heterozygous   Having two different alleles in a gene pair. Compare with **homozygous.**

holistic   Assuming an interrelationship among the parts of a subject. Anthropology is a holistic discipline.

hominids Modern human beings and our ancestors, generally defined as the primates who habitually walk erect. Technically, the members of family Hominidae.

homologies Traits shared by two or more species through inheritance from a common ancestor. Such traits need not serve the same function. An example would be the arms of a human and the wings of a bat. We assume that many similar behaviors among humans and chimpanzees are also homologies. Compare with **analogies.**

homozygous Having two of the same allele in a gene pair. Compare with **heterozygous.**

human ecology A specialty of anthropology that studies the relationships between humans and their environments.

hunter-gatherers Societies that rely on naturally occurring sources of food. They have no domestic plants or animals except, perhaps, dogs.

hypotheses Educated guesses to explain natural phenomena. In the scientific method, hypotheses must be testable. See also **theory.**

inclusive fitness The idea that fitness is measured by the success of one's genes, whether possessed by the individual or by that individual's relatives.

independent assortment When genes on different chromosomes segregate to gametes independently of one another.

induction Developing a general explanation from specific observations. The step in the scientific method that generates hypotheses. See also **deduction.**

inheritance of acquired characteristics The incorrect idea, associated with Lamarck, that adaptive traits acquired during an organism's lifetime can be passed on to its offspring.

inorganic A molecule not containing carbon. Compare with **organic.**

intelligence The relative ability of the brain to acquire, store, retrieve, and process information.

intelligent design The idea that an intelligent designer played a role in some aspect of the evolution of life on earth, usually the origin of life itself. Generally, a thinly disguised version of scientific creationism.

knuckle walking Walking on the backs of the knuckles of the hand, typical of the African apes.

law of parsimony A principle that relies on using the simplest explanation in formulating a scientific hypothesis. Another name for Ockham's razor.

Levallois technique A tool technology involving striking uniform flakes from a prepared core. See **core tools** and **flake tools.**

life history The study of the timing of life cycle events such as fertility, growth, and death.

linkage When genes occur on the same chromosome and are inherited together.

luminescence dating An absolute dating technique that measures trapped electrons by releasing their energy in the form of light. Can be used to date fired clay, pottery, brick, and burnt stones. It may have some application in soil dating.

macroevolution The branching of new species from existing species.

macromutations Mutations with extensive and important phenotypic results. The mutations for sickle cell anemia and Down syndrome are examples.

meiosis The process of cell division in which gametes are produced, each gamete having one-half the normal complement of chromosomes and, therefore, only one allele of each original pair. See also **mitosis.**

melanin The pigment largely responsible for human skin color.

melanocytes Specialized skin cells that produce the pigment melanin.

menarche A woman's first menstrual period.

Mendelian genetics The basic laws of inheritance discovered by Gregor Mendel in the nineteenth century.

menopause The end of a woman's reproductive cycle.

messenger ribonucleic acid (mRNA) The molecule that carries the genetic code out of the nucleus for translation into proteins. See also **transfer RNA.**

microevolution Evolutionary change within a single species through time.

microsatellites Long repetitious strings of noncoding DNA. Their length and the fact that they are not influenced by selection make them good genetic landmarks for DNA comparisons.

mitochondrial DNA (mtDNA) The genetic material found in the cell's mitochondria rather than in the cell's nucleus. The mtDNA does not play a role in inheritance and thus may give a more accurate measure of the genetic differences among populations.

mitosis The process of cell division that results in two exact copies of the original cell. See also **meiosis.**

monogenic A trait coded for by a single gene. The ABO blood group system is a monogenic trait. Compare with **polygenic.**

Mostly-Out-of-Africa model The hypothesis that *Homo sapiens* is about 2 million years old as a species but that most of the genetic variation and phenotypic features of modern humans have an African origin.

Mousterian technique A toolmaking tradition associated with the European Neandertals.

Multiregional Evolution (MRE) model The hypothesis that *Homo sapiens* is about 2 million years old and that modern human traits evolved in geographically diverse locations and then spread through the species. Compare with **Recent African Origin model.**

mutation Any mistake in an organism's genetic code.

natural selection Evolutionary change based on the differential reproductive success of individuals within a species.

niche The environment of an organism and its adaptive response to that environment.

nocturnal Active at night. Compare with **diurnal.**

notochord A stiff cartilaginous rod that supports the body and protects the dorsal nerve. The evolutionary precursor of the vertebral column.

nuclear DNA The genetic material in the nucleus of a cell.

nucleotide The basic building block of DNA and RNA, made up of a sugar, a phosphate, and one of four bases.

Oldowan A toolmaking tradition from Africa associated with early *Homo.*

omnivore An organism with a mixed diet of animal and vegetable foods. Compare with **carnivore.**

opposability The ability to touch (oppose) the thumb to the tips of the other fingers on the same hand.

organic Molecules that are part of living organisms. They are based on the chemistry of carbon and contain mostly hydrogen, oxygen, carbon, and nitrogen. Even carbon-based molecules that are not found in living things are sometimes referred to as organic. Compare with **inorganic.**

oscillating selection Adaptive variation around a norm, rather than in one direction, in response to environmental variation in a species' habitat.

osteology The study of the structure, function, and evolution of the skeleton.

Out-of-Africa model Another name for the Recent African Origin model.

paleoanthropology A specialty that studies the human fossil record.

paleopathology The study of disease and nutritional deficiency in prehistoric populations, usually through the examination of skeletal material.

Pangea The supercontinent that included parts of all present-day landmasses. It formed around 280 mya and began breaking up around 200 mya.

particulate The idea that biological traits are controlled by individual factors rather than by a single all-encompassing hereditary agent.

petrified Turned to stone. As the organic material of a fossil decays, it is slowly replaced by minerals, leaving a cast in stone of the organism or some of its parts.

phenetic taxonomy A classification system based on existing phenotypic features and adaptations. Compare with **cladistics.**

phenotype The chemical or physical results of the genetic code. See also **genotypes.**

photosynthesis The process by which plants manufacture their own nutrients from carbon dioxide and water, using chlorophyll as a catalyst and sunlight as an energy source.

physical anthropology The traditional name for biological anthropology.

plate tectonics The movement of the plates of the earth's crust, caused by their interaction with the molten rock of the earth's interior. The cause of continental drift.

Pleistocene The geological time period, from 1.6 mya to 10,000 ya, characterized by a series of glacial advances and retreats. See **glaciers.**

point mutations Mutations of a single base of a codon. The mutation that causes sickle cell anemia is an example. Compare with **chromosomal mutations.**

polygenic A trait coded for by more than one gene. Skin color is a polygenic trait. Compare with **monogenic.**

polymorphisms Variations in the genetic code within a species.

polytypic A species with physically distinguishable regional populations.

postnatal dependency The period after birth during which offspring require the care of adults to survive.

postorbital constriction A narrowing of the skull behind the eyes, as viewed from above.

potassium/argon (K/Ar) dating A radiometric dating technique using the rate at which radioactive potassium, found in volcanic rock, decays into stable argon gas. See also **argon/argon dating.**

prehensile Having the ability to grasp.

primates Large-brained, mostly tree-dwelling mammals with three-dimensional color vision and grasping hands. Humans are primates.

primatology A specialty of anthropology that studies nonhuman primates.

prognathism The jutting forward of the lower face and jaw area.

progressive In evolution, the now-discounted idea that all change is toward increasing complexity.

prosimian A primate with primitive features most closely resembling the ancient primates.

proteins Molecules that make cells and carry out cellular functions. Proteins are made of amino acids.

protein synthesis The process by which the genetic code puts together proteins in the cell.

provenience The precise location where a fossil or artifact was found.

pseudoscience Scientifically testable ideas that are taken on faith, even if tested and shown to be false. Scientific creationism is a pseudoscience.

punctuated equilibrium The view that species tend to remain stable and that evolutionary changes occur fairly suddenly through the evolution of new species branching from existing ones. Compare with **Darwinian gradualism.**

quadrupedal Walking on all four limbs.

races In biology, the same as subspecies. In culture, cultural categories to classify and account for human diversity; see **folk taxonomies.**

racism Judging an individual based solely on his or her racial affiliation.

radiocarbon dating A radiometric dating technique using the decay rate of a radioactive form of carbon found in organic remains.

radiometric Referring to the decay rate of a radioactive substance. See **argon/argon dating; radiocarbon dating;** and **potassium/argon dating.**

Recent African Origin (RAO) model The hypothesis that *Homo sapiens* recently evolved as a separate species in Africa and then spread to replace more archaic populations. Compare with **Multiregional Evolution model.**

recessive The allele of a heterozygous pair that is not expressed. For a recessive allele to be expressed it must be homozygous. Compare with **dominant.**

recombination The exchange of genetic material between pairs of chromosomes during meiosis. An important source of genetic variation. See also **crossing over.**

reification Translating a complex set of phenomena into a single entity such as a number. IQ test scores are an example.

relative dating technique A dating method that indicates the age of one item in comparison to another. Stratigraphy provides relative dates by indicating that one layer is older or younger than another. Compare with **absolute dating technique.**

replication The copying of the genetic code during cell division.

reproductive isolating mechanism Any difference that prevents the production of fertile offspring between members of two populations. Necessary for the production of separate species.

reproductive strategies   Behaviors that evolve to maximize an individual's reproductive success.

RNA   See **messenger RNA** and **transfer RNA.**

sagittal crest   A ridge of bone, running from front to back along the top of the skull, for the attachment of chewing muscles.

sagittal keel   A sloping of the sides of the skull toward the top, as viewed from the front.

sampling error   When a sample chosen for study does not accurately represent the population from which the sample was taken. See **gamete sampling.**

savanna   The open grasslands of the tropics. The savannas of Africa are important in early hominid evolution.

science   The method of inquiry that requires the generation, testing, and acceptance or rejection of hypotheses.

scientific creationism   The belief in a literal biblical interpretation regarding the creation of the universe, with the connected belief that this view is supported by scientific evidence. An example of a pseudoscience.

scientific method   The process of conducting scientific inquiry. See **science.**

segregation   In genetics, the breaking up of allele pairs in the production of gametes.

semispecies   Populations of a species that are completely isolated from one another but have not yet become truly different species.

sex   The biological categories and characteristics of males and females. Compare with **gender.**

sexual dimorphism   Physical differences between the sexes of a species not related to reproductive features. See **sex.**

sexually   Reproducing by combining genetic material from two individuals. Compare with **asexually.**

shared derived characteristics   Phenotypic features shared by two or more taxonomic groups that are derived from a common ancestor and that are not found in other groups.

single nucleotide polymorphism (SNP)   A single base pair of the genetic code that displays variable expressions among individuals.

sites   Locations that contain fossil and archaeological evidence of human presence.

sociobiology   The scientific study that examines evolutionary explanations for social behaviors within species.

specialized   Species that are adapted to a narrow range of environmental niches. Compare with **generalized.**

speciation   The evolution of new species.

species   A group of organisms that can produce fertile offspring among themselves but not with members of other groups. A closed genetic population, usually physically distinguishable from other populations.

stereoscopic vision   Three-dimensional vision; depth perception.

strata   Layers; here, the layers of rock and soil under the earth's surface. Singular, *stratum.*

stratigraphy   The study of the earth's strata.

subspecies   Physically distinguishable populations within a species. See **races.**

superposition   The principle of stratigraphy that, barring disturbances, more recent layers are superimposed over older ones.

symbiosis   An adaptive relationship between two different species, often, but not necessarily, of mutual benefit.

symbolic   A communication system that uses arbitrary but agreed-upon sounds and signs for meaning.

systematists   Another name for taxonomists.

taphonomy   The study of how organisms become part of the paleontological record—how fossils form and what processes affect them through time.

taxa   Categories within a taxonomic classification; singular, *taxon.* See **taxonomy.**

taxonomists   Scientists who classify and name living organisms.

taxonomy   A classification based on similarities and differences. In biology, the science of categorizing organisms and of naming them so as to reflect their relationships. Compare with **cladistics,** and see **phenetic taxonomy.**

theory   A well-supported general idea that explains a large set of factual patterns. In science, theory is a positive term.

torus   A bony ridge at the back of the skull, where the neck muscles attach.

transcription   The process during which mRNA is formed from the DNA code.

transfer ribonucleic acid (tRNA)   RNA that lines up amino acids along mRNA to make proteins. See also **messenger RNA.**

translation   The process during which the mRNA code builds a protein using amino acids supplied by tRNA.

trephination   Cutting a hole in the skull, presumably to treat some illness, a practice within some societies with prescientific knowledge.

tundra   A treeless area with low-growing vegetation and permanently frozen ground. Located in the Arctic today, tundras were found during the Pleistocene in the vicinity of glaciers far to the south.

uniformitarianism   The idea that present-day geological and biological processes can also explain the history of the earth and its life. See also **catastrophists.**

velocity curve   A graph that compares the rate of change in some variable at different points in time, for example, rate of growth at different ages. Compare with **distance curve.**

vertebrates   Organisms with backbones and internal skeletons.

zygote   The fertilized egg before cell division begins.

References

Aiello, L., and C. Dean. 1990. *An introduction to human evolutionary anatomy.* London: Academic Press.

Aiello, L. C. 1993. The fossil evidence for modern human origins in Africa: A revised view. *American Anthropologist* 95 (1): 73–96.

Aldhous, P., and A. Abbot. 2000. Battling the killer proteins. *Nature* 408:902–3.

Alexander, R. McN. 1995. Standing, walking and running. In *Gray's anatomy.* 38th ed. New York: Churchill Livingston.

Allen, T. B. 1996. The silk road's lost world. *National Geographic* 189 (3): 44–51.

Appleman, P. 1979. *Darwin: A Norton critical edition.* 2nd ed. New York: Norton.

Armelagos, G. 1998. The viral superhighway. *The Sciences* 38 (1): 24–29.

Armelagos, G., K. C. Barnes, and J. Lin. 1996. Disease in human evolution: The re-emergence of infectious disease in the third epidemiological transition. *AnthroNotes* 18 (3): 1–7.

Asfaw, B., W. H. Gilbert, Y. Beyene, W. K. Hart, P. R. Renne, G. Wolde-Gabriel, E. S. Vrba, and T. D. White. 2002. Remains of *Homo erectus* from Bouri, Middle Awash, Ethiopia. *Nature* 416:317–20.

Asfaw, B., T. White, O. Lovejoy, B. Latimer, S. Simpson, and G. Suwa. 1999. *Australopithecus garhi:* A new species of early hominid from Ethiopia. *Science* 284:629–35.

Attenborough, D. 1979. *Life on earth.* Boston: Little, Brown.

Avise, J. C. 2001. Evolving genomic metaphors: A new look at the language of DNA. *Science* 294:86–87.

Bahn, P. G. 1995. Last days of the Iceman. *Archaeology,* May–June, 66–70.

Balter, M. 2001a. Scientists spar over claims of earliest human ancestor. *Science* 291:1460–61.

———. 2001b. Anthropologists duel over modern human origins. *Science* 291:1728–29.

Balter, M., and A. Gibbons. 2002. Were "little people" the first to venture out of Africa? *Science* 297:26–27.

Barfield, A. 1976. Biological influences on sex differences in behavior. In *Sex differences,* ed. M. S. Teitelbaum. Garden City, NY: Anchor Press/Doubleday.

Barinaga, M. 1992. "African Eve" backers beat a retreat. *Science* 255:686–87.

Bass, W. 1971. *Human osteology: A laboratory and field manual of the human skeleton.* Columbia: Missouri Archaeological Society.

Beall, C. M., and A. T. Steegmann, Jr. 2000. Human adaptation to climate: Temperature, ultraviolet radiation, and altitude. In *Human biology: An evolutionary and biocultural perspective,* ed. S. Stinson et al., 163–224. New York: Wiley-Liss.

Becker, L. 2002. Repeated blows. *Scientific American,* March: 77–83.

Begun, D. R. 2000. Knuckle-walking and the origin of human bipedalism. Paper delivered at the 69th Annual Meeting of the American Association of Physical Anthropologists, San Antonio, TX.

———. 2003. Planet of the apes. *Scientific American,* August: 74–83.

Behe, M. J. 1996. *Darwin's black box.* New York: Touchstone.

Benedict, J. 2003. *No bone unturned: The adventures of a top Smithsonian forensic scientist and the legal battle for America's oldest skeletons.* New York: HarperCollins.

Berger, L. 1998. Redrawing our family tree? *National Geographic* 194 (2): 90–99.

Bermúdez de Castro, J. M., J. L. Arsuaga, E. Carbonell, A. Rosas, I. Martinez, and M. Mosquera. 1997 A hominid from the Lower Pleistocene of Atapuerca, Spain: Possible ancestor to Neandertals and modern humans. *Science* 276: 1392–95.

Binford, L. 1985. Ancestral life ways: The faunal record. *Anthroquest* 32 (1): 15–20.

Binford, L., and K. Chuan. 1985. Taphonomy at a distance: Zhoukoudian, "The cave home of Beijing Man." *Current Anthropology* 26:413–43.

Binford, L., and N. M. Stone. 1986. Zhoukoudian: A closer look. *Current Anthropology* 27:435–76.

Binford, L. R. 1987. *Bones: Ancient men and modern myths*. Orlando, FL: Academic Press.

Bloch, J. I., and D. M. Boyer. 2002. Grasping primate origins. *Science* 298:1606–9.

Blumenschine, R. J., et al. 2003. Late Pliocene *Homo* and hominid land use from Western Olduvai Gorge, Tanzania. *Science* 299:1217–21.

Boaz, N. T., and R. L. Ciochon. 2001. The scavenging of "Peking Man." *Natural History* 110 (2): 46–51.

Boesch, C. 1999. A theory that's hard to digest. *Nature* 399 (17 June): 653.

Boesch, C., and H. Boesch-Achermann. 1991. Dim forest, bright chimps. *Natural History*, September, 50–57.

Bogin, B. 2001. Book review. *Evolutionary Anthropology* 114 (2): 172–74.

Bogin, B., and B. H. Smith. 2000. Evolution of the human life cycle. In *Human biology: An evolutionary and biocultural perspective*, ed. S. Stinson et al. New York: Wiley-Liss.

Bordes, F. 1972. *A tale of two caves*. New York: Harper & Row.

Bower, B. 1995. Human genetic origins go nuclear. *Science News* 148:52.

———. 1997a. Ancient roads to Europe. *Science News* 151 (4 January): 12–13.

———. 1997b. Ancient ape shuffles to prominence. *Science News* 152 (18 October): 244.

———. 1999. Fossil may expose humanity's hybrid roots. *Science News* 155:295.

Bowlby, J. 1990. *Charles Darwin: A new life*. New York: Norton.

Boyd, R., and J. B. Silk. 1997. *How Humans Evolved*. New York: Norton.

Bramblett, C. A. 1994. *Patterns of primate behavior*. 2nd ed. Prospect Heights, IL: Waveland.

Bräuer, G., and C. Stringer. 1997. Models, polarization, and perspectives on modern human origins. In *Conceptual issues in modern human origins research*, ed. G. A. Clark and C. M. Willermet. New York: Aldine de Gruyter.

Bräuer, G., Y. Yokoyama, C. Falguères, and E. Mbua. 1997. Modern human origins backdated. *Nature* 386:337.

Brown, G. C. 2000. Symbionts and assassins. *Natural History* 109 (6): 66–71.

Brown, R. A., and G. J. Armelagos. 2001. Apportionment of racial diversity: A review. *Evolutionary Anthropology* 10 (1): 34–40.

Brunet, M. 2002. Reply to Wolpoff et al. 2002. *Nature* 419:582.

Brunet, M. et al. 2002. A new hominid from the Upper Miocene of Chad, Central Africa. *Nature* 418:145–55.

Buchan, J. C., S. C. Alberts, J. B. Silk, and J. Altmann. 2003. True paternal care in a multi-male primate society. *Nature* 425:179–81.

Byrne, R. W., and J. M. Byrne. 1988. Leopard kills of Mahale. *Natural History* 97 (3): 22–26.

Cann, R. L., M. Stoneking, and A. C. Wilson. 1987. Mitochondrial DNA and human evolution. *Nature* 325:31–36.

Cartmill, M. 1992. New views on primate origins. *Evolutionary Anthropology* 1 (3): 105–11.

———. 1997. The third man. *Discover*, September: 56–62.

Cavalieri, P., and P. Singer. 1993. *The great ape project: Equality beyond humanity*. New York: St. Martin's.

Cavalli-Sforza, L. L. 1991. Genes, peoples, and languages. *Scientific American* 265:104–10.

Cavalli-Sforza, L. L., and F. Cavalli-Sforza. 1995. *The great human diasporas: The history of diversity and evolution*. Reading, MA: Addison-Wesley.

Cavalli-Sforza, L. L., P. Menozzi, and A. Piazza. 1994. *The history and geography of human genes*. Princeton, NJ: Princeton University Press.

Cavallo, J. A. 1990. Cat in the human cradle. *Natural History* 99 (2): 53–60.

Chaimanee, Y., D. Jolly, M. Benammi, P. Tarroueau, D. Duzer, I. Moussa, and J-J. Jaeger. 2003. A Middle Miocene hominoid from Thailand and orangutan origins. *Nature* 422:61–65.

Ciochon, R., J. Olsen, and J. James. 1990. *Other origins: The search for the giant ape in human prehistory.* New York: Bantam Books.

Ciochon, R. L., and J. G. Fleagle, eds. 1993. *The human evolution source book.* Englewood Cliffs, NJ: Prentice Hall.

Clark, G. A., and C. M. Willermet, eds. 1997. *Conceptual issues in modern human origins research.* New York: Aldine de Gruyter.

Clark, J. D., et al. 2003. Stratigraphic, chronological and behavioral contexts of Pleistocene *Homo sapiens* from Middle Awash, Ethiopia. *Nature* 423:747–52.

Cohen, J. E. 1996. Ten myths of population. *Discover,* April, 42–47.

Collard, M., and L. C. Aiello. 2000. From forelimbs to two legs. *Nature* 404:339–40.

Conroy, G. C. 1997. *Reconstructing human origins: A modern synthesis.* New York: Norton.

Conway Morris, S. 1998. *The crucible of creation: The Burgess Shale and the rise of animals.* New York: Oxford.

Conway Morris, S., and S. J. Gould. 1998–1999. Showdown on the Burgess Shale. *Natural History* 107 (10): 48–55.

Coon, C. 1962. *The origin of races.* New York: Knopf.

Cooper, R. S., C. N. Rotimi, and R. Ward. 1999. The puzzle of hypertension in African-Americans. *Scientific American,* February: 56–63.

Coppens, Y. 1994. East side story: The origin of humankind. *Scientific American* 270:88–95.

Couzin, J. 2002. Small RNAs make big splash. *Science* 298:2296–97.

Cowen, R. 1995. *History of life.* 2nd ed. Boston: Blackwell Scientific Publications.

Crossette, B. 2001. Against a trend, U.S. population will bloom, U.N. says. *New York Times,* 28 February, A6.

Crow, T. J., ed. 2002. *The speciation of modern* Homo sapiens. Oxford: Oxford University Press (for The British Academy).

Culotta, E. 1999a. A new human ancestor? *Science* 284:572–73.

———. 1999b. Anthropologists probe bones, stones, and molecules. *Science* 284:1109–11.

Cummins, H., and C. Midlo. 1961. *Finger prints, palms, and soles: An introduction to dermatoglyphics.* New York: Dover.

Darwin, C. R. 1898. On the origin of species by means of natural selection. 1872. 6th ed. New York: Appleton.

De Bonis, L., and G. D. Koufos. 1994. Our ancestor's ancestor: *Ouranopithecus* is a Greek link in human ancestry. *Evolutionary Anthropology* 3 (3): 75–83.

Defleur, A., T. White, P. Valensi, L. Slimak, and E. Crégut-Bonnoure. 1999. Neanderthal cannibalism at Moula-Guercy, Ardèch, France. *Science* 286:128–31.

de Heinzelin, J. J., D. Clark, T. White, W. Hart, P. Renne, G. Wolde-Gabriel, Y. Beyene, and E. Vrba. 1999. Environment and behavior of 2.5-million-year-old Bouri hominids. *Science* 284:624–29.

de Waal, F., and F. Lanting (photographer). 1997. *Bonobo: The forgotten ape.* Berkeley: University of California Press.

de Waal, F. B. M. 1995. Bonobo sex and society. *Scientific American,* March, 82–88.

Diamond, J. 1991. Curse and blessing of the ghetto. *Discover,* March, 60–65.

Dickson J. H., K. Oeggl, and L. L. Handley. 2003. The Iceman reconsidered. *Scientific American,* May: 70–79.

DiPietro, L. 2000. Tackling race and sports. *Scientific American,* May: 73–76.

Dobzhansky, T. 1970. *Genetics of the evolutionary process.* New York: Columbia University Press.

Dolhinow, P., and A. Fuentes, 1999. *The nonhuman primates.* Mountain View, CA: Mayfield.

Donnelly, C. A. 2000. Likely size of the French BSE epidemic. *Nature* 408: 787–88.

Donnelly, P., S. Tavaré, D. J. Balding, and R. C. Griffiths. 1996. Technical comments: Estimating the age of the common ancestor of men from the ZFY intron. *Science* 272:1357–58.

Dorit, R. L., H. Akashi, and W. Gilbert. 1995. Absence of polymorphism at the ZFY locus on the human Y chromosome. *Science* 268:1183–85.

Duarte, C., J. Mauricio, P. B. Pettiee, P. Souto, E. Trinkhaus, H. Van der Plicht, and J. Zilhão. 1999. The early Upper Paleolithic human skeleton from the Abrigo od Lagar Velho (Portugal) and modern human emergence in Iberia. *Proceedings of the National Academy of Sciences* 96:7604–9.

Dunham, I., N. Shimizu, B. A. Roe, S. Chissoe, et al. 1999. The DNA sequence of human chromosome 22. *Nature* 402:489–95.

Eaton, S. B., and M. Konner. 1985. Diet: Paleolithic genes and twentieth-century health. *Anthroquest,* The L. S. B. Leakey Foundation, 1985.

Eldredge, N. 1991. *The miner's canary: Unraveling the mysteries of extinction.* New York: Prentice Hall.

———. 1995. *Dominion.* New York: Holt.

Entine, J. 2000. *Taboo: Why black athletes dominate sports and why we're afraid to talk about it.* New York: PublicAffairs Books.

Epstein, P. R. 2000. Is global warming harmful to health? *Scientific American,* August: 50–57.

Fagan, B. 1994. *In the beginning: An introduction to archaeology.* 8th ed. New York: HarperCollins.

Fagan, B. M. 1990. *The journey from Eden: The peopling of our world.* London: Thames and Hudson.

Fausto-Sterling, A. 1993. The five sexes. *Sciences,* March–April, 20–24.

———. 2000. The five sexes, revisited. *The Sciences* July–August: 18–23.

Feder, K. L. 1996. *The past in perspective: An introduction to human prehistory.* Mountain View, CA: Mayfield.

———. 1997. Indians and archaeologists: The conflicting views of myth and science. *Skeptic* 5 (3): 74–80.

———. 1999. *Lessons from the past: An introductory reader in archaeology.* Mountain View, CA: Mayfield.

———. 2001. *Frauds, myths, and mysteries: Science and pseudoscience in archaeology.* 4th ed. Mountain View, CA: Mayfield.

Feder, K. L., and M. A. Park. 2001. *Human antiquity: An introduction to physical anthropology and archaeology.* 4th ed. Mountain View, CA: Mayfield.

Fedigan, L. M., and L. Fedigan. 1988. *Gender and the study of primates: Curricular module for the Project on Gender and Curriculum.* Washington, DC: American Anthropological Association.

Ferris, Timothy. 1988. *Coming of age in the Milky Way.* New York: Morrow.

Fleagle, J. G. 1988. *Primate adaptation and evolution.* San Diego: Academic Press.

Fortey, R. 1998. *Life: A natural history of the first four billion years of life on earth.* New York: Knopf.

Fossey, D. 1983. *Gorillas in the mist.* Boston: Houghton Mifflin.

Fouts, R., with S. T. Mills. 1997. *Next of kin: What chimpanzees have taught me about who we are.* New York: Morrow.

Fouts, R. S., and D. H. Fouts. 1999. Chimpanzee sign language research. In *The nonhuman primates,* ed. P. Dolhinow and A. Fuentes. Mountain View, CA: Mayfield.

Francione, G. L. 1996. *Rain without thunder: The ideology of the animal rights movement.* Philadelphia: Temple University Press.

Frayer, D. W., M. H. Wolpoff, A. G. Thorne, F. H. Smith, and G. G. Pope. 1993. Theories of modern human origins: The paleontological test. *American Anthropologist* 95 (1): 14–50.

———. 1994. Getting it straight. *American Anthropologist* 96:424–38.

Fu, Y-X, and W-H Li. 1996. Estimating the age of the common ancestor of men from the ZFY intron. *Science* 272:1356–57.

Gaffney, E. S., L. Dingus, and M. K. Smith. 1995. Why cladistics? *Natural History* 104 (6): 33–35.

Galdikas, B. 1995. *Reflections of Eden: My years with the orangutans of Borneo.* Boston: Little, Brown.

Gebo, D. L., M. Dagosto, K. C. Beard, T. Qi, and J. Wang. 2000. The oldest known anthropoid postcranial fossil and the early evolution of the higher primates. *Nature* 404:276–78.

Gebo, D. L., L. MacLatchy, R. Kityo, A. Deino, J. Kingston, and D. Pilbeam. 1997. A hominoid genus from the early Miocene of Uganda. *Science* 276:401–4.

Gee, H. 2001. Return to the planet of the apes. *Nature* 412:131–32.

Gibbons, A. 1997a. Tracing the identity of the first toolmakers. *Science* 276:32.

———. 1997b. A new face for human ancestors. *Science* 276 (30 May): 1331–33.

———. 1997c. Doubts over spectacular dates. *Science* 278:220–22.

———. 1997d. Y chromosome shows that Adam was an African. *Science* 278:804–5.

———. 1998a. Genes put mammals in age of dinosaurs. *Science* 289:675–76.

———. 1998b. Which of our genes makes us human? *Science* 281:1432–34.

———. 2001. The peopling of the Pacific. *Science* 291:1735–37.

Gish, Duane T. 1979. *Evolution: The fossils say no!* San Diego: Creation-Life Publishers.

Glausiusz, J. 1995. Unfortunate drift. *Discover*, June, 34–35.

Goldman, E. 2003. Puzzling over the origin of species in the depths of the oldest lakes. *Science* 299:654–55.

Goodall, J. 1971. *In the shadow of man.* Boston: Houghton Mifflin.

———. 1986. *The chimpanzees of Gombe: Patterns of behavior.* Cambridge, MA: Belknap.

———. 1990. *Through a window: My thirty years with the chimpanzees of Gombe.* Boston: Houghton Mifflin.

Gore, R. 1989. Extinctions. *National Geographic* 175 (6): 662–99.

———. 1993. The Cambrian period: Explosion of life. *National Geographic* 184 (4): 120–36.

———. 1997a. Expanding worlds. *National Geographic* 191 (5): 84–109.

———. 1997b. The first Europeans. *National Geographic* 192 (1): 96–113.

———. 2002a. The first pioneer? *National Geographic* 202 (August): xxxvii–xlvii.

———. 2002b. New find. *National Geographic* (August).

Goudsmit, J. 1997. *Viral sex: The nature of AIDS.* New York: Oxford University Press.

Gould, S. J. 1977. *Ever since Darwin.* New York: Norton.

———. 1980. *The panda's thumb.* New York: Norton.

———. 1983. *Hen's teeth and horse's toes.* New York: Norton.

———. 1985. *The flamingo's smile.* New York: Norton.

———. 1989. *Wonderful life: The Burgess Shale and the nature of history.* New York: Norton.

———. 1991. *Bully for brontosaurus.* New York: Norton.

———. 1992. What is a species? *Discover*, December: 40–45.

———, ed. 1993a. *The book of life.* New York: Norton.

———. 1993b. *Eight little piggies.* New York: Norton.

———. 1994a. The evolution of life on the earth. *Scientific American* 271 (4): 84–91.

———. 1994b. In the mind of the beholder. *Natural History* 103 (2): 14–23.

———. 1995a. *Dinosaur in a haystack: Reflections in natural history.* New York: Harmony.

———. 1995b. Of tongue worms, velvet worms, and water bears. *Natural History* 104 (1): 6–15.

———. 1995c. Evolution by walking. *Natural History* 104 (3): 10–15.

———. 1996a. *Full house: The spread of excellence from Plato to Darwin.* New York: Harmony.

———. 1996b. *The mismeasure of man.* 2nd ed. New York: Norton.

———. 1997–1998. The paradox of the visibly irrelevant. *Natural History* 106 (11): 12–18, 60–66.

———. 1998. *Leonardo's mountain of clams and the Diet of Worms: Essays on natural history.* New York: Harmony.

———. 1999. *Rocks of ages: Science and religion in the fullness of life.* New York: Ballantine.

———. 2000. *The lying stones of Marrakech: Penultimate reflections in natural history.* New York: Harmony.

———. 2002a. *I have landed: The end of a beginning in natural history.* New York: Vintage.

———. 2002b. *The structure of evolutionary theory.* Cambridge, MA: Belknap.

Grant, P., and R. Grant. 2000. Non-random fitness variation in two populations of Darwin's finches. *Proceedings of the Royal Society of London* 267 (1439): 131–38.

Grant, P. R., and B. R. Grant. 2002. Unpredictable evolution in a 30-year study of Darwin's finches. *Science* 296:707–11.

Greene, J. C. 1959. *The death of Adam.* New York: Mentor.

Groves, C. P. 1997. Thinking about evolutionary change: The polarity of our ancestors. In *Conceptual issues in modern human origins research*, ed. G. A. Clark and C. M. Willermet, 319–26. New York: Aldine de Gruyter.

Guth, A. H. 2000. Genesis: The sequel. *Natural History* 109 (1): 77–79.

Hahn, B. H., G. M. Shaw, K. M. De Cock, and P. M. Sharp. 2000. AIDS as a zoonosis: Scientific and public health implications. *Science* 287:607–14.

Haile-Selassie, Y. 2001. Late Miocene hominids from the Middle Awash, Ethiopia. *Nature* 412:178–81.

Hammer, M. F., and S. L. Zegura. 1996. The role of the Y chromosome in human evolutionary studies. *Evolutionary Anthropology* 5 (4): 116–34.

Hansen, J. P., J. Meldgaard, and J. Nordqvist. 1985. The mummies of Qilakitsoq. *National Geographic* 167 (2): 191–207.

Harpending, H., and J. Relethford. 1997. Population perspectives on human origins research. In *Conceptual issues in modern human origins research*, ed. G. A. Clark and C. M. Willermet. New York: Aldine de Gruyter.

Harris, C. L. 1981. *Evolution: Genesis and revelations.* Albany: State University of New York Press.

Harrison, G. A., and A. J. Boyce, eds. 1972. *The Structure of human populations.* Oxford: Clarendon.

Harrison, G. A., J. S. Weiner, J. M. Tanner, and N. A. Barnicot. 1977. *Human biology: An introduction to human evolution, variation, growth, and ecology.* 2nd ed. Oxford: Oxford University Press.

Hawks, J., and M. H. Wolpoff. 2001. Brief communication: Paleoanthropology and the population genetics of ancient genes. *American Journal of Physical Anthropology* 114:269–72.

Hedges, S. B., S. Kumar, K. Tamura, and M. Stoneking. 1992. Technical comments. *Science* 255:737–39.

Henshilwood, C. S., F. d'Errico, R. Yates, A. Jacobs, C. Tribolo, G. A. T. Duller, N. Mercier, J. C. Sealy,

H. Valladas, I. Watts, and A. G. Wintle. 2002. Emergence of modern human behavior: Middle stone age engravings from South Africa. *Science* 295:1278–80.

Hern, W. M. 1993. Is human culture carcinogenic for uncontrolled population growth and ecological destruction? *BioScience* 43 (11): 768–73.

Herrnstein, R. J., and C. Murray. 1994. *The bell curve: The reshaping of American life by difference in intelligence.* New York: Free Press.

Hill, K. 1993. Life history theory and evolutionary anthropology. *Evolutionary Anthropology* 2 (3): 78–88.

Holden, C. 1998. No last word on language origins. *Science* 282:1455–58.

———. 1999. Patrimony debate gets ugly. *Science* 285:195.

———. 2001a. Oldest human DNA reveals Aussie oddity. *Science* 291:230–31.

———. 2001b. Dinner in a mound. *Science* 291:587.

Holliday, T. W. 1997. Postcranial evidence of cold adaptation in European Neandertals. *American Journal of Physical Anthropology* 104:245–58.

Holloway, R. 1980. Indonesian "Solo" (Ngandong) endocranial reconstructions: Preliminary observations and comparisons with Neandertal and *Homo erectus* groups. *American Journal of Physical Anthropology* 53:285–95.

———. 1981. The Indonesian *Homo erectus* brain endocasts revisited. *American Journal of Physical Anthropology* 55:503–21.

Hostetler, J. A. 1974. *Hutterite society.* Baltimore: Johns Hopkins University Press.

Huyghe, P. 1988. No bone unturned. *Discover* (December).

Ingman, M., H. Kaessmann, S. Pääbo, and U. Gyllensten. 2000. Mitochondrial genome variation and the origin of modern humans. *Nature* 408:708–13.

Ingmanson, E. 1996. Tool-using behavior in wild *Pan paniscus*: Social and ecological considerations. In *Reaching into thought: The minds of the great apes*, ed. A. Russon, K. Bard, and S. Taylor. Cambridge: Cambridge University Press.

Ingmanson, E., and H. Ihobe. 1992. Predation and meat eating by *Pan paniscus* at Wamba, Zaire.

Paper delivered at the 61st Annual Meeting of the American Association of Physical Anthropologists, Las Vegas, NV.

Ingmanson, E., and T. Kano. 1993. Waging peace. *International Wildlife*, November–December, 30–37.

International HapMap Consortium. 2003. The international HapMap project. *Nature* 426:789–96.

International SNP Map Working Group. 2001. A map of human genome sequence variation contains 1.42 million single nucleotide polymorphisms. *Nature* 409:928–33.

Jablonski, N. G., and G. Chaplin. 2000a. Do theories of bipedalization stand up to anatomical scrutiny? Paper delivered at the 69th Annual Meeting of the American Association of Physical Anthropologists, San Antonio, TX.

———. 2000b. The evolution of human skin coloration. *Journal of Human Evolution* 39 (1): 57–106.

———. 2002. Skin deep. *Scientific American*, October: 74–81.

Jaeger, J.-J., et al. 1999. A new primate from the Middle Eocene of Myanmar and the Asian early origin on anthropoids. *Science* 286:528–30.

Janus, C. 1975. *The search for Peking Man*. New York: Macmillan.

Jegalian, K., and B. T. Lahn. 2001. Why the Y is so weird. *Scientific American*, February, 56–61.

Jensen, A. R. 1969. How much can we boost IQ and scholastic achievement? *Harvard Educational Review* 39 (1, Winter): 1–123.

Jobling, M. A., and C. Tyler-Smith. 1995. Fathers and sons: The Y chromosome and human evolution. *Trends in Genetics* 11:449–56.

Johanson, D., and J. Shreeve. 1989. *Lucy's child: The discovery of a human ancestor*. New York: Morrow.

Johanson, D. C., and M. A. Edey. 1981. *Lucy: The beginnings of humankind*. New York: Simon & Schuster.

Johnson, T. C., C. A. Scholz, M. R. Talbot, K. Kelts, R. D. Ricketts, G. Ngobi, K. Beuning, I. Ssemmanda, and J. W. McGill. 1996. Late Pleistocene dessication of Lake Victoria and rapid evolution of cichlid fishes. *Science* 273 (23 August): 1091–93.

Jolly, A. 1985. *The evolution of primate behavior*. New York: Macmillan.

———. 1988. Madagascar's lemurs: On the edge of survival. *National Geographic* 174 (2): 132–61.

Junta de Castilla y León. 2003. *The first Europeans: Treasures from the hills of Atapuerca*. New York: Junta de Castilla y León.

Kano, T. 1990. The bonobos' peaceable kingdom. *Natural History*, November, 62–71.

Kay, R. F., C. Ross, and B. A. Williams. 1997. Anthropoid origins. *Science* 275 (7 February): 797–804.

Ke, Y., et al. 2001. African origin of modern humans in East Asia: A tale of 12,000 Y chromosomes. *Science* 292:1151–53.

Keith, A. 1927. *Concerning man's origin*. London: Watts.

Kennedy, K. A. R. 1976. *Human variation in space and time*. Dubuque, IA: Brown.

Kerr, R. A. 2001. Evolutionary pulse found, but complexity as well. *Science* 293:2377.

King, M-C, and A. Motulsky. 2002. Mapping human history. *Science* 298:2342–43.

Kingston, J. D., B. D. Marino, and A. Hill. 1994. Isotopic evidence for neocene hominid paleoenvironments in the Kenya Rift Valley. *Science* 264:955–59.

Kirkpatrick, M. 2000. Fish found in *flagrante delicto*. *Nature* 408:298–99.

Korber, B., M. Muldoon, J. Theiler, F. Gao, R. Gupta, A. Lapedes, B. H. Hahn, S. Wolinsky, and T. Bhattacharya. 2000. Timing the ancestor of the HIV-1 pandemic strains. *Science* 288:1789–96.

Krings, M., H. Geisert, R. W. Schmitz, H. Krainitzki, and S. Pääbo. 1999. DNA sequence of the mitochondrial hypervariable region II from the Neandertal type specimen. *Proceedings of the National Academy of Sciences* 96 (10): 5581–85.

Krings, M., A. Stone, R. W. Schmitz, H. Krainitzki, M. Stoneking, and S. Pääbo. 1997. Neandertal DNA sequences and the origin of modern humans. *Cell* 90 (1): 19–30.

Kunzig, R. 1997. The face of an ancestral child. *Discover* 18 (12): 88–101.

Lack, D. 1947. *Darwin's finches: An essay on the general biological theory of evolution*. Cambridge: Cambridge University Press.

Leakey, M. G., C. S. Feibel, I. McDougall, and A. Walker. 1995. New four-million-year-old hominid species from Kanapoi and Allia Bay, Kenya. *Nature* 376:565–71.

Leakey, M. G., F. Spoor, F. H. Brown, P. N. Gathogo, C. Kiarie, L. N. Leakey, and I. McDougall. 2001. New hominid genus from eastern Africa shows diverse Middle Pliocene lineages. *Nature* 410: 433–40.

Leakey, M. G., F. Spoor, F. H. Brown, P. N. Gathogo, and L. N. Leakey. 2003. A new hominin calvaria from Ileret (Kenya). Paper delivered at the 72nd Annual Meeting of the American Association of Physical Anthropologists, Tempe, AZ.

Leakey, R., and R. Lewin. 1992. *Origins reconsidered: In search of what makes us human.* New York: Doubleday.

———. 1995. *The sixth extinction: Patterns of life and the future of humankind.* New York: Doubleday.

Lemonick, M. D. 1994. One less missing link. *Time,* 3 October, 68–69.

Leonard, W. R. 2002. Food for thought. *Scientific American,* December: 106–15.

Lewin, R. 1991. The biochemical route to human origins. *Mosaic* 22 (3): 46–55.

Lewontin, R. 1982. *Human diversity.* New York: Scientific American Books.

Lindenbaum, S. 1979. *Kuru sorcery: Disease and danger in the New Guinea highlands.* Mountain View, CA: Mayfield.

Livingstone, F. B. 1958. Anthropological implications of sickle cell gene distribution in West Africa. *American Anthropologist* 60:533–62.

Lyell, C. 1873. *The geological evidences of the antiquity of man.* London: Murray.

Madigan, M. T., and B. L. Marrs. 1997. Extremophiles. *Scientific American,* April, 82–87.

Malik, K. 2000. Sporting colours. *Nature* 407:131–32.

Malthus, T. R. 1789. *An essay on the principles of population as it affects the future improvement of society with remarks on the speculations of Mr. Godwin, M. Condorcet and other writers* (facsimile of the first edition, 1926), London: Macmillan.

Maples, W. R., and M. Browning. 1994. *Dead men do tell tales.* New York: Doubleday.

Marks, J. 1994. Book reviews. *Human Biology* 66: 1113–17.

———. 1995. *Human biodiversity: Genes, race, and history.* New York: Aldine de Gruyter.

———. 2002. *What it means to be 98% chimpanzee: Apes, people, and their genes.* Berkeley: University of California Press.

Marks, J., and R. B. Lyles. 1994. Rethinking genes. *Evolutionary Anthropology* 3 (4): 139–46.

Martin, M. K., and B. Voorhies. 1975. *Female of the species.* New York: Columbia University Press.

Martin, R. D. 1993. Primate origins: Plugging the gap. *Nature* (20 May): 223–24.

McCollum, M. A. 1999. The robust australopithecine face: A morphogenic perspective. *Science* 284:301–4.

McCrossin, M. L. 1997. New postcranial remains of *Kenyapithecus* and their implications for understanding the origins of hominoid terrestriality. Paper delivered at the 66th Annual Meeting of the American Association of Physical Anthropologists, St. Louis, MO.

McGrew, W. C. 1998. Culture in nonhuman primates? *Annual Review of Anthropology* 27:301–28.

Menon, S. 1997. Neanderthal noses. *Discover,* March: 30.

Mercader, J., M. Panger, and C. Boesch. 2002. Excavation of a chimpanzee stone tool site in the African rainforest. *Science* 296:1452–55.

Mettler, L. E., T. G. Gregg, and H. E. Schaffer. 1988. *Population genetics and evolution.* Englewood Cliffs, NJ: Prentice Hall.

Miller, K. R. 1999. *Finding Darwin's god.* New York: HarperCollins.

Mills, C. 1997. The deadliest virus. *Sciences,* January– February, 34–38.

Minugh-Purvis, N. 1995. The modern human origins controversy: 1984–1994. *Evolutionary Anthropology* 4 (4): 140–47.

Molnar, S. 1992. *Human variation: Races, types, and ethnic groups.* 3rd ed. Englewood Cliffs, NJ: Prentice Hall.

Montagu, A., ed. 1964. *The concept of race.* New York: Collier.

Morris, H. M. 1974. *The troubled waters of evolution.* San Diego, CA: Creation-Life Publishers.

Mosko, S., C. Richard, J. McKenna, S. Drummond, and D. Mukai. 1997. Maternal proximity and infant CO_2 environment during bedsharing and possible implications for SIDS research. *American Journal of Physical Anthropology* 103 (3): 315–28.

Mowat, F. 1987. *Woman in the mists.* New York: Warner.

Muchmore, E. A., S. Diaz, and A. Varki. 1998. A structural difference between the cell surfaces of humans and great apes. *American Journal of Physical Anthropology* 107:187–98.

Müller, W., H. Fricke, A. N. Halliday, M. T. McCulloch, and J-A. Wartho. 2003. Origin and migration of the Alpine Iceman. *Science* 302:862–65.

Nafte, M. 2000. *Flesh and bone.* Durham, NC: Carolina Academic Press.

Nanda, S. 1990. *Neither man nor woman: The hijras of India.* Belmont, CA: Wadsworth.

Nesse, R. M., and G. C. Williams. 1998. Evolution and the origins of disease. *Scientific American,* November: 52–58.

Nichols, M., J. Goodall, G. B. Schaller, and M. G. Smith. 1993. *The great apes: Between two worlds.* Washington, DC: National Geographic Society.

Normile, D. 2001. Gene expression differs in human and chimp brains. *Science* 292:44–45.

O'Brien, S. J., and R. Stanyon. 1999. Ancestral primate revealed. *Nature* 402 (25 November): 356–66.

Oliwenstein, L. 1995. Dr. Darwin. *Discover,* October: 111–17.

Olshansky, S. J., B. A. Carnes, and A. Désesquelles. 2001. Prospects for human longevity. *Science* 291:1491–92.

Omohundro, J. T. 2001. *Careers in anthropology.* 2nd ed. Mountain View, CA: Mayfield.

Orgel, L. E. 1994. The origin of life on the earth. *Scientific American* 271 (4): 76–83.

Ovchinnikov, I., A. Götherström, G. Romanova, V. Kharitonov, K. Lindén, and W. Goodman. 2000. Molecular analysis of Neandertal DNA from the northern Caucasus. *Nature* 404:490–92.

Pääbo, S. 2001. The human genome and our view of ourselves. *Science* 291:1219–20.

Park, M. A. 1979. Dermatoglyphics as a tool for population studies: An example. Ph.D. dissertation, Department of Anthropology, Indiana University, Bloomington.

———. 1982–1983. Palmistry: Science or hand-jive? *The Skeptical Inquirer* 7 (2): 21–32.

———. 1999. The homegoing. In *Lessons from the past,* ed. K. L. Feder, 80–83. Mountain View, CA: Mayfield.

———. 2002. *Biological anthropology: An introductory reader.* 3rd ed. New York: McGraw-Hill.

———. 2003. *Introducing anthropology: An integrated approach.* 2nd ed. New York: McGraw-Hill.

Partridge, T. C., D. E. Granger, M. W. Caffee, and R. J. Clarke. 2003. Lower Pliocene hominid remains from Sterkfontein. *Science* 300:607–12.

Passingham, R. 1982. *The human primate.* New York: Freeman.

Pearson, O. M. 2000. Postcranial remains and the origin of modern humans. *Evolutionary Anthropology* 9 (6): 229–47.

Pennisi, E. 2001. Malaria's beginnings: On the heels of hoes? *Science* 293:416–17.

Perry, W., and M. Blakey. 1999. Archaeology as community service: The African Burial Ground Project in New York City. In *Lessons from the past,* ed. K. L. Feder, 45–51. Mountain View, CA: Mayfield.

Pfeiffer, J. 1969. *The emergence of man.* New York: Harper & Row.

———. 1996. When *Homo erectus* tamed fire, he tamed himself. *New York Times Magazine,* December 11.

Pilbeam, D. 1984. The descent of the hominoids and hominids. *Scientific American* 250 (3): 84–96.

———. 1986. Human origins. *David Skomp Distinguished Lecture in Anthropology.* Bloomington: Indiana University.

Podolefsky, A., and P. J. Brown, eds. 1994. *Applying anthropology: An introductory reader.* 5th ed. Mountain View, CA: Mayfield.

Podos, J. 2001. Correlated evolution of morphology and vocal signal structure in Darwin's finches. *Nature* 409:185–87.

Post, P. W., F. Daniels, Jr., and R. T. Binford. 1975. Cold injury and the evolution of "white" skin. *Human Biology* 47:65–80.

Potts, R. 1984. Home bases and early hominids. *American Scientist* 72:338–47.

———. 1996. Evolution and climate variability. *Science* 273 (16 August): 922–23.

———. 1998. Variability selection in hominid evolution. *Evolutionary Anthropology* 7:81–96.

Power, M. 1991. *The egalitarians—human and chimpanzee: An anthropological view of social organization.* Cambridge: Cambridge University Press.

Prag, J., and R. Neave. 1997. *Making faces: Using forensic and archaeological evidence.* College Station: Texas A&M University Press.

Prum, R. O., and A. H. Brush. 2003. Which came first, the feather or the bird? *Scientific American,* March: 84–93.

Prusiner, S. B. 1997. Prion diseases and the BSE crisis. *Science* 278 (10 October): 245–51.

Raby, P. 1996. *Bright paradise: Victorian scientific travellers.* Princeton: Princeton University Press.

Ragir, S. 2000. Diet and food preparation: Rethinking early hominid behavior. *Evolutionary Anthropology* 9 (4): 153–55.

Reinhard, J. 1996. Peru's ice maidens. *National Geographic* 189 (6): 62–81.

———. 1997. Mummies of Peru. *National Geographic* 191 (1): 36–43.

———. 1999. Frozen in time. *National Geographic* 196 (5): 36–55.

Relethford, J. H. 2001. *Genetics and the search for modern human origins.* New York: Wiley-Liss.

———. 2003a. *The human species: An introduction to biological anthropology.* 5th ed. New York: McGraw-Hill.

———. 2003b. *Reflections of our past: how human history is revealed in our genes.* Boulder, CO: Westview.

Relethford, J. H., and H. C. Harpending. 1995. Ancient differences in population size can mimic a recent African origin of modern humans. *Current Anthropology* 36 (4): 667–74.

Rhine, S. 1998. *Bone voyage: A journey in forensic anthropology.* Albuquerque: University of New Mexico Press.

Rhodes, R. 1997. *Deadly feasts: Tracking the secrets of a terrifying new plague.* New York: Simon & Schuster.

Richmond, B. G., and D. S. Strait. 2000. Evidence that humans evolved from a knuckle-walking ancestor. *Nature* 404:382–85.

Ridley, Mark. 1996. *Evolution.* 2nd ed. Boston: Blackwell Scientific Publications.

Ridley, Matt. 1999. *Genome: The autobiography of a species in 23 chapters.* New York: HarperCollins.

Roberts, D. 1993. The Ice Man. *National Geographic* 183 (6): 36–67.

Robey, B., S. O. Rutstein, and L. Morris. 1993. The fertility decline in developing countries. *Scientific American,* December: 60–67.

Robins, A. 1991. *Biological perspectives on human pigmentation.* Cambridge: Cambridge University Press.

Rogers, J., P. B. Samollow, and A. G. Comuzzie. 1996. Estimating the age of the common ancestor of men from the ZFY intron. *Science* 272:1360–61.

Rosenberg, N. A., J. K. Pritchard, J. L. Weber, H. M. Cann, K. K. Kidd, L. A. Zhivotovsky, and M. W. Feldman. 2002. Genetic structure of human populations. *Science* 298:2381–85.

Rowe, N. 1996. *The pictorial guide to the living primates.* East Hampton, NY: Pogonius.

Rowen, L., G. Mahairas, and L. Hood. 1997. Sequencing the human genome. *Science* 278 (24 October): 605–7.

Ryan, F. 1997. *Virus X: Tracking the new killer plagues out of the present and into the future.* Boston: Little, Brown.

Sagan, C. 1977. *The dragons of Eden: speculations on the evolution of human intelligence.* New York: Random House.

———. 1996. *The demon-haunted world: Science as a candle in the dark.* New York: Random House.

Sargis, E. J. 2002. Primate origins nailed. *Science* 298:1564–65.

Savage-Rumbaugh, E. S., S. Shanker, T. J. Taylor, and S. Savage-Rumbaugh. 1998. *Apes, language, and the human mind.* Oxford: Oxford University Press.

Savage-Rumbaugh, S., and R. Lewin. 1994a. Ape at the brink. *Discover,* September: 91–98.

———. 1994b. *Kanzi: The ape at the brink of the human mind.* New York: Wiley.

Schadewald, R. 1981–1982. Scientific creationism, geocentricity and the flat earth. *Skeptical Inquirer* 6 (2): 41–48.

———. 1986. Creationist pseudoscience. In *Science confronts the paranormal*, ed. Kendrick Frazier. Buffalo, NY: Prometheus.

Schick, K. D., and N. Toth. 1993. *Making silent stones speak: Human evolution and the dawn of technology.* New York: Morrow.

Schoeninger, M. J. 1995. Stable isotope studies in human evolution. *Evolutionary Anthropology* 4 (3): 83–98.

Scholz, M., L. Bachmann, G. J. Nicholson, J. Bachmann, I. Giddings, B. Rüschoff-Thale, A. Czarnetzki, and C. M. Pusch. 2000. Genomic differentiation of Neanderthals and anatomically modern man allows a fossil DNA-based classification of morphologically indistinguishable hominid bones. *American Journal of Human Genetics* 66:1927–32.

Schultz, E., and R. Lavenda. 1998. *Anthropology: A perspective on the human condition.* 2nd ed. Mountain View, CA: Mayfield.

Schuster, A. M. H. 2001. World's oldest woodworking? *Archaeology Online News* 31 January.

———. 2001. World's earliest woodworking? *Archaeology Online News,* January 31. www.archaeology.org/online/news.

Schwartz, J. H. 1995. *Skeleton keys: An introduction to human skeletal morphology, development, and analysis.* New York: Oxford University Press.

Science. 2003. Iceman fights back. *Science* 301:1043.

Semaw, S., P. Renne, J. W. K. Harris, C. S. Feibel, R. L. Bernor, N. Fesseha, and K. Mowbray. 1997. 2.5-million-year-old stone tools from Gona, Ethiopia. *Nature* 385 (23 January): 333–36.

Service, R. F. 2000. Where dead men really do tell tales. *Science* 289:855–57.

Sewa, G., B. Asfaw, Y. Beyene, T. D. White, S. Katoh, S. Nagaoka, H. Nakaya, K. Uzawa, P. Renne, and G. WoldeGabriel. 1997. The first skull of *Australopithecus boisei. Nature* 389 (2 October): 489–92.

Sharer, R. J., and W. Ashmore. 1993. *Archaeology: Discovering our past.* 2nd ed. Mountain View, CA: Mayfield.

Shea, J. 1989. A functional study of the lithic industries associated with hominid fossils in Kebara and Qafzeh Caves, Israel. In *The human revolution: Behavioural and biological perspectives in the origins of modern humans,* ed. P. Mellars and C. Stringer, 611–25. Princeton, NJ: Princeton University Press.

Shermer, M. 2002. *In Darwin's shadow: The life and science of Alfred Russel Wallace.* New York: Oxford University Press.

Sherwood, R. J. 2000. The status of early *Homo.* Paper delivered at the 69th Annual Meeting of the American Association of Physical Anthropologists, San Antonio, TX.

Shipman, P. 1981. *Life history of a fossil: An introduction to taphonomy and paleoecology.* Cambridge, MA: Harvard University Press.

———. 1984. Scavenger hunt. *Natural History* 93 (4): 20–27.

———. 1986. Scavenging or hunting in early hominids: Theoretical frameworks and tests. *American Anthropologist* 88:27–43.

———. 2001. *The man who found the missing link: Eugene Dubois and his lifelong quest to prove Darwin right.* New York: Simon & Schuster.

Shipman, P., and J. Rose. 1983. Evidence of butchery and hominid activities at Torralba and Ambrona: An evaluation using microscopic techniques. *Journal of Archaeological Science* 10:465–74.

Shreeve, J. 1994. *Erectus* rising. *Discover,* September: 80–89.

———. 1995. The Neanderthal peace. *Discover,* September: 70–81.

———. 1996. Sunset on the savanna. *Discover* 17 (7): 116–25.

———. 1999. Secrets of the gene. *National Geographic* 196 (4): 42–75.

Simerly, C., et al. 2003. Molecular correlates of primate nuclear transfer failures. *Science* 300:297.

Simons, E. L., and T. Rasmussen. 1994. A whole new world of ancestors: Eocene anthropoideans from Africa. *Evolutionary Anthropology* 3 (4): 128–39.

Simons, M. 1996. New species of early human reported found in Africa. *New York Times,* 23 May, A8.

Smail, J. K. 1999. Beyond population stabilization: The case for dramatically reducing global human numbers. *Politics and Life Sciences* 16 (2):183–92.

Small, M. F. 1992. A reasonable sleep. *Discover,* April: 83–88.

Smith, B. H. 1993. Life history and the evolution of human maturation. *Evolutionary Anthropology* 1 (4): 134–42.

Smith, F. H. 1994. Samples, species, and speculations in the study of modern human origins. In *Origins of anatomically modern humans*, ed. M. Nitecki and D. Nitecki, 227–52. New York: Plenum.

Smith, F. H., A. B. Falsetti, and S. M. Donnelly. 1989. Modern human origins. *Yearbook of Physical Anthropology* 32:35–68.

Smith, J. M. 1984. Science and myth. *Natural History* 93 (11): 10–24.

Smith, S. L., and F. B. Harrold. 1997. A paradigm's worth of difference? Understanding the impasse over modern human origins. *Yearbook of Physical Anthropology* 40:113–38.

Smuts, B. 1985. *Sex and friendship in baboons.* Hawthorne, NY: Aldine de Gruyter.

———. 1995. Apes of wrath. *Discover,* August: 35–37.

Snow, C. C., and J. L. Luke. 1970. The Oklahoma City child disappearances: Forensic anthropology in the identification of skeletal remains. In *Applying anthropology*, ed. A. Podolefsky and P. J. Brown. Mountain View, CA: Mayfield.

Sokolove, M. 2004. The lab animal. *New York Times Magazine,* 18 January: 28–33, 48, 54, 58.

Specter, M. 1999. Decoding Iceland. *New Yorker,* 18 January, 40–51.

Sponheimer, M., and J. A. Lee-Thorp. 1999. Isotopic evidence for the diet of an early hominid, *Australopithecus africanus. Science* 283:368–69.

Stanford, C. 1999. *The hunting apes: Meat eating and the origins of human behavior.* Princeton: Princeton University Press.

Stanford, C. B. 1995. To catch a colobus. *Natural History* 104 (1): 48–55.

Stern, J. T., Jr. 2000. Climbing to the top: A personal memoir of *Australopithecus afarensis. Evolutionary Anthropology* 9 (3): 113–33.

Steudel, K. 1996. Limb morphology, bipedal gait, and the energetics of hominid locomotion. *American Journal of Physical Anthropology* 99 (2): 345–56.

Stinson, S. 2000. Growth variation: Biological and cultural factors. In *Human biology: An evolutionary and biocultural perspective*, ed. S. Stinson et al. New York: Wiley-Liss.

Stinson, S., B. Bogin, R. Huss-Ashmore, and D. O'Rourke, eds. 2000. *Human biology: An evolutionary and biocultural perspective.* New York: Wiley-Liss.

Stone, R. 2000. Ice Man warms up for European scientists. *Science* 289:2253–54.

Stoneking, M. 1993. DNA and recent human evolution. *Evolutionary Anthropology* 2 (2): 60–73.

———. 2001. From the evolutionary past . . . *Nature* 409:821–22.

Strait, D. S., and F. E. Grine. 1999. Cladistics and early hominid phylogeny. *Science* 285:1210.

Stringer, C. 1994. Out of Africa: A personal history. In *Origins of anatomically modern humans*, ed. M. H. Nitecki and D. V. Nitecki, 149–72. New York: Plenum.

———. 2003. Out of Ethiopia. *Nature* 423:692–95.

Stringer, C., and P. Andrews. 1988. Genetic and fossil evidence for the origin of modern humans. *Science* 239:1263–68.

Stringer, C., and C. Gamble. 1993. *In search of the neanderthals: Solving the puzzle of human origins.* London: Thames and Hudson.

Stringer, C., and R. McKie. 1996. *African exodus: The origins of modern humanity.* New York: Holt.

Strum, S. 1987. *Almost human.* New York: Random House.

Susman, R. L. 1994. Fossil evidence for early hominid tool use. *Science* 265 (9 September): 1570–73.

Sussman, R. W. 1997. Exploring our basic human nature: Are humans inherently violent? *Anthro-Notes* 19 (3).

———, ed. 1999. *The biological basis of human behavior: A critical review.* 2nd ed. Upper Saddle River, NJ: Prentice Hall.

Suwa, G., et al. 1997. The first skull of *Australopithecus boisei. Nature* 389:489–92.

Takai, M., F. Anaya, N. Shigehara, and T. Setoguchi. 2000. New fossil materials of the earliest New World monkey, *Branisella boliviana*, and the problem of platyrrhine origins. *American Journal of Physical Anthropology* 111:263–81.

Tattersall, I. 1992. The many faces of *Homo habilis. Evolutionary Anthropology* 1 (1): 33–37.

———. 1993. *The human odyssey: Four million years of human evolution.* New York: Prentice Hall.

———. 1994. What do we mean by human—and why does it matter? *Evolutionary Anthropology* 3 (4): 114–16.

———. 1995. *The last neanderthal: The rise, success, and mysterious extinction of our closest human relatives.* New York: Macmillan.

———. 2001. How we came to be human. *Scientific American,* December: 56–63.

Tattersall, I., and J. Schwarz. 2000. *Extinct humans.* Boulder, CO: Westview.

Tavaré, S., C. R. Marshall, O. Will, C. Soligo, and R. D. Martin. 2002. Using the fossil record to estimate the age of the last common ancestor of extant primates. *Nature* 416:726–29.

Teitelbaum, M. S., ed. 1976. *Sex differences.* Garden City, NY: Anchor Press/Doubleday.

Templeton, A. R. 1993. The "Eve" hypothesis: A genetic critique and reanalysis. *American Anthropologist* 95:51–72.

———. 1996. Gene lineages and human evolution. *Science* 272:1363.

———. 1997. Testing the Out of Africa replacement hypothesis with mitochondrial DNA data. In *Conceptual issues in modern human origins research,* ed. G. A. Clark and C. M. Willermet. New York: Aldine de Gruyter.

———. 2002. Out of Africa again and again. *Nature* 416:45–51.

Thieme, H. 1997. Lower Paleolithic hunting spears from Germany. *Nature* 385:807–10.

Thompson, M. J., and D. W. Harsha. 1984. Our rhythms still follow the African sun. *Psychology Today,* January, 50–54.

Time-Life Books, eds. 1973. *The first men.* New York: Time-Life Books.

Tishkoff, S. A., E. Dietzsch, W. Speed, A. J. Pakstis, J. R. Kidd, K. Cheung, B. Bonné-Tamir, A. S. Santachiara-Benerecetti, P. Moral, M. Krings, S. Pääbo, E. Watson, N. Risch, T. Jenkins, and K. K. Kidd. 1996. Global patterns of linkage disequilibrium at the CD4 locus and modern human origins. *Science* 271:1380–87.

Todd, T. W. 1920. Age changes in the pubic bone. *American Journal of Physical Anthropology* 3: 285–384.

Toth, N. 1985. The Oldowan reassessed: A close look at early stone tools. *Journal of Archaeological Science* 2:101–20.

Tuchman, B. W. 1978. *A distant mirror: The calamitous fourteenth century.* New York: Knopf.

Tullar, R. M. 1977. *The human species: Its nature, evolution, and ecology.* New York: McGraw-Hill.

Ubelaker, D., and H. Scammell. 1992. *Bones: A forensic detective's casebook.* New York: HarperCollins.

Underwood, J. H. 1979. *Human variation and human microevolution.* Englewood Cliffs, NJ: Prentice Hall.

Van Blerkom, L. M. 2003. Role of viruses in human evolution. *Yearbook of Physical Anthropology* 46: 14–46.

van Schaik, C. P., et al. 2003. Orangutan cultures and the evolution of material culture. *Science* 299:102–5.

Vekua, A., et al. 2002. A new skull of early *Homo* from Dmanisi, Georgia. *Science* 297:85–89.

Venter, J. C., et al. 2001. The sequence of the human genome. *Science* 291:1304–51.

Verheyen, E., W. Salzburger, J. Snoeks, and A. Meyer. 2003. Origin of the superflock of cichlid fishes from Lake Victoria, East Africa. *Science* 300:325–29.

Videan, E. N., and W. C. McGrew. 2000. Bipedality in chimpanzees and bonobos: Testing hypothesized selection pressures. Paper delivered at the 69th Annual Meeting of the American Association of Physical Anthropologists, San Antonio, TX.

Vignaud, P., et al. 2002. Geology and palaeontology of the Upper Miocene Toros-Menalla hominid locality, Chad. *Nature* 418:152–55.

Wade, N. 1998. Human or chimp? 50 genes are the key. *New York Times,* 20 October, F1, 4.

Walsh, P. D., et al. 2003. Catastrophic ape decline in western equatorial Africa. *Nature* 422:611–14.

Ward, C., M. Leakey, and A. Walker. 1999. The new hominid species *Australopithecus anamensis. Evolutionary Anthropology* 7 (6): 197–205.

Ward, S., B. Brown, A. Hill, J. Kelley, and W. Downs. 1999. *Equatorius:* A new hominoid genus from the Middle Miocene of Kenya. *Science* (27 August) 285:1382–86.

Watson, A. 2000. A new breed of high-tech detectives. *Science* 289:850–54.

Weaver, K. F. 1985. The search for our ancestors. *National Geographic* 168:560–623.

Weaver, R. F. 1984. Changing life's genetic blueprint. *National Geographic,* December: 818–47.

Weiner, J. 1994. *The beak of the finch: A story of evolution in our time*. New York: Knopf.

Weiss, G., and A. von Haeseler. 1996. Estimating the age of the common ancestor of men from the ZFY intron. *Science* 272:1359–60.

Weiss, K. M., and A. V. Buchanan. 2000. Rediscovering Darwin after a Darwinian century. *Evolutionary Anthropology* 9 (5): 187–200.

White, F. J. 1996. *Pan paniscus* 1973 to 1996: Twenty-three years of field research. *Evolutionary Anthropology* 5 (1): 11–17.

White, T. D. 2001. Once we were cannibals. *Scientific American*, August: 58–65.

———. 2003. Early hominids—diversity or distortion? *Science*, 299:1994–97.

White, T. D., B. Asfaw, D. DeGusta, H. Gilbert, G. D. Richards, G. Suwa, and F. C. Howell. 2003. Pleistocene *Homo sapiens* from Middle Awash, Ethiopia. *Nature* 423:742–47.

White, T. D., and P. A. Folkens. 1991. *Human osteology*. San Diego: Academic Press.

White, T. D., G. Suwa, and B. Asfaw. 1994. *Australopithecus ramidus*, a new species of early hominid from Aramis, Ethiopia. *Nature* 371 (22 September): 306–12.

Whiten, A., and C. Boesch. 2001. The cultures of chimpanzees. *Scientific American*, January: 60–67.

Whiten, A., J. Goodall, W. C. McGrew, T. Nishida, V. Reynolds, Y. Sugiyama, C. E. G. Tutin, R. W. Wrangham, and C. Boesch. 1999. Cultures in chimpanzees. *Nature* 399 (17 June): 682–85.

Wilford, J. N. 1994. Fog thickens on climate and origin of humans. *New York Times*, 17 May, C1, 8.

Wilmut, I. 1998. Cloning for medicine. *Scientific American*, December: 58–63.

Wilmut, I., A. E. Schnieke, J. McWhir, A. J. Kind, and K. H. S. Campbell. 1997. Viable offspring derived from fetal and adult mammalian cells. *Nature* 385 (27 February): 810–13.

Wilson, A. C., and R. L. Cann. 1992. The recent African genesis of humans. *Scientific American* 266 (4): 68–73.

Wilson, E. O. 1992. *The diversity of life* (College edition with study materials). New York: Norton.

———. 1998. *Consilience: The Unity of Knowledge*. New York: Knopf.

Winchester, S. 2002. *The map that changed the world: William Smith and the birth of modern geology*. New York: HarperCollins/Perennial.

Wolpoff, M. 1989. Multiregional evolution: The fossil alternative to Eden. In *The human revolution: behavioural and biological perspectives in the origins of modern humans*, ed. P. Mellars and C. Stringer, 62–108. Princeton, NJ:Princeton University Press.

———. 1994. What do we mean by human—and why does it matter? *Evolutionary Anthropology* 3 (4): 116–17.

Wolpoff, M., and R. Caspari. 1997. *Race and human evolution: A fatal attraction*. New York: Simon & Schuster.

Wolpoff, M. H., J. Hawks, D. W. Frayer, and K. Hunley. 2001. Modern human ancestry at the peripheries: A test of the replacement theory. *Science* 291:293–97.

Wolpoff, M. H., B. Senut, M. Pickford, and J. Hawks. 2002. Brief communication. *Nature* 419:581–82.

Wong, K. 1998. Ancestral quandary. *Scientific American* 278 (1): 30–32.

———. 2000a. The caveman's new clothes. *Scientific American*, November: 32–34.

———. 2000b. Paleolithic pit stop. *Scientific American*, December: 18–20.

———. 2003. An ancestor to call our own. *Scientific American*, January: 54–63.

Wood, B. 2002. Hominid revelations from Chad. *Nature* 418:133–35.

Wood, B., and M. Collard. 1999. The human genus. *Science* 284:65–71.

Woodruff, D. S., and P. A. Morin. 1995. Geneticists out on a limb. *Natural History* 104 (1): 54.

Yoon, C. K. 1996a. Lake Victoria's lightning-fast origin of species. *New York Times*, 27 August, C1, 4.

———. 1996b. Parallel plots in classic evolution. *New York Times*, 12 November, C1, 7.

———. 1998. Iguanas sail from Guadeloupe to Anguilla and into history. *New York Times*, 8 October.

Zhu, R. X., et al. 2001. Earliest presence of humans in northeast Asia. *Nature* 413:413–17.

Zimmer, C. 1995. Tooling through the trees. *Discover*, November: 46–47.

———. 2001. After you, Eve. *Natural History* 110 (2): 32–35.

Photo and Illustration Credits

National Geographic Society Image Collection; 10.12, from *Lucy: The Beginnings of Humankind*. Copyright © 1981 Luba Dmytryk Gudz/David L. Brill. Reprinted with permission; 10.13, © John Reader/Science Photo Library/Photo Researchers, Inc.; 10.14, © Institute of Human Origins, photography by W.H. Kimbel. Used with permission; 10.16 left, © John Reader/Science Photo Library/Photo Researchers, Inc.; 10.16 right, Neg. #4744(5). Photo by D. Finnin/C. Chesek. Courtesy Department of Library Services, American Museum of Natural History; 10.17, © National Museums of Kenya; 10.18, © Patrick Robert/Sygma Collection/Corbis; 10.20, © Emory Kristof/National Geographic Society Image Collection; 10.21, Courtesy Transvaal Museum, D.C. Panagos; 10.22, Micrographs courtesy of Dr. Frederick E. Grine, SUNY, Stony Brook. Photographed by Chester Tarka; 10.23, © Alan Walker/National Geographic Society Image Collection; 10.24, Courtesy Transvaal Museum, D.C. Panagos; 10.25, © The National Museums of Kenya.

Chapter 11 CO11, Courtesy Comité Départemental du Tourisme de la Dordogne; 11.2, © Eric Delson; 11.4, © The National Museums of Kenya; 11.5, Courtesy Dr. Pat Shipman; 11.7 top, © National Museum of Natural History, Leiden; 11.7 bottom, Neg. #319781. Courtesy Department of Library Services, American Museum of Natural History; 11.8, Neg. #315446. Photo by Charles H. Coles. Courtesy Department of Library Services, American Museum of Natural History; 11.9, © The National Museums of Kenya; 11.11, © David L. Brill, 1985; 11.12, © Geoffrey Clifford/Woodfin Camp and Associates; 11.14, © AP/Wide World Photos; 11.15 left, © Boltin Picture Library; 11.15 middle, 11.15 right, Courtesy K.L. Feder; 11.16, from Wu Rukland and Lin Shenglong, "Peking Man," *Scientific American*, June 1983. Illustration reprinted by permission of Patricia J. Wynne; 11.17, © John Reader/Science Photo Library/Photo Researchers, Inc.; 11.18, from "The Anatomy of Human Speech," by Jeffrey Laitman, *Natural History*, vol. 93, 1984. Hugh Thomas, illustrator; 11.20, © Javier Trueba/Madrid Scientific Films; 11.22, © Dr. Christopher B. Stringer/Natural History Museum, London; 11.23, © The Natural History Museum, London; 11.24, Courtesy Dr. Ian Tattersall, From *The Human Odyssey*; 11.25, © H. Lilienthal/Landschaftsverband Rheinland; 11.27 left, © The Field Museum, Neg. #A66700; 11.27 right, © Paul Jaronski/University of Michigan Photo Services; 11.28, from *In Search of the Neanderthals* by Clive Gamble and Christopher Stringer. Reprinted by permission of Thames & Hudson, Ltd.; 11.29, Courtesy American Museum of Natural History Library;

11.30, Courtesy K.L. Feder; 11.31, Courtesy Phototheque du Musée de l'Homme, Paris. M. Lucas, photographer; 11.32, © John Reader/Science Photo Library/Photo Researchers, Inc.; 11.34, Courtesy Phototheque du Musée de l'Homme, Paris; 11.35, © David L. Brill; 11.36 top, © Peabody Museum, Harvard University. Photograph by Hillel Burger. Photo No. N26470; 11.36 bottom left, Photo by A.R. Hughes. Courtesy Professor P.V. Tobias, University of the Witwatersrand, Johannesburg, South Africa; 11.36 bottom right, Courtesy B. Vandermeersch, Laboratoire d'Anthropologie, Universite de Bordeaux; 11.37, from Singer and Wymer, *The Middle Stone Age at Klasies River*. Reprinted by permission of The University of Chicago Press; 11.38, Courtesy K.L. Feder; 11.39, Neg. #39686. Photo by Kirschner. Courtesy Department of Library Services, American Museum of Natural History; 11.40, Courtesy Comité Départemental du Tourisme de la Dordogne.

Chapter 12 CO12, © Anthony Bannister/Animals Animals/Earth Scenes; 12.3, adapted from *Nature*, Volume 416, March 2002. Reprinted by permission of *Nature*, Macmillan Magazines Limited; 12.4, © Charles P. Mountford/National Geographic Society Image Collection; 12.5, Courtesy Mark Stoneking, Pennsylvania State University; 12.6, © Anthony Bannister/Animals Animals/Earth Scenes; 12.8, *Nature*, Volume 416, March 2002, page 48. Reprinted by permission of *Nature*, Macmillan Magazines Limited.

Chapter 13 CO13, © Bruce Dale/NGS Image Collection; 13.10 left, Neg. #231604. Photo by D.B. MacMillan. Courtesy Department of Library Services, American Museum of Natural History; 13.10 right, © Bruce Dale/NGS Image Collection; 13.13 from John Relethford, *The Human Species*, p. 436. Copyright © 2003 The McGraw-Hill Companies. Reprinted by permission of The McGraw-Hill Companies.

Chapter 14 CO14, 14.1, © 1996 George Steinmetz; 14.3, Courtesy Dr. Serena Nanda; 14.4, © Johnny Johnson/DRK Photo; 14.5, Maps redrawn from originals, Canadian Museum of Nature. Reprinted by permission of National Geographic Society; 14.6, from Ridley, *Evolution*, 1993, page 411. Reprinted by permission of Blackwell Publishers; 14.8, adapted from King & Mitulsky, *Science* 298, December 2002, page 2343. Reprinted by permission of Mary-Claire King and Amo G. Motulsky; 14.9, © The Granger Collection, New York.

Chapter 15 CO15, © Kenneth Garrett/NGS Image Collection; 15.1, © Gerha Hinterleitner/Gamma; 15.2, © Kenneth Garrett/NGS Image Collection; 15.3, © Irven DeVore/Anthro-Photo.

Exercises Exercise 2, Photos courtesy of the author.

Index